explore

BRITAIN

Tim Locke

AA Publishing

Cover picture: Polperro harbour, Cornwall

Page 3: Looe harbour, Cornwall

Page 4: the essence of rural Devon

Page 5(a): Stonehenge, near Salisbury, Wiltshire

Page 5(b): a morris dancer's unusual head-gear

Page 5(c): Mousehole harbour, Cornwall

Page 6: the Cuillin Hills, Isle of Skye, Scotland

Page 7(a): royalty-watching, The Mall, London

Page 7(b): Inveraray Castle, Argyll & Bute, Scotland

Page 8(a): Ambleside from Kirkstone Road

Page 23(b): Wheal Coats, St Agnes Head

Page 111: detail, Banbury Cross

Page 211: Black Watch Memorial, River Tay

Written by Tim Locke, Richard Cavendish and Barnaby Rogerson
Additional writing by Nia Williams

Reprinted Oct 1998
Revision verified by Tim Locke 1994, 1996, 1998
Revised third edition 1998
First published 1994

Edited, designed, produced and distributed by AA Publishing, Norfolk House, Priestley Road, Basingstoke, Hampshire RG24 9NY.
Maps © The Automobile Association 1994, 1996, 1998

A CIP catalogue record for this book is available from the British Library.

ISBN 0 7495 1598 8
Published by AA Publishing (a trading name of Automobile Association Developments Limited, whose registered office is Norfolk House, Basingstoke, Hampshire RG24 9NY. Registered number 1878835).

Printed and bound in Italy by Printer Trento srl

Titles in the Explorer series:
Australia • Boston & New England • Brittany
California • Caribbean • China • Costa Rica • Crete
Cyprus • Egypt • Florence & Tuscany • Florida • France
Germany • Greek Islands • Hawaii • Indonesia • Ireland
Israel • Italy • Japan • London • Mexico
Moscow & St Petersburg • New York • New Zealand
Paris • Portugal • Prague • Provence • Rome
San Francisco • Scotland • Singapore & Malaysia
South Africa • Spain • Thailand • Turkey • Venice • Vietnam

How to use this book

This book is divided into five main sections:

❏ Section 1: *Britain Is*

discusses aspects of life and living today, from politics to pubs

❏ Section 2: *Britain Was*

places the country in its historical context and explores those past events whose influences are felt to this day

❏ Section 3: *A to Z Section*

is divided into regional chapters, and covers places to visit, including walks and drives. Within this section are the Focus-on articles, which consider a variety of subjects in greater detail

❏ Section 4: *Travel Facts*

contains the strictly practical information vital for a successful trip

❏ Section 5: *Hotels and Restaurants*

lists recommended establishments throughout Britain, giving a brief résumé of their attractions and facilities

How to use the star rating
Most of the places described in this book have been given a separate rating:

▶▶▶　　**Do not miss**

▶▶　　**Highly recommended**

▶　　**Worth seeing**

　　Not essential to see

Map references
To make the location of a particular place easier to find, every main entry in this book has a map reference to the right of its name. This comprises a number, followed by a letter, followed by another number, such as *176B3*. The first number (*176*) refers to the page on which the map can be found, the letter (*B*) and the second number (*3*) pinpoint the square in which the main entry is located. The maps on the inside front cover and inside back cover are referred to as IFC and IBC respectively.

Contents

Quick reference

This quick-reference guide highlights the features of the book you will use most often: the maps; the introductory features; the Focus on articles; the walks; and the drives.

7

My Britain by Tim Locke

From my house in Sussex, I can look upon Lewes Castle, an administrative headquarters set up in Norman times. The town's main street slopes down between numerous Georgianised timber-framed buildings, past the White Hart Hotel – where Tom Paine held meetings in the 18th century – to family-run Harvey's brewery, little changed in over a hundred years. A short walk away are the sheep-grazed slopes of the South Downs, dotted with ancient remains. On one slope is the site of the Battle of Lewes, where in 1264 Simon de Montfort defeated Henry III, and forced him to grant rights that paved the way for parliamentary democracy.

I find this sense of continuum an impressive feature of Britain: its landscapes, both rural and urban, pock-marked with historical incident. I often wonder what else would strike me about Britain if I had never seen it before. I imagine being confronted with a series of cameos: a sheep auction in Mid Wales, with cloth caps and ruddy Celtic faces in abundance; the light qualities of East Anglia which make virtually any view never seem quite the same twice; a county cricket match at the spa town of Tunbridge Wells; or the hypnotic patter of a trader at London's atmospheric Brick Lane market.

Britain has probably been written about and travelled in more than any other corner of the Earth. This book is my personal selection of the most rewarding places in the kingdom. It doesn't include every city or tourist attraction, but aims for a balance between the well known and the less obvious.

It constantly surprises me that in an age ever tending towards standardisation, so many aspects of Britain have remained almost intact: its communities, its lifestyles, its idiosyncrasies. The threats are still there, but there has been a realisation that we need our heritage as a point of reference to tell us who we are. It would take a great deal to erode away that national persona.

Tim Locke has contributed to *Boston and New England*, *Thailand* and *Germany* in the AA *Explorer* series, as well as to other guides on Britain. Richard Cavendish has had numerous books and articles published on Britain, including *The Complete Book of London*, published by the AA, and was the consultant editor on the AA British Isles Database. Barnaby Rogerson, an experienced travel writer, is the author of AA *Essential Scotland*.

■ **Britain is by no means a uniform entity: it presents the amiable paradox that the more one travels, the more one realises there is to see. Within its 228,000 square kilometres (88,000 square miles) Britain shows an astonishingly rich variety of landscape, architecture, micro-climate, regional accents, cultural traditions, social make-up and economic activity.** ■

Great Britain has a great heritage as a stronghold of invention, literature, naval and imperial might, and individualism. This is the land of William Shakespeare, Thomas Hardy, William Wordsworth, Beatrix Potter and Winnie-the-Pooh, the land of Edward Elgar, Benjamin Britten, Gilbert and Sullivan, the Beatles and the Sex Pistols, the land of Scotch whisky, Yorkshire pudding, real ale, fish and chips, Scottish haggis, Welsh cakes, and Chinese and Indian take-aways, the land of seaside piers, cricket, semi-detached houses, greyhound racing, the early Industrial Revolution, stately homes, lawns and herbaceous borders, porches, chimneypots, village fêtes, the royal family and the Loch Ness monster.

The diversity Many newcomers are constantly surprised by how abruptly the urban scene can change to deeply rural countryside. Significant factors are the compactness of many urban centres, a restrictive planning system, and the constant variations in the physical environment. One key to Britain's diversity is the complex geology which makes for subtle and sudden changes in landforms and land use: low-level arable fens, rolling hedgerow-lined pastures, craggy dales, blustery moorland tops, postglacial mountain scenery, rugged cliffs and shingle shores. This in turn has given rise to numerous types of local or vernacular architecture: sometimes the bedrock supplies the building material, as in the Cotswolds, Cornwall, rural Wales, the Scottish Highlands, and the Pennines, while elsewhere timber and/or bricks predominate.

Twentieth-century progress has eroded some of the finer distinctions in various locales (such as hi-tech agricultural landscapes and the sadly standardised, chain-store dominated British high street), but much has been carefully preserved or has survived.

Regional accents, for instance, continue to thrive, and a well-trained ear will distinguish from which side of the Pennines, Scotland or even London the speaker originates. In fact, accents are now fashionable.

Britain's greatest assets for the visitor include its accessibility, sense of history and wealth of variety. The curious explorer will be well served.

Market day (this is Norwich) – a colourful experience in every way

■ **The British system of government is by parliamentary democracy, one of the nation's great gifts to the world. There is no written constitution, but the system has developed gradually over many centuries, and continues to do so. All adults, except 'peers, lunatics and certain criminals', have the right to vote in general and local elections, but this is a comparatively recent development. Universal male suffrage in Britain dates only from 1918 – and women did not get the right to vote until 1928.** ■

❏ Let not England forget her precedence of teaching other nations how to live.
     John Milton (1644) ❏

Britain has a confusing variety of names. The British Isles are the two islands of Britain and Ireland, and all their offshore islands. (Great) Britain constitues England, Wales and Scotland. Wales was conquered by England in the 13th century. The King of Scots succeeded to the English throne in 1603 and the political union between the two dates from 1707.

The United Kingdom is England, Wales, Scotland and Northern Ireland, the latter being the six counties of Ulster (predominantly Protestant in religion) which refused to join the rest of Ireland in breaking away from Britain in 1921. The United Kingdom is a highly centralised state. Scotland, Wales and Northern Ireland are ruled, like England, from London, though Scotland has its own legal system.

The seat of power The head of state is the Queen and much of the ceremony of British life revolves round the monarchy, dating from a time when the monarch actually ruled the country. Today power rests with the democratically elected government answerable to **parliament**, and principally to the **House of Commons**, the main legislating body. The unelected **House of Lords** is for peers, and is primarily a revising chamber. Britain's relationship with the European Union, however, and the consequences for British sovereignty and the supremacy of parliament is a matter of debate.

❏ Great Britain has lost an empire and has not yet found a role.
     Dean Acheson (1962) ❏

The British people

■ Class distinctions are still profoundly important in British life and involve the most acutely discriminating judgements – about people's houses and furnishings, clothes, cars, jobs, education, manners and personal tastes. The simplest clue to class is regional accent – the writer, George Bernard Shaw once made the now famous remark that an Englishman 'cannot open his mouth without making some other Englishman despise him'. ■

The population of Great Britain numbers about 56 million. A small and densely populated country, it would fit neatly inside the American state of Oregon, which has a population of only 3 million. Or, keeping the comparison within Europe, the country has about the same number of people as France, in an area less than half the size.

Early ancestry The British are a nation of mongrels, principally a mixture of Germanic and Celtic strains. The original English, or Anglo-Saxons, came across the North Sea in their dragon-prowed longships

from northwest Germany and southern Denmark some 1,500 years ago. They subjugated most of the native Celtic people, whom they dismissively called Welsh, which means 'foreigners'.

More Germanic invaders came from Denmark and Norway in the Viking Age and the Norman Conquest of England in 1066 eventually gave all areas of the British Isles a new and initially French-speaking ruling class. From the 16th to 18th centuries, thousands of French Protestants, known as 'Huguenots', came to England to escape religious persecution. The 19th century brought substantial Irish immigration to Britain, and an influx of Jewish families fleeing from persecution in Russia and Eastern Europe. After World War II, fresh waves of immigrants came from the West Indies, the Indian subcontinent, Cyprus and many Commonwealth countries.

Over the centuries, these incomers have enriched the British population and the British way of life.

Ethnic and religious mix Despite the presence of many ethnic and religious minorities, statistics show that more than 80 per cent of the UK population is classified as English, about 10 per cent Scottish, 2½ per cent Irish and 2 per cent Welsh. Britain is 95 per cent white, with West Indians, Indians and Pakistanis numbering about 1 per cent each. There are tiny percentages of Bangladeshis and Chinese. Of the ethnic minority population, close to 50 per cent was born in Britain.

The population is overwhelmingly Christian, or thinks of itself that way. More than 85 per cent regard themselves as Christians, but fewer than one person in five goes regularly to church or chapel. The Muslim population is about 2 per cent and practising Jews total about 1 per cent.

Males and female members of the population are today nearing equality in numbers. Throughout this century, the British birth rate has increased extremely slowly, and during the 1970s the UK population actually fell for a time.

❏ Arthur Koestler, a foreign writer who lived in Britain for many years, described the average Englishman as 'an attractive hybrid between an ostrich and a lion': keeping his head in the sand for as long as possible, but when forced to confront reality, capable of heroic deeds. ❏

A national character? Whether there is anything that can be called a British national character is open to question. The Scots, the Welsh and the Irish have retained their separate identities despite (or because of) English domination. Even in England itself, people from London, Yorkshire, Lancashire, the Northeast, the West Country and other areas cherish their regional identities.

As seen by outsiders, at least, qualities of the typical Englishman include reserve and politeness, helpfulness, a gift for understatement and awkwardness with women and children (particularly in the upper and middle classes). The English pride themselves on fair play and a genius for compromise. Profoundly conservative by temperament, they suspect intellectuals and ideologies, change, professionalism, and fads and fancies. They like gardens, dogs and horses. They love the countryside, but mostly do not live in it. They love sport and taught the rest of the world organised games.

Perhaps the most fundamental trait the British have in common is an ironic sense of humour, which lends itself to self-caricature. Yorkshire folk, for instance, have been described by a distinguished Yorkshireman as being like the Scots but without the generosity.

■ If anything causes the British more gloom, complaint, anxiety and frustration than the weather, it is the economy. In the Victorian Age, Britain was the most powerful industrial nation on earth, with a mighty economy based on coal, iron and steel, heavy machinery, textiles, shipbuilding and foreign trade. She also ruled the largest empire in history. This commanding position has been lost – and with it the vigorous self-confidence of Victorian Britain. ■

The British economy today is based on private enterprise; in the 1980s many of the nationalised industries were restored to private ownership. Heavy industry has since steeply declined, while the service sector has grown. Britain used to import raw materials for its factories, now it is an importer of manufactured goods from countries which make them better and cheaper. The balance of trade, along with unemployment and inflation, is an ongoing problem.

❏ The change which has come over Britain can be observed in the mining valleys of South Wales, where King Coal once raised his grimy sceptre above teeming pits and spoil heaps. Today not a nugget of coal is mined in the Rhondda Valley, famed in song and story, and the valleys are being extensively 'greened'. ❏

Trade and resources On the other hand, the UK has rich energy resources – coal, North Sea oil and natural gas. A strong financial sector achieves substantial invisible exports. Less food is imported and more grown at home, though only 2 per cent of the working population is employed in agriculture. The once flourishing fishing industry is hampered by European Union and government restrictions. In 1973, belatedly, Britain joined the European Community, which now accounts for more than half her trade.

The UK was the sixth richest country in the world in 1950, while 30 years later it only reached 22nd. All the same, by the early 1990s, with two-thirds of British households buying their own homes and owning their own cars, Britons had a higher standard of living than they had ever had before.

The Bank of England, at the heart of the City of London

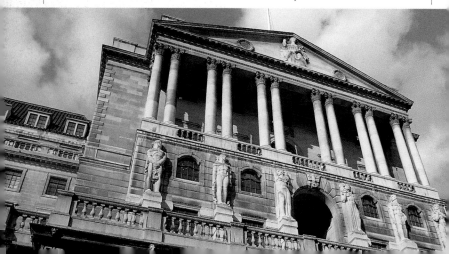

■ **Pubs are much more than just places in which to drink. They are enclaves of laughter and gossip, arenas for playing games and competing, havens of sympathy in time of trouble, refuges, and bolt-holes. A good pub has its own distinctive atmosphere and its own resident local characters.** ■

> ❏ When you have lost your inns drown your empty selves, for you will have lost the last of England.
> **Hilaire Belloc (1870–1953)** ❏

Some pubs are dedicated to thoughtful imbibing and peaceful conversation, others to deafening piped music and clattering slot machines. There are venerable half-timbered Tudor hostelries, leaning about at all angles and apparently held up as much by the strength of the ale consumed in them over the centuries as by their massive black timbers. There are ample, beaming Georgian coaching inns, glittering Victorian gin palaces, and dubious little backstreet taverns. There are pubs with romantic tales to tell of smugglers and highwaymen, rose-wreathed pubs idyllically set by rivers and canals, lobster-potted inns gazing over pretty fishing harbours and patronised by sailing enthusiasts, while grim-faced pubs inured to wind and weather are perched high on remote moors and frequented by booted ramblers in water-repellent jackets.

Then and now

Today's neighbourhood pub is descended from the local alehouse of Anglo-Saxon and medieval England, an ordinary house whose occupants brewed and sold ale. In the 12th and 13th centuries, inns began to open up, providing overnight accommodation for travellers. Recent years have seen momentous changes in the pub: the vastly increased importance of food,

There are town pubs, village pubs country pubs ... and boaty pubs

the return of real ale (old-fashioned, properly brewed beer, once threatened with extinction by the big commercial brewers). Most pubs have become less aggressively masculine, and women can feel quite comfortable in them.

What's in a name? The tradition of the pictorial sign which graphically explains the pub's name and hangs over the door dates from days when few people could read. Some names are derived from heraldry, such as the White Hart and the Red Lion. Stoutly patriotic, pubs are often named after royalty, as in the Crown or the King's Head. Other names reflect country life – the Plough or the Fox and Hounds, and there are strange and enigmatic names: the Leg of Mutton and Cauliflower, the Hand in Hand. All are part of an engaging richness and variety.

■ **Gardens and gardening are a national passion throughout Britain. Whether their patch of land is the tiniest cottage garden or the grandest estate, the British have always found opportunities for self-expression and creativity. The selection of gardens open to the public given below indicates the vast scope and diversity of the nation's 'backyards'.** ■

The British garden dates from Roman times, when every upwardly mobile villa-owner aspired to an atrium with a small garden. Monastic gardens were merely practical affairs for growing food or cultivating herbs and plants for dyes or medicinal purposes. With the first great houses of the 16th century came the first true pleasure gardens, with their knots of herbs and flowers. In the next century the aristocratic classes toured France and Italy and saw the formal creations of Le Nôtre; topiary and water parterres were the rage.

The classical age of English landscaping in the 18th century saw formality rejected in favour of the naturalistic contrivances of Lancelot 'Capability' Brown and others, who designed green expanses fringed by woodlands, interrupted by lakes and punctuated by classical follies. Victorian times saw formal rockeries, ferneries, roseries and other horticultural extravaganzas back in fashion.

Meanwhile the working classes tended allotments where they grew their own vegetables, and middle-class suburban villas sported lawns and herbaceous borders. In their back gardens, people found a private haven from the outside world, and whether it is to satisfy a creative urge or as an antidote to the stresses of daily life, toiling in the garden has become a national pastime.

The West Country Subtropical species thrive in the gardens of **Tresco Abbey**, in the Isles of Scilly. On the Cornish mainland, **Glendurgan** (NT), **Penjerrick** and **Trebah** are neighbouring subtropical havens; **Trelissick** (NT) is noted for rhododendrons and azaleas with colour all year round; paths wind down to the waterside with glimpses of Pendennis Castle. At **Trewithen** magnolias, rhododendrons and rare shrubs surround a Georgian mansion. Meanwhile, **Stourhead** (NT), in Wiltshire, is a splendid example of 18th-century landscaping.

Southern England and London
Kew Gardens in London is the king of all botanic gardens. The collection of rare specimens from all over the world owes much to the 19th-century botanist Sir Joseph Banks. Don't miss the elegant Palm House and the Princess of Wales Conservatory. **Wisley Garden** in Surrey, was set up in 1904 as experimental gardens for the Royal Horticultural Society: it has

Stourhead in Wiltshire, the quintessential landscaped garden

Late spring at Sissinghurst in Kent

many scarce species and an excellent garden centre. **Winkworth Arboretum** in Surrey, has a superb tree collection, splendid for spring and autumn colours. In East Sussex, **Sheffield Park Garden** (NT) enjoys lakes, azaleas, rhododendrons and more, while **Wakehurst Place** (NT) has rare trees and shrubs in a lakeside setting. In Kent the gardens of **Hever Castle** are strongly Italian in feel and those of **Scotney Castle** (NT) are in picturesque-romantic style in a lake and island setting. **Sissinghurst Garden** (NT) is the wonderful 1930s creation of Harold Nicholson and Vita Sackville-West.

The Heart of England and Eastern England Barnsley House, Hidcote Manor (NT), Kiftsgate Court, Miserden Park, Painswick Rococo Garden and Westonbirt Arboretum are all in the Cotswolds, each offering something different (see panels, pages 118 and 120). **Rousham House**, Oxfordshire, is an excellent example of an 18th-century romantic rural idyll by William Kent. **Anglesey Abbey** (NT), in Cambridgeshire, has a charming Georgian garden.

Wales Powis Castle in Powys is set amid fine 18th-century terraces. At Bodnant, Conwy, is a garden of sublime inspiration based on five Italianate terraces with the mountains of Snowdonia behind.

Northern England Chatsworth in Derbyshire is a masterly marriage of parkland, landscaped by Lancelot 'Capability' Brown, and gardens full of surprises that owe much to Joseph Paxton, head gardener from 1827. **Studley Royal** (NT), North Yorkshire, is an ultra-romantic creation around Fountains Abbey.

Scotland Culzean Country Park in South Ayrshire boasts a landscaped park and woodland. At **Edzell Castle** in Stirling is a 17th-century 'pleasaunce', while **Branklyn**, near Perth, is a modest, well-stocked suburban garden. **Crathes Castle** in Aberdeenshire is both enchanting and innovative. In the wilds of the Highlands, **Inverewe** is a spectacular oasis in a mild gulf-stream climate.

❑ The National Gardens Scheme is an umbrella organisation for gardens throughout Britain. Included are many private gardens whose owners open them to the public just one or two days a year, offering the chance of a peep into their personal Edens. Details are given in the booklet *Gardens of England and Wales*. ❑

■ The national calendar of events ranges from the offbeat activities of Mayday dancing and Shrove Tuesday pancake-racing to the royal pageantry of Trooping the Colour and the great sports fixtures at Wembley Stadium, Royal Ascot and Lord's Cricket Ground. Local tourist information offices stock details of what's on where and when. ■

Pageantry and spectacle Trooping the Colour, which is the celebration of the Queen's official birthday, takes place in June in Horse Guards' Parade in London and shows off the best of royal pageantry. The Lord Mayor's Show in November features the new mayor of London in procession in a stunning gold coach. Among other spectacles are Cruft's Dog Show (March, Birmingham), the International Air Show (September, even-numbered years, Farnborough, Hampshire) and the Chelsea Flower Show (May, London).

The Randwick Wap, a Cotswolds mayor-making ceremony

Arts festivals The major arts festival is the Edinburgh Festival in August/ September; other venues include Bath, Brighton and Glasgow, as well as Gloucester, Herefordshire or Worcestershire for the Three Choirs Festival (see panel on page 117), and Llangollen for the International Eisteddfod in Wales (see page 163). The Promenade Concerts ('Proms') at London's Royal Albert Hall take place in summer, with newly commissioned as well as established classical music being performed.

Sports Professional soccer matches are held every Saturday between August and April; the FA (Football Association) Cup Final in May is the big match. Cricket, the gentle summer game, is subtler than it looks at first sight; try a one-day county game first. The Wimbledon Lawn Tennis Championships are held in Wimbledon, London, during the last week of June and first week of July. As for horse racing, the Grand National is a notoriously tough steeplechase run at Aintree (near Liverpool) in April, and the ultra-fashionable Royal Ascot meeting takes place in June (women's hats are the focus here). Regattas are rowed at Henley in Berkshire and Fowey in Cornwall, and a round-the-island yacht race takes place at Cowes in the Isle of Wight. In March the University Boat Race (Oxford versus Cambridge) is rowed on the Thames in west London.

Numerous traditional sports get an annual airing: variants of medieval football are played in the streets of St Columb Major in Cornwall and Ashbourne in Derbyshire, while Cumberland Wrestling takes place in the Lake District. In Scotland the summer Highland Games at Braemar and elsewhere feature caber-tossing, mountain races and pipe bands.

Shows and fêtes County shows have an agricultural emphasis with livestock and horticultural competitions, but also sport and entertainment. Village fêtes offer tombolas, cake competitions, fairground sideshows, bric-à-brac stalls, and sometimes sheep-dog trials – essential for anyone wanting to see the real rural Britain.

Folk and religious customs The only nationally celebrated event unique to England is Guy Fawkes Night, on 5 November, when firework displays are held and effigies of Guy Fawkes, the anarchist caught attempting to blow up the Houses of Parliament in 1605, are set alight on top of vast bonfires.

Locally, an amazing variety of folk customs is celebrated. Some of the oldest owe their origins to Mayday fertility rites, including maypole dancing (widespread) and, in Cornwall, the Furry Dance in Helston and the 'Obby 'Oss festival at Padstow. Elsewhere, you can take your pick from such oddities as oyster-blessing at Whitstable (Kent), a pancake race at Olney (Buckinghamshire) or face-pulling through a horse-collar at Egremont (Cumbria). Church customs include rush-bearing (dating from times when churches needed rushes to cover earthen floors) and, in the Peak District, well-dressing, when wells are decorated with elaborate pictures made of flowers.

The 'Obby 'Oss festival, Padstow

■ The Industrial Revolution began in Britain in the late 18th and 19th centu-ruries, and its legacy is phenomenal. In the late 20th century, Britain's heavy industrial base continues to decline, although muse-ums which heighten the awareness of this aspect of the national heritage are a boom industry. You don't have to be just a fan of rusty sprockets and cogwheels to appreciate and learn from them. ■

Listed here is a selection of the best museums to visit. However, it must not be forgotten that the numerous industrial communities and disused relics that are a vital aspect of the landscape are in themselves evoca-tive reminders of Britain's industrial past. The most rewarding of these include the textile mill towns of West Yorkshire, the valleys of South Wales, the factory villages of Port Sunlight and Saltaire, and numerous abandoned mining landscapes, such as the tin mines of Cornwall and the lead mines of Swaledale.

Many of the sites mentioned below are described more fully in the A to Z section of this guide.

The West Country Coldharbour Mill, at Cullompton in Devon, is an old wool mill that recalls the heyday of the Devon woollen industry; the processes of carding, drafting and spinning are shown, and there are some fine, old machines. **Poldark Mine**, at Wendro, in Cornwall, includes an underground tin-mine tour, reconstructed cottages and

children's amusements. At **Wheal Martyn** in St Austell, Cornwall's still-active china clay industry is explained, with a tour around an abandoned site and a fine view into the moonscape that results from the extraction process.

Southern England At the **Amberley Museum** in West Sussex, watch craftsmen at work in a former chalk pit and lime works. The **Royal Naval Dockyard**, at Chatham in Kent, has the country's longest brick building (the rope works) and the world's old-est corrugated iron structure.

The Heart of England The Black Country Museum, Dudley (West Midlands), is a skilful reconstruction of an industrial Black Country com-munity of yesteryear, with a colliery, redbrick cottages, a canal where you can try 'legging' along the tunnel in the time-honoured fashion, and an old-style fairground. The **Ironbridge Gorge Museum** (in Shropshire), the birthplace of the Industrial Revolu-tion, is the star of Britain's distinguished industrial museums.

Wales Visit the **Big Pit Museum** at Blaenavon, Torfaen, to get the full experience of going down into a coal mine in the heart of the Welsh val-leys. **Sygun Copper Mine** in Beddgelert, Gwynedd, and **Llechwedd Slate Caverns** in Blaenau Ffestiniog, Gwynedd, offer imaginatively conceived tours of the old mines, and the **Welsh Slate**

The Museum of Iron at Ironbridge Gorge, a World Heritage Site

The Black Country Museum

Museum, Llanberis, is an evocative semi-abandoned slate quarry. The **Museum of the Welsh Woollen Industry**, at Drefach Felindre in western Wales, has fabric-making demonstrations, factory trails and bygone tools and machinery. You even can try your hand at spinning.

Northwest England Cromford Mill, Cromford in Derbyshire, is an exciting monument to Richard Arkwright on the site of his first water-powered cotton mill. In The Potteries area (around Stoke-on-Trent, Staffordshire), the **Royal Doulton**, **Wedgwood** and **Spode** factories are open to visitors. The **Gladstone Pottery Museum** at Longton, Staffordshire, is an authentic Victorian pottery. The **Paradise Silk Mill and Museum** in Macclesfield, Cheshire, gives the story of the town's heyday when the fashion was to wear Macclesfield silk buttons. **Quarry Bank Mill**, Styal, Cheshire, is an excellent restoration of an 18th-century water-powered cotton mill in a fine verdant setting, while authentically clanking old machines can be seen, and heard, at the **Helmshore Textile Museums,** in the heartland of the former Lancashire cotton-making country.

At **Stott Park Bobbin Mill** in Finsthwaite, Cumbria, former mill workers explain the process of one of the last bobbin mills to be operational in England – it functioned from 1835 until 1971.

Northeast England At Abbeydale **Industrial Hamlet**, Sheffield, South Yorkshire, a courtyard is surrounded by 18th-century workshops, where scythes were forged in the River Sheaf. The sense of period and sheer atmosphere are most impressive. The **North of England Open Air Museum**, Beamish, Co. Durham, is a clever evocation of the early 1900s.

Southern Scotland New Lanark Mills at Lanark in South Lanarkshire, is a well-preserved factory village; there is not much in the way of working machinery, but further work is in progress; the village has a dramatic setting near waterfalls. At Newtongrange in Midlothian, the **Scottish Mining Museum** has a fine working steam engine used for winding. Ambitious displays cover the lives of the miners and some of the colliery buildings can be visited; its sister site at Prestongrange features a beam engine and locomotives.

Gladstone Pottery Museum

■ Often taken for granted, the 'semi' is a major component of the physical make-up of the British nation. Rapidly and cheaply built in the 1930s, and inexpensive to buyers, semi-detached houses were laid out in neat rows, avenues and crescents. Within two decades, a large part of Britain's countryside had given way to genteel suburbia. The 'semi' may never have been particularly chic, but it has proved admirably adaptable for modern living. ■

Mention the word 'suburbia' in Britain, and it is the 'semi' that springs to mind. Throughout the length and breadth of the country, semi-detached houses line the roads that lead into many major towns. To the passer-by, each may look superficially the same as the other, but closer inspection will reveal certain marks of individuality. For an Englishman's home is his castle, and never more so than his semi.

Rise of the semi The terraced house had been the dominant feature of 19th-century popular housing in England and Wales (Scottish cities specialised more in tenements); inexpensive and quick to build, the terrace provided housing for the artisan classes. Wealthier folk, meanwhile, aspired to semi-detached or detached properties.

The semi-detached house was a feature of the urban scene in Victorian and Edwardian times, but it was in the 1930s Depression years that it really came into its own. Labour was cut-price and plentiful and cheap materials readily available. Speculative builders created new estates in the verdant fringes of London and other major cities, and improved rail and road links made commuting easier. House advertisements promised a rural idyll.

The building boom With this boom came the uni-plan semi: a square plan, a common pitched roof, one party wall, a front and back garden and often a garage built on to one side. The semi was available to virtually anyone with a reasonable income; cash deposits were modest. Rustic and fanciful flourishes were added to the basic design: leaded windows, gables sporting Tudor-style half-timbering, tile-hung walls, stained-glass windows, sunrise-motifs. Interior plans varied little: three or four bedrooms and a bathroom, a lounge (or sitting room) and a small kitchen (after all, in the new labour-saving age of convenience foods, who needed a big kitchen?). Three-piece suites (a sofa for the children, an armchair for each parent) exemplified Edwardian solidity.

And more than half a century on, the semi has shown itself readily adaptable, with new porches, picture windows and extra rooms over the garage being frequent alterations.

A typical semi, in Basingstoke

■ England's 'green and pleasant land' is not a natural phenomenon, but the product of 200 generations of hard work. Britain's underlying geology – drastically oversimplified – divides the country into a highland zone in the north and west, including Scotland, the Pennines, the Lake District and Wales, and a lowland zone in the south and east. No matter what the geology, however, hardly any part of the landscape is unaltered by human hand. ■

The first people to make a mark on the landscape were the mesolithic people, nomadic hunters who burned forests and cleared large areas in order to control and concentrate herds of wild animals. This lifestyle gradually became more settled as neolithic peoples introduced crops, farming and domesticated animals. To make fields for growing crops and pasture for their cattle, sheep and pigs, they made permanent clearings that eventually resulted, over 4,000 years ago, in landscapes not unlike those we see today, although the actual use of the land was substantially different. Generally, small groups lived in hamlets of a few huts, surrounded by an earth bank or a wooden palisade, with fields outside. These were the forerunners of subsequent centuries of village life.

A well-preserved Roman road on Wheeldale in the North York Moors

❑ The stone axes with which neolithic farmers cleared the land were far more effective implements than is generally realised. Experiments indicate that one man working alone could have cleared a quarter-hectare (half an acre) a week. ❑

The earliest communities Over many centuries, villages grew up where there was fertile soil and an adequate water supply. The 'typical' English village of houses clustered round a village green and duckpond is only one of several types (in Wales and Scotland the green is not a common feature). Other villages are stretched out along a road, or have more than one centre, or sprawl about in a congenial muddle.

Each village was a service centre for the surrounding countryside, providing a church, a drinking house, craftsmen, and a marketplace. The more successful ones had a geographical advantage – they were by a ford, or an important road junction – and developed into towns. Others were founded by landowners looking for profit.

Tracks and roads The earliest roads were created by farmers and their livestock, and many of today's country lanes, lying deep between high banks, are thousands of years old. Trade also had its part to play and a network of prehistoric 'high roads' can still be traced. It was the

❏ Britain's human history stretches back over a vast period of time to the arrival of manlike beings over 300,000 years ago. It is conventionally divided into the periods shown here, but the dates are rough approximations.

Period	Dates	Outstanding example
Palaeolithic (Old Stone Age)	to 12000 BC	
Mesolithic (Middle Stone Age)	12000–4500 BC	
Neolithic (New Stone Age)	4500–2500 BC	Belas Knap, Winchcombe
Bronze Age	2500–750 BC	Stonehenge
Iron Age	from 750 BC	Maiden Castle hillfort, Dorchester
Roman invasion of Britain	AD 43	Roman Baths, Bath ❏

Oak woodlands near Butts Lawn in Hampshire's ancient New Forest

Romans who introduced the first centrally planned road network, and today, just a few feet beneath many long straight stretches of highway, lies a Roman road. The Roman network sufficed until a new era of road building began in the 1700s.

❏ The great charm ... of English scenery is the moral feeling that seems to pervade it. It is associated in the mind with ideas of order, of quiet, of sober well-established principles, hoary usage and reverend custom. Everything seems to be the growth of ages of reverend and peaceful existence.
　　Washington Irving (1820) ❏

Forest and woodlands As well as clearing forest for agriculture, neolithic people managed woodlands very successfully. Coppicing is a good example: the tree is cut down to ground level so that it throws up several shoots to replace the lost one. Over several years this produces a crop of poles of just the right size for whatever use the woodsman decides upon, and coppiced trees live on almost indefinitely so long as coppicing continues. It is a perfect self-regenerating system. After World War II, skills such as these, first learned over 4,000 years ago, were still being used and refined.

Today, however, most woodlands are unmanaged, since management is seen as expensive, and the skills have all but disappeared. Wildlife suffers as a result: flowers are shaded out, and butterflies have lost the glades that they need.

Landscape today Despite the changes of the 20th century, the British landscape presents a remarkable historical tableau. Early settlers slashed and burned down the primeval forests, exhausting the soil and leaving moorlands that still cover much of upland Britain. Agricultural and much common land was then subject to enclosure from medieval times to the 19th century; the old 'open field' system, where several farmers worked strips within a large single field, was abandoned in favour of smaller enclosures. During that period the hedges and drystone walls that dominate so much of the lowlands today changed the face of the country.

■ **Gaunt and grey in the British countryside, the shells and ruins of formidable medieval strongholds still defy time and weather. They were sited at strategic points – to control a river crossing, a hill pass or a harbour, for example. Many of them saw little or no action, which is testimony to their effectiveness. They were not built to provoke attack, but to deter it.** ■

The Norman Conquest of England made 1066 one of the key dates of British history. The triumphant William the Conqueror – known in his own time, though not to his face, as William the Bastard – parcelled England out among his Norman, French, Breton and Flemish followers. The more important built castles to secure their grip on their new estates, and by 1100 there were some 500 of these strongholds in England. The early ones consisted of a mound of earth (the motte), built by conscript labour, with a yard (the bailey) round its base, enclosed by an earth rampart and ditch. Wooden buildings housed the castle's lord, his family and his small private army. The local villagers could take refuge in the bailey in time of danger.

Bastions of stone Many of these primitive fortresses were soon replaced by daunting strongholds of stone. A hulking keep was erected on the mound, its walls as much as 30m (99ft) high and 6m (20ft) thick at the base,

Stark and strong, Corfe Castle in Dorset was built by the Normans

pierced by tiny windows through which archers and crossbowmen could fire. The living quarters were in the keep, with the ground floor used for storage and dungeons. Outer curtain walls kept besiegers at a distance, and around them might be a water-filled moat, crossed by a drawbridge. Castles became ever more elaborate as time went by.

> ❏ The rich man in his castle,
> The poor man at his gate,
> God made them high and lowly,
> And ordered their estate.
> **19th-century hymn** ❏

The **Tower of London**, originally built for William the Conqueror, is a particularly impressive specimen.

In Wales, Norman and native warlords built themselves castles, and when Edward I of England conquered the country, a chain of powerful fortresses, which could be supplied by sea, cemented his hold. **Caernarfon**, **Harlech**, **Conwy** and **Beaumaris** castles still testify to the skill of his military engineer, James of St George. Scotland, where central authority was never as strong, bristles with ferocious and romantic strongholds, led by **Edinburgh** and **Stirling**, high on their lofty crags.

The manorial estate Castles were extremely costly and only the richest magnates could afford them. In medieval England, the basic landholding unit was the manor, ruled by its lord. Often a manor was a village with its surrounding countryside, but some manors contained more than one village, while others covered

Harlech Castle, impregnable monument to King Edward I

only part of one. The villagers cultivated the land, while the lord's function was to protect them and to keep order. Above the lord, in what is now called the 'feudal system', a chain of greater lords led up to the king himself, each link in the chain owing support to the one above it and protection to the one below.

The lord lived in the manor house, a bigger version of the timber-and-mud hovels of his villagers. By the 13th century, manor houses were being built of stone and the fortified manor house appeared – cheaper and more comfortable than a castle, but defensible. They centred on one main room, the hall, where the household ate and slept, while the dogs gnawed their bones on the straw- or rush-covered floor and the smoke from a central hearth drifted out through a hole in the roof.

Over the centuries, the medieval lord of the manor's descendants evolved into the less omnipotent, though still dominating figure of the country squire. Just as the power of kings has ebbed away, so the title of lord of the manor has become an attractive but empty honour.

❏ Perhaps England's best example of a fortified manor house is Stokesay Castle, near Shrewsbury in Shropshire (see page 124), which has almost completely preserved its medieval atmosphere. ❏

■ At the same time as being beautiful and satisfying to the senses, churches were originally built as earthly houses for God, symbols of the God-given order of the world and the true purpose of human life. Through the centuries, generations have worshipped in them, joined in the community's spiritual life, been baptised and married and finally, after life's fitful fever, have been carried to sleep in eternal peace in the churchyard. ■

From the humblest parish church to the most sumptuous cathedral, in country and town alike, churches are a familiar and essential element of the British scene.

Almost all of them have been altered, enlarged or rebuilt many times over.

Styles of architecture A few Anglo-Saxon churches are still standing. Small and plain, they are the oldest English ecclesiastical buildings to survive to this day. The Normans built on an altogether more massive and powerful scale, with thick, round columns supporting the roof and round arches above small doors and windows.

The Saxon church at Greensted, Essex, is built of split oak logs

The Gothic style, which arrived in Britain in the 12th century, was lighter, airier, more slender, and more uplifting to the spirit. Its earliest phases, Early English and the more ornate Decorated, introduced the pointed arch, the flying buttress and the tall spire that pointed to heaven as humanity's goal. These churches were alive with elaborate decoration, carvings in wood and stone, stained-glass windows, statues and wall paintings – the religious textbooks of an age that could not read. Much of this decoration, however, was destroyed or painted over by the Puritans under the Commonwealth in the 17th century, with the result that many churches are notably plain. In the 14th century came the Perpendicular style, named after the strong vertical lines that carry the eye up to the roof. Tall, soaring shafts support a web of fan-vaulting and enormous windows of the most delicate tracery, while graceful towers rise to a riot of pinnacles. The style reached its apogee in the astonishing stone cobweb of King's College Chapel, Cambridge.

The monastic movement Among the most haunting legacies that the Middle Ages left to Britain are the now ruined monasteries – Fountains, Rievaulx, Glastonbury, Tintern and many more. Medieval abbeys and priories ran a rough-and-ready welfare system for the poor, treated the sick, kept scholarship and art alive, and gave hospitality to travellers, but their primary function was as centres of prayer and worship. At eight services a day, from matins long before dawn to vespers at sunset and compline at bedtime, the monks paid human-kind's tribute of devotion to God.

The church was always the biggest and finest building in a monastery, usually standing at one side of a quadrangle. Around the other sides were the refectory for meals, the kitchen, the dormitory and the infirmary. The monks themselves took vows of poverty, but monasteries accumulated large estates and ran farms. Fountains Abbey in Yorkshire, for example, was the North of England's biggest wool producer.

During the 16th century, the **Reformation** created the Church of England as a separate body, no longer owing allegiance to the pope, and in the 1530s the monasteries were all closed down (the church, however, was often retained by the community as a parish church). The purpose was to boost the king's income, but most of the monastic land ended up in the hands of the aristocracy and the country gentry, not only enriching them but making it quite certain that the Dissolution of the Monasteries would never be reversed.

Today empty, roofless shells stand quietly where generations of monks once lived and prayed.

The soaring ruins of Tintern Abbey

❏ Guidebooks often use the following terms for early and medieval styles of architecture in Britain. The dates should only be considered as rough indications.

Style	Dates	Outstanding example
Saxon	650–1066	Church of St Andrew, Greensted-juxta-Ongar, Essex
Norman (or Romanesque)	1066–1190	Durham Cathedral
Gothic: Early English	1190–1275	Salisbury Cathedral
Decorated	1275–1375	Exeter Cathedral
Perpendicular	1375–1485	King's College Chapel, Cambridge
Classical	17th–18th centuries	St Paul's Cathedral, London
Gothic Revival	19th century	Truro Cathedral ❏

■ **A record of largely peaceful development since the 1500s has left Britain virtually without equal in the number of gracious and historic houses open to the public to enjoy, packed from floor to ceiling with treasures of art and triumphs of decoration – paintings, sculptures, furniture, porcelain, books and clocks. Surrounded by exquisite gardens and sumptuously landscaped parks, these historic legacies testify to five centuries of wealth, taste and security. Many are run by the National Trust.** ■

Ordinary people's houses in the Middle Ages were made of sticks, mud and thatch, easily built and, when they fell down, easily replaced. The comparatively few medieval buildings which have survived are the important ones – castles, churches, monasteries – constructed massively of stone.

Tudor Chenies Manor House, near Amersham in Buckinghamshire

The Elizabethan age The Tudor era was one of peace and prosperity in which the rich Englishman's home no longer needed to be a castle. The wealthy built ostentatious houses, Cardinal Wolsey and Henry VIII leading the way with the huge brick palace of **Hampton Court**.

Capacious bay windows gazed out upon the countryside, while the fantastically elaborate chimneystacks of grand houses of the 16th and 17th centuries joined the gables, turrets and balustrades that enlivened the

roofline to impress the neighbours with the depth of the owner's purse.

Much Tudor building was in brick, but in areas where there was plenty of timber – as in the southeast and the western Midlands – houses were half-timbered, with rectangular wooden frames enclosing panels of whitewashed plaster or brick. The most lavish examples, like **Little Moreton Hall** in Cheshire, are a riot of zebra-striped patterns.

❑ The stately homes of England,
How beautiful they stand,
To prove the upper classes
Have still the upper hand.
Noel Coward (1899–1973) ❑

The classical ideal Outside these houses, a formal symmetrical garden was a sign that the Renaissance enthusiasm for classical Greek and Roman architecture was infiltrating from the continent. The first really famous individual British architects – **Inigo Jones** and **Sir Christopher Wren** in the 17th century – were influenced by classical ideals.

The charming Queen Anne style employed red brick to create a simple, symmetrical mansion with large sash windows and a four-sided roof behind a parapet. As the 18th century unfolded, **Sir John Vanbrugh** piled the colossal baroque palaces of **Castle Howard** in North Yorkshire and **Blenheim** in Oxfordshire upon the groaning earth, both domed and porticoed in princely splendour. Most of the English upper class, however, preferred the restrained elegance of the Palladian style of mansion, with its straight lines and pleasing proportions, its classical pillars and pediments. Around the house would stretch a noble park, as smooth lawns escorted the eye to carefully positioned groups of trees, an artificial lake, a bridge, and a temple.

Georgian elegance The same style, imposing a calm order upon unruly Nature, created some of Britain's most satisfying townscapes – in Bath, London, Edinburgh and other cities. From the 1760s the interiors of Georgian houses were opulently enriched by the genius of **Robert Adam** and his many imitators, who reintroduced colour and glamour into mansions like **Syon House** in Middlesex, in rooms never intended for living in, but for entertaining, intrigue, gossip and politics.

Victorian exuberance A powerful enthusiasm for medieval Gothic Christian architecture gave many Victorian houses an ecclesiastical look, with turrets, pointed windows and stained glass, while Scots magnates built themselves mock baronial palaces. Victorian architects and their patrons took the whole past as their province. They adopted whatever architectural style took their fancy and blended characteristics from different styles to romantic and sometimes wildly over-the-top effect. In the Edwardian period came

Kiftsgate Court, Gloucestershire: a Georgian house in a lovely garden

❏ All through the 19th century, the Gothic and the classical styles vied for supremacy. In Yorkshire, for instance, the city fathers of Leeds built a magnificent classical temple as their town hall, while rival Bradford erected a Gothic town hall of mammoth proportions. ❏

a revival of the Queen Anne style and traditional English 'vernacular', or countryside, styles, led by **Richard Norman Shaw** and **Sir Edwin Lutyens**.

Changing ideals A fierce reaction against Victorian and Edwardian 'pastiche' followed in the 20th century as the modern movement in architecture adopted an austere simplicity of straight lines and concrete, carrying over not infrequently into totalitarian brutishness. A reaction has now developed against these high-rise concrete egg boxes, with a return to a more romantic approach.

The vernacular Just as fascinating as the range of styles displayed in Britain's great houses and public buildings is the variety of regional style seen in the country's vernacular buildings. These – the houses of the ordinary people in particular, but also their agricultural and industrial buildings – were constructed following local traditions and in whatever material was readily to hand, be it stone, flint or cob, thatch, slate or pantile. It is perhaps these buildings above all which give Britain such an excitingly diverse architectural heritage.

31

Kings and queens

■ **Few Britons today know much about their medieval rulers. The kings and queens whose memories still live are those of the Tudor, Stuart, Hanoverian and Windsor dynasties, which have reigned for the last 500 years. Figures such as Henry VIII, Elizabeth I, Mary, Queen of Scots and the Young Pretender are remembered in a popular mingling of history and romance.** ■

The modern history of Britain dates from 1485, the year when a shrewd Welshman called Henry Tudor seized the throne of England by force to make himself King Henry VII. His son, **Henry VIII**, with a massive frame and small eyes so famously depicted in the Holbein portrait, is known for his treatment of his six wives. The rhyme goes 'Divorced, beheaded, died, divorced, beheaded, survived'. His changing desires for wives have shaped aspects of the legal and religious systems of today.

Elizabeth Tudor It was typical of Henry's daughter, **Elizabeth I**, that when a deputation arrived in 1558 to tell her she was queen, the 25-year-old princess was sitting under an oak tree demurely reading an improving book. She always had a genius for public relations. A consummate politician, with her father's physical and intellectual vigour allied to grace and charm, she steered her country safely through 44 dangerous years.

Henry VIII with Anne of Cleves, his fourth wife

Elizabeth I, 'Virgin Queen'

❑ Mr Speaker, we perceive your coming is to present thanks to us. Know I accept them with no less joy than your loves can have desire to offer such a present, and do more esteem it than any treasure or riches; for those we know how to prize, but loyalty, love and thanks, I account them invaluable. And though God hath raised me high, yet this I account the glory of my crown, that I have reigned with your loves.

> Queen Elizabeth I, the 'golden speech' to her last parliament, 1601 ❑

The Stuarts Scotland, meanwhile, had seen a long succession of kings of the Stuart dynasty, who since 1371 had struggled to impose their authority on their turbulent aristocracy. The beautiful **Mary, Queen of Scots** was forced to abdicate in

A Van Dyck portrait of Charles I

1567. She escaped to England, where she was politely kept prisoner for 20 years until executed at Fotheringay Castle in 1587.

Her son, **James VI of Scots**, succeeded the childless Elizabeth I in 1603 as **James I of England**. The house of Stuart fared little better in England than in Scotland. **Charles I**, attempting to uphold royal power against parliament, was defeated in the **Civil War** and executed on a cold January day in London in 1649. **Charles II** was restored to the throne in 1660, after a deeply unpopular interregnum of republican rule. He is remembered for his charm, his cynicism and his sex life. **James II**, Charles' brother, was dethroned for his Roman Catholic sympathies in 1688 and his daughter, **Queen Anne**, was the last Stuart ruler.

The Hanoverians On Anne's death in 1714, the Elector of Hanover became king as **George I**. Although he was a German who could not speak a word of English, as a Protestant he was preferred to the Stuart claimants, who made a bloody, but unsuccessful throw for their lost throne in 1745, led by

Prince Charles Edward, saccharinely known as **Bonnie Prince Charlie**.

It was during poor mad **George III**'s time – he was much liked for his hearty geniality – that the American colonies broke away to become an independent nation. His granddaughter, **Queen Victoria**, enjoyed the longest reign of any British sovereign – 64 years from 1837 to 1901. Clad invariably in black after the death of her beloved Prince Consort, Albert, in 1861, the widowed queen was ruler of the largest empire in history, and became immensely popular as a symbol of British power and influence at their peak.

The House of Windsor Victoria's grandson, **George V**, sensitive about the dynasty's German connections during World War I, decided to change the family name to the House of Windsor. Windsor Castle remains the favourite residence of **Queen Elizabeth II**.

❑ Walk wide o' the Widow at Windsor,
For 'alf o' Creation she owns.
Rudyard Kipling (1892) ❑

■ **The fact that Britain is an island has formed and coloured its whole history and character. Britain's greatness was built on sea-borne trade, and the British Empire rested on the Royal Navy's command of the sea, celebrated in popular patriotic songs from *Rule Britannia* and *Hearts of Oak* to *All the Nice Girls Love a Sailor*. The sea and seafaring are in Britain's blood.** ■

Nelson's flagship, HMS Victory

The sea has played contradictory roles in British history, as both barrier and bridge. Whatever poets may say, Britannia has always needed her 'towers along the steep', coastal fortifications against attack by sea. They can be seen bristling along England's southern and southeastern shoreline, ranging from Roman forts of the Saxon Shore to medieval and Tudor castles, Martello towers and Palmerston forts against the French, and World War II defences.

Overseas trading At the same time, while the sea has served Britain as a defensive moat, it has also been by sea that people, ideas and trade have moved between Britain and the rest of the world. In prehistoric times, ships from the Mediterranean came to Cornwall for tin, and in Roman days, Britain exported slaves, oysters and hunting dogs to the continent and imported wine.

The great medieval 'wool churches' of England stand as testimony to the wealth generated by the export trade in wool and cloth. It remained a major factor in the economy into the 16th century, when merchants forged thriving trade links with the world beyond Europe – Asia, Africa and the Americas. The piratical **Sir Francis Drake** sailed away in 1578 in a cockleshell of a ship, which was only the second to circumnavigate the globe. Gleefully plundering Spanish possessions on the way, he returned in 1580 with loot estimated at £25 million in today's money.

In command of the seas It was Drake, along with two other formidable Elizabethan seadogs, Hawkins and Frobisher, who sent the ponderous Spanish Armada packing in 1588. In fact, the British navy can trace its history back to **Alfred the Great** in the 9th century, the first English king to lead his own squadron in battle, against the Danes. In medieval times, ships and crews were supplied for the royal fleet by the **Cinque Ports** of southeast England – Dover, Sandwich, Hythe, New Romney and Hastings.

❏ Britannia needs no bulwarks,
No towers along the steep;
Her march is o'er the mountain waves,
Her home is on the deep.
 Thomas Campbell, *Ye Mariners of England* (1800–01) ❏

The Tudor and Stuart kings built up a more effective and powerful force.

Between 1700 and 1780, Britain's foreign trade almost doubled. The port of Bristol took a leading part in the slave trade, which shipped millions of Africans to the American plantations. Meanwhile Britain became the world's leading colonial power in a struggle against the French in which command of the sea was of paramount importance. The French were driven from India and North America, and the British built up the empire on which the sun never set. The 'wooden walls' – the Royal Navy's implacable three-deckers – kept **Napoleon** at arm's length. 'I do not say they cannot come,' said Admiral Lord St Vincent of the French invasion barges, 'I only say they cannot come by sea.'

Illustrious names The navy was the guardian of British liberty and a succession of naval heroes etched their names on the British consciousness – Anson, Rodney, Hood, Howe, St Vincent, Collingwood, Cochrane. The most admired and loved of them all was **Horatio Nelson**, killed at the battle of Trafalgar in 1805 as HMS *Victory* bore down upon the foe. The great ship is lovingly preserved in Portsmouth.

> ❑ A willing foe and sea room. The Royal Navy's Friday night toast ❑

The British Empire would eventually cover a quarter of the land surface of the globe, stretching across the world's heaving waters from Canada to India, Australia, New Zealand and remote islands in the Pacific. It could not be sustained, however, and World War II demonstrated that command of the sea had passed from Britain to the United States.

A martello tower on the south coast, one of many built to counter the threat of a Napoleonic invasion

■ Many places in Britain are linked with famous writers and their work. The village of Chawton in Hampshire shelters the modest house where Jane Austen wrote (*Pride and Prejudice, Sense and Sensibility, Emma ...*), hiding her papers when any of the household came in. Near by at Selborne is the home of Gilbert White, doyen of English country writers. Each year, Rochester in Kent honours Charles Dickens, who lived near by. George Bernard Shaw's home can be explored at Ayot St Lawrence in Hertfordshire, as well as Lord Byron's and D H Lawrence's homes near Nottingham, Rudyard Kipling's at Bateman's in Sussex, and Dr Johnson's in Lichfield and London. ■

William Shakespeare is without rival as a crowd-puller among English writers, and the town of Stratford-upon-Avon in Warwickshire is the most visited British tourist destination outside London. The Bard's birthplace attracts more than half a million visitors a year.

Literary shrines In West Yorkshire the once-grim little town of Haworth is thronged with pilgrims to the parsonage, home of Charlotte, Emily and Anne **Brontë** and their unsatisfactory brother Branwell. Out on the desolate moorland is the ruined farmhouse that may have been the original *Wuthering Heights*.

The Lake District also draws literary pilgrims, to **William Wordsworth**'s homes at Dove Cottage and Rydal Mount, and the Lakeland scenes which inspired great poetry. **John Ruskin**, the Victorian art critic and social reformer, owned a house with a magical view over Coniston Water. **Sir Hugh Walpole**'s romantic 'Herries' novels were set in the Derwent Water area, as was **Arthur Ransome**'s *Swallows and Amazons*. **Beatrix Potter** lived at Near Sawrey.

At Laugharne in South Wales the most famous Welsh poet of this century is fondly remembered at **Dylan Thomas**' Boathouse, where he wrote.

Scotland's national poet, **Robert Burns**, is cherished at the humble cottage where he was born in the outskirts of Ayr. The 'immortal memory' is also honoured in Dumfries, where Burns spent his last years. **Sir Walter Scott**'s engaging collection of historical curios – Rob Roy's sword, a lock of the Young Pretender's hair and so on – can be admired at Abbotsford, his home in his beloved Scottish Borders, while at Kirriemuir is the birthplace of **Sir James Barrie**, author of *Peter Pan*.

John Bunyan's iron violin is on show in the museum in Bedford devoted to the author of *Pilgrim's Progress*. At Coxwold in North Yorkshire is the house where **Laurence Sterne** created the humours of *Tristram Shandy,* and **Milton** completed *Paradise Lost* at Chalfont St Giles in Buckinghamshire.

❏ Selborne, Nov 22, 1777
This sudden summer-like heat was attended by many summer coincidences; for on those two days the thermometer rose to sixty-six in the shade; many species of insects revived and came forth; some bees swarmed ... the old tortoise ... awakened and came forth out of his dormitory.
  Gilbert White (1720–93),
  The Natural History and Antiquities of Selborne ❏

Resting places Interesting literary connections can frequently be found in churchyards. **T S Eliot** is buried at East Coker in Somerset, **John Buchan** at Elsfield, near Oxford. The country churchyard of **Thomas Gray**'s famous *Elegy* can be found at Stoke Poges in Buckinghamshire. The memory of the evil **Count Dracula**, Bram Stoker's creation, vampirishly haunts the Yorkshire graveyard of Whitby. In London, Westminster Abbey's south transept is affectionately known as **Poets' Corner** because Chaucer, Edmund Spenser, Tennyson, Browning and many other famous poets are buried or have memorials there.

Monuments to Shakespeare, Milton, Wordsworth, Burns, Keats

> ❏ The curfew tolls the knell of parting day,
> The lowing herd winds slowly o'er the lea,
> The ploughman homeward plods his weary way,
> And leaves the world to darkness and to me.
> 　　**Thomas Gray** (1716–71),
> 　　*Elegy in a Country Churchyard* ❏

and Shelley cluster close to memorials to Byron, T S Eliot, W H Auden and Dylan Thomas.

' ... my country still' Some writers are associated with a whole area of countryside, seen through their eyes and peopled with their characters. **Thomas Hardy** Country extends over much of Dorset and the museum in Dorchester has an excellent Hardy collection. The 'blue remembered hills' of Shropshire are inseparably linked with the melancholic poetry of **A E Housman**.

Tennyson is particularly cherished in his native county of Lincolnshire, and there is a statue of him outside Lincoln Cathedral. The centre of the **George Eliot** industry is Nuneaton in Warwickshire, and the southern part of Tyne and Wear calls itself **Catherine Cookson** Country after the best-selling romantic novelist.

> ❏ The first fire since the summer is lit, and is smoking into the room;
> The sun-rays spread it through, like woof-lines in a loom.
> Sparrows spurt from the hedge, whom misgivings appal
> That winter did not leave last year for ever, after all.
> 　　**Thomas Hardy** (1840–1928),
> 　　*Shortening Days at the Homestead* ❏

Sometimes it is the characters more than the author who cast the spell. It is hardly possible to explore Exmoor without recalling **Lorna Doone**, Cornwall without thinking of the heroes and heroines of **Daphne du Maurier** and **Winston Graham** or Dartmoor without memories of Sherlock Holmes, Doctor Watson and the Hound of the Baskervilles.

Thomas Hardy's statue at the top of the high street in Dorchester, the 'Casterbridge' of his novels

■ **Britain's most characteristic contribution to western art lies in a long tradition of landscape painting, which inspired such artists as Gainsborough, Constable and Turner. It is this tradition which created the British idea, not so much of what the landscape looks like, as of what it ideally ought to look like. Visitors enjoying the British countryside today still tend to see it through the eyes of the great painters of the past.** ■

The British tradition of landscape painting was founded by **Richard Wilson**, who was born in Wales in 1714 and was deeply impressed by the work of the French painter Claude Lorraine. Battling against incomprehension, neglect and poverty, he struggled to introduce to the British eye the novel impression that wild scenery could be beautiful; his paintings of his native Welsh mountains looming above limpid lakes have a classic grandeur and serenity.

The great names Far more successful financially was **Thomas Gainsborough**, who came from Suffolk. He made his money as a fashionable portrait painter in Bath and London, but his passion was for landscapes – often generalised and idyllic, rather than depicting a particular place. The great Victorian critic John Ruskin said of him: 'His touch was as light as the sweep of a cloud and swift as the flash of a sunbeam.'

John Constable, arriving on the scene 50 years later, came from the Suffolk–Essex border and his paintings of hayfields, church towers, river scenes, carthorses and wagons have remained hugely popular ever since. Salisbury Cathedral, Stonehenge and the South Coast were also favourite subjects of his. He believed in the most minute study of Nature, to render, as he said, 'light – dews – breezes – bloom – and freshness' with loving accuracy, and he broke free of the formal Claude-inspired landscape.

Constable's contemporary, the prodigious **Joseph Mallord William Turner**, travelled all over Britain, painting romantic landscapes, castles, cathedrals and great houses. He followed in Richard Wilson's footsteps in Wales, painted extensively at Petworth in Sussex and in the Thames Valley, and rejoiced in the scenery of the Lake District and Wharfedale in Yorkshire. He grew increasingly fascinated by effects of light – in his paintings of Norham Castle in Northumberland the ruined fortress and the grazing cattle almost disappear into abstraction in the glowing sunlit mist.

❏ He saw that there were more clouds in every sky than had ever been painted, more trees in every forest, more crags on every hillside, and set himself with all his strength to proclaim the great quantity of the universe.

John Ruskin (1819–1900), on Turner ❏

Places of inspiration Other painters drawn to the Lake District included **Philippe de Loutherburg** and **Joseph Wright of Derby**, and much later, oddly enough, the German Dada artist **Kurt Schwitters**, who settled at Ambleside after World War II. **L S Lowry** painted Lake District scenes, too, though he is better known for his northern industrial townscapes.

Some areas have inspired groups of artists, like the **Norwich School** of painters in the early 19th century. **Bristol**'s flourishing school of artists

Flatford Mill in Suffolk, still recognisable from Constable's paintings

The young J M W Turner

was dominated by **Francis Danby** in the 1820s. The **Newlyn School** of artists, based in Cornwall's premier fishing port, was led by **Stanhope Forbes** from the 1880s, while **St Ives** in Cornwall was later a base for **Barbara Hepworth**, **Ben Nicholson** and the great potter **Bernard Leach**.

The mystical painter **Samuel Palmer** settled at Shoreham in Kent in the 1820s to explore his 'Valley of Vision'. **John Singer Sargent** painted Worcestershire landscapes in the 1880s, **Graham Sutherland** painted in Pembrokeshire before and after World War II, while Cookham in Berkshire owes its fame to the paintings and parables of **Sir Stanley Spencer**.

In every generation since the 18th century, artists have found inspiration in the British landscape.

❏ There was not a picturesque clump of trees nor even a single tree of any beauty, no, not a hedgerow, stem or post in or around my native town that I did not treasure in my memory from earliest years.

Thomas Gainsborough (1726–88) ❏

■ **Crowded, noisy, dirty and packed with life, Manchester was the archetype of the new cities created in Britain by the Industrial Revolution. Instead of a skyline offering church spires, hundreds of factories belched out smoke and fumes. Though horrified by the city's abominable slums and its turbid rivers crawling with filth, many visitors saw Manchester as the symbol of a dawning new age of intense creativity and vitality.** ■

40

The Industrial Revolution was revolutionary not so much in its speed, but in its consequences. The century between 1750 and 1850 ushered in the machine age of factories, mass production and the assembly line, the industrial town and the industrial working class. Why it should all have started in Britain is a disputed question, but the country had ample resources of coal and iron as well as a growing empire overseas which provided a captive market for British-made products.

The textile industry The industries most affected in the early stages were textiles, iron and steel, coal mining and pottery. In textiles, a succession of inventions provided increased output with less expenditure of human energy, transforming the making of cloth from a small-

scale operation, carried on by skilled workmen and their families at home, to large-scale production in factories where unskilled workers, many of them women and children, toiled as acolytes of the insatiable machines. In 1765 **James Hargreaves** patented the 'Spinning Jenny' – named after his wife – which could spin several threads simultaneously. Four years later a formidable Lancashire-man called **Richard Arkwright**, who became the first great industrial tycoon, patented a spinning frame powered by water. He built a cotton mill and company town at Cromford in the beautiful Derbyshire valley of the Derwent, where his workers laboured in 12-hour shifts as the machines clattered on day and night.

Titus Salt's vast 1853 mill and his model village at Saltaire, Bradford

> ❏ And if here man has made of the very daylight an infamy, he can boast that he adds to the darkest night the weird beauty of fire and flame-tinted cloud. From roof and hill you may see on every side furnace calling furnace with fiery tongues and wreathing messages of smoke.
> **Arnold Bennett**
> *The Potteries* (1898) ❏

The power of steam Arkwright's machinery was powered by water, but in 1779 **Samuel Crompton** invented 'the mule', a spinning machine that could be powered by water or steam.

Steam was the driving force of the Industrial Revolution, and the most important figure in its development, the Scots inventor **James Watt**, patented the first modern steam engine in 1769.

Steam was used to drive machinery in factories and mines, and later to propel railway locomotives and ships, as a transport revolution developed in the 19th century.

> ❏ Since the introduction of inanimate mechanism into British manufactories, man, with few exceptions, has been treated as a secondary and inferior machine.
> **Robert Owen**, *A New View of Society* (1813) ❏

Coal and iron Steam required coal. Britain's coal production doubled between 1750 and 1800, and then grew by a factor of 20 by the end of the 19th century. **Abraham Darby** initiated the mass production of iron ore at Ironbridge and new industrial regions grew up close to the principal coalfields in the **Midlands**, the **North of England**, Scotland's **Clydeside** and **South Wales**, where the flow of coal from the valleys turned sleepy little fishing villages like Cardiff, Barry and Swansea into busy, blackened ports. At the entrance to the Great Exhibition of 1851 in London's Hyde Park there stood, appropriately, a towering 24-tonne block of coal.

Towns like Manchester, Birmingham, Glasgow, Leeds, Bradford and Sheffield covered their surrounding countryside with terrace upon terrace of back-to-back workers' housing and many a lush valley became an inferno of blast furnaces, spoil heaps and 'Satanic mills'. A new Iron Age introduced iron buildings, iron machines, iron bridges, iron boats, even iron tombstones – as well as the iron regimentation of the assembly line.

Victorian Britain was 'the workshop of the world', but other countries took the same path and began to overtake, notably Germany and the United States. In the 1880s Britain enjoyed 37 per cent of the world's trade in manufactured goods, but by 1913 the figure was down to 25 per cent. A new phase of the Industrial Revolution had opened, based on steel, chemicals and electricity, and Britain was unable to keep up.

41

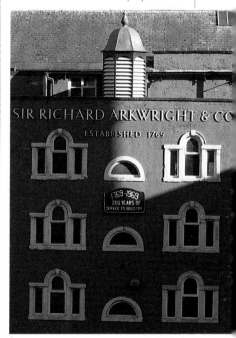

The cotton mill built by Richard Arkwright in Cromford, Derbyshire

LONDON

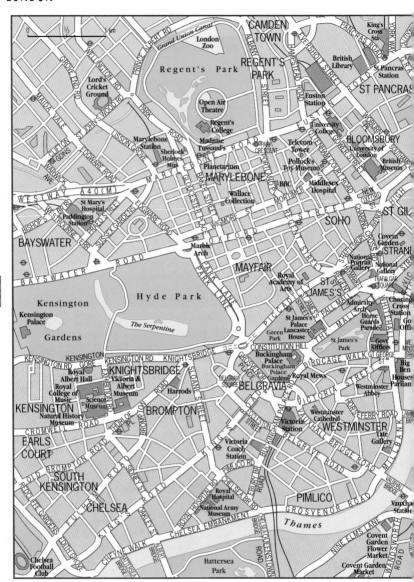

London With a population of over seven million in Central London (12 million in Greater London), it is not an easy city in which to get your bearings; even many Londoners think of the capital in terms of the Underground map, and have little idea of how one neighbourhood leads into another. Stand on Hampstead Heath and you get an idea of the city's sprawling form, across a great basin dissected by the meandering River Thames. Despite this, it is still a highly rewarding city for exploration on foot.

The West End The bulk of the capital's attractions are to be found in the **West End**. **Trafalgar Square►►►** is the undisputed centre of London, where a statue of Nelson

A to Z
LONDON

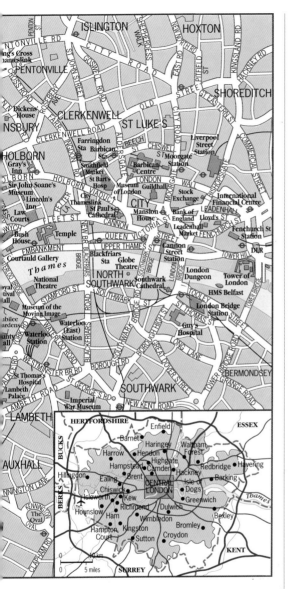

CITY HIGHLIGHTS ◄◄◄◄◄

TRAFALGAR SQUARE *see pages 42 and 52*

COVENT GARDEN *see pages 44 and 52*

BRITISH MUSEUM *see pages 45 and 47*

TOWER OF LONDON AND TOWER BRIDGE *see pages 45, 49 and 53*

GREENWICH *see pages 46, 47 and 57*

MUSEUM OF LONDON *see pages 46 and 49*

ST PAUL'S CATHEDRAL *see pages 46 and 54*

SOUTH KENSINGTON MUSEUMS *see pages 48 and 49*

TATE GALLERY *see page 49*

HAMPTON COURT *see page 51*

stands high on a column guarded by lions modelled by the artist E H Landseer. **St Martin-in-the-Fields church►** and the **National Gallery►►►** take up two sides of the square; Admiralty Arch leads through a third into The Mall, the grand approach to **Buckingham Palace►►** (begun 1825), the main residence of the Queen. In August and September a series of 19 rooms is open to the public, including the Throne Room, Picture Gallery, State Dining Room and Music Room; adjacent are the Royal Mews and Queen's Gallery. **St James's Park►►** is a seductive expanse with a lake and bandstand concerts in summer.

The hub of **Westminster** is Parliament Square, dominated by the clocktower housing the huge bell, Big Ben,

Taking a break by the fountains of Trafalgar Square with the National Gallery (left) and St Martin-in-the-Fields church (right)

London: A potted history Part 1: Romans to Wren
Becomes the Roman settlement of *Londinium* after the Roman invasion of Britain in AD 43; London Bridge built across the Thames (not until 1738 was a second bridge built across the river, at Westminster).
Hit by the Black Death in 1348–50 and the Plague in 1665–6. The Great Fire in 1666 destroys four-fifths of the city, taking the slums, rats and plague with it. Sir Christopher Wren rebuilds St Paul's Cathedral and a host of city churches.

which is part of London's most photographed building, the splendid Gothic Revival **Houses of Parliament▶▶▶**. The symbol of the seat of government, they were remodelled by Charles Barry and Augustus Pugin after fire destroyed an earlier building in 1834. When parliament is sitting, the Strangers' Gallery can be visited (*Open* Mon–Thu 5.30–10.30pm, Fri 9.30am–3pm). Across the square is **Westminster Abbey▶▶▶**.

To the west, some of the best addresses in London are in **Mayfair**, chic **Chelsea,** elegant **Knightsbridge** and **Kensington**. Here there is a preponderance of 19th-century stucco in addition to the familiar yellow-grey London brick. **South Kensington** is the primary museum area. **Hyde Park** and adjacent **Kensington Gardens** constitute a green swathe north of the Royal Albert Hall and the Albert Memorial (which is currently swathed in long-term scaffolding).

Covent Garden▶▶▶, the former fruit and vegetable market hall, was converted in 1974 and has been imaginatively revamped into a lively piazza, with boutiques, buskers and craft stalls. Covent Garden Piazza, laid out by Inigo Jones in 1631, was the first true square in London. The name Covent Garden also includes the Royal Opera House (closed for rebuilding until 1999).

Soho▶▶, further west, is the centre of the Chinese community (around Gerrard Street the streetnames are in Chinese) as well as a lively mix of Italian delicatessens, high-class restaurants, nightclubs and sex shops.

Bloomsbury▶ represents the hub of intellectual London: blue plaques (placed on buildings throughout London) indicate the former houses of the famous, including the homes of Charles Dickens (a memorial museum is at 48 Doughty Street) and Virginia Woolf and her 'Bloomsbury Set'. Bloomsbury still has a gracious atmosphere, and is a good illustration of how residential London developed into formal squares and terraces in Georgian and

Regency times; Bedford Square continues to be as fashionable as when it was first laid out in 1775. Landmarks include the **British Museum►►►** (within whose former Reading Room Karl Marx wrote *Das Kapital*) and the unusual **British Telecom Tower**, built in 1964.

Regent's Park►► is a gracious tract laid out by Regency architect John Nash in conjunction with the supremely elegant stucco terraces on its east side; within the park is London Zoo, a boating lake and an open-air theatre, a memorable venue for summer productions. Nash's scheme included Regent Street and Piccadilly Circus; he was under royal instructions to make London the rival of Napoleon's Paris.

Legal London revolves around **Holborn**, with its Gothic Revival High Courts in the Strand and the Central Criminal Courts of the Old Bailey; both have public galleries within the courtrooms. Barristers are attached to chambers within the **Inns of Court►►** (Lincoln's Inn, the Temple etc), where aspiring lawyers are trained.

The City The 'square mile' of the ancient city of London, the City is where the major financial institutions are concentrated; it retains its medieval street pattern, and though the city wall has largely disappeared its gateways live on in placenames (such as Ludgate, Aldersgate, Moorgate); these gates, plus plinths bearing the City griffin (holding the flag of St George, patron saint of England) still mark the City boundaries. It is best approached from London Bridge, which has a perfect view of **Tower Bridge►►►** and the **Tower of London►►►**.

The **Monument►**, designed by Sir Christopher Wren to commemorate the Great Fire of 1666, is a good viewing platform for those fit enough to manage the narrow steps. The **Lloyd's Building►** in Lime Street is London's most innovative contribution to hi-tech architecture. The **Bank of England** (museum inside), the central bank of the UK, stands at a meeting of seven streets opposite the

45

Whitehall
Linking Trafalgar Square and Parliament Square, this street contains grandiose 19th-century government offices. London's main royal residence was Whitehall Palace until it was destroyed by fire in 1698; the Banqueting House (designed by Inigo Jones in 1622), with its superb painted ceiling by Rubens, is the sole survivor. The archway at the Horse Guards is the former entrance into the palace: traditionally dressed soldiers still keep watch; the Changing of the Guard occurs daily at 11.30am April to August, and every other day from September to March.

St Paul's Cathedral was begun in 1675 and completed 35 years later

*Canary Wharf Tower,
completed in 1991,
rises to 240m (800ft)*

46

Mansion House, the official residence of the Lord Mayor. Lombard Street, leading east, is London's Wall Street.

Near **St Paul's Cathedral▶▶▶**, the **Barbican** development comprises 21 high-rise concrete apartment blocks and a confusing maze of walkways; within is the Barbican Arts Centre, home of the London Symphony Orchestra and London base of the Royal Shakespeare Company, as well as the commendable **Museum of London▶▶▶**.

To the west, the quiet streets of **Smithfield▶** are a different world, with an endearingly workaday look. The Smithfield Meat Market is an outstanding example of a Victorian market building; adjacent Cloth Fair has a rare wooden house, a survivor of the Great Fire, while the **Church of St Bartholomew the Great▶▶** represents London's most impressive Norman church architecture.

The suburbs Docklands▶ is Europe's biggest urban development area. Once the heart of the docklands of the East End, it is now a futuristic cityscape of gleaming office blocks and waterside housing. The area embraces Rotherhithe to the south of the Thames and the Isle of Dogs and North Woolwich to the north. The best way to see it is by the toylike Docklands Light Railway (DLR), which runs along an elevated section from Island Gardens to **Canary Wharf Tower** (Britain's tallest building).

Greenwich▶▶▶ The former centre of the maritime world (see panel, page 47), Greenwich Park occupies a hillside above the Thames, and within it are the Greenwich meridian line, and the old **Royal Observatory** of 1676▶▶. Just below, the **National Maritime Museum▶▶** and **Queen's House** (begun 1616) form a supreme early classical composition by Wren and Inigo Jones. The former **Royal Naval College** was designed by Wren, and the **painted hall▶▶**, open in the afternoons, has a superb painted ceiling by Thornhill. Beside the river, the *Cutty Sark* and *Gipsy Moth IV* can be boarded.

Hampstead and Highgate▶▶ Hampstead Heath remains pleasantly countrified, with hollows, glades and grassland. Parliament Hill Fields attracts kite-fliers and has a wonderful view over central London. Hampstead village developed as an 18th-century spa, and is one of the most fashionable residential districts; psychologist Sigmund Freud and poet John Keats were among its residents – both men's houses can be visited. **Highgate Cemetery▶▶** has a spectacular derelict area (*guided tours*) where many rich and famous are buried, including the writer George Eliot and the poet Christina Rossetti.

Richmond and Chiswick▶▶ These charming riverside villages, now affluent suburbs, are best seen by taking the summer boat service (from the piers at Putney Bridge, Kew Bridge and Richmond Bridge) or by walking along the river, for example west from Hammersmith Bridge along Chiswick Mall to **Chiswick House▶** (see page 51) or from Kew to Richmond, where there is a handsome green by the remains of the palace of Henry VII. The towpath continues west past **Ham House▶** (see page 51).

Richmond Park▶▶ is a former royal hunting park, enclosed by Charles I in 1635 and still inhabited by deer; within is the renowned Isabella Plantation, famous for azaleas and heathers. For **Kew Gardens▶▶▶** (*Admission charge* unless otherwise stated) see page 16.

Getting around
Forget the car and use public transport.
Day travelcards can be purchased at underground and railway stations, as well as from many newsagents, and allow freedom of travel by train, underground and bus (except night bus services).
Zone 1 tickets cover the centre. The Underground (or 'tube') is the easiest to understand, but double-decker buses give excellent views (route 11 is recommended); free bus maps are available from tourist offices.
The *A–Z Street Atlas* is useful for exploring the centre and suburbs.
(For organised tours see page 271.)

Museums and art galleries

The principal museums and galleries to be found in central London are listed below, grouped together in geographical areas. Those outside the central area are described in the side panels on pages 47–9.

Piccadilly Circus and Trafalgar Square►►► In Piccadilly Circus itself are **Sega World►** (in the Trocadero Centre), which promises futuristic virtual-reality rides; and **Rock Circus**, London Pavilion, where Elvis, the Beatles and many more are brought to life with animated mannequins and music.

The **National Gallery►►►** (*Guided tours* daily at 11.30am and 2.30pm, Sat 2pm and 3.30pm from the foyer of the Sainsbury Wing. *Admission free*) Trafalgar Square, WC2, has a superb collection of paintings, many of which will be instantly familiar, from early Renaissance to French Impressionists.

Around the corner, in St Martin's Place, WC2, is the **National Portrait Gallery►►**, as complete a collection of faces in British history, science and the arts as you will find.

Covent Garden►►► and Bloomsbury The art gallery of the **Courtauld Institute►►**, Somerset House, Strand,

WC2, contains one of Britain's finest selections of French Impressionist paintings. In Covent Garden Piazza is the **London Transport Museum►►**, an enthralling place which traces the development of London's buses, trams, trains and 'tubes', with exhibits you can climb. Near by, the **Theatre Museum►**, 1e Tavistock Street, Covent Garden, WC2, exhibits stage memorabilia aptly located in London's theatreland. It works hard to involve visitors (especially children) in the magic of the theatre. (See *Houses*, page 50 for **Sir John Soane's Museum►►**.)

The **British Museum►►►** (*Admission free*), Great Russell Street, WC1, is one of the greatest collections in the world. Its most famous artefacts include the Rosetta Stone (which helped to decode hieroglyphics), Egyptian mummies, the Elgin marbles from the Parthenon in Athens, and the Mildenhall and Sutton Hoo treasures. The latter, one of the finest archaeological finds of all time, is the contents of a 7th-century ship burial, thought to be of Redwald, King of the Angles. **Pollock's Toy Museum►**, Scala Street, W1, has tin soldiers, mechanical curios and toy theatres in a collection for children of all ages.

Greenwich
Greenwich Pier, SE10, is home to the 'tea-clipper' *Cutty Sark*, launched in 1869 and the last of her kind to survive, and *Gipsy Moth IV*, a ketch in which Sir Francis Chichester sailed around the world single-handed in 1966–7. Both vessels can be boarded.

In Greenwich Park, the *National Maritime Museum*, Romney Road, celebrates Britain's long maritime history, with nautical clocks, sea paintings and ship models. Also here is the *Old Royal Observatory*, designed by Wren, with astronomical and navigational exhibits. Adjacent is the *Greenwich Meridian* (0° longitude), where you can have one foot in each hemisphere. Greenwich is proposed to host the huge Millennium Exhibition.

The London Transport Museum

EXCURSIONS SHORTLIST
Here we highlight some recommended day-trip excursions that can easily be made by rail.
Castles: Dover, Windsor.
Historic cities: Cambridge, Canterbury, Oxford, Salisbury, Winchester.
Industrial, railway and naval interest:
Amberley Chalkpits Museum, Bluebell Railway (near Haywards Heath), Chatham Dockyard, Portsmouth, Watercress Line (Alton to Alresford).
Roman remains:
Fishbourne Palace (near Chichester), Lullingstone Villa (near Eynsford), Verulamium (St Albans).
By the sea: Brighton, Broadstairs, Eastbourne, Hastings.
Small towns: Arundel, Rye, Lewes, Sandwich, Tunbridge Wells.

Changing exhibitions of art and design
Major venues for art exhibitions are the *Hayward Gallery* on the South Bank, SE1, the *Royal Academy* in Piccadilly, W1, the *ICA* in the Mall, SW1, and the *Barbican Centre*, Silk Street, EC2. The latest aspects of design are on show at the *Design Centre* in Haymarket.

The Natural History Museum's riot of coloured terracotta and French Romanesque elements was the creation of the architect Alfred Waterhouse

48

Wembley Stadium
The FA Cup final (the highlight of the domestic English football season) and most England internationals are held at Wembley Stadium in northwest London; it is also a venue for major pop concerts. The guided tour around the stadium takes visitors into the changing rooms, hospital, TV studio and up the hallowed 39 steps to the Royal Box where they can lift a replica FA cup; tours take place daily (10am–3pm in winter; 10am–4pm in summer); Wembley Park tube (Metropolitan and Jubilee lines).

Regent's Park and Baker Street London Zoo►► in Regent's Park, NW1, is one of the world's great animal collections and an important research centre. It places emphasis on breeding endangered species, as well as on education.

In Marylebone Road, NW1, **Madame Tussaud's►** tops the charts as a paying tourist attraction; be photographed alongside politicians, pop stars, murderers, sportsmen and actors. Queues can be long. Its annexe, **the Spirit of London►** is a 'sight, sounds and smells' journey in replica London taxi-cabs through 400 years of London: experience the Great Fire, the swinging sixties and more.

Next door, at the **Planetarium►** the sky at night is projected on to a dome; a commentary guides you around the constellations.

The **Sherlock Holmes Museum** at 221b Baker Street, W1, displays memorabilia of the eponymous great sleuth at the address used in Conan Doyle's stories.

The **Wallace Collection►►** (*Admission free*), in 18th-century Hertford House, Manchester Square, W1, is a treat for the eye, containing a dazzling collection of paintings and furniture, bequeathed to the nation in 1897.

South Kensington Prince Albert headed the Royal Commission that purchased the museum sites in what was dubbed 'Albertopolis'. The **Victoria and Albert Museum►►►** (the 'V & A') (*Admission charge*), Cromwell Road, SW7, is a treasurehouse of applied art, displayed by theme (such as musical instruments, costume, furniture etc) and by civilisation (Japan, China, India etc). There is something for everyone but too much for one visit.

Across the road, the **Natural History Museum►►►**, Cromwell Road, SW7, exhibits dinosaurs, evolution, blue whales ... just about everything in this splendid Victorian building. Transformed from antiquated glass cases to

Museums and art galleries

hi-tech displays, the collection is popular with enthusiasts, semi-enthusiasts and children.

The **Science Museum**▶▶▶, Exhibition Road, SW7, is suitable for most tastes and interests, despite the obvious technical bias of many exhibits. Children can conduct their own experiments at the 'Launch Pad'. There is space technology, air transport and much more.

Chelsea and Westminster The **National Army Museum** (*Admission free*), Royal Hospital Road, SW3, tells a 500-year story of soldiers through the ages. The **Cabinet War Rooms**▶ in King Charles Street, SW1, was the subterranean emergency accommodation for Winston Churchill and his cabinet during World War II; the Map Room and the Transatlantic Telephone Room remain intact.

The **Tate Gallery**▶▶▶ on Millbank, SW1, is the nation's greatest collection of British and modern art. Usually entry is free, but admission is charged for special exhibitions. The **Queen's Gallery**▶ at Buckingham Palace, SW1, has items from the royal collection on display.

South of the river The **Imperial War Museum**▶▶, Lambeth Road, SE1, covers the wars that Britain has been involved in since 1914. There is a Blitz reconstruction and a trench dug-out, in addition to weapons, memorabilia, uniforms and an excellent collection of paintings by war artists. The **Museum of the Moving Image (MoMI)**▶▶ on the South Bank, SE1 (by the National Film Theatre), has entertaining hi-tech displays and hands-on exhibits on everything to do with film and television.

In Southwark, on Bankside, the thatched, circular **Globe Theatre** is a faithful reconstruction of the venue where many of Shakespeare's plays were performed in his own lifetime. There are summer performances, guided tours and an exhibition. The **Design Museum**▶ at Butler's Wharf, 28 Shad Thames, SE1, is a stylish riverside building housing changing thematic exhibitions of 20th-century design from a potato peeler to cars.

At the **London Dungeon**▶, Tooley Street, SE1, gloomy vaults reveal the dark stories of punishment, torture and witchcraft. Next door, **Britain at War**▶ evokes London at the height of the Blitz, with the smells and sounds of an air raid. Moored on the Thames (Tower Bridge, The Thames Path, SE1) is **HMS *Belfast*▶**, the last of the Royal Navy's big World War II gunships, launched in 1938.

Tower Hill and the City The **Tower of London**▶▶▶ on Tower Hill, EC3, is the greatest Norman castle in the kingdom, standing silent sentinel in the shadow of Tower Bridge. The Tower has had a long and gory history since Roman times, and was the site of several beheadings, including Anne Boleyn. Traditionally dressed Beefeaters still patrol the grounds. The White Tower is the main Norman feature, housing St John's Chapel and the Armouries. The Crown Jewels are in the Jewel House. **Tower Hill Pageant**▶, Tower Hill Terrace, EC3, offers a 'ride through history' from Roman times to today's Docklands.

At the **Museum of London**▶▶▶, London Wall, EC2, a time-walk display begins with Roman London, passes a cell door from Newgate prison, a panorama of the Great Fire, and a street of Victorian shops.

The East End
The *Bethnal Green Museum of Childhood*, Cambridge Heath Road, Bethnal Green, E2, is an entertaining offshoot of the Victoria and Albert Museum (*Admission free*). Toys of all ages and countries are here; among the exhibits are a wonderful collection of dolls' houses, a surreal display of dolls' heads and a group of puppet theatres.
The *Geffrye Museum* occupies a row of early 18th-century almshouses in Kingsland Road, Hackney, E2. Each of a series of rooms is furnished in a different period style from the Elizabethan era to the 1960s. It is a succinct summary of furniture styles through the ages.

North London suburbs
Sited on the former Hendon airfield, the *Royal Air Force Museum*, Hendon, NW9 (*Admission charge*) has over 60 aircraft and galleries on military aviation and the RAF. Next door, the *Battle of Britain* and *Bomber Command* museums cover related themes.
The *Musical Museum*, 368 High Street, Brentford, has a large collection of musical instruments, with hour-long demonstrations.

The White Tower at the Tower of London

Houses

A suburban overview: commuterdom
Most Londoners live outside the centre and commuterdom extends far into the Home Counties (that is, the counties surrounding London). The suburbs are much-expanded villages, joined together for the most part by somewhat anonymous 19th- and 20th-century building, but seen from the air it is the greenery that impresses. Several ancient commons (originally common grazing grounds) have been retained as public open spaces and there are literally millions of trees in back gardens, suburban roads and parks.

Where the famous lie at rest
Inner London's churchyards were so crowded by the early 1800s that they had become dangerously unsanitary. To relieve this, massive cemeteries were created further from the centre, which are the resting places of some of London's most famous citizens. Emmeline Pankhurst, the Suffragette leader, is buried in Brompton Cemetery; the music-hall queen Marie Lloyd in Hampstead Cemetery; Isambard Kingdom Brunel and Anthony Trollope at Kensal Green; and George Eliot and Karl Marx in Highgate.

Hampton Court's Pond Gardens started life as fishponds to supply the royal kitchens

London has a diverse selection of houses open to the public, from grand palaces built for monarchs to the more personal homes of the famous or eccentric.

Hundreds of buildings in London carry blue plaques, marking where famous people lived and died, such as 25 Brook Street, W1, where Handel lived for 25 years until his death in 1759, or 45 Berkeley Square, W1, where Clive of India cut his throat in 1774. The plaques add an extra piquancy to a stroll through streets and squares.

Central London Sir John Soane's Museum►► (*Guided tours Sat 2.30pm. Admission free*) 13 Lincoln's Inn Fields, WC2, is a wonderfully eccentric house, whose exterior gives away nothing of the astonishing creation by Soane, the architect (1753–1837), who designed it around his collection of artefacts. The house is full of inventive lighting effects and quirky details, and some great treasures, in particular the paintings of *A Rake's Progress* and *An Election* by Hogarth.

At **Dickens' House►**, 48 Doughty Street, WC1, the famous scribe wrote *Oliver Twist*, the *Pickwick Papers* and *Nicholas Nickleby*.

Dr Johnson's House, 17 Gough Square, EC4, hidden away in an alley off Fleet Street, is the house where Dr Johnson resided between 1749 and 1759, and where he completed his celebrated dictionary.

Apsley House►►, Hyde Park Corner, W1, was the London home of the Duke of Wellington, built in 1778 by Robert Adam with 19th-century alterations by James Wyatt. Its interior is notably grand and houses mementoes of the Iron Duke and his campaigns, as well as his collection of paintings.

Kensington Palace►► (*Open* May–Oct, daily 10–5. Palace due to close during 1998 for refurbishment, so

check before setting out), Kensington Gardens, W8, was remodelled by Christopher Wren and William Kent. It was the birthplace of Queen Victoria; it is now the residence of Princess Margaret, and was that of Diana, Princess of Wales. Inside are the royal collection of art and furniture, a set of magnificent court costumes. Hunt out the statue of Peter Pan nearby in Kensington Gardens.

Leighton House▶ (*Admission free*), 12 Holland Park Road, W14, is the charmingly offbeat Victorian house of Lord Leighton, former president of the Royal Academy, who added antique Islamic tiles to the Arab Hall. Pre-Raphaelite paintings, William de Morgan ceramics and Leighton's own canvases are on show.

Buckingham Palace▶▶ is now open to the public.

Hampstead Kenwood House▶ (*Admission free*), Hampstead Lane, NW8, is on the edge of Hampstead Heath, the quasi-rural oasis in north London. Robert Adam gave the house its classical proportions; within is a collection of old masters and portraits, including works by Reynolds and Gainsborough. Outdoor summer concerts, often with fireworks, attract big crowds on Saturday evenings.

Hampstead's oldest house, and one of the grandest, is **Fenton House▶** in Windmill Hill, NW3. Owned by the National Trust, it contains a collection of antique keyboard instruments, paintings and furniture. (**Keats'** and **Freud's** houses can also be visited.)

South and west Hampton Court▶▶▶, East Molesey, Surrey, is best reached by riverboat from Westminster Pier. The palace was begun in the early 16th century by Cardinal Wolsey and later presented to Henry VIII to curry favour; it is an enjoyable mix of styles and history, with a hammer-beamed hall, Wren's Fountain Court and carvings by Grinling Gibbons. The grounds contain a famous maze. **Ham House▶**, Ham Street, Ham, by the Thames towpath close to Richmond Park, is owned by the National Trust, and is an outstanding example of Jacobean architecture, built in 1610.

Kew Palace▶▶ was built in 1631 for a London merchant and subsequently leased by George II for Queen Caroline. Since its purchase in 1781 by George III, the house has changed little, and retains panelling and portraits. A visit here ties in nicely with **Kew Gardens** (see page 16) and a walk along the Thames towpath to Richmond.

On the other side of the river is **Syon House▶**, Isleworth. Founded in 1415 as a monastery, the house underwent remodelling in the 18th century, and was given crisp interiors by Robert Adam and grounds by Capability Brown. Next to it in Syon Park are a major gardening centre, a butterfly park and a collection of historic vehicles.

Chiswick House▶, Chiswick Park, Chiswick, is a small, formal Palladian villa (1729) once used for soirées and as a library rather than a house. Modelled on Palladio's Villa Capra in Italy, it stands in delightful parkland, landscaped in what came to be regarded as the English manner.

Osterley Park▶▶, off Great West Road (A4), Osterley, is a gracious manor house with Tudor origins set in parkland, all but engulfed by the suburbia of London's western fringes. It provides an excellent opportunity to see Robert Adam's interiors at their richest.

Kensington Palace became a royal residence when asthmatic William III elected to move away from the unhealthy riverside air of Whitehall Palace

Robert Adam
The state rooms at Syon House and Osterley House are among the finest examples of Robert Adam interiors in the country. The brilliant Scottish designer was born at Kirkcaldy in 1728 and was trained, along with his three brothers, by his architect father, William. He set up in practice in London in 1758 and three years later was appointed principal architect to George III. His elegant and graceful classical interiors, lightening the austere accepted Palladian style, were soon all the rage and widely copied. Charlotte Square in Edinburgh (see page 224) is one of his most notable works in his native Scotland. He died in London in 1792.

LONDON WALKS

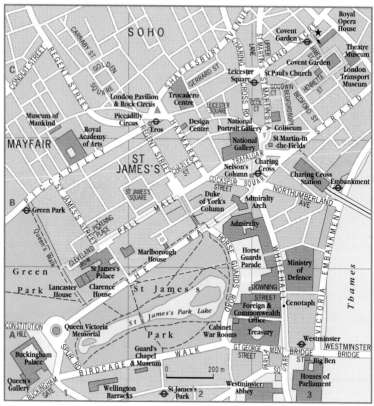

Walk **Covent Garden, royal London and Westminster**

Start from Covent Garden tube station. Walk down James Street to **Covent Garden►►**, the former fruit and vegetable market, now transformed to a stylish shopping piazza and popular meeting place. The **Theatre Museum►** and **London Transport Museum►►** are close by. From Henrietta Street, an archway on the right leads into the churchyard of St Paul's, the innovative design of Inigo Jones. At the heart of London's theatreland, St Paul's is known as the **actors' church►** and its interior walls are covered with plaques in memory of stars of stage and screen. Leave the churchyard via a gate into Bedford Street; off the next street to the west, Bedfordbury, an arch leads into

Goodwin Court, where bow-windowed houses have changed little since the 18th century. As you reach St Martin's Lane, opposite is Cecil Court, part of the secondhand bookshop quarter. Enter Trafalgar Square at the end of St Martin's Lane, the great pigeon-populated piazza with **St Martin-in-the-Fields church►►** on the right and the **National Gallery►►►** on the left.

Cross over to Admiralty Arch and enter the Mall. Steps lead up to the right past the Duke of York's column. Walk along Pall Mall, past the long-established concentration of exclusive gentlemen's clubs, distinguished by unobtrusive signs at the entrances. Take a detour to look at

Big Ben, Britain's most famous timepiece, and Parliament Square

the east side of St James's Street with its trio of old-fashioned shops –

Lock's the hat-makers, Berry and Rudd's wine merchants, and Lobb's, makers of bespoke shoes. Pickering Place was once used for sword duels.

Cleveland Row skirts **St James's Palace▶**, residence of Prince Charles and others; leave by gates into Queen's Walk, fringing Green Park. Return to the Mall: **Buckingham Palace▶▶**, the main residence of the Queen, is to the right; the Changing of the Guard takes place daily at 11.30am April to August and every other day September to March. Cross the Mall and enter St James's Park, keeping left. Leave by the gate and pass through the arch into **Horse Guards' Parade▶▶** and turn right into Whitehall; Downing Street to the right, is permanently guarded, because the prime minister lives at No 10. Parliament Square is presided over by Big Ben, part of the **Houses of Parliament▶▶▶**. Across the square is **Westminster Abbey▶▶▶**. Return from Westminster tube.

Walk **Along the South Bank to Tower Hill**

Start from Westminster Bridge. The above walk can be extended by following the South Bank (there is a walkway for much of the way) from Westminster Bridge to the **Royal Festival Hall▶**, where the **riverbus** can be taken to London Bridge. The walkway continues east of the bridge past an impressive modern office development, with outstanding views of the City. At **HMS *Belfast*▶** it is necessary to divert away from the river to Tooley Street, but a path leading through a small park takes

you to **Tower Bridge▶▶**, which can be crossed (a museum inside the bridge explains its workings and history); to the right you can see Canary Wharf, Britain's tallest building. On the other side, circuit the moat of the **Tower of London▶▶▶**. Signs to the World Trade Centre lead you to **St Katharine's Dock▶**, a yacht haven with a collection of historic boats. Return from Tower Hill tube station.

St Katharine's Dock

Churches

Southwark Cathedral is noted for the many monuments that survived from its days as a monastic church. That of poet John Gower, above, is dated 1408

Sir Christopher Wren (1632–1723)
Wren, one of the most celebrated of English architects, was responsible for the rebuilding of St Paul's Cathedral (in which his monument appears as *lector, si monumentum requiris, circumspice* – 'reader, if you seek my monument, look around') and the City churches. He drew up an ambitious plan for the rebuilding of London with continental-style avenues, but the complexities of land ownership prevented its realisation. MP for Weymouth in Dorset, he used the local Portland stone liberally in his buildings.

Another great architect of the day was Inigo Jones, who designed Covent Garden piazza, the first piazza in London.

The dome of St Paul's Cathedral

Although the Great Fire of 1666, the Blitz of 1940 and constant rebuilding have changed London's face repeatedly, the legacy of church architecture is an impressive one, dating from Norman times. There are particularly fine examples of designs of the master architects from the 17th and 18th centuries: Wren, Hawksmoor and Inigo Jones. Here we shortlist the undoubted masterpieces.

The earliest churches The only large-scale church of the Norman period in London is **St Bartholomew the Great**►► in West Smithfield, EC1. It is the survivor of a 12th-century Augustinian Priory and although the apsidal east end is a 19th-century rebuilding, the atmosphere is one of great antiquity. **Southwark Cathedral**►, Montague Close, SE1, the cathedral for the South Bank, was founded as the Augustinian priory church of St Mary Overie in 1106. Although much restored in the 19th century, it is the most substantial medieval artefact in the district of Southwark. Previously it was known as St Mary Overie (meaning 'over' the water from the City). The building attained cathedral status in 1905.

Sir Christopher Wren Wren's domed masterpiece, **St Paul's Cathedral**►►►, Ludgate Hill, EC4, replaced the Gothic cathedral that perished in the Great Fire of 1666. It no longer dominates the skyline as it did until the mid-20th century, but when seen close up the proportions are overwhelming. Inside the dome, the Whispering Gallery plays acoustic tricks (whispered sounds carry around the great void). The tombs of Wren, Nelson, Wellington, Turner and Reynolds are in the crypt, amd other highlights are the views from the Golden Gallery, woodwork by Gibbons, and ironwork by Tijou.

After the Great Fire, **Sir Christopher Wren** graced the City with 51 **churches**►► (some were restored after World War II bombing). Among the most celebrated are St Bride's (Fleet Street), St Margaret's (Lothbury), St Martin Ludgate (Ludgate Hill), St Mary Abchurch (Cannon Street), St Mary-at-Hill (Eastcheap) and St Stephen Walbrook (Walbrook).

Other great churches St **Martin-in-the-Fields**►, Trafalgar Square, WC2, is an 18th-century rebuilding by James Gibbs, and a particularly satisfying example of the temple-like architecture of the period, with a characteristic galleried interior.

At **Westminster Abbey**►►► in Parliament Square, SW1, British sovereigns are crowned and many great men and women are buried, among them monarchs, statesmen, poets and scientists. It also has cloisters, a treasury, brass-rubbing centre and the oldest garden (*Open* Thu) in the country.

Westminster Cathedral►, in Ashley Place, off Victoria Street, SW1, is Britain's premier Roman Catholic cathedral, a vast Byzantine brick creation, completed in 1903. A strong layer of incense pervades the dark, cavernous interior.

Nightlife

Theatre There are dozens of theatres to choose from, offering everything from Shakespeare to Lloyd Webber musicals, and there is an impressive legacy of Victorian theatre architecture. Half-price tickets for the day of performance are available from the SWET ticket booth in Leicester Square (see panel).

Nightspots Soho and Covent Garden constitute the heart of clubland with the Hippodrome and Empire discotheque by Leicester Square, and The Wag in Wardour Street. Nightspots come and go, but Ronnie Scott's (47 Frith Street, W1) is a well-established jazz venue, and Heaven (under Charing Cross Station) is a leading gay club. Cabaret and alternative comedy is at The Comedy Store in Leicester Square. Away from the centre of town is the highly esteemed Fridge, at Town Hall Parade, Brixton Hill, SW2. Watch listings (see panel) for pop concerts at the Hammersmith Odeon and Brixton Academy.

Classical music London has five resident orchestras. The Royal Festival Hall on the South Bank (plus the smaller Purcell Room and Queen Elizabeth Hall) and the Barbican Hall, Silk Street (Moorgate tube) are major venues. Wigmore Hall in Wigmore Street has Sunday morning coffee concerts and often hosts performances by up-and-coming artists. Summer visitors should try to take in a performance at the Promenade Concerts ('the Proms', see page 18), Europe's biggest music festival. Operas at the Royal Opera House in Covent Garden are performed in the original language with 'surtitles' projected above (the Opera House is closed for rebuilding until 1999 – telephone 0171-304 4000 for details of venues), while the English National Opera, in the Coliseum in St Martin's Lane, gives performances in English.

Film The big first-release venue is the Odeon on Leicester Square, with a huge main cinema, and a cinema organ. There are also other multi-screen cinemas on Leicester Square. The National Film Theatre (NFT) on the South Bank near Waterloo Bridge is the leading repertory cinema; programmes change daily and day membership is available.

Listings and bookings
The weekly magazine *Time Out* gives listings for all London's entertainments, events and exhibitions, and has excellent previews. The *London Theatre Guide*, updated every two weeks, lists theatrical events and is available free of charge from West End theatres, libraries and tourist information centres.
Book direct to cut out commissions. Ticket agencies include Ticketmaster (tel: 0171-334 4444) and First Call (tel: 0171-240 7200); check for credit card surcharges. Never buy tickets from street touts or unofficial agencies. The SWET (Society of West End Theatres) ticket booth opens at 12 noon for matinées and 2.30pm for evening performances for the same day.

The lights of Leicester Square

James Smith's redoubtable stick and umbrella store

The principal shopping areas Most of the West End department stores are in **Oxford Street** – Selfridges is the largest. John Lewis (whose 'never knowingly undersold' policy guarantees a refund if you find the same goods on sale cheaper elsewhere) has a fine stock of furnishings, fashions and decorative items, while the ubiquitous Marks and Spencer is known for good-value clothing and good food halls. Virgin Megastore and HMV have big selections of CDs and cassettes.

Around the corner, **Regent Street** comes into its own in the weeks running up to Christmas when the illuminations are switched on by a celebrity; during this period, Hamleys, the undisputed king of toyshops, fills to bursting and has spectacular displays. Nearby is Liberty, renowned for Liberty print fabrics and stylish clothes; the mock-Tudor building itself is worth a look.

Hi-fi and electrical goods are available at discounted prices in the shops along **Tottenham Court Road**. At the corner of Goodge Street and Charlotte Street, Nice Irma's has Indian-inspired candlesticks, cushion covers and more. Further east at 53 New Oxford Street, James Smith, umbrella manufacturers, has an eye-catching Victorian shopfront boasting 'Life Preservers, Jagger Canes and Swordsticks'.

Charing Cross Road constitutes the heart of London's bookshop territory: Foyles, the largest, has an impressive stock, though the layout can be confusing as books are displayed alphabetically by publisher (not by author). There is a fascinating array of specialist secondhand bookshops just off Charing Cross Road in Cecil Court.

Just to the west, **Soho** is densely packed with ethnic food shops, including Chinese supermarkets in Chinatown, and numerous Italian delicatessens.

Shopping

Covent Garden has an absorbing variety of shops, including the Tea Shop in Neal Street, a cheese shop and bakery in Neal's Yard and a dolls' house shop in the piazza itself.

St James's Street, off Piccadilly, has a clutch of old-fashioned shops offering finely made wine, hats, shoes and shirts. Close by, in Jermyn Street, Paxton and Whitfield (London's most irresistibly aromatic shop?) sells hundreds of cheeses.

Kings Road in Chelsea is the place for chic fashions, interior design and people-watching; a smart antiques market (Monday to Saturday) extends along one part.

Great for window shopping Harrods, Knightsbridge, is the grandest department store of them all; many visitors go just to collect a carrier bag. Harrods prides itself on its range and quality of stock; the food-halls conjure up Edwardian splendour.

Burlington Arcade, off Piccadilly, is a perfectly preserved Regency shopping arcade retaining its early 19th-century air with considerable dignity. An immaculately attired beadle patrols the alley and notices forbid 'hurrying or whistling'. Chic galleries and boutiques attract the rich.

Fortnum and Mason, Piccadilly, is the food store *par excellence*, with high-priced hampers for those who can afford them, and other exclusive foods. The famous exterior clock features Mr Fortnum and Mr Mason, who bow to each other on the hour.

Street markets always provide good entertainment. Easily the most atmospheric is **Brick Lane** (Sunday mornings), off Bethnal Green Road in the heart of Cockney London, now the heart of the Bengali community. It is unashamedly shabby and hugely crowded, and the mish-mash of wares is bizarre, ranging from cheap hi-fi to bargain CDs to secondhand junk. Don't miss the bagel store. (Note this is not the same as the nearby Petticoat Lane Market.) Weekend-long antiques markets are at **Camden Lock** and **Greenwich▶▶▶**.

Portobello Road, W11, operates Monday to Saturday (junk stalls on Friday, antiques on Saturday).

Speakers' Corner
At the corner of Hyde Park, close to Marble Arch at the western end of Oxford Street, Speakers' Corner is a bastion of free speech. It provides memorable free entertainment at lunchtime Monday to Friday, and is at full throttle on Sunday morning. Anyone can set up a soapbox and speak on anything he or she likes as long as there is no blasphemy, defamation, treason or breach of the peace laws.

Only the best: a selection of Fortnum and Mason's gift baskets

Accommodation

Hotels London is one of the most expensive European capitals for hotel accommodation. Those who can afford high prices will not be disappointed by the style and service found at such long-established and prestigious establishments as the Ritz, Claridge's, the Savoy and the Connaught; be prepared for a high degree of formality, however, and do not expect air-conditioning as a matter of course. The top modern hotels are in the same price bracket. Among the best areas to stay are the West End (W1, NW1, SW1, WC2), Bloomsbury (WC1), Kensington (W2, W8, W11), Knightsbridge (SW1) and Chelsea (SW3).

Reserving accommodation
The London Tourist Board has accommodation lists and operates a reservation service. For help dial 0891 505487; calls are charged at 45p/50p per minute. For general information dial 0171-938 3000.

In a city where accommodation is generally not cheap, London's top hotels can be very expensive

Service at its most discreet ...

Bed and Breakfast More modest bed and breakfast (B&B) accommodation comes at roughly double the price you would expect to pay outside London; there is a reasonable selection around Victoria (SW1) and Bloomsbury (WC1); the King's Cross area (WC1) is cheap, but has a reputation as a red-light and drugs-peddling district. To the west, Hammersmith (W6) has some large hotels and good underground connections to the centre; the immediate area is unprepossessing, however. Small hotels and B&Bs exist in many suburbs, and can cut the accommodation bill; aim for a location convenient for the underground, and check the journey time and the timing of the last train back.

Hostels and campsites Budget travellers are catered for by youth hostels; the central locations are in Noel Street, W1, Bolton Gardens, SW5, Holland Park, W8, and Carter Lane, EC4; three more hostels are at Highgate West Hill, N6, Wellgarth Road, NW11 and Salter Road, Rotherhithe, SE16. All these get heavily booked, especially in summer, and reservations are advised (National YHA tel: 01727 855215). Additionally, many colleges offer accommodation in the summer; halls of residence at White Hart Lane, N17, and Wood Green, N22 (both in the northern suburbs) are run as summer hostels. The International Students Hostel at Frognal House, 99 Frognal, NW3 (tel: 0171-794 6893), is a female-only establishment in Hampstead.

Campsites are further from the centre; Crystal Palace Caravan Site, SE19, is pleasantly located, with good public transport links.

Eating out

Breakfast For a leisurely start to the day, plump for breakfast at one of the big hotels such as the Savoy (the Strand, WC2; tel: 0171-836 4343). Devotees of Chinese *dim sum* brunch should look no further than New World (1 Gerrard Place, W1; tel: 0171-734 6631).

Lunch For quick lunches, sandwich bars and simple restaurants are a good bet; there is a particular concentration of these in the West End. Many pubs and wine bars offer food, though some get crowded and smoky; the long-established Gordon's Wine Bar (47 Villiers Street, WC2; tel: 0171-930 1408) is set in a subterranean vault by the Thames. Look in Soho and Covent Garden for the many oriental restaurants which offer good-value set lunches. Big museums and galleries, including the National Gallery, Tate Gallery and Festival Hall, have good self-service cafeterias. A number of inexpensive southern Indian vegetarian restaurants are along Drummond Street, NW1, handy for Regent's Park. Panton Street, WC2, off Leicester Square, has several good-value budget eateries. You can lunch at some of the top restaurants for roughly half the price of an evening meal.

Afternoon tea Tea is served with considerable flair at such prestigious hotels as the Ritz (reservation advisable; Piccadilly, W1; tel: 0171-493 8181) and Brown's (Dover Street, W1; tel: 0171-493 6020), although prices are quite high and there is a formal dress code. A much less expensive option, and less formal, is the Charing Cross Hotel (Strand, WC2; tel: 0171-839 7282), or the Café Royal (68 Piccadilly W!; tel: 0171-437 9090).

The evening For a special evening, try one of the great French restaurants such as Bibendum (Michelin House, 81 Fulham Road, SW3; tel: 0171-581 5817) in the eye-catching Michelin building, or Nico Central (35 Portland Street, W1, tel: 0171-436 8846). Those who wish to live it up in style without breaking the bank will like Kettner's (29 Romilly Street, W1; no reservations) in the heart of Soho, part of the excellent Pizza Express chain. Among the residential districts, Hampstead, Camden Town, Islington, Bayswater, Kensington and Chelsea have a good choice of places to eat. (See also London's restaurants, page 282.)

Pubs in London
Pubs of special character include the *Cittie of York* (with Britain's longest bar – 22 High Holborn, WC2); the *Lamb and Flag* (in Covent Garden – 33 Rose Street, WC2); the *Museum Tavern* (near the British Museum – Museum Street, WC1); the *Princess Louise* (spectacular Victorian tiled interior – 208 High Holborn, WC1); the *Lamb* (Bloomsbury, with old fittings – Lamb's Conduit Street); *Ye Olde Cheshire Cheese* (ancient tavern, former haunt of writers Dickens and Johnson – Wine Office Court, 145 Fleet Street, EC4); the *Black Friar* (London's finest art-nouveau pub interior – 174 Queen Victoria Street, EC4, opposite Blackfriars station); and the *Dove* (riverside pub with terrace – 19 Upper Mall, Chiswick). Fuller's and Young's are two excellent 'real ale' London brews.

The Ritz was London's first steel-framed building when it was built in 1906

THE WEST COUNTRY

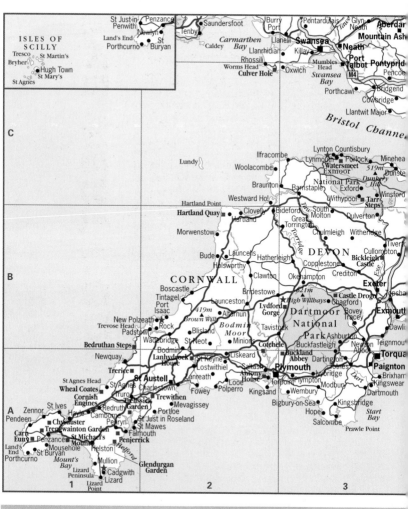

ISLES OF SCILLY

Tresco, St Martin's
Bryher
Hugh Town
St Mary's
St Agnes

St Just-in-Penwith · Penzance
Land's End · Newlyn · St
Porthcurno · St Buryan

Saundersfoot
Tenby
Caldey

Carmarthen Bay

Burry Port · Pontardulais
Llanelli · Glyn-Neath · Aberdar
Killay · Swansea · Mountain Ash
Mumbles Head · Port Talbot · Neath · Pontypridd
M4 · Pencoe
Porthcawl · Bridgend
Cowbridge
Llantwit Major

Rhossili
Worms Head · **Culver Hole** · Oxwich
Llanrhidian
Swansea Bay

Bristol Channel

C

Lundy

Ilfracombe · Lynton Countisbury
Lynmouth · Porlock · Minehea
Woolacombe · **Watersmeet** · 519m · Dunste
Braunton · **Exmoor** · Dunkery Hill
National Park · Exford · Winsford
Barnstaple · Withypool · **Tarr Steps**
Westward Ho! · South Molton · Dulverton
Hartland Point
Hartland Quay · Clovelly · Bideford · Great · Withridge · Tiver
Morwenstow · Hartland · Torrington · Chulmleigh
Bude · Holsworthy · Hatherleigh · Copplestone · Crediton · Cullompton
CORNWALL · Clawton · Okehampton · **Bickleigh Castle**
Boscastle · Launceston · Bridestowe · **Exeter**
Tintagel · 419m · 621m · Castle Drogo · Topsha
Port Isaac · **Brown Willy** · Altarnun · High Willhays · Chagford · **Exmout**
New Polzeath · **Lydford Gorge** · **Dartmoor** · Bovey Tracey
Trevose Head · Rock · Blisland · Tavistock · **National** · Dawli
Padstow · Wadbridge · **Bodmin Moor** · **Park** · Ashburton · Newton Abbot · Teignmou
Bedruthan Steps · Bodmin · St Neot · Minions · Cotehele · Buckfastleigh
Newquay · **Lanhydrock House** · St Keyne · Liskeard · **Buckland Abbey** · Dartington · **Torqua**
Trerice · Lostwithiel · **Plymouth** · Ivybridge · Totnes · **Paignton**
St Austell · Lanreath · Looe · Saltash · Brixham
Wheal Coates · Charlestown · Fowey · Polperro · **Antony House** · Torpoint · Ivybridge · Modbury · Kingswear
Cornish Engines · Truro · **Trelissick Garden** · Kingsand · Wembury · Dartmouth
Trewithen · Mevagissey · Bigbury-on-Sea · Kingsbridge
St Ives · Redruth · Portloe · Hope · Salcombe · **Start Bay**
Zennor · Hayle · Camborne · St Just in Roseland · Prawle Point
Pendeen · **Chysauster** · Penryn · St Mawes
Carn Euny · **Trengwainton Garden** · Falmouth · **Penjerrick**
Land's End · Penzance · **St Michael's Mount** · **Penjerrick**
Porthcurno · St Buryan · Mousehole · Helston
Mullion · Cadgwith · **Glendurgan Garden**
Mount's Bay · Lizard · Lizard
Lizard Peninsula · Lizard Point

B

A

1 · 2 · 3

★ Walk start point

| 0 | 10 | 20 | 30 | 40 | 50 km |
| 0 | | 10 | | 20 | 30 miles |

4   5

The West Country The tapering southwest peninsula of England culminates in the rugged clifflands of western Cornwall, where Land's End forms the big toe of Great Britain. The West Country is the term given to this region, an area that offers perhaps a fuller range of activities, landscapes and experiences than any other in Britain.

In essence it is a set of several distinct regions, and this rich diversity is a key to the area's enduring appeal. The only downside is of course that it is very popular, and the crowds are sometimes overwhelming, though concentrated in the summer months.

The climate is mild and the sprawling resorts of Torquay and Bournemouth head the sunshine league; this is also a major retirement area. To many, the West Country is synonymous with dairy country; the locals are Britain's big cheese-eaters, and you can gorge on a cream tea or even send clotted cream, a cholesterol-watcher's nightmare, by post. Further temptation is provided by lardy cake, a gooey raisin-topped speciality largely confined to the southern and western counties.

Land's End, Cornwall

THE WEST COUNTRY

Cornwall Until the opening of the Tamar railway bridge in the 19th century, Cornwall was the most remote county in England. This may be hard to believe at the peak of summer, as tourists converge in the coastal villages and the narrow lanes jam with traffic, but the area still has a distinct sense of locale – partly real, partly manufactured by the heritage industry. The Cornish language has gone, the tin mines are all but defunct, and Tintagel has but a tenuous link with King Arthur's Camelot (a link reinforced by interested hoteliers and shopkeepers). But plenty is real enough: Cornish placenames live on, the silhouettes of mining relics haunt the skylines, the Methodist tradition is still strong, and the superlative coastline encompasses awe-inspiring headlands and secret coves that bring to life oft-repeated tales of smugglers and shipwrecks.

Cornwall is a summer playground, ideal for watersports and family fun, and more interesting for its archaeology, holy wells and ancient stone crosses than for its architecture. It is not as good for scenic drives as the roads seldom follow the coast closely enough. Cornish villages are plain and sturdy-looking with granite walls beneath Delabole slate roofs. There is nothing very ancient about much of central Cornwall, which largely grew up around the mining and china clay industries. No part of the county is further than half an hour from the coast (in normal driving conditions). Take a walk along the coast path, and you will find comparative solitude and great beauty.

Devon Devon is a county of many faces. South Devon has the best beaches (such as Blackpool Sands (near Stoke Fleming) and Bigbury-on-Sea) and some popular, pleasant seaside resorts – Torquay, Paignton, Teignmouth, Dawlish, Brixham and Exmouth. Sidmouth has a conspicuously well-preserved Regency seafront, and is a popular retirement town. Much of the interest focuses around the estuaries, notably the grand finale of the River Dart at Dartmouth, and the Kingsbridge Estuary.

Of central Devon, Dartmoor is by far the best-known part, a world of windswept wastes and wilderness, tors and relics of early settlers. Granite is the predominant building material, although on the peripheries you will see cob walls and thatched roofs, a Devon vernacular hallmark. Exeter, sadly, was bombed in World War II and you have to search for its best corners; but the city repays exploration (particularly the cathedral) and makes a good base. The rest of central Devon is less well known, a terrain of hilly farmlands, sandstone walls and swift-flowing rivers. In the far north, moorland meets the sea in Exmoor National Park, with its primeval grandeur, England's highest cliffs, and Devon's longest stretch of unspoilt coast.

Somerset While the Somerset coast has little to speak of outside Exmoor National Park (which straddles the Devon border), there is much to explore inland, in the little-visited Quantock Hills, with their fine heritage of country churches, and the Mendip Hills, with Wells, the Cheddar Gorge and Burrington Combe.

Southwards lie the Levels, a flat, drained fenland once beneath the sea; Glastonbury Tor and the low-rise Polden Hills protrude above the far side. Taunton, the county town in the heart of cider-making country, has a bland streetscape redeemed by an impressive church and an absorbing museum.

Bath is the obvious first choice among cities to visit in Somerset (although until recently it was in the county of Avon, named after the river that flows through it, but now renamed). It is a delightful city for wandering but an ordeal to drive in. Bristol (now in its own county of Bristol) is a fascinating city, and large port, with a great maritime heritage and an elegant suburb, somewhat like Bath, in Clifton, as well as an excellent university.

Dorset The home of Dorset Blue Vinny cheese, Dorset often has the tag 'Hardy's Wessex' applied to it, though the ancient kingdom of Wessex in fact extended into Wiltshire, Somerset and Hampshire. There is scarcely a corner that does not appear under a pseudonym in Thomas Hardy's literary output. Although over three-quarters of the county's heathlands have disappeared since 1945, the inland areas still have a traditional appearance, with sweeping downs, clumps of beech trees, thatched villages and prehistoric burial sites (tumuli) and hillforts. Villages such as Abbotsbury and Corfe Castle make delightful bases for the best of the remarkably varied and largely unspoilt coast.

SHORTLIST: WHERE TO GO
(continued from page 62)
Dorset: Lyme Regis under-cliff, Chesil Beach, Isle of Portland, Lulworth Cove, St Albans Head, Old Harry Rocks, Poole Harbour.
WALKING The 800km (500-mile) South West Coast Path follows the coast from Minehead (Somerset) to Poole (Dorset); Exmoor, north Cornwall and east Dorset are the most dramatic bits; Dartmoor is best for inland walking; otherwise inland Exmoor, the Dorset downs, the Mendips, the Quantocks.
OFFSHORE ESCAPISM Isles of Scilly, Lundy Island.
PREHISTORIC SITES Wiltshire downs, west Cornwall.

63

Wiltshire An inland county, Wiltshire has a gentle physique of prairie-like chalk downlands, with its northern reaches of honey-stone villages just inside the Cotswolds. Most of its interest is manmade, such as the curious hill 'carvings' of horses and regimental badges on the hillsides. More famous is the legacy of early settlers, notably at Stonehenge and perhaps even more memorably at Avebury. Salisbury Cathedral is the pinnacle of Early English style; a bus service from Salisbury station to Stonehenge makes a good day-trip from London.

Wiltshire's largest town, Swindon, grew up in the railway era (its railway museum is a magnet for train buffs) and witnessed an economic boom in the 1980s; smaller places, including Devizes, Marlborough and Bradford on Avon, are much more attractive.

Thatched roofs and whitewashed walls in Lustleigh: the unspoilt face of Devon

'There is in the Cornish character, smouldering beneath the surface, ever ready to ignite, a fiery independence, a stubborn pride'.
   Daphne du Maurier
   Vanishing Cornwall (1967)

Walks

Cheddar Gorge, Somerset *61C4*
Car park adjacent to Butchers Arms near gorge entrance. Walk along the road at the bottom of the gorge; at the far end (1.5km/1 mile), opposite the gate into a nature reserve, take the West Mendip Way on the right, up through woods. Fork right to follow the top edge of the gorge; the views are astonishing. Drop down by steps at Prospect Tower. (2 hours)

Lizard, Cornwall *60A1*
Start at Lizard village. For the best of this celebrated coast, take the road east to Church Cove and turn right along the coast path, past Lizard Point, the southernmost point on the mainland, and to idyllic Kynance Cove. Follow the toll road inland, branching right by a National Trust sign on to a path back to Lizard village. (2 hours)

Lulworth Cove, Dorset *61B5*
Car park at Lulworth Cove. Take the steep path above the cove, which gives a good aerial view. Then head west, taking the path from the car park, along the coast to Durdle Door, a natural arch eroded by the waves. The rugged coast east of the cove, once rife with smuggling, extends across Worbarrow Bay and Bindon Hill to Kimmeridge; this is army training land, but is open most weekends, at Easter and all of August. (Allow 1 to 2 hours)

Lydford Gorge, Dartmoor National Park, Devon *60B3*
Car parks by gorge; entrance fee. A densely wooded gorge with the White Lady Waterfall at one end and the Devil's Cauldron, where the River Lyd swirls in a gloomy chasm, at the other. The full trail takes 1½ hours, or you can take short walks from the car parks.

Valley of Rocks, Exmoor National Park, Devon *60C3*
Start at Lynton. Take the small road between the Valley of Rocks Hotel and the church; it becomes the coast path. The Valley of Rocks and its feral goats soon come into view. Climb Castle Rock, the most prominent feature, for the view and return along the road, branching left after 400m by a stone shelter to ascend Hollerday Hill and then drop into Lynton. (1½ hours)

Avebury's stones stand silent as daily life goes on around them

Built in a perfect circle around a covered reservoir, the houses that comprise Bath's elegant Circus were variously home to the missionary explorer David Livingstone, Lord Robert Clive ('Clive of India') and the artist Thomas Gainsborough

Prehistoric landmarks at Avebury
Avebury's stone circle, which can be entirely walked around, connects to the so-called *Stone Avenue*, parallel rows of stones that lead south to the site of another circle, the *Sanctuary*.
A path leading south from opposite the main car park passes close by suet-pudding shaped *Silbury Hill*, the largest prehistoric earthwork in Europe; it is thought to have played an astronomical or religious role. The path continues south of the A4 to *West Kennet Long Barrow*, an ancient burial chamber, which can be entered.

▶▶▶ Avebury   61C5

Avebury is encompassed by a huge Bronze Age stone circle – the largest such monument in Europe – which, like Stonehenge (see page 84), seems to have been erected for a mystical or ceremonial purpose (see panel). The Alexander Keiller Museum (EH) expounds Avebury's archaeology; an aisled manorial barn houses the Great Barn Museum of Wiltshire Life, with rural bygones and crafts. Avebury Manor, dating back 900 years, is open to visitors.

▶▶▶ Bath   61C5

A spa centre since Roman times, Bath regained its popularity in the 18th century as a place for taking the waters and it remains the finest Georgian town in Britain. Parks, classical terraces, squares, an architectural 'circus' and a Royal Crescent, much of it the design of John Wood the Elder and Younger (father and son), were laid out in the time of Beau Nash, archetypal English dandy, who was the master of ceremonies and led fashionable society. The city has an elegant uniformity owing to the use of the golden-hued Bath stone. Jane Austen stayed here and drew on her company as material for her novels, including *Northanger Abbey.*

Bath delights as a place for casual wandering. Museums include an outstanding **Museum of Costume▶▶▶** within the Assembly Rooms, the **Bath Industrial Heritage Centre▶** with its re-creation of a Victorian brass foundry, the **Building of Bath Museum▶** (with the **British Folk Art Collection▶** next door), the **Victoria Art Gallery** and the **Holburne Museum▶** of fine arts; on the edge of town at Claverton Manor is the **American Museum▶**, where 17th- to 19th-century interiors are re-created.

The **Pump Room▶▶**, the **Roman Baths▶▶▶** and **Bath Abbey▶▶** form the historical *raison d'être* at the heart of the city (see Walk on following page).

Corsham Court▶▶, near Chippenham, has magnificent state rooms. Capability Brown, usually known as a landscape gardener, worked on the house in the 1740s.

BATH

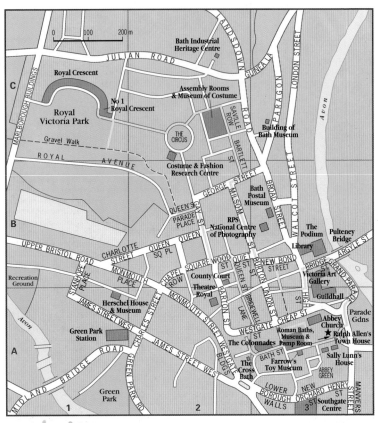

Walk **Bath city centre**

From the **abbey▶▶**, (the west front depicts Bishop Oliver's dream of angels which inspired him to rebuild the abbey in 1499), pass the **Roman Baths▶▶▶**, Britain's finest Roman remains: baths, cold plunges, a hypocaust room and part of a Temple to Sulis, goddess of the springs, can be seen. Adjacent is the **Pump Room▶▶**, the epitome of Bath's timeless spirit; sip afternoon tea to the strains of chamber music beneath the statue of Beau Nash.

Carry on along Old Lilliput Alley. **Sally Lunn's House**, a bakery producing the original Sally Lunn cakes from a secret recipe, is the oldest house in Bath (1482); a kitchen museum tells the story. Follow Grand Parade as far as **Pulteney Bridge▶▶** (1774, designed by Robert Adam), with shops along both sides. In Milsom Street pass the **National Centre of Photography**, and walk up Saville Row past the **Assembly Rooms and Museum of Costume▶▶▶**. Walk around **The Circus▶▶▶** (begun 1754) and continue into **Royal Crescent▶▶▶** (John Wood the Younger, 1767–74), No 1 is open to the public. Go through Royal Victoria Park to Queen's Parade Place, and on past **Queen Square** (1729–36); the novelist, Jane Austen stayed at No 13 in 1799. Return via Bath Street to the abbey.

▶ Bodmin Moor 60B2

The roof of Cornwall resembles a smaller version of Dartmoor, its bleak open moors dotted with granite tors, ponies and sheep. Brown Willy 419m (1,377ft) is the county's highest point. Tracks on to the moor from the windswept hamlet of **Minions** give excellent views and lead past the **Hurlers Stone Circle▶** (Bronze Age). At nearby Darite, **Trethevy Quoit▶** is a Bronze Age burial chamber with its capstone still in place. **Altarnun▶** is a tranquil haven off the busy A30; its spacious church has magnificent 16th-century bench ends with carvings of jester, piper and dancers. In **Trewint**, a tiny cottage is a simple shrine to John Wesley, father of Methodism, while **St Neot** church has the finest medieval stained glass in Cornwall.

Launceston▶ occupies a hilltop crowned by a mighty Norman castle keep; twisting streets, a town-wall gateway, a steam railway and a local museum head its other attractions. Huge **Lanhydrock House▶** (NT) epitomises high living back at the turn of the century.

▶▶ Bradford on Avon 61C5

A charming base for the southern Cotswolds, this stone-built town rises steeply, terrace by terrace, with flagged steps connecting its narrow lanes. Former cloth merchants' mansions and humble medieval and 18th-century

weavers' cottages set the theme; oddly named Top Rank Tory is the street with the best views. In Barton Farm Park stands a splendid 14th-century **tithe barn.**

Lacock Abbey▶ (NT), some 14km (9 miles) northeast, retains 13th-century cloisters, chapter house and sacristy. A barn houses the Fox Talbot Museum, in memory of the pioneer photographer who lived here from 1827 to 1877. The village itself, preserving an 18th-century time warp feeling, is owned by the National Trust. It has been used recently for the filming of *Pride and Prejudice*, *Emma* and *Moll Flanders*.

**Bodmin Moor:
three curious collections**
Jamaica Inn, signed from the A30, is the setting for Daphne du Maurier's eponymous novel of lawless days and smugglers. Its upper storey is home to Potter's Museum of Curiosities, a collection of oddities that includes tableaux of stuffed animals playing cricket, attending village school and so on. At Lanreath is an ever-growing folk museum of familiar and not-so-familiar objects of everyday and yesterday. Near St Keyne, the Paul Corrin Musical Collection focuses on old-style mechanical musical instruments – pianolas, fairground organs etc, which are demonstrated by the owner.

Bradford on Avon's nine-arched Town Bridge dates from the 14th century; two of its original arches remain

A lost church
Bradford on Avon's Church of St Laurence, thought to be 7th–8th century, is one of Britain's most complete Saxon churches, yet it lay completely forgotten for many years. Looking over the town from a house above the church, a 19th-century vicar noticed the cruciform shape of the building, parts of which had been incorporated into a school, a house and a factory wall. In 1858, restoration was carried out and its interior can once more be seen.

■ **The harsh Atlantic gusts buffet a wild, rocky coast, a graveyard for hundreds of ships, while eerie ruins of tin mines perch on treeless hillsides. The long coast is popular for its scenery, sights, and excellent bathing and surfing beaches. Accordingly, you have to be prepared for crowds at the peak of the season, and more than just the occasional unsightly holiday development, especially between Padstow and Newquay. But it's easy to get away from it all if you are prepared to walk a mile or two along the stunning coast path. ■**

Penwith's rich archaeology
Inland Penwith is peppered with reminders of early settlers. Major sites include two Iron Age villages, Carn Euny and Chysauster (both well signposted), where the wall layout has survived intact. Chûn Castle is an Iron Age fort with visible stone ramparts, while Lanyon Quoit is a good Bronze Age burial chamber and Men-an-Tol is a stone hoop of unknown purpose, used in recent times as a folk-remedy for rickets; all three sites lie near the Madron–Morvah road. Close by St Buryan, near the road, Merry Maidens stone circle is Bronze Age; the maidens supposedly turned to stone for dancing on the Sabbath.

One foot forward ...
Not everyone who sets out on the 1,600km (1,000-mile) walk from Land's End to John o'Groats, at the other end of Britain, makes it; one unfortunate managed to trip over the starting sign he had put up and thus broke his leg with his very first stride.

The Devon border to Padstow The village of Morwenstow▶ bears the indelible stamp of Reverend Robert Hawker, Celtic poet and priest here from 1834 to 1875. He adorned the vicarage with chimneypots in the form of miniature church towers, and on the cliffs near by erected a driftwood shack for meditation and opium-smoking (it still stands). His memorial is in the church, which has Norman arches and 16th-century bench ends.

Bude is an unremarkable resort town and a major surfing base, with a large beach; a small museum on the quay tells the story of the Bude Canal, which ends here. Inland, Launcells Church▶, standing all by itself, escaped the fervour of Victorian restorers, and little has changed since the 15th century. Boscastle▶ occupies a craggy, precipitous creek; the best views are from the clifftop just west of the harbour. Tintagel▶ achieved fame for its legendary connections with King Arthur (was it really here that Arthur lived at Camelot?); the ruined medieval castle postdates Arthur, but the site is nevertheless magnificent, above an impregnable headland, reached by a steep staircase. The adjacent village is a tourist trap, redeemed by the Old Post Office (NT), a small-scale manor house preserved as an outstanding example of Cornish domestic architecture. Port Isaac▶▶ may stake a claim as the most authentic-feeling Cornish fishing village, a hotchpotch of cottages and narrow alleyways, with a wholesome whiff of seaweed.

Padstow▶ is a busy resort town of considerable charm. It lacks a beach (try Harlyn Bay, west of town) but has a harbour packed with brightly painted craft; fresh fish are on sale at quay warehouses and served at a number of good seafood restaurants. Prideaux Place, at the top of the town, looks Elizabethan but house tours in the summer months reveal whimsical Strawberry Hill Gothick (see Shobdon, page 122) alterations as well as the original plaster ceilings. The adjacent Camel Estuary offers sailing and gentle walks.

Bedruthan Steps to Land's End West from Padstow the summer crowds thicken rapidly. Many of Cornwall's safest and cleanest beaches are found between Padstow and Newquay. The immediate hinterland is spoilt by modern development, but Bedruthan Steps▶▶ is an impressive coastal feature, comprising massive rock buttresses, detached from the cliff itself. **Newquay** is brash and bustling: night spots, loud-music pubs, theme parks and surf shops, but offers good beaches, a well-stocked zoo and a pretty harbour. Out of town, **Trerice►** (NT) is a handsome Elizabethan manor house with a minstrels' gallery and intricate plasterwork ceilings.

St Ives►►, a delightful port turned resort, has attracted artists and bucket-and-spade holidaymakers for a century. Although it has been considerably cleaned up since its heyday as a fishing port, its back streets have an unmistakably haphazard Cornish character. Sculptress Barbara Hepworth was one of many 20th-century artists who settled here; her studio is now a museum with her sculptures gracing the garden. A branch of the Tate Gallery features the St Ives school of artists in one of the most striking settings of any gallery.

Cornwall's westernmost knob of land is known as **Penwith►►►** and has some of the most dramatic coastal scenery in England, with lonely heather moors inland. At **Zennor** a folk museum has an appealing selection of Cornish bygones while the church is home to a legendary mermaid, carved on an ancient bench end. **Land's End** (see panel page 68), Britain's southwesternmost mainland point, is the place to come if you collect geographical extremities. A signpost gives distances to places throughout the world (add your home town and pose for the photo); the crowds and theme park dwindle within ten minutes' walk along the cliff southwards, where the scenery gets better and better. The outdoor **Minack Theatre►** clings to a breathtaking cliff site at Porthcurno, while to the east the mighty headland of **Treryn Dinas**, near Treen, is one of the most dramatic features of Cornwall's coastline. **Mousehole** (pronounced 'Mouzal') as quaint as its name suggests, was the home of the last sole Cornish speaker, who died in 1777 at the age of 102.

A shopkeeper shows off Cornish pasties (traditional meat and vegetable pies)

Mining in Cornwall
Up to the last century Cornwall was a world leader in copper and tin production; lead was also produced. The evidence of its active past is everywhere, from the settlements of the Bronze Age people who exploited surface deposits of tin, to the 19th-century mining towns of Camborne, Redruth and St Just, as well as the haunting legacy of abandoned mines and engine houses such as Wheal Coates near St Agnes Head. In medieval times, tin was weighed and stamped at 'stannary towns', which included Penzance and Truro. Cornish innovations which made the job easier included Sir Humphry Davy's miner's safety lamp, Richard Trevithick's steam-powered beam engine, and the rock drill.

St Ives' distinctive Mediterranean quality of light attracted artists such as Naum Gabo, Ben Nicholson and Bernard Leach

■ **Eastwards from Penzance, the coast gets more sheltered; the cliffs are less mighty, the seaboard is lusher and more populated than the north coast. Deep-water harbours are packed with craft: industrial ships, private yachts and ferries – every village and town seems to have a board advertising fishing and sharking trips by boat. Visitors in spring and early summer will be nicely in time for Cornwall's justly famous gardens.** ■

Lizard transmitters

The Lizard peninsula plays a historic and living role as an important telecommunications centre. A memorial near Poldhu Cove commemorates the birth of transatlantic transmissions – it was from here that in 1901 Marconi sent three dots (a morse 'S') to Newfoundland; his first message which followed was 'What hath God wrought'. Inland, Lizard is dominated by the space-age form of the Goonhilly Downs Earth Station, the receiving centre for satellite-relayed telephone calls. A tour of the site takes you into an old control tower and you can see the nerve centre of the whole operation.

Penzance to Falmouth The town of **Penzance** has been knocked about by the 20th century, but it retains corners of Georgian streetscape, at its best in Chapel Street with its wildly capricious Egyptian House, an early 19th-century precursor to art deco. The National Lighthouse Centre records the essential function of lighthouses on a perilous coast. Surveying the main street is the statue of Sir Humphry Davy, inventor of the miner's safety lamp and the town's foremost son in its tin-mining heyday.

St Michael's Mount►►► (NT) shimmers ethereally in the sea, an isle capped by a castle. Those who have seen Mont St Michel in Brittany can be excused a sense of *déjà vu*; the Benedictines from Brittany founded a church on the site, which became a fortress after the Dissolution; the owners today are the same family who snatched possession after the Civil War. At low tide you can walk to it along a causeway across the sands; at other times take the little ferry. It has a tremendous view from the roof terrace and an intriguing warren of rooms inside.

The **Lizard peninsula** juts out to form Britain's southernmost acres. Its inland portion is flat and bleak. **Kynance Cove►** epitomises the best of the tumbledown cliffscape of the western Lizard, with a wonderfully sited beach amid the so-called serpentine rocks. There are several rock workshops at **Lizard** village, itself of little appeal. Eastern Lizard, beyond **Cadgwith►**, with its thatched cottages sloping down to the sea, has secretive,

Nowadays fishing boats in Mevagissey are still busy, but tourism is the main source of income

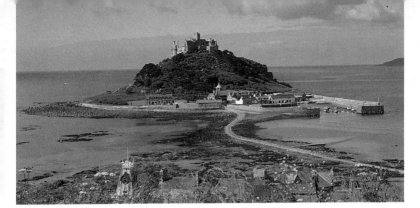

verdant creeks in the vicinity of the **Helford River**, including the tiny estuarine village of Helford itself.

Falmouth, Cornwall's largest town, is no great beauty but abuts Carrick Roads, alternatively known as the Fal Estuary▶; boat trips are the thing here, and include excursions upriver to **Truro**, the Cornish capital (not itself of major interest, although it has a 19th-century cathedral). Perfectly preserved Tudor castles, St Mawes and Pendennis, guard the great estuary. Subtropical plants abound at the delicious churchyard of **St Just in Roseland**▶, which dips down to the water's edge.

Portloe to the Tamar Portloe▶ is an unspoilt fishing hamlet, hard to get to – and long may it continue to be; it has real character and nothing to attract large-scale commercialisation. **Veryan**, inland, is known for its five early 19th-century round houses. **Charlestown**▶, a carefully preserved port, is still used by the china clay industry, whose white spoil heaps dominate the area.

Fowey▶▶ rises terrace by terrace above the deep-anchorage Fowey Harbour, with Polruan across the water. Blockhouses that used to guard the harbour stand silent sentinel. A delightful holiday base, Fowey comes to life during the late summer regatta.

Mevagissey has become too popular for some people's tastes, with coachloads of visitors cramming into its little harbour, but the place resumes its quiet charm when they have gone; ice cream, fish and chips, a model railway and the Gardens of Heligan – a Victorian garden gradually being restored – pander to daytrippers' needs. **Polperro**▶▶▶ is distinctly prettier and more groomed, though no less popular, with an appealing mêlée of alleys around its photogenic harbour; you may prefer to park at Talland Bay to the east and walk in along the level coast path rather than struggle with the traffic jams.

The **Tamar Estuary** forms the Devon/Cornwall border; the river can be explored by boat trip from Plymouth. **Antony**▶ (NT) is the earliest and finest classical-style house in Cornwall, with fine woodland gardens. **Cotehele**▶▶ (NT) is an extraordinary medieval survival, a completely unmodernised house; its estate buildings (saddler, smithy, wheelwright etc) are well preserved. By the Tamar is moored the last Tamar barge in existence.

The **Mount Edgcumbe estate**▶, tucked in the far corner of southeastern Cornwall is a country park looking across to Plymouth with paths through its grounds, which lead towards quietly characterful Kingsand and Cawsand.

St Michael's Mount acquired its monastery after a vision of St Michael had appeared in AD 495 to local fishermen

Subtropical gardens
Penjerrick, Glendurgan (NT), and Trebah gardens, close together west of Falmouth, were all the creation of the Foxes, a Quaker family, who aimed to create Paradise on Earth. They came close to succeeding, for each garden displays spectacular subtropical species. For other gardens to visit in south Cornwall, see Gardens, page 16.

Looe, a lively resort in a pleasant setting

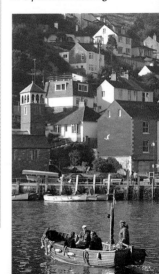

Lundy Island

A popular day-trip by ferry from Bideford (in summer also from Barnstaple) is to Lundy, a little island 19km (39 miles) north of Hartland Point. Its cliffs are a major site for birdlife; over 400 species are recorded, including puffins (*lunde* being Norse for puffin). From 1925 to 1954, Lundy's owner Martin Harman tried to make it a separate kingdom; he did not succeed, but the island still issues its own stamps. Lundy's isolation in the Bristol Channel has given it a long history of smuggling. The Marisco Tavern serves beer brewed on the island.

When Brunel's superlative Clifton Suspension Bridge was completed in 1864, its 214m (702ft) span was the world's greatest

►► Bristol   61C4

The city centre was badly bombed in 1940 and postwar planning was unimaginative. However, careful searching reveals many gems, among them **Christmas Steps**, a 17th-century survival, the **Church of St Mary Redcliffe►** with its majestic proportions, the **cathedral►** (begun 1142), notable for its Norman chapter house and organ case carved by Grinling Gibbons, and the **New Room**, Britain's first Wesleyan chapel. Outside the Exchange in Corn Street are the famous **Bristol Nails**, four small bronze pedestals upon which city merchants completed their financial deals, 'paying on the nail'. A curious architectural folly, the **Cabot Tower►** provides an excellent city view.

Docking activity is now concentrated in Avonmouth, but the revamped dockland area still has a boaty atmosphere, with sailing dinghies, a July regatta and boat tours around the harbour. Here too is the **Industrial Museum**, which acknowledges the life of Isambard Kingdom Brunel, the 19th-century engineer who designed the first ocean-going propellor ship, **SS *Great Britain►***. Launched here in 1843, it is now on public show in the dry dock where she was built. The docks are also home to the **Arnolfini** arts centre, the **Industrial Museum** and the **Marine Heritage Centre**.

Clifton►►, an elegant Georgian suburb, has honey-stone squares, crescents and terraces, including Royal York Crescent. Brunel's **Clifton Suspension Bridge**, constructed between 1836 and 1864, spans the Avon Gorge in quite spectacular fashion. Near by an 18th-century **camera obscura** offers views over Bristol.

Don't drop your Ls

The hallmark of Bristol speech is the adding of the letter *L* to the ends of words. Thus *area* becomes *areal*, *Australia* becomes *Australial* and *Bristowe*, the old city name, becomes *Bristol*.

► Clovelly   60B2

A captivating, if self-conscious fishing village, Clovelly is so steep that cars have to be left at the top. The Hobby Drive was constructed by a 19th-century owner of Clovelly Court as a scenic road (and is well worth the modest toll). In high season the village simply teems with visitors, and smaller boats take visitors from Lundy Island to Clovelly in rough winter weather.

Hartland Quay►►, to the east, gives access to some of the most formidable cliffs in the West Country, the strata fantastically contorted into bizarre cross-sections.

▶▶▶ Dartmoor National Park   *60B3*

Southern England's largest area of wild country, Dartmoor is a great expanse of blustery moors punctuated by weathered granite outcrops known as tors. Sheep and Dartmoor ponies graze the open grasslands, wandering between Bronze Age hut circles and burial mounds. The moor can be a bleak place – there is no higher place in England south of the Pennines – but there are cosy cob-and-thatch villages to come down to in the lusher valleys (some offering Devon cream teas) and some good country-house style hotels. Indoor attractions are few: this is a place to be outdoors – picnicking, touring, walking or riding horseback.

On Dartmoor's east side, lush farmland meets the barren moors. **Hay Tor▶▶** is the most visited viewpoint, easily accessible. **Hound Tor▶▶**, close by, is well signposted and lies next to a well-preserved abandoned medieval village; signs explain the layout and you can still make out the fireplaces. West of **Buckland**, whose church clock has the letters MY DEAR MOTHER instead of numerals, **Bel Tor** presides over the Webburn Valley. The **Dart Valley▶** is full of choice corners, including Combestone Tor and the medieval stone 'clapper' bridge at Dartsmeet, junction of the West and East Dart rivers.

Widecombe in the Moor▶ draws visitors for its valley setting, its fame from the folksong 'Widecombe Fair' and for its church, the 'cathedral of the moor'. **North Bovey▶** is much quieter and quite uncommercialised, with a pretty green, thatched cottages, stone cross and village pump. **Chagford** is a large but sleepy village; **Moretonhampstead**, a crossroads town, is a shade busier and has a fine row of 17th-century almshouses; to the west, on the B3212, the **Miniature Pony Centre** shows several rare farmyard breeds (not just ponies).

In northeast Dartmoor the River Teign has carved a course through a deep valley with an enchanting deciduous forest. From **Fingle Bridge▶**, an old packhorse bridge, paths lead along the river and up on to moorland viewpoints; the Hunter's Path passes the back entrance to **Castle Drogo▶▶** (NT), architect Edwin Lutyens's early 20th-century masterpiece, an improbable marriage of granite medievalism and Edwardian Arts and Crafts style. The main entrance is near **Drewsteignton**, which has a charming village square.

Two main roads cross the central moor; the B3212 passes through **Postbridge**, with its notable medieval 'clapper bridge', and grim **Princetown**, dominated by the high-security prison, originally built for Napoleonic prisoners of war. The northwest moor is the highest and most remote landscape of all; it is used for army training, but on certain days (including most weekends) you can drive along the **army road▶** from Okehampton Camp.

Two outstanding features justify a visit to the western fringes: **Brent Tor▶**, a plain church on a huge rock and looking far into Cornwall, and **Lydford Gorge▶▶** (*Admission charge*) (see Walks, page 64), a deep and tortuous ravine with a waterfall and whirlpool.

The towns encircling Dartmoor National Park are not of great interest, although **Ashburton** has some attractive streets and **Buckfastleigh** boasts a modern Benedictine abbey, a butterfly park and otter sanctuary, and the termi-

Weathering has attacked the joints in the great granite outcrops, such as Hound Tor, that dominate the wastes of Dartmoor

Dartmoor's letterboxes
Many visitors to Dartmoor in the 19th century liked to try to locate Cranmere Pool, scarcely more than a puddle and remotely situated in the moors above Chagford. Someone had the idea of placing a letterbox here, so that a self-addressed postcard would be left here by one walker and picked up and sent on by the next. The fad caught on and now there are some 400 boxes in various places. Today you can record your visit with the rubber stamp provided.

Prehistoric processional routes
Rows of stones erected in the Bronze Age are believed to have marked processional routes. Above the Erme Valley in south Dartmoor, one of these stretches 3km (2 miles) from Stall Moor to Green Hill.

Early settlers on Dartmoor
The moorland gravels yielded copious quantities of tin, exploited by Bronze Age settlers. Among the most striking of their relics are *Scorhill Stone Circle*, on Shovel Down above Gidleigh (near Chagford), a Bronze Age stone circle of 23 uprights, and *Spinsters' Rock*, off the A382 south of its junction with the A30, a neolithic tomb with its capstone held in place by three uprights.
Grimspound, between Widecombe in the Moor and the B3212, reached by a path up from the road on to Hamel Down, is a large walled enclosure with 24 discernible hut circles.

nus of the steam-powered South Devon Railway which wends its way 11km (7 miles) to Totnes. A museum of Dartmoor life at **Okehampton** tells of country life and ways; a fragment of a medieval castle caps a hillock on the edge of town.

Buckland Abbey▶, a former Cistercian monastery, was once home to Sir Francis Drake, born at nearby Tavistock. The house has some relics from his famous ship, *Golden Hind,* (including a drum and banners) but it was more Sir Richard Grenville, an earlier occupant, who stamped his character on the house; he added the intricate plasterwork in the Great Hall.

▶▶ Dartmouth 60A3

An old naval town, attractively set on steep slopes which drop to the River Dart, Dartmouth has real atmosphere, with small craft on the river and in the little harbour and a maze of back streets. The August regatta sees the town at its most exuberant.

Beside Duke Street is the arcaded **Butterwalk**, a former dairy market and now a local museum. In the quayside gardens stands the world's first steam pumping-engine, built in 1725 by Thomas Newcomen, a Dartmouth resident. Two Tudor castles guard either side of the harbour entrance; **Dartmouth Castle▶** has a magnificent view from its roof terrace.

Dartmouth is well placed for excursions, including **Totnes▶** (best reached by boat) with its Norman castle and steep medieval streets, and **Salcombe▶**, a yachting centre finely sited on an estuary. Ferries cross the Dart to Kingswear, where steam loco-hauled trips can be taken on the **Dart Valley Railway** to Paignton.

Dartmouth quay: boat trips can be taken up river or out to sea

▶ Dorchester · 61B4

Dorchester is the centre of the countryside in Thomas Hardy's novels, in particular *The Mayor of Casterbridge*, in which the town features as Casterbridge; it is often visited for that reason. It has a good local museum celebrating numerous aspects of the county and displaying Hardy's study and a collection of materials relating to him. As well as a writer, Hardy was a trained architect and designed **Max Gate** (NT), which is open to the public; he lived there from 1885 until his death in 1928.

Dorchester, a typical country town, is still recognisable as Thomas Hardy's 'Casterbridge', which features in The Mayor of Casterbridge *and his other Wessex novels*

Maiden Castle▶ is a huge earthwork on the southwestern edge of Dorchester; its massive concentric ramparts date from the 1st century BC.

Hardy's Birthplace▶ (view from outside; interior by appointment only) is the humble, thatched cottage where Thomas Hardy was born in 1840, and can be reached via a short walk along a track from a signposted car park at Higher Bockhampton. A marked trail leads to Duddle Heath, a fragment of the 'untamed and untamable wild' of the Egdon Heath of Hardy's writings. Although Hardy's body was buried at Westminster Abbey, his heart is buried here in the family plot at **Stinsford Church▶**, near the grave of Cecil Day Lewis, a former Poet Laureate.

A prominent tower some 8km (5 miles) southwest of Dorchester, confusingly called the **Hardy Monument▶**, commemorates Admiral Thomas Hardy, Nelson's flag-captain at the Battle of Trafalgar. From here the view extends over Chesil Beach and the Isle of Portland.

THOMAS HARDY COUNTRY

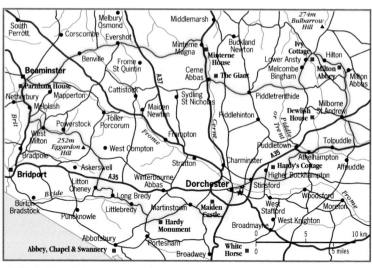

Drive **Thomas Hardy Country**

This tour (approx. 110km/70 miles) explores the heartland of the countryside immortalised in the writings of Thomas Hardy: the way of life has changed beyond recognition but many elements are still there – thatched villages, rolling downlands, manor houses, ancient monuments.

From **Dorchester** take the A35 east, branching off for **Stinsford**▶ and detouring to Hardy's Birthplace at **Higher Bockhampton**▶ (see page 75). At **Tolpuddle** the cottage museum pays homage to the Tolpuddle Martyrs who formed a trade union and were transported for their pains. Take minor roads north to **Milton Abbas**▶▶, an 18th-century estate village of rustic thatch and whitewash: the owner of Milton Abbey house near by (now a school) had the village rebuilt here to improve the view from his house. The abbey church and finely roofed Abbot's Hall are open.

Take lanes west to **Cerne Abbas**▶▶ to look at the famous Giant, best seen from a lay-by on the A352 road north. Follow the A352 to **Minterne**

Magna, where a turn-of-the-century house harbours a fine collection of trees and shrubs (open in season).

❑ The demure village of Cerne Abbas is brusquely overlooked by an extraordinary prehistoric hill-carving of a naked club-bearing man (the Cerne Giant) revealing all for the world to see. Its origins and purpose are unclear, but it is thought to be a fertility or cult symbol. ❑

Continue west to **Beaminster**▶, a delightful scene of small-town rural England with an attractive square, and past **Parnham House**▶. Drunken lanes meander southeast through **Powerstock**, attractively placed on a hillside, and past **Eggardon Hill**▶, an impressively bleak Iron Age hillfort site. Continue through **Littlebredy** and up to the **Hardy Monument**▶ (see page 75). Carry on east via the B3159 and minor roads to pass **Maiden Castle**▶ (car park on Dorchester side). The A354 leads northwards into Dorchester.

Lulworth Cove, a great semicircular scoop in the coast, displays layers of chalk, sandstone and Portland limestone

▶▶▶ Dorset Coast   61B4–B5

Dorset's varied seaboard comes as a refreshing tonic: the cliffs are mighty roller-coasters and their largely unspoiled hinterlands seem only recently to have emerged from the primeval past.

Dorset's coast is famous particularly for fossils, no place more than **Lyme Regis▶▶**, a charming resort beloved of novelist Jane Austen. The narrow lanes and Regency seafront cottages have changed little since her visits at the turn of the 19th century. Huge ammonite fossils can be seen in garden walls and in specialist fossil shops. The thatched honey-stone village of **Abbotsbury▶▶** crouches beneath a hillock crowned by a lone chapel; dedicated to St Catherine, it was once the property of the Benedictine abbey which gave the village its name. A great tithe barn and the swannery (very much alive) are other abbey survivals.

Close by, **Chesil Beach** (or Bank) is one of the most extraordinary features of the British coastline. **Weymouth▶**, an elegant resort with an early 19th-century flavour, made popular by George III, lies behind a curving bay.

Further east lies **Lulworth Cove▶▶▶**, abutted by amazing cliffs that offer ideal cross-sections for the aspiring geologists who flock here along with fishermen and skin-divers, and walkers heading for **Durdle Door** (see Walks, page 64), a natural arch. East of Lulworth, army ranges permit only occasional access to impressively rugged cliffs as far as Kimmeridge. **St Aldhelm's Head** juts into the sea and has a primitive chapel on its summit. Beyond the resort of **Swanage** lie **Old Harry Rocks▶**, chalk stacks detached from the cliff, and the multicoloured sands of **Studland**, with its fine Norman church; the village lies by the largest remaining heathlands in Dorset. Seawards, views extend to the Isle of Wight. Inland, the **Purbeck Ridge** offers a panorama of Poole Harbour. The ridge is interrupted dramatically at **Corfe Castle▶▶**, where the jagged pinnacle of a Norman castle rises above the grey-stone village.

The Fowles connection
At Lyme Regis a sinuous sea-wall known as The Cobb gained fame through the film of John Fowles' novel *The French Lieutenant's Woman*, where crazed Sarah Woodruff stared out to sea in despair while Charles Smithson explored natural history in the undercliff just west of town. The Cobb is of medieval origin, and the undercliff, still a wild place and riddled with landslips, is designated a National Nature Reserve.

The Chesil Beach phenomenon
The 29km (18-mile) shingle bank was created by the deposition of millions of pebbles through the process of long-shore drift, the lateral shift of material as a result of the waves meeting the shore at an oblique angle. The beach links the Isle of Portland to the mainland and encloses a lagoon known as the Fleet, a peaceful haven for birds. Because of the steeply shelving seaward side of the beach, it attracts anglers (but swimmers must stay clear: this is one of Britain's most dangerous beaches). The pebbles increase in size from west to east.

Tarr Steps, an ancient packhorse bridge, was allegedly built in a single night by the Devil when challenged to a show of strength by a local giant

Exeter Arts Festival
Exeter's arts festival lasts for two weeks some time during May, June or July. Classical music, including opera and ballet, predominates but there are also plays, films, poetry readings and children's events.

Threats to Exmoor
The primeval moorland of Exmoor was once much larger than it is now. The former royal hunting forest was acquired in the early 19th century by one John Knight, who created huge farmlands and introduced new breeds. From 1945 to the 1970s, the moorland dwindled further as agriculture and forestry took over, despite Exmoor's elevation to National Park in 1954. With the end of subsidies for putting moorland under the plough, and with the introduction of voluntary management agreements, the remaining moor now looks to have a permanent future.

► **Exeter**   *60B3*

Prior to destruction in a World War II 'Baedeker' raid (one of a series targeted on historic sites), Exeter was one of southern England's most attractive ancient cities.

Amazingly the **cathedral►►►** escaped almost unscathed, and justifies a visit to the otherwise largely rebuilt city centre. The twin towers are Norman, its nave displays the longest span of Gothic vaulting in the world. Look too for the astronomical clock in the north transept, the bishop's throne and the intricately carved misericords.

The porticoed **guildhall** in the high street is England's oldest municipal building. Within **Boots Arcade** is the entrance to a 13th-century underground water system, which you can explore by guided tour. The pick of the museums is the **Maritime Museum►►** with its collection of over 100 historic vessels brought from the world over; many can be boarded.

►► **Exmoor National Park**   *60C3*

A small but varied national park, Exmoor encompasses unspoilt coast, moors and quiet farmland straddling the Devon and Somerset borders. The coast provides the main focus of interest, but inland there are lonely moors and fine river valleys. Unusually for England, the moors often reach the clifftops, and the Exmoor coast is rich in diverse walks, where you can set off on the coast path and return over windswept hillsides.

The Coast Road (A39) In the northwest of the National Park, **Parracombe's Church of St Petrock►** is a completely unaltered medieval building, threatened with demolition in the last century but preserved thanks to a campaign led by John Ruskin, influential writer, critic and social reformer. Trentishoe church has a tiny musician's gallery (notice the notch cut out to allow for the double bass's bow), and just east, Heddon's Mouth is a charming, walkers-only valley which leads from the isolated Hunter's Inn to a disused lime kiln on a pebbly beach.

At **Lynton**, a sleepy but amiable resort, strange shaped crags adorn the **Valley of Rocks►**, where feral goats sniff the sea breezes (see Walks, page 64); **Heddon Valley** is another popular area for walks.

A cliff railway connects Lynton with **Lynmouth** below, prettily situated by a small harbour and, in season, more animated than its neighbour. Eastwards, the River Lyn lines a magnificent wooded valley; you can walk along the river to an idyllically sited café at **Watersmeet►►**, at the joining of the East Lyn River and Farley Water, or head on to the hills for the best views; close by, the cliffs near **Countisbury** exceed 300m (1,000ft) and are some of England's highest. **Oare** and **Malmsmead** are at the heart of Doone Country, the setting of R D Blackmore's *Lorna Doone*, based on a real family of outlaws (see panel below). **Culbone**, north of the main road, has England's smallest church, alone in the woods. **Allerford▶** has a pretty packhorse bridge and a fascinating amateur-run local museum within its old school, while tiny **Selworthy▶** has a group of immaculate thatched cottages and a large church with a fine wagon roof.

Inland Exmoor Sheep and ponies roam the breezy hills, red deer the eastern forests. Over the years the moors have dwindled in extent in the face of agricultural improvement and then enclosure, but recent National Park measures have safeguarded what remains. A road tour from Dunkery Hill to Exford, then to Dulverton and west along the Park boundary to Twitchen gives a good idea of the moor. **Winsford▶**, **Exford** and **Withypool** are three attractive villages in this area; **Dulverton▶** has heaps of small-town charm. South of Withypool, **Tarr Steps▶** is a 1,000-year-old clapper bridge, the finest of its kind in the country, spanning the River Barle. **Dunkery Beacon▶▶** is an easily climbed hill, a 10-minute walk from the road, which on a clear day offers a far-ranging view across Devon and Somerset and over the Bristol Channel into South Wales.

Dunster▶▶▶ rates as one of the most perfect small towns in England, with its ancient yarn market at the hub of its tapering street of medieval buildings, and the castle towering above. The fashionable 19th-century architect Salvin upgraded the castle interior, but it retains earlier features, including a 17th-century staircase and leather wall-hangings that tell the story of Antony and Cleopatra.

Stag hunting on Exmoor
From Norman times Exmoor was a royal hunting forest, and forest laws were enforced by special wardens. The red deer live on, and are the subject of the controversial Exmoor hunts; the Devon and Somerset staghounds are kennelled at Exford, with meets held from August to April. With the hardening of public attitudes against bloodsports, the National Trust, a major landowner hereabouts, recently balloted its members on the subject. The majority vetoed the continuation of the hunts, but the Trust decided against an immediate ban.

Lorna Doone
Blackmore's Victorian adventure novel takes place in the wilds of Exmoor. The hero, John Ridd, seeks to avenge the Doones for shooting his father, and is in love with Lorna Doone, whom the Doones have kidnapped in order to claim her inheritance by marrying her off to one of the Doone family. Tragedy later strikes at Lorna's wedding at Oare Church. Despite failing to sell for more than a year after publication, Lorna Doone has become a minor classic that for many is synonymous with Exmoor.

Dunster, an important cloth centre in the 16th century, is dominated by the octagonal yarn market, where Somerset cloths – 'Dunsters', 'Tauntons', and 'Bridgwaters' used to be sold. 'Dunster ' later became 'duster'

THE WEST COUNTRY

Sir Francis Drake
It was Drake (*c*1541–96), as every schoolchild knows, who finished off that famous game of bowls on Plymouth Hoe before turning his attention to the Spanish Armada. Devon-born, he was the first Englishman to sail around the world and, as a darling of Elizabeth I, was knighted for his efforts. In 1588 he achieved the great victory over the Armada. The weather played a major role, with a third of the Spanish vessels being shipwrecked. This was Drake's last great naval exploit, although he pioneered a leat (channel) bringing fresh water from Dartmoor to Plymouth.

Gilded ceilings and other adornments at Longleat House were added in the 19th century by the 4th Marquess of Bath

▶▶ **Glastonbury** 61C4

This market town huddles around the base of Glastonbury Tor, a green hillock capped by the tower of St Michael's Chapel. Visible from far around, the Tor was an island in early times, when the sea extended across the Somerset Levels. The **abbey▶**, which fell into spectacular ruins with Henry VIII's Dissolution of the Monasteries, has long been a place of pilgrimage: the Legend of Glastonbury records Joseph of Arimathea burying the chalice used in the Last Supper. There are links too with Arthurian legend: Arthur's corpse was brought here by Sir Lancelot.

▶▶ **Longleat** 61C5

'We have seen the lions of Longleat' proclaim the car stickers; the hugely popular safari park and allied attractions (Butterfly Park, Dr Who display and more) have made Longleat a household name. The house, completed in 1580, was ahead of its time: it looks out to the park rather than gazing into a courtyard, with a uniform design on its four sides. Inside are 16th-century tapestries, portraits, and rare manuscripts; 19th-century embellishments – marquetry, fireplaces and gilded ceilings – were added by Italian craftsmen. Capability Brown landscaped the gardens in 1757; they feature the world's largest maze.

▶ **Plymouth** 60A2

A major naval base for many centuries, Plymouth's centre suffered under World War II bombing. Head for the old area west of Sutton Harbour, with the **Merchant's House**, the timber-framed **Elizabethan House**, the **Black Friars Distillery** (where Plymouth Dry Gin has been made since 1793) and the **Pilgrim Fathers Memorial**.

Most famous of all is the waterfront area known as **The Hoe▶**. Here is **Smeaton's Tower**, a re-erected form of the Eddystone lighthouse; close by are the excellent **Aquarium of the Marine Biological Association** and the 17th-century **Royal Citadel**, a vast fortress. In Finewell Street, 15th-century **Prysten House**, with displays including a model of 17th-century Plymouth, is a museum. West of the centre, the two **Tamar bridges** cross into Cornwall: the graceful 1961 road suspension bridge and Brunel's 1859 railway bridge.

English placenames

■ **In Dorset you can walk from Ryme Intrinseca to Beer Hackett; in Kent you can try getting your tongue around Trottiscliffe (pronounced Trozlee); in County Durham you can go to Pity Me; while in Worcestershire, there is a pukka-sounding village called Upton Snodsbury. England's placenames have amused and bemused visitors and locals alike, inspiring both affectionate parody and rhapsodic verse.** ■

Historical pointers By the time of the Norman invasion in 1066, the settlement pattern in England was already largely established. Placenames give a host of clues as to how and when England developed. Generally the suffix gives the key element, with the prefix acting as a descriptive defining element – Doncaster, for example, tells us of a Roman camp (*castra*) on the River Don.

Settlers from the East As Saxons began to settle in England, they introduced their own placenames rather than using the existing Celtic ones – the only native placenames to have survived adopted natural features such as hills, rivers and valleys. Early Saxon names included heathen names such as those of gods, for instance Woden (Wednesbury) and Thunor (Thunderfield). The suffix *-ing* survives from that period, particularly in Surrey and East Anglia, while later Saxon names included the commonest suffixes, *-ham* (home) and *-ton* (enclosure, farm or manor).

That Scandinavian settlers ensconced themselves in eastern England is shown by a concentration of names ending with *-by* (Grimsby, Whitby, Wragby etc): the vast majority are in the eastern counties. Remote areas had names unto themselves: Lympne and Lyminge in east Kent and numerous Cornish names (Trelissick, Marazion, Nanjizal) are unique to those parts. The suffix Chipping (Chipping Campden, Chipping Sodbury, Chippenham etc) indicates a market place; the word is related to the German *kaufen* (to buy) and appears to be the root of Copenhagen.

Later changes In the 19th century, mining and other industrial settlements created new names – ranging from matter-of-fact New Mills to the intriguing likes of Indian Queens and Booze. The Somerset seaside resort of Weston upgraded itself into Latin, and was renamed Weston-super-Mare. The odd euphemism took place – the Devil's Arse cave was tamed to Peak Cavern, and Pigg Hill became Peak Hill. Craven Arms in Shropshire was originally just a pub; a railway town grew around it and the name stuck.

Placename quirks
● Some places were merely cartographical accidents: Unnear appears on several early 19th-century maps of Mid Wales, but was no more than the corruption of a map-maker's query – Quaere.
● Few 20th-century placenames exist; the new towns of Peterlee (named after a trade union leader) and Telford (after Thomas Telford, the engineer) are exceptions.
● Westward Ho! is Britain's only placename bearing an exclamation mark.
● Coldharbour (meaning a shelter from bad weather) is the commonest minor placename.

81

Salisbury Cathedral

► **Quantock Hills** 61C4

This is a truly forgotten corner of rural England. Hedges grow high around the sunken, drunkenly crooked lanes, churchyards hide behind banks of cow parsley, and private manor houses lurk behind estate walls. Villages are sleepy, typically of sandstone and colour-washed cottages, and dense woodlands cloak the lower slopes. On the top is a plateau of heather moors crossed by ancient trackways.

Medieval wool-trade prosperity left a legacy of fine churches in the Quantocks: 16th-century carved bench ends are a speciality; the best include those at **Broomfield**, **Spaxton**, **Crowcombe** and **Bicknoller**.

William Wordsworth and his sister Dorothy stayed in 1797 at Alfoxton Park at **Holford**, keeping fellow poet Coleridge company (see panel). The latter lived for some years at **Nether Stowey►**, where his cottage has been restored by the National Trust and filled with mementoes of his life and works.

The **West Somerset Railway►**, the longest private line in Britain, operates steam and diesel trains from Bishop's Lydeard (near Taunton) to Minehead. Washford station has a small museum devoted to railway memorabilia.

►► **Salisbury** 61C5

Salisbury's **cathedral►►►** displays faultless uniformity, and was built mostly between 1220 and 1258 in Early English Gothic. Its noble spire, added 1334–80, soars to 123m (405ft), higher than any other in the country. On clear days, it is worth preserving enough energy to climb the tower to the base of the spire. Reached through the cloisters, the octagonal chapter house boasts a superb medieval carved frieze depicting scenes from the books of *Genesis* and *Exodus*, and has the best preserved of four manuscripts of the *Magna Carta*, the first bill of rights foisted on King John by barons in 1215.

England's largest **cathedral close** surrounds the precincts; houses open to the public here are the 13th-century **King's House**, now home to the Salisbury and South Wiltshire Museum (exhibits relate to Stonehenge and Old Sarum, ceramics, and a pre-National Health Service surgery); **Redcoats in the Wardrobe** (regimental

Old Sarum
Old Sarum (EH), the original site of Salisbury, was finally abandoned in Norman times because of its exposed hilltop position. Old Sarum Church was founded in 1078, but five days afterwards was struck by lightning and largely destroyed. The town upped and moved to New Sarum (present day Salisbury) soon after, yet up to 1832 it was the classic 'rotten borough' returning two Members of Parliament (including, towards the end, the Elder Pitt) to serve a non-existent electorate. Old Sarum is on the edge of Salisbury.

museum); **Malmesbury House**; and **Mompesson House** (NT), a fine Queen-Anne house with a walled garden, period furnishings and a rare collection of English drinking glasses. The rest of town, laid out on a spacious grid plan by Bishop Poore in the 13th century, also has many attractive corners.

Wilton House▶▶, the 17th-century home of the earls of Pembroke in nearby Wilton, is not on a grand scale, but shows exemplary taste. Inigo Jones designed most of it, including the Double Cube Room, hung with Van Dijk portraits. Here too is the room where some of the D-Day invasion planning took place.

▶▶▶ Scilly, Isles of 60C1

An idyllic retreat beyond the southwestern tip of the British mainland, 'the Scillies', as they are often known, comprise five inhabited islands. Each is surprisingly different from the other and there is much to interest the naturalist, particularly birdlife. Daffodils, narcissi, iris and tulips are commercially grown.

Hugh Town is the principal township on **St Mary's**, the largest island (only 5km/3 miles wide at its maximum girth); Star Castle, built 1593–4 as a fortress against a possible Spanish invasion, is now a hotel. Paths follow the coastline, and there is a remarkable concentration of prehistoric burial chambers to explore, while at Peninnis Head are curiously weathered rocks. The island of **Bryher** is windswept, with simple facilities and gorse-clad hillsides that dazzle with yellow in spring. **St Agnes**, the smallest inhabited island, has an old lighthouse of 1680 (now a private house but still providing flashes). Troy Town Maze, a curious piece of folk art with stones laid out on the turf, may have been created by an 18th-century lighthouse-keeper with time on his hands. **St Martin's** is treeless, with a prominent day-mark cone (1683) on its highest point, and has splendid beaches; Higher and Lower Towns between them muster a population of around 100. **Tresco▶▶** is renowned for its sub-tropical gardens of Tresco Abbey, the major attraction of the Scillies, created by Dorrien Smith. The island is fun to explore (no cars, just tractors), with a trio of forts and several white-sand beaches.

Scilly practicalities
The archipelago, 45km (28 miles) west of Land's End, is reached from Penzance heliport (just out of town on the A330) by a 20-minute helicopter trip, by plane from Land's End aerodrome, or by a 2½-hour boat ride to St Mary's. There is a good boat service between the other islands. Bicycles can be hired on St Mary's.

Stonehenge, compellingly immense and silent

Stonehenge – the facts
Stonehenge began as a simple ditch and bank (2800 BC); sarsen stones from Wiltshire and stones from the Preseli Hills in Wales were added around 2000 BC. In the Bronze Age, around 1600–1500 BC, the whole was remodelled with uprights and cross-lintels. The central axis aligns with the sun on Midsummer's Day and other alignments may have enabled the circle to perform a calendar function.

Stonehenge – the enigma
Archaeologists may never know the precise mystical, religious or cere-monial significance of Stonehenge. More extreme theories have included notions of inspira-tions from beings from outer space, a creation by King Arthur and his circle of models of male and female sexuality, a bird trap, a model of the solar system, and a cosmic scheme related to the Egyptian pyramids and built by the people of Atlantis.

▶▶▶ Stonehenge   61C5
Britain's most famous prehistoric stone circle, a World Heritage Site, stands alone on Salisbury Plain, a sparsely populated area of chalk downland that is studded with mementoes of early settlers. Its origins and purpose remain a mystery (see panel).

Visitors flock here in their thousands; plans are in hand for the diversion of the main road and for a much-needed upgrading of its facilities.

▶▶ Stourhead   61C5
In 1741, inspired by a Grand Tour of Europe, Henry Hoare II, the son of a wealthy banker, returned home to Stourhead and decided to improve his grounds with clas-sical temples, a triangular lake and rare plants. He created one of the highest achievements of English landscape gardening. The Palladian mansion suffered a fire in 1902 but still has good Chippendale furniture, paintings and a library. This and the adjacent village of Stourton are owned by the National Trust.

▶▶▶ Wells   61C4
England's smallest cathedral city is set near the eastern end of the Mendip Hills. The handsome streets of lime-stone houses are dwarfed by the magnificence of the **cathedral▶▶▶**, significant above all for the richness of its early 13th-century west front (recently restored), adorned with 356 statues. Building started on the choir in about 1180 and finished with the cloisters in 1508, all to the design of Bishop Reginald de Bohun. A problem of sub-sidence at the crossing was resolved by the remarkable innovation of inverted 'scissor' arches, which despite the obvious Gothic provenance look curiously timeless in style. Here too is the world's second oldest clock, with its 14th-century face showing phases of the moon and the position of the sun. The stained glass, chapter house and carving deserve time to be savoured in full.

Close by is the moated **Bishop's Palace▶** with its draw-bridge and turrets and ruined medieval hall. **Vicar's Close** is the best of Wells' streets. The **Church of St Cuthbert's** has a fine Perpendicular tower and roof; beasts and angels feature among the roof bosses. Built in 1348, Vicars Close is home to the Vicars Choral and is said to be the oldest complete street in Europe.

Cheddar Gorge►►► is the most spectacular feature of the Mendip Hills, themselves a gently rolling whaleback plateau perforated with limestone caverns – some have collapsed to form gorges. A road follows the bottom of Cheddar Gorge beneath the massive grey cliffs; fanciful names have been given to many of the crags. A staircase at the entrance to the gorge, on its south side, leads up to a ramshackle tin prospect tower; views are even better from above. (See also Walks, page 64.) Also by the gorge entrance are the **Cheddar Caves►**, of which Gough Cave is recommended for its weird limestone formations. Cheddar itself has a fine medieval market cross.

Axbridge► is a pleasing, small town that sees far fewer visitors than Cheddar Gorge or Wells. Its attractive, rather irregular central square is overlooked by the timber-framed King John Hunting Lodge, a 15th-century merchant house that is home to a local history museum.

Burrington Combe► is a lesser version of Cheddar Gorge. During a storm here in 1792, Reverend Augustus Toplady sheltered beneath a rock and composed the hymn *Rock of Ages*. **Dolebury Warren►**, a grassy ridge between Burrington Combe and the A38, has splendid views from its Iron Age hillfort, extending over the Severn Estuary to South Wales and southwards towards Bath. Jutting out into the Severn Estuary just south of Weston-super-Mare, **Brean Down►►** gives phenomenal panoramic views of hills and estuary; this too has the site of an ancient hillfort on its summit.

Wookey Hole► is a colourfully lit cavern, said to have housed the witch of Wookey (her alabaster ball and comb and the bones of her goat are kept in the town museum in Wells). It is a good place for children, with waxworks and vintage penny-in-the-slot machines, and Britain's oldest complete skeleton – with a re-creation of 'his' world 9,000 years ago. Near by, Ebbor Gorge is a secretive limestone ravine with a nature trail through charming woods.

Cheddar cheese
Cheddar itself is of course best known for Cheddar cheese. The hard cows' milk cheese was first made here in the early 12th century, perhaps even earlier. The traditional method is to 'cheddar', or cut, the firm curd into small pieces and to drain the whey before packing the residual matter into cylinders some 30–38cm (12–15in) in diameter; the cheese is then wrapped in muslin and coated with wax. It is left to mature (originally this was done in local caves) for anything from three months to two years according to the strength desired. The Cheddar Gorge Cheese Co Rural Village, at Cheddar, makes the authentic product.

85

A genre of folk art: antique merry-go-round horses in the old Papermill at Wookey Hole

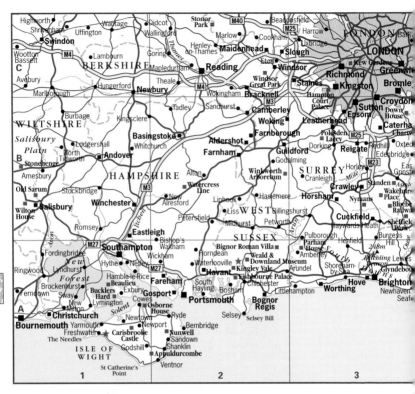

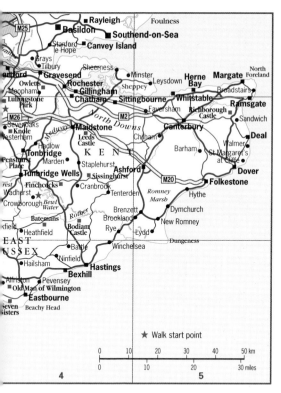

★ Walk start point

```
0        10      20      30      40      50 km
0        10              20              30 miles
```

4   5

Southern England The southeastern counties constitute a comparatively affluent corner of Britain. Proximity to the capital and a green-belt policy restricting growth around London have increased property prices in this cherished ring of countryside, so that the villages and towns have become affluent commuter areas. Beyond the green belt spreads suburbia. Yet for all the urban pressures, the region has surprisingly deep pockets of rural countryside; west Kent, southern Surrey and much of Sussex represent some of the most varied lowlands in Britain.

The Weald The area between the North and South Downs is known as the Weald, a word related to the German word *Wald,* or 'forest', which suggests an area once covered with woodlands; even today the tree cover is appreciable, but pasture fields, enclosed by hedgerows, are the predominant feature. A mirror-image geology makes the Weald easy to comprehend: the two outlying flanks of chalk downs are the remnants of a great chalk dome that once covered southern England; it has been breached in the middle and the underlying greensand exposed, appearing as ridges running through Kent and Surrey; Wealden clays cover the low levels in between the hills. Accordingly, the Wealden landscape is complicated and varied, a patchwork of hedge-lined pastures, small woodlands and the odd patch of heath. The North and South Downs rise abruptly from the plain, the

Wye Downs, part of the North Downs, in Kent

steeper escarpments sporting rough grassland, coppiced woods and scrubs. But modern agriculture has removed much of the herb-rich grassland from the South Downs, where the plough has turned downs into flinty fields of earth and crops. Wealden buildings traditionally have timber frames and are often hung with pantiles. Square and circular oast houses, built as kilns for drying hops, are an important component of the Kentish scene, although they are no longer used for that purpose. Hop-gardens (easily identifiable as fields of regimented wooden poles, upon which hops are grown) and orchards are declining in number, but are still striking features. The area is particularly rich in grander houses and gardens; the best are listed on pages 16–17 and 102–3.

Kent, East and West Sussex and Surrey Kent is indeed a mixed bag; the north coast is part marshy, part industrial, although the historic dockyard in Chatham and the centre of Rochester make a good day's outing. Inland Kent has numerous pretty villages such as Penshurst, Chilham, Chiddingstone and Shoreham; of its inland towns, Canterbury, Tunbridge Wells and Tenterden stand out. On the coast, Dover deserves more than a fleeting glance for its castle, and Broadstairs and (to a lesser extent) Folkestone are pleasant resorts. The Channel Tunnel runs from Folkestone to Sengatte, near Calais (see panel, page 98).

The Sussex shoreline is almost entirely built up, much of it with 20th-century residential development, and the beaches are not as good as elsewhere. The curious traveller may like to pay a visit to the assembly of houseboats on the tidal mudflats at Shoreham in West Sussex, or to the De La Warre Pavilion, a Bauhaus-inspired design in Bexhill. The most rewarding coastal town is Brighton, a recently renovated resort with a fun and lively atmosphere. The Royal Pavilion rates as one of the country's most extravagant follies. Hastings and Eastbourne are also rewarding, in contrasting styles, but both abutting fine cliffs. Chichester Harbour is the yacht haven of Sussex, and the town of Chichester, Sussex's cathedral city, has on its outskirts the county's finest Roman survival, Fishbourne Palace.

SHORTLIST: WHERE TO GO
HISTORIC CITIES
Canterbury, Rochester, Winchester.
CASTLES AND ROYALTY
Berkshire: Windsor.
Hampshire: Portchester, Solent defences at Portsmouth, Southsea etc.
Isle of Wight: Carisbrooke, Osborne House.
Kent: Deal, Dover, Rochester, Walmer.
Sussex: Bodiam, Pevensey.
ROMAN REMAINS
Kent: Lighthouse and painted house at Dover, Lullingstone Villa (near Eynsford), Richborough Castle (near Sandwich).
Sussex Bignor Villa (near Amberley), Fishbourne Palace (near Chichester).
SMALL TOWNS
Arundel, Chichester, Cranbrook, Faversham, Lewes, Petworth, Rye, Sandwich, Tunbridge Wells.
SEASIDE TOWNS
Brighton, Broadstairs, Eastbourne, Hastings.
NAVAL HERITAGE
Chatham, Portsmouth.
COASTAL SCENERY
Sussex: Seven Sisters and Beachy Head (near Eastbourne), Fairlight Cove (Hastings).
Kent: Cliffs between Folkestone and Walmer.

Oast houses are peculiar to Kent and the Hereford and Worcester areas

SOUTHERN ENGLAND

In recent years, a number of small-scale vineyards have opened in the south, producing white wines, typically with a flowery aroma

In quitting the great Wen [London] we go through Surrey … There are erected within these four years, two entire miles of stock-jobbers' houses on this one road, and the work goes on with accelerated force! … What at once horrible and ridiculous thing this country would become, if this thing could go on only for a few years!
William Cobbett (1822), *Rural Rides*

Much of inland Sussex is genteel, with smart villages and an abundance of historic buildings, teashops and antique shops, as in Arundel, Amberley, Lewes and Alfriston. By contrast, the Ashdown Forest in East Sussex is an exhilarating heathland, almost upland in feel; this is the landscape of the *Winnie the Pooh* stories of A A Milne, with idyllic glades and sandy tracks – excellent picnic country.

Surrey, Britain's most wooded county, has been heavily developed as an affluent commuter area, but has some delightful countryside, ideal for walking, notably in the greensand country around Haslemere and the vicinities of Shere and Leith Hill, the highest point in the southeast at 294m (965ft).

Hampshire and Berkshire The county of **Hampshire** rolls gently inland, the best of its country in the far east around Selborne and in the far west by the heaths and woodlands of the New Forest. Winchester has a compact but fascinating medieval centre. The coast offers little aesthetically, but Portsmouth has an important naval heritage and Southampton, although much bombed in the Second World War and overtly a large industrial and commercial centre, has a few corners of historic interest (medieval town walls, Tudor House and the oldest bowling green in the world) as well as aviation and maritime museums and a fine art gallery.

Both these towns, and Lymington, have ferries to the **Isle of Wight**, a pleasant base, with plenty to tempt families and walkers, despite the urbanisation that has crept along its eastern coast. The island has an excellent public transport system (you may prefer to leave the car on the mainland), and its south coast is one of Britain's sunniest spots.

Berkshire has a split identity, divided north–south by the M4, with downlands merging into Wiltshire and Hampshire to the west, while at its eastern edge is Windsor Great Park.

At Windsor Castle you can see inside the state apartments of the Queen's favourite residence; crowds throng the town all year round, and a number of side-attractions have sprung up; you can escape from the bustle by taking a boat trip along the Thames or a walk into Eton or the park.

The Thames defines Berkshire's northern border from Windsor to Streatley; the river, which it shares with Buckinghamshire and Oxfordshire, has a placid beauty and a boating scene that is quintessentially English.

REGION HIGHLIGHTS ◄ ◄ ◄ ◄

BRIGHTON *see pages 90–1*
CANTERBURY *see page 93*
BEACHY HEAD *see page 98*
DOVER CASTLE *see page 98*
THE WEALD *see pages 102–3, 106–7*
PORTSMOUTH *see page 104*
RYE *see pages 104–5*
WINCHESTER *see pages 107–8*
WINDSOR *see page 109*

I will go out against the sun
Where the rolled scarp retires,
And the Long Man of Wilmington
Looks naked toward the shires;
And east till doubling Rother crawls
To find the fickle tide,
By dry and sea-forgotten walls,
Our ports of stranded pride.
Rudyard Kipling (1865–1936), on the Sussex landscape

The period charm of Horsted Keynes station on the preserved Bluebell Line – so called because of the bluebell woods through which the railway passes

Brighton's beginnings
In 1754, Dr Richard Russell came to what was then the fishing village of Brighthelmstone and pre-scribed sea water as a cure for a variety of com-plaints. Many heeded his advice and the village acquired spa status. Georgian and Regency terraces followed as the élite followed in the foot-steps of the Prince Regent. Once a playground for the rich, Brighton later acquired a reputation as a rather sleazy town. Graham Greene's novel *Brighton Rock* is based on the seedy world of 1930s gang warfare.

►► **Bluebell Railway** 86B3

In 1960 the Bluebell was the first standard-gauge steam railway to be re-opened as a tourist attraction; in many ways it is the pick of the bunch, with some of its carriages dating from the 1890s and the stations evocatively fur-nished with Victorian advertising signs, fire buckets and gas-lamps. Its 27km (18-mile) round trip takes an hour (special restaurant trains and other events at weekends) and currently runs between Sheffield Park and Kingscote via Horsted Keynes (there are bus links to East Grinstead, to which, it is hoped, the line will eventually run). Sheffield Park Garden (see page 17), owned by the National Trust, makes a pleasant destination.

►►► **Brighton** 86A3

This is the oldest and in many ways the most interesting British seaside resort. The Prince Regent, later King George IV, came here after his secret marriage to Mrs Fitzherbert, and initiated the fashion for seaside holidays and bathing machines. He converted a farmhouse bought in 1784 into his wildly capricious **Royal Pavilion**►►►, an oriental extravaganza covered with minarets and onion domes; inside, the exoticism continues at full throttle to create one of the most extraordinary interiors in Europe. Chandeliers and gilt, *chinoiserie* trappings and rich décor are prolific.

Brighton's **seafront**►►, the legacy of its elegant hey-day, is still impressive. **West Pier**, Britain's finest such structure, has long been derelict, half wrecked, but a recent National Lottery award has been allocated to help restore it. Meanwhile, the newer **Palace Pier** is very much alive, with fish and chips, souvenirs and fortune-tellers. Summer weekends draw crowds to the amusements, aquarium and privately run seafront train, one of the oldest electric railways in the world. The nudist beach, Britain's first, lies discreetly out of sight from the pier; the main beach is shingle. Cream and sky blue period streetlamps and white stucco terraces proliferate: the best streets lie to the east at **Kemp Town►**, an outstanding example of early 19th-century town planning, with a crescent at its hub. To the west, along with seafront, **Hove** has similarly attractive buildings.

The Lanes►► survive from the once humble fishing village of Brighthelmstone, but is now upmarket Brighton, with antiques and jewellery shops, pavement cafés, restaurants and galleries in its warren of narrow alleys. Brighton's main **museum►** has some eye-catching furniture, including art-nouveau pieces and a famous sofa by Salvador Dalí representing a gigantic version of Mae West's lips.

A conspicuously attractive town by the South Downs, to the northeast of Brighton, **Lewes►►** is graced with some pleasing streets and paths known as 'twittens', which include steep, cobbled Keere Street. The hilltop castle is Norman, and was adapted into a romantic garden feature in the 18th century; it gives a fascinating rooftop view. Many of the timber-framed houses were given a fake brick veneer, fashionable in the 18th century, with the widespread use of 'mathematical tiles', thin fascia tiles resembling bricks. The town is famed for the best and heartiest November 5 fireworks night in the country, and it also has a notable concentration of antiques emporia and auction rooms.

►► Broadstairs   *87C5*

The prettiest of the seaside resorts in Thanet, East Kent, Broadstairs has a pleasantly old-fashioned air and concentrates its charms on the seafront, with seven miniature sandy coves beneath low cliffs. It's an amalgam of sedate holidaymaking and fishing; you can still watch fish unloaded and eat shellfish on the harbour wall. Charles Dickens knew and loved Broadstairs well, and spent several summers at what has since been named 'Bleak House', where you can see the desk at which he penned *David Copperfield*.

Almost joined to Broadstairs, **Ramsgate►** is more run down, but merits a visit for some of the Regency streets. The coastal walk from Broadstairs to Ramsgate takes about 30 minutes.

Bloomsbury connections
Three places associated with the Bloomsbury Group are found in the South Downs, around Lewes. *Monk's House* at Rodmell (south of Lewes) was the home of Leonard and Virginia Woolf. *Charleston Farmhouse*, near Alciston, was the home of Duncan Grant and Clive and Vanessa Bell (Virginia's sister), and its walls and furniture are still decorated with their paintings, while the garden recalls the Bloomsbury days. The group added further decorations in the form of murals in *Berwick Church*.

At this desk at 'Bleak House', Dickens completed David Copperfield. *Miss Mary Strong, the original Betsey Trotwood of his story, lived in Dickens House in nearby Victoria Parade*

Walks

Tennyson Down, Isle of Wight
86A1

Start from Freshwater Bay. The coast path leads west along a grassy ridge, with views of the sea on three sides. Pass the Tennyson monument and continue to the island's western tip; an old fort, Needles Old Battery, gives views of The Needles, a set of rock pinnacles battered by the waves. Return the same way. (2½ hours)

Ditchling Beacon, West Sussex
86A3

Start from car park adjacent to Ditchling Beacon. Here the South Downs rise to their third highest point and are capped by the site of an Iron Age hillfort. Follow the South Downs Way west along the escarpment edge. After 3km (2 miles), you reach the famous Jack and Jill windmills. Return the same way. (2½ hours)

Bewl Water, Kent/East Sussex border
87B4

Start from visitor centre car park. An attractive reservoir, Bewl Water is the largest lake in the southeast and has a well-marked and scenically varied path encircling it. It is too long for a day's walk, but pleasant for strolls.

Lullingstone Park, Kent
87C4

Start from car park at visitor centre off the A225. A popular outing for Londoners, trails from the centre take in river, woodland and grassland landscapes (about 1½ hours). Longer walks in the vicinity incorporate the pretty villages of Shoreham, Otford and Eynsford.

Ashdown Forest, East Sussex
87B4

Start at the Poohsticks Bridge car park in Ashdown Forest (take the B2026 south of Hartfield (2km/1¼ miles), turning west at junction with minor road; the car park is 180m (200yds) on north side of road). This is the heartland of of A A Milne's *Winnie the Pooh* stories. A path leads to the bridge where the game of Poohsticks was played; return to the car park and follow the gravel track eastwards, ignoring left forks. Cross the road and take a path rising on to heathland (where Piglet supposedly lived). Continue up to the monument to Milne on Gill's Lap: this is the 'Enchanted Place' of the stories, a spot with a view encapsulating the splendour of the 'forest'. Return the same way. (1½ hours)

Poohsticks Bridge, Ashdown Forest

▶▶▶ Canterbury   87B5

Canterbury has witnessed two very dark hours. One was the murder of Thomas à Becket in the cathedral in 1170, the other a World War II 'Baedeker raid' in 1942 (so called because targets were historic rather than military). The medieval city centre was destroyed but miraculously the cathedral, seat of the Archbishop of Canterbury and the premier church of England, was unscathed.

Yet today the city's sense of history is as compelling as ever. You can walk through the **West Gate** (museum inside), as countless pilgrims have done for eight centuries, and pass a number of charitable hospitals founded in medieval times as places to accommodate pilgrims (St Thomas' Hospital and the **Poor Priests' Hospital▶** are open to the public, the latter housing a hi-tech city heritage museum). The old city centre is largely contained within the **city wall**, but just outside lie **St Augustine's Abbey**, founded by St Augustine in 597, its church and cloister foundations still apparent, as well as **St Martin's Church**, England's oldest church in continuous use and the erstwhile headquarters of St Augustine.

The **cathedral▶▶▶** precincts are entered by Christ Church Gate, much ornamented with heraldic motifs. The cathedral, built in Caen limestone, boasts several outstanding features, among them Bell Harry, the 72m (236ft) high central tower, an outstanding collection of 12th- and 13th-century stained glass, a Norman crypt and the Black Prince's tomb. Adjacent is the 15th-century Great Cloister, where you can find a stone marking the death-place of Thomas à Becket. Just behind the cathedral, Green Court is fronted by the Norman Staircase, the ruins of the monks' dormitory and the graceful buildings of the **King's School**, a prestigious private establishment. The **Roman Museum▶**, under street level, in Longmarket, features the remains of a Roman townhouse and a mosaic floor.

Northwest of Canterbury, **Faversham▶** is a well-preserved country town with a wealth of timber-framed and rendered buildings, some restored gunpowder mills and an absorbing volunteer-run heritage centre.

The village of **Chilham▶▶** has a handsome half-timbered square, with the church at one end and the castle entrance at the other.

Canterbury's rich architectural heritage is in evidence around the early 16th-century Christ Church Gate

The Canterbury Tales
In Chaucer's *Canterbury Tales*, the apogee of English medieval literature, a party of pilgrims meet at the Tabard Inn, Southwark (now part of London). They agree to travel together and to tell stories to pass the time:
  'And specially, from every shires ende
  Of Engelonde to Caunterbury they wende.'
Chaucer's works are brought to life in theme-park fashion, with tableaux and re-created sounds and smells, in *The Canterbury Tales* in St Margaret's Street.

■ The seaside holiday is a great British invention, which, like other good things, has spread down the class ladder. In the 18th century, the only people who could afford a holiday of more than one day were the aristocracy and the wealthy. Later, resorts like Bournemouth and Eastbourne were planned to attract middle-class custom. The arrival of the railways and the invention of the Bank Holiday in Victorian times spurred the development of the brash, cheerfully vulgar resort for the working class – such as Blackpool, Margate and Skegness. ■

Beach belles
When the fashion for sea bathing began in the 18th century, men and women customarily bathed naked, but as it spread, so did modesty. The bathing machine carried people, shielded from view, right out among the waves but, even so, women took to wearing all-enveloping flannel gowns tied with a drawstring at the neck. Elaborate Victorian and Edwardian costumes made of flannel, worsted or serge looked much like day dresses, with frilly caps, stockings and shoes. The one-piece costume for ladies came in before World War I, with sleeves and reaching to the knees.

94

Before the 18th century, people occasionally bathed in rivers and lakes, but eyed the sea with suspicion. It was dangerous and it tasted nasty. Even in the Royal Navy, a seaman who could swim was a rarity. When seabathing began, it was for health rather than pleasure. An illustration from 1735 shows men and women in the sea at Scarborough, a health spa with a mineral spring on the Yorkshire coast. The spring was good for business for the local doctors, and it seems to have occurred to them that perhaps the rolling ocean, so plentifully at hand with its salt-laden water and brisk North Sea breezes, might be profitably exploited as well.

'So bracing' Certainly this exploitation worked on the Sussex coast, where the obscure fishing hamlet of Brighthelmstone was transformed into glamorous **Brighton**, queen of the sea. A doctor called Richard Russell, who moved there in 1753, proclaimed the virtues of crabs' eyes, cuttlefish bones and woodlice washed down with a hearty pint of seawater. His successor, an Irishman called Anthony Relham, opportunely discovered the salubrious qualities of fresh sea air, heightened, he said, by Brighton's fortunate lack of noxiously perspiring trees.

The effect of all this twaddle was to draw well-to-do invalids and hypochondriacs to the Sussex shore, and when the Prince Regent took to visiting and built himself an oriental pleasure dome, the Royal Pavilion, the new resort's success was assured.

Some fishing villages and minor ports grew gradually into resorts, while others were planned for profit by shrewd local landowners and developers. **Llandudno**, on the North Wales coast, was

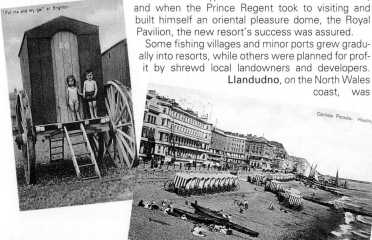

"For me and my gal" at Brighton.

Carlisle Parade. Hastings

Above: ice cream and beach huts, Walton on the Naze. Below right: just sitting, Brighton Palace Pier

Piers of the realm

The pier, that familiar feature of the seaside, is descended from the much earlier quay, built to land cargo and passengers on an open shore. In 1823 Brighton constructed its famous Chain Pier, like a suspension bridge tiptoeing gracefully into the English Channel (which destroyed it in a storm in 1896). Though built for boat-passengers to and from Dieppe, it was a pleasure pier as well. It had souvenir shops and a camera obscura and was appreciated as a way of enjoying the sea without being seasick. Sadly, piers are an endangered species now, desperately expensive to repair and maintain.

laid out by the local Mostyn family and remains a charming Victorian resort, queening it over brash **Rhyl** and **Prestatyn**, which developed later for Lancashire millhands. In the 1870s, at **Skegness** on the Lincolnshire coast, the Earl of Scarborough built a resort to lure the middle classes, but the Great Northern Railway brought hordes of holidaymakers from the Midlands industrial towns and Skegness instead became a leading working-class resort. The first of the chain of Butlin's holiday camps opened there in 1937.

Places with a sandy beach naturally cashed in, as did towns with a mild climate and plenty of summer sun. The Thames Estuary resorts of **Margate** and **Southend** enjoy Britain's highest July/August temperatures, followed by those along the south coast from Torquay to Folkestone. The highest sunshine figures are presently held by **Shanklin** and **Sandown** and on the Isle of Wight.

'Beside the seaside' Health remained a factor – 'Skegness is *So* Bracing', the posters proclaimed – but sheer fun took precedence as resorts sprouted piers and promenades, illuminations, funfairs, cliff railways, zoos, flowery gardens, bandstands, dance halls, freak shows, tattoo parlours, saucy postcards, fortune tellers' booths, eel and whelk stalls, ice-cream and rock kiosks to spice up the simpler pleasures of swimming, sunbathing, sand castles and donkey rides.

The seaside landlady became an archetypal figure of fun and dread, with her iron gentility, strictly regulated mealtimes and parlour aspidistra. On August Bank Holiday Monday in 1937 more than half a million people swarmed into Blackpool in 50,000 motor vehicles and 700 trains, the earliest of which arrived at 3.55am.

Since World War II, with growing affluence, more cars and much longer holidays, patterns have changed. Some people still go faithfully to the same resort every year. Blackpool and Brighton are still both very popular, but most British seaside resorts have not been able to compete with inexpensive package holidays abroad, and adverse publicity about polluted beaches has not helped. The traditional seaside holiday seems increasingly a pleasure of the past.

All the way through

One of the traditional seaside delights is rock, a stick of mint confectionery which is usually white in colour with the resort's name in pink or red letters, mysteriously running through the stick's whole length. Blackpool and Morecambe both claim to have invented the delicacy, but there is also a tradition that it originated in the inland mining town of Dewsbury in the 1860s. As late as the 1970s Blackpool was manufacturing two tons of rock a day in the summer.

The Medway towns
The three Medway towns of Rochester, Chatham and Gillingham together form a large industrial conurbation in the north of Kent. The most historic of these is Rochester. Pre-industrial Rochester is compact but impressive, with a medieval cathedral, an absorbing museum within the Guildhall, and the ruins of a Norman castle giving mighty panoramas over the River Medway below. The writer Charles Dickens lived in Rochester for a period; the Charles Dickens Centre is in Tudor House, which features in the *Pickwick Papers* and *Edwin Drood.*

Kingley Vale
Europe's largest yew forest spreads over a shoulder of the South Downs, a wonderful ancient-feeling place, dark and eerie, where trees have collapsed and then continued to grow from their horizontal positions, making a bizarre collection of shapes and forms. A nature trail circles the site. The forest's origins are a mystery; could it have been a plantation? Yews were once valued for making bows and arrows. The view from the Bronze Age bell barrows (burial mounds) on the summit extends over Chichester Harbour.

Half-timbering and pantile hanging are among the vernacular building styles on show at the Weald and Downland Open Air Museum at Singleton

▶▶ **Chatham Dockyard** 87C4

The historic dockyard was once a naval centre of shipbuilding and fitting; today it incorporates Britain's largest concentration of listed buildings. Warehouses, shipbuilding sheds, a dockyard church, and a rope-works and flag-loft (the longest brick structure in the world when it was built) have been opened up together with a visitor centre. Combined with Rochester (see panel), this makes an excellent day out (there are fast rail services from London).

▶ **Chichester** 86A2

The cathedral city for Sussex is based on a simple criss-cross layout centred on a fine 16th-century Butter Cross and, with ancient city walls and handsome Georgian streets, it is an enjoyable place to explore.

Its medieval **cathedral**▶ (early Norman with Early English additions) is unusual in not being tucked away in its own close, and in having a detached belfry. The interior has some distinguished modern features: a tapestry by John Piper, a painting by Graham Sutherland and glass by Chagall. The Mechanical Music and Doll Collection is the most offbeat of the city's museums, while Pallant House specialises in modern British art, displayed within an elegant, early 18th-century house.

On the edge of Chichester, **Fishbourne Roman Palace**▶▶ is thought to have been built for one Cogidubnus, a Briton who supported the Romans and was made senator. Now much has been re-created, with a dining room, mosaics in full view, and the garden laid out as it probably once was. The palace, built in four wings around a courtyard, was begun in AD 75, and burnt down in 280. The partition walls, heating system, bath and hypocaust have been excavated.

Southwest of the town, **Chichester Harbour**▶ is a big yachting centre. Extending over a huge area, its east side is mostly unspoilt mudflats and complex, marshy inlets. **Bosham** is one of the best places to appreciate the setting: the much-painted village has a picturesque church steeple, waterfront cottages and boating scenes. East Head juts into the southeast corner of the harbour: here sand dunes and saltmarshes make for an exhilarating stroll. Daily boat tours from Itchenor take 1½hrs (for a recorded timetable tel: 01243 786418).

Due north of Chichester is the **Weald and Downland Open Air Museum**▶▶, Singleton, an exemplary rural

Fishbourne's unearthing
In 1939 some children who had been learning about Roman Britain at school decided to dig on the farmland at the bottom of their garden beside the Fishbourne road. They hit the jackpot straight away, finding a black and white mosaic. However, the owner of the field, who did not want archaeologists all over his land, made them fill it in and told them to keep quiet – which they did (until fairly recently). Then a workman cutting a water-main trench in 1960 came across some ancient-looking building rubble; he reported it and it was then that archaeologists really focused on this, the largest known Roman residence in Britain.

museum with reconstructed vernacular buildings rescued from all over Kent and Sussex – including a farmhouse, toll cottage, smithy, school and watermill.

A sleepy, unblemished village, much of it thatched, **Amberley▶▶** is beautifully set below the South Downs, some 20km (13 miles) northeast of Chichester. Glimpse through the churchyard gate to the 16th-century manor within a massive medieval curtain wall. The former residence of the bishops of Chichester, the old castle was dismantled by Cromwell's men. It perches on the edge of Amberley Wild Brooks, an area of watermeadows known for its rich birdlife and marshland plants. Near the station at the south end of the village, the Amberley Museum has displays of small-scale Sussex industries and crafts, located in a former chalk pit; here are a blacksmith, potter, boat-builder, printer, narrow-gauge railway, vintage buses, wheelwright, and even a collection of antique wirelesses. Near by is the Elizabethan manor house **Parham House▶**, begun in 1577 by Sir Thomas Parham, who later sailed with Sir Francis Drake to Cadiz; its deer park has lakes and a walled garden.

Arundel▶▶ is a handsome, compact town. The main street climbs from the River Arun up to the sprawling medieval-Victorian castle (home of the dukes of Norfolk and their ancestors for over 700 years) and the nearby Roman Catholic cathedral. The castle and adjoining park are open to the public.

At the Wildfowl Reserve just north of town, visitors can observe the birdlife at close quarters from specially constructed hides. The English cricket season traditionally sees the touring team playing its first match against Lavinia, Duchess of Norfolk's XI at Arundel.

A little to the north, **Bignor Roman Villa▶**, one of Britain's largest Roman houses, has splendid mosaic floors (depicting gladiators, Ganymede and the eagle etc). The villa was occupied during the 2nd to 4th centuries and was discovered during ploughing in 1811. Stane Street, a Roman road now relegated to a path, cuts straight across the beautiful downland close by. Its finest section starts from the car park on Bignor Hill (reached by a narrow, bumpy lane).

Chichester: flint walls in St Richard's Walk

The Channel Tunnel

The project to build a link from England to France has been germinating since Napoleonic times. The current Anglo-French venture; a rail tunnel from Folkestone to Calais, created many complications. Naturalists were aghast at the spoil dumped near Dover, and errors were made over a high-speed rail link to London. The tunnel was completed in 1994 at a cost of £10 billion, and now *Le Shuttle* takes cars between Folkestone and Calais, and the *Eurostar* passenger train runs non-stop from London, Waterloo to Paris, Lille and Brussels. The Eurotunnel Exhibition Centre in Folkestone gives an overview.

Eastbourne's Victorian pier

 Dover 87B5

The major cross-Channel port since Roman times (when it was known as *Dubris*), Dover has long assumed a military role. It was badly bombed during World War II and re-development has been lacklustre. But the famous white cliffs of Dover (a symbol of homecoming for Britons) still beckon across the Channel.

The **castle**▶▶ (EH), high above town, stands proudly as one of Britain's finest examples of an intact Norman keep; an 'All the Queen's Men' exhibition and a model of the Battle of Waterloo enliven a musty interior. The shell of the **Pharos**, a Roman lighthouse, is close by, and Kent's major **Saxon church**, adorned by Victorian encaustic tiles, completes the trio of Dover's finest buildings. Nineteenth-century ramparts and barracks surround the castle, a reminder of its recent military use, and an extensive **tunnel system** underneath the castle is open to the public.

In the town centre, a few Georgian and Regency terraces remain unscathed, but the major sight is the **Roman Painted House**▶, with its complex central heating system and its modestly painted walls on display.

The **White Cliffs Experience**▶ gives an interactive view of Dover's history: row a Roman galley and walk through a Blitz-damaged street.

The French coast looks surprisingly near on a clear day: Cap Gris Nez, a chalk headland in Picardie, is the most prominent feature.

The first cross-Channel flight

The cliff walk northeast from Dover passes Blériot's monument, commemorating the first powered flight across the Channel. Louis Blériot (1872–1936), whose early flying experiments included towing gliders along the River Seine, made the historic flight from Calais to Dover on 25 July 1909.

Deal and Walmer▶ are both on the coast to the north of Dover, and both have castles built by Henry VIII in the plan of a Tudor rose. Walmer has villas and shingle; Deal has a pretty ex-fishermen's quarter of narrow streets.

 Eastbourne 87A4

A well-heeled town of chintzy hotels, genteel stucco, and brass bands on the prom, Eastbourne is as neatly preserved an example of a middle-class 19th-century English seaside resort as you will find. The beach is shingle.

The South Downs end in style just west of Eastbourne at **Beachy Head and the Seven Sisters**▶▶▶. There's a sheer drop of 160m (525ft) at Beachy Head, the chalk cliffs towering above a lighthouse. Further west, the

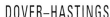

Seven Sisters are a series of dry valleys chopped off by the sea to form a roller-coaster cliff. There is access to the coast path at **Birling Gap** and at **Seven Sisters Country Park** by Cuckmere Haven. Beware the unfenced edge.

Alfriston▶▶ is a village with a strong medieval atmosphere, with old houses, cafés and antique shops. The 14th-century Clergy House, a pre-Reformation vicarage, was the first building acquired by the National Trust, and is a carefully restored half-timbered house with its original clay floor. Adjacent, the church, dubbed 'Cathedral of the Downs', has good 14th-century features. In the street are two fine inns, the Star and the George, and the stump of a market cross as a memento of busier days.

Near by and best seen from south of Wilmington village is the **Long Man of Wilmington▶▶**, an enigmatic chalk carving on the downs of a man bearing a staff in either hand. 'He' is probably Anglo-Saxon or earlier, although no written record before the 18th century has been found. The Norman-Tudor priory in **Wilmington** now houses a worthwhile agricultural museum.

Eastwards along the coast from Eastbourne is **Pevensey Castle▶**. Its 4th-century Roman fort walls enclose a medieval castle and keep. William the Conqueror landed here in 1066 to launch his invasion of Britain at the Battle of Hastings (see panel).

▶ **Hastings** 87A4

Hastings itself is an endearingly seedy seaside resort, recommended if you like places oozing with decaying grandeur. The picturesque and distinctly warren-like **old town** lies in a valley east of the commercial centre; the former fishermen's quarter lies close by a group of curious tall wooden sheds, called 'deezes', built for storing fishing nets, and there are caves and a castle to visit.

Pleasant walks on to the sandstone cliffs extend eastwards to **Fairlight Cove** along a surprisingly wild coastline; a cliff railway carries you up the steep slope of the old town.

St Leonards on Sea, into which Hastings merges, has some particularly fine and well-cared-for Regency terraces.

Bodiam Castle▶▶ (NT), 19km (12 miles) inland from Hastings, dates from the 14th century. Surrounded by a wide moat filled with water lilies and with walls at their original height, the ruins are substantial enough to be able to picture the building at its prime.

The Battle of Hastings
Every British schoolchild knows the date 1066, when the Battle of Hastings between William of Normandy and King Harold took place at Battle (as it is now called). Oddly, the great turning point in English history was a surprisingly haphazard affair: the English (Saxons) should have trounced the French, who were vastly outnumbered and fighting uphill. However, they made a strategic blunder in storming downhill when they thought some of the Normans were retreating; this left a hole in the Saxon defences on the top of the slope, which the Normans promptly filled.

Battle Abbey
William I, 'the Conqueror', vowed that if he was victorious he would found an abbey here, on the battlefield where he defeated Harold's English forces; the high altar marks the spot where Harold is said to have fallen, pierced through the eye by a Frenchman's arrow. Today a battlefield trail and an audiovisual display detail the story of the battle. Of the abbey, the gatehouse of 1338 and the east range are intact.

Low tide at Birling Gap gives access to the beach below the brilliant-white Seven Sisters

SOUTHERN ENGLAND

The Royal Yacht Squadron has its headquarters at Cowes

Some island houses to visit
Osborne House (EH) was built as a retreat for Queen Victoria in 1845 and she died here in 1901. The State Apartments provide a rewarding insight into Victoria's lifestyle. Dating from the 18th century, *Appuldurcombe House* (EH) stands as a partial skeleton, with a triumphal gateway to nowhere in its Capability Brown landscaped grounds. *Arreton Manor* is a graceful stone house built around 1600, with furnishings and panelling of the period. Among several museums it incorporates is the National Wireless Museum, acknowledging the work of Marconi, who made his pioneering transmission experiments near by.

The Tennyson connection
Alfred Lord Tennyson ensconced himself at Farringford Park House (now a hotel) near Freshwater Bay; his Victorian fan club (autograph hunters and all) tracked him down here and he is still remembered by the monument on Tennyson Down.

Cowes High Street

►► Isle of Wight *86A1*

This diamond-shaped island is reached by ferry or catamaran from Portsmouth (for Ryde and Fishbourne), Southampton (for Cowes) and Lymington (for Yarmouth). Although much built up and geared to tourism, the island has plenty of scenic variety, with chalk downs inland and some splendid coastal cliffs. Public transport is excellent; many visitors prefer to leave their cars on the mainland.

On the south coast, grassy whaleback hills provide outstanding views for walkers; at the western end of **Tennyson Down►►** (see Walks, page 92) is a set of fragile chalk pinnacles known as **The Needles**. Close by, the multicoloured sands of Alum Bay are sold in souvenir glass bottles of every shape and size. The island's southernmost point, **St Catherine's Point►** has a lighthouse open to visitors; St Catherine's Hill is capped by an oratory in the tower of a 14th-century chapel, once used as a beacon. Further north, **Yarmouth►** is the most appealing town on the island, a pretty port with whitewashed cottages and one of the numerous Solent forts built by Henry VIII. The coast and rivers have some attractive marshy landscapes, as found along the **River Yar** and **Newtown Estuary.**

The east coast is much developed: **Ryde, Shanklin, Sandown** and **Bembridge** are suburban-looking resorts, well attuned to gentle seaside holidaying. Shanklin has preserved its old village near Shanklin Chine, a gorge leading to the sea. **Cowes** has a yachty atmosphere; in late June, the Round the Island Yacht Race features over 1,000 competitors, and in August Cowes hosts a regatta. **Ventnor** snuggles beneath an undercliff.

The only inland town, **Newport** is the island's capital. Near by are the impressive remains of **Carisbrooke Castle►►**, one of the best-preserved Norman shells in the kingdom, with inner rooms dating from 1470; Charles I spent time here pending his execution. The castle has Britain's only surviving donkey wheel, once used to haul water from a deep well. **Godshill►** is a self-consciously pretty village of stone and thatch, with a model village among its tourist attractions; its church has a rare 15th-century wall painting of the 'Lily Cross', which shows the crucifix as a lily.

▶ New Forest 86A1

The New Forest, in western Hampshire, is a freakish survival. Established in 1079 as a hunting forest for Norman royalty, it has retained a remoteness that is rare for this part of England. Essentially it is a tract of lowland heath and mixed forest, much in 'inclosures' (plantations); it is splendid territory for walking, camping and picnics. There are no major hills, but there is enough variety for it to be of interest; it tends to be more open on the west side. Wild ponies and red deer are commonly seen; the former graze on heathlands and are owned by commoners who hold historic grazing rights. The **New Forest Museum** at Lyndhurst sets the scene.

Lined with conifers planted in the 19th century are two forest drives, the **Bolderwood** and **Rhinefield ornamental drives▶**. Species to be seen include giant fir, redwood and swamp cypress. Lord Montagu's **National Motor Museum▶▶** at Beaulieu (pronounced 'bewlee'), the finest collection of its kind, celebrates the golden age of motoring; adjacent are **Beaulieu Abbey▶** and **Palace House▶**, Lord Montagu's stately home (complete with monorail and vintage bus rides). Downriver, **Bucklers Hard▶** is a pretty hamlet with a nautical flavour; the story of this former boat-building centre is told in the Maritime Museum. **Exbury Gardens** includes a celebrated collection of azaleas, rhododendrons, magnolias and camellias.

Rhinefield, in the New Forest

101

More offbeat is **Peterson's Tower**, Sway, built in the 1870s to show off the virtues of concrete. It is now a hotel.

▶ Petworth 86B2

This attractive town features clusters of timber houses and enticing back streets next to the park of **Petworth House▶▶**. This grand mansion was built by the Duke of Somerset in the late 17th century, and has been in the Percy family since Norman times. Today the National Trust maintains its interior, which includes virtuoso woodcarving by Grinling Gibbons and a superb collection of paintings by J M W Turner, Rembrandt and others.

Squatters' rights
A few scattered thatched hamlets are found in New Forest clearings. Typically such settlements owe their origins to squatters' rights, whereby common land could be occupied by anyone building a house within one day, provided smoke was seen to be rising from the chimney by dusk.

Houses of the Weald

■ The counties of Kent, West Sussex, East Sussex and Surrey boast a remarkably varied range of houses that are open to the public. Many of those described below make pleasant day trips from London. (Several are also included in the Drive on pages 106–7.) Some houses may be closed during winter months and it is always worth checking on opening times with local tourist information centres before starting out on your visit. ■

102

The National Trust (NT)
The National Trust is a major landowner; it was formed in 1895 to safeguard Britain's places of historic interest and natural beauty. Property it acquires is inalienable, held on trust for the nation. Many of the NT's hundreds of country houses, gardens and other places of interest are open to the public. Cards giving free admission to any property are available, on payment of a membership fee, from these and from NT information centres, or by post from PO Box 39, Bromley, Kent BR1 1NH.

The Italian Garden at Hever Castle: part of Astor's 20th-century design

Polesden Lacey► (NT), near Dorking, Surrey was built by Thomas Cubitt in 1824 and remodelled in Edwardian times for Mrs Greville, a society hostess. The house has a lovely rural outlook from its North Downs perch, and fine gardens. Exhibits include photographs from Mrs Greville's collection.

Standen► (NT), near East Grinstead, West Sussex, is a delightful Arts and Crafts house, designed in the 1890s by Philip Webb, a friend of leading artist-craftsman William Morris. It still has its original electric light fittings and has a collection of ceramics by William de Morgan. Towards Tonbridge, **Penshurst Place►►**, Penshurst, Kent, lies amid charming lowland countryside, an outstanding example of domestic 14th-century architecture, owned by the Sidney family, earls of Leicester, whose forebears include Sir Philip Sidney, the Elizabethan poet. It has a splendid hall with a chestnut ceiling, and a fine, long gallery. Nearby **Hever Castle►►**, Hever, Kent, was the birthplace of Anne Boleyn, second wife of Henry VIII. The moated Tudor house owes much of its present appearance to the 20th-century adaptations by William Waldorf Astor, a wealthy American. He added mock-medieval features and laid out delightful grounds with great avenues of chestnuts and limes, a yew maze, yew topiary in the form of chessmen, and an Italian garden filled with sculpture. **Chartwell►►** (NT), 8km (5 miles) north, near Westerham, Kent, was Sir Winston Churchill's home from 1922 until his death in 1965. The house appears as it was when Churchill and his family lived here in the 1920s and 30s, a comfortable, homely place filled with mementoes of one of the greatest men of the century. Timed tickets avoid the problem of long queues. General Wolfe, general of the British

army at the capture of Quebec from the French, was born in 1726 at **Quebec House▶** (NT), Westerham, Kent; an exhibition illustrates his role in the campaign.

Charles Darwin lived for the last 40 years of his life at **Down House▶** near Downe, Kent, and here wrote his

seminal work *On the Origin of Species* (1859), the book that changed mainstream thinking on evolution.

Immediately southeast of Sevenoaks, Kent, **Knole ▶▶▶** (NT) is England's largest house, with 365 rooms, 7 court-yards and 52 corridors; little has been altered since the early 17th century. A former archbishop's palace which later fell into the hands of Henry VIII, Knole has been in the hands of the Sackvilles from the time of Elizabeth I. Its sheer size requires mental stamina. The huge deer park is always open to the public. **Ightham Mote▶▶▶** (NT), near Shipbourne, Kent, is one of the finest houses of its period in this region, a 14th-century moated building of immense character, with a Tudor chapel with painted ceiling, a splendid Great Hall, and a 14th-century chapel and crypt.

Near the North Downs in northern Kent, **Owletts▶** (NT), near Cobham, is a restrained redbrick Carolean house, which boasts a plasterwork ceiling and a staircase of the same period. Do not miss the collection of memorial brasses in Cobham church. Near the village of Shoreham in Kent's Darent valley, **Lullingstone Castle▶** is a family mansion with state rooms and one of the earliest brick gateways in the country; a visit can be combined with Lullingstone Roman Villa.

Leeds Castle▶▶, to the east of Maidstone, Kent, was once a residence of Henry VIII, but is not as genuine a stately home as some, as the furniture and contents have been acquired with the aim of re-creating a country house. The grounds and building themselves are real enough, however, and the place has warmth and an idyllic lake setting. About 20km (13 miles) south near Goudhurst in Kent (not far from **Sissinghurst**, see Gardens, page 17), is **Finchcocks▶**, an early Georgian house noted for its collection of keyboard instruments, while 20km (12 miles) south at Burwash, East Sussex, is **Bateman's▶** (NT), the 17th-century house where author Rudyard Kipling lived from 1902 to 1936 and completed *Puck of Pook's Hill* and *Rewards and Fairies*. The mill next door houses one of the oldest water-driven turbines, still grinding flour for sale. Kipling's 1928 Rolls Royce is on show.

The Arcadian beauty of Penshurst Place, famous for its medieval Baron's Hall. The house inspired Sir Philip Sidney (1554–86), who was born here, to pen his poem, Arcadia

The Wealden forests

The Weald has not always been the countryside of fine mansions, charming villages, rich farms and hop-fields that we see today. In centuries gone by, it was deeply forested, its oaks supplying the timber that built the British Navy. The trees were also felled by charcoal burners to smelt the Sussex iron. Patches of this ancient forest remain, in the forests of St Leonards and Ashdown.

*On Nelson's flagship,
HMS* Victory, *you
can learn about
the appalling living
conditions of the
crew*

Portsmouth's historic ships

HMS *Victory* was Nelson's
flagship at Trafalgar and is
still in commission (thus
manned by serving
officers). Henry VIII's
favourite battleship, the
Mary Rose, keeled over in
1545 in the harbour, in
sight of the king. In 1982
the wreck was recovered
and is now kept under
special conditions, an
intriguing time capsule of
Tudor life. HMS *Warrior*
was the world's first iron-
hulled warship, now
restored to its former
glory; visitors can walk
around the decks.

Naval defences at Portsmouth

Among those which can
be visited are Southsea
Castle, built in 1544, which
still has tunnels (exhibits
include fish-bone ship
models made by
Napoleonic prisoners of
war); Spitbank Fort, out to
sea and reached by a short
boat trip, with a labyrinth
of passages; Fort Nelson at
Fareham; and Fort
Brockhurst at Gosport.

Church Square, Rye

▶▶▶ Portsmouth   86A2

A sprawling port and industrial city, much bombed in
World War II, Portsmouth is unique among British towns
in being built on its own island. This has been a major
naval base since the 12th century, and in 1495 was host
to the world's first dry dock. At its peak, some 25,000
were employed in building and serving the fleet. In 1982
the South Atlantic Task Force was prepared here for the
Falklands War. For the visitor, Portsmouth rates alongside
Greenwich (see page 46) as the centre for finding out
about Britain's maritime history.

The **Historic Dockyard▶▶▶**, by Portsmouth Harbour
station, is the chief attraction, where a trio of famous
warships are berthed (see top panel). The **Royal Naval
Museum** (*entry fee separate, or combined with ticket for
HMS* Victory) charts naval history from 1485 to the
Falklands War, and features the stories of the Trafalgar
campaign and the Siege of Malta. **Port cruises** operate
between April and October, weather permitting.

Eastwards lies **Southsea**, an Edwardian seaside resort,
where the **D-Day Museum▶** commemorates the Allied
invasion of Normandy on 6 June 1944 with the sights and
sounds of Britain at war and the 80m (260ft) Overlord
Embroidery (a latter-day Bayeux Tapestry). The **Royal
Marines Museum** traces the 300-year history of the
marines and has an Arctic display, junior commando
assault course and Falklands multimedia cinema. Also in
Southsea, the **Portsmouth Sea Life Centre** is an enterprising aquarium with a ceiling-high 'window on to the
ocean'. The extensive **Solent defences** were developed
during Henry VIIIs reign and again in the 19th century (see
lower panel) to counter threats to the naval base.

Elsewhere in town are **Charles Dickens' birthplace**
(Commercial Road), where the writer was born in 1812,
now a three-room museum; **Portchester Castle▶▶**, from
which the Romans co-ordinated the defence of southeast
England, and which include remains of a Norman church
and a palace built by Richard II; the **City Museum** (Museum Road); old shopfronts and more.

▶▶▶ Rye   87B4

This small town of cobblestones and timber-framed
houses perches on a rise above Romney Marsh. Mermaid
Street is one of the prettiest thoroughfares in southeast
England. Originally a Cinque Port (see panel, page 105),
Rye now lies inland by some 3km (2 miles). In medieval

times the town was frequently attacked by the French, who set fire to it in 1377; the Ypres Tower is a rare pre-fire survival and now houses the local museum. Medieval Landgate guards what was once the only landward entrance. The Gun Garden below looks down the River Rother towards Rye Harbour. The novelists Henry James and E F Benson lived at Lamb House at different times; many of Benson's Lucia stories are set in Rye. Antiques hunters should head for the shops near the old quay.

To the northeast lies **Romney Marsh►**. The sea has receded, leaving the marsh, now drained and fertile farmland grazed by chunky Romney sheep. A long way inland, the old Saxon shore is visible as an abrupt escarpment edge; at its foot runs the Royal Military Canal, built in Napoleonic times as a defence. Romney Marsh is sparsely populated but has some good medieval churches, including the drunkenly askew one at **Brookland**, with its detached belfry. **Camber Sands** offers one of the cleanest beaches in the southeast.

Winchelsea►► is a quiet hilltop village southeast of Rye, still ranged around its medieval grid plan, with many handsome old houses and a superb church. The original town was much plundered by the French in the 14th and 15th centuries. Three town gates survive.

Beyond Romney Marsh, the **Romney, Hythe and Dymchurch Railway**, a mere 38-cm (15-inch) gauge, runs between the picturesque hillside town of **Hythe** (there's a bizarre collection of human skulls in the church crypt) and **Dungeness**, a most surreal place, where fishermen's shacks and converted railway carriages crouch on a vast shingle bank beneath the shadow of Dungeness B Nuclear Power Station (*Guided tours* free).

►► Sandwich   87B5

Though of modest size, Sandwich has a remarkably intact medieval centre, all the better for being off the tourist track. You can walk alongside the river on the earth ramparts, taking in the Barbican, a toll bridge-cum-gateway. Notable among public buildings are a Tudor guildhall and three medieval churches.

Northwest of town and on the bank of the Stour, is **Richborough Castle►**, a Roman fort for legions crossing the English Channel and heading along Watling Street to London and beyond.

The Cinque Ports
During the reign of Edward the Confessor (1042–66) a confederation of Channel ports was formed for the defence of the coast, and for 300 years these Cinque Ports had the monopoly on the supply of ships and men for the royal fleet, enjoying certain privileges in return. The original five ports – Sandwich, Hastings, Hythe, New Romney and Dover – were later joined by Winchelsea and Rye, and several other towns were also attached. After the 14th century, as harbours silted up and the coastline shifted, the Cinque Ports declined in importance. Today, only Dover is an active port.

105

Martello Towers
A feature of the Kent and Sussex coasts is the string of 74 Martello Towers, built 1805–12 to resist a possible French invasion; some are derelict, others have been converted into private houses; English Heritage maintains one at Dymchurch, in Romney Marsh (Kent), and opens it to the public in summer.

Fishing boats on the beach at Dungeness

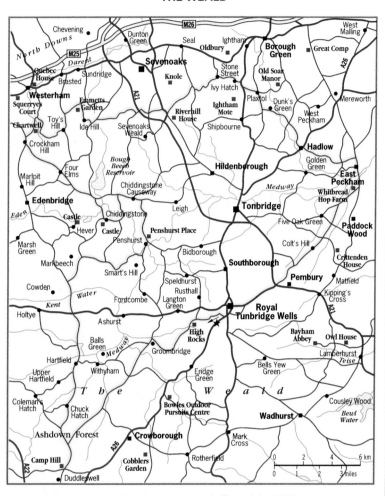

THE WEALD

The Pantiles, an attractive shopping area in Tunbridge Wells

Drive The Weald

Starting at Royal Tunbridge Wells, this is a circular tour of approximately 110km (70 miles). You will see the weatherboarded and pantile-hung cottages, the undulating woodlands and unspoilt farmland of the Weald and you can visit a host of country houses and attractive gardens. Allow plenty of extra time if you plan to stop at all the places mentioned.

Start at **Tunbridge Wells►**, a pleasant old spa town with echoes of its 18th-century heyday, including the delightful Pantiles, a Regency arcade. Leave by the A26, but soon fork right and then left to pass **High Rocks►**, a popular place for climbers.

At **Groombridge** take the B2188 which rises on to the sandy heathlands of the **Ashdown Forest►**, the landscape of A A Milne's *Winnie the Pooh* stories. Detour south along the B2026 – just before the next junction, Camp Hill on the right is a fine

viewpoint. Return north along the B2026 through **Hartfield** and turn off past Cowden railway station to take lanes to **Penshurst►►**, with its great house (see page 102) and pretty cottages.

Continue by the B2176 and a minor road to **Chiddingstone►**, where a splendid half-timbered group owned by the National Trust includes the Castle Inn, close by an eye-catching Gothic castle.

Weave around minor lanes past **Chartwell►►**, Churchill's house (see page 102), through pretty **Ide Hill** village, with its spacious green, around the south side of **Knole Park►►►** and close to **Ightham Mote►►►** (see page 103). Return via Plaxtol, **Hadlow**, with its ruinous 19th-century folly tower, and **East Peckham,** where oast houses mark the site of Whitbread Brewery's demonstration hop farm (*Open*).

The Round Table in Winchester names King Arthur's knights – but was made 700 years after his death

►►► Winchester   86B1

The capital of Saxon England, Winchester became a major religious and commercial centre in medieval times. Its importance has drastically ebbed, but its substantial medieval core is well preserved and its long-established College remains one of Britain's great public schools.

SOUTHERN ENGLAND

Winchester College

Students of Winchester College, one of the country's leading public schools (see panel on Eton College, page 109), are known as Wykehamists, harkening to its 14th-century foundation by the Bishop of Winchester, William of Wykeham. Seventy scholars were prepared here, originally in classics and other disciplines, before studying at New College, Oxford (another Wykeham foundation). The school probably was used as a model for Eton College, founded by Henry VI. Both have quaranggles, a chapel and a hall.

The Watercress Line

Also known as the Mid-Hants Railway, the privately owned 16km (10-mile) railway runs through the Hampshire countryside from New Alresford to Alton (where it connects with British Rail), giving a good feel for rail travel in the age of steam. The carriages are old BR ones, the staff dress in period costume and the stations look and feel right. The watercress beds which gave the line its nickname are still to be seen around New Alresford and watercress soup is served on the line's evening diner train.

Visitors will spend most of their time in the vicinity of the cathedral▶▶▶, the longest medieval cathedral in Europe. It has an outstanding Norman crypt, much Perpendicular work and monuments to Jane Austen and Isaak Walton, of *Compleat Angler* fame; the chantry of William Wykeham, who funded restoration work, is perhaps the finest monument of all. Walton resided in No 7 in the cathedral close, a charming precinct between the flying buttresses of the cathedral and the rambling half-timbered Cheyney Court (dating from 1148). Close by is the City Museum▶, with a strong Roman section.

The High Street and Broadway have been the main axes of the city since Roman times. At the top end, West Gate, one of two surviving city gates, occupies a Roman site; a small museum upstairs has a drawing of Wren's scheme for a royal palace (which never got off the ground). Near by is the Great Hall, where hangs 'King Arthur's Round Table', a resplendent medieval fake. Down along Broadway is the tall statue of King Alfred, King of Wessex, who is buried near by, and the Abbey Gardens, a quiet haven close to the Gothic revival guildhall (1871) housing the tourist information centre. The half-timbered City Mill straddles the River Itchen near by. In College Street, a plaque records the house in which Jane Austen died in 1817, aged just 42.

Winchester College▶ can be visited by guided tour between April and September: it has a 'quad' like those found at Oxford and Cambridge university colleges. Wolvesey Castle▶ (EH), a gaunt shell of a bishop's palace built in 1130 and dismantled by Parliamentarians in the Civil War, stands next to elegant Wolvesey Palace (1684), which superseded it.

A 15–20 minute walk along the watermeadows to the south brings you to St Cross Hospital▶▶, founded in 1136 as a charitable almshouse institution, an extraordinary place apparently in a time warp, with a fine Norman chapel and an antiquated kitchen. By an ancient rule of the charitable trust, Wayfarer's Dole – bread and ale – is still given to anyone who asks for it specifically.

On the banks of the River Test, 16km (10 miles) southwest of Winchester, is the pleasant town of Romsey, well worth a visit for its wonderful Norman abbey▶▶, built mainly in the 12th century by Henry de Blois, Bishop of Winchester, and full of little treasures.

Winchester Cathedral, built of Quarr stone from the Isle of Wight, contains the remains of Canute, successor to King Alfred

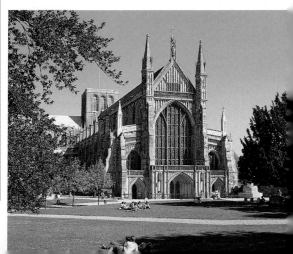

Eton College rowers with Windsor Castle beyond

86C2

Too innovative for some
Windsor's 17th-century guildhall, started by Sir Robert Fitch and completed by Sir Christopher Wren, needed no structural columns beneath its raised floor. The alarmed town burghers insisted that Wren supplied some; this he did, but deliberately built them too short, to prove they were unnecessary.

▶▶▶ **Windsor and Eton**

The two towns are a short walk apart, separated only by the Thames. It is an easy trip by train from London, but it needs a very full day to get round the sights. Visitors to Windsor and Eton often tie in a trip to the gardens at Wisley (see page 16). Open-top buses run between the main sights in Windsor and Eton every 15 minutes.

The pleasant town of **Windsor** is dominated by the presence of **Windsor Castle▶▶▶**, Europe's largest, a royal family residence which opens its doors to visitors. Times of the daily Changing of the Guard are posted near by (generally 11am). St George's Chapel, the State Apartments and the incredibly detailed Queen Mary's Dolls' House are high points. Parts of the castle were badly damaged in a major fire in 1992, but have now been restored, funded by money raised from occasionally opening Buckingham Palace to the public (see page 43). **Windsor Park▶▶▶** is worth exploring on foot (there is public access to most of it), with follies, lakes and a totem pole to discover. The **Legoland** theme park includes a Lego traffic driving school and a Miniland re-creation of Amsterdam, London, Brussels and Paris.

Another royal site is **Frogmore House** (*Open* occasionally), the 17th-century home of Queen Charlotte and Queen Victoria's mother, as well as the burial place of Victoria herself.

Over the river lies **Eton**, its appealing main street fronted by **Eton College▶▶**. The chapel is a very fine example of 15th-century Perpendicular style, reminiscent of King's College Chapel, Cambridge. The quad has a strong Oxford and Cambridge look about it too. The Museum of Eton Life celebrates the life and times of Eton College.

From **Windsor**, boat trips run to **Bray Lock** in the heart of the **Thames valley▶▶**. The river has a classic quality of Edwardian summer days. At **Maidenhead**, fanciful villas and spacious gardens back on to the river, and Sunday afternoon walkers stroll along the towpath to **Boulter's Lock**. The village of **Cookham▶** has been immortalised by the works of artist Stanley Spencer, and a gallery here has a number of his works. **Henley-on-Thames▶** is famed as the focus of the Royal Regatta, first rowed in 1839.

Eton College
This is the most famous of Britain's 'public schools' (rather a misnomer since they are prestigious, private, fee-paying establishments), and was founded by Henry VI in 1440. The high street has numerous barbers and tailors; one of them, T Brown, has changed little over the years. Here, the boys are fitted out at the start of term in long-tailed jackets and wing-collars. Presidents of societies are entitled to wear specially designed parti-coloured waistcoats.

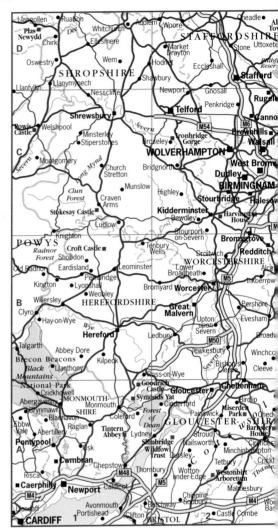

The map shows locations including:

Ilkeston, NOTTINGHAM, Bingham, DERBY, Stapleford, West Bridgford, Grantham, Long Eaton, Castle Donington, Kegworth, Burton upon Trent, Shepshed, Loughborough, Barrow upon Soar, Melton Mowbray, Ashby-de-la-Zouch, Coalville, LEICESTERSHIRE, RUTLAND, Measham, Ibstock, Birstall, Oakham, Stamford, Lichfield, M42, Tamworth, Desford, LEICESTER, Rutland Water, Burghley, Atherstone, M69, Oadby, Uppingham, Sutton Coldfield, Wigston, Narborough, Coleshill, Hinckley, Nuneaton, Market Harborough, Oundle, M6, Bedworth, M1, COVENTRY, Lutterworth, Husband's Bosworth, Desborough, Rothwell, Kettering, Thrapston, Solihull, Kenilworth, Rugby, NORTHAMPTONSHIRE, Raunds, M45, Brixworth, Wellingborough, Rushden, M40, Leamington Spa, Warwick, Southam, Daventry, Northampton, WARWICKSHIRE, Wellesbourne, Weedon, Bozeat, Stratford-upon-Avon, Byfield, M1, Olney, Bradford-on-Avon, Farnborough, Towcester, Bedford, Hidcote Manor, Shipston-on-Stour, Silverstone, Newport Pagnell, Chipping Campden, Broughton Castle, Banbury, Milton Keynes, Ampthill, Moreton-in-Marsh, Deddington, Buckingham, Brackley, Bletchley, Woburn Abbey, Chipping Norton, Stow-on-the-Wold, Rousham House, Bicester, Leighton Buzzard, Dunstable, Bourton-on-the-Water, OXFORDSHIRE, BUCKINGHAMSHIRE, Waddesdon Manor, Whipsnade, Northleach, Blenheim Palace, Woodstock, Aylesbury, Burford, Witney, Kidlington, Wendover, Tring, Minster Lovell, Oxford, Waterperry, Princes Risborough, Hemel Hempstead, Fairford, Eynsham, Thame, Chesham, Chenies, Lechlade, Chinnor, Amersham, M25, Buscot Park, Faringdon, Abingdon, West Wycombe, Highworth, Didcot, Stonor Park, High Wycombe, Beaconsfield, Lavenham, Uffington, Wantage, Wallingford, Marlow, Cookham, Swindon, Goring, Henley-on-Thames, Maidenhead, Slough, Lambourn, BERKSHIRE, Reading, M4, Eton, Windsor, Mapledurham

Scale: 0 10 20 30 40 km / 0 10 20 miles

The Heart of England
This is a region that reflects, as deeply as any other, the elusively diverse nature of the English landscape: for it includes both the Cotswolds, the epitome of rural England, and the more workaday face of the industrial 'Black Country', the economic hub of the Midlands.

The Black Country
The area known as the Black Country falls within the county of **West Midlands**, which is dominated by the conurbation of West Bromwich, Wolverhampton and others; adjacent is Birmingham, Britain's largest city after London. There are tangible signs that Birmingham, nicknamed 'Brum', has turned the corner and is witnessing a cultural awakening. Visually it has little to offer apart from a few survivals of Victorian splendour and an extensive canal network (larger than that of Venice) – the city is mostly a jungle of flyovers,

The post office,
Eastnor, below the
Malvern Hills

trading estates and 19th- and 20th-century suburbs. One spearhead of the revival has been the City of Birmingham Symphony Orchestra, based at the Symphony Hall, which has emerged as one of the world's great orchestras; the D'Oyly Carte Opera Company, which specialises in the satirical Victorian operettas of Gilbert and Sullivan, has made the Alexandra Theatre its home. The National Exhibition Centre and International Convention Centre bring in many business travellers. The excellent Black Country Museum at Dudley evokes life in an industrial village in the 1900s, and Cadbury World (the Chocolate Experience) gives a look inside the factory established at Bournville by the Cadburys, a Victorian Quaker family. The City Museum and Art Gallery has the world's finest collection of Pre-Raphaelite paintings. Other indoor attractions include Jacobean Aston Hall, the Barber Institute (art collection), the Museum of Science and Industry, Blakesley Hall (a 16th-century farmhouse), the Jewellery Quarter Discovery Centre, the Birmingham Sealife Centre, with its walk-through tube (the sharks and others swim around and over you), Birmingham Railway Museum, Selly Manor Museum and Sarehole Mill (an 18th-century watermill, said to be the inspiration for J R R Tolkien's fantasy novel *The Hobbit*). East of Birmingham, the ancient city of Coventry had its heart knocked out by bombing in 1940, and its ruined medieval cathedral stands beside Basil Spence's innovative postwar replacement.

The English Marches Shropshire, Herefordshire and Worcestershire encompass much unspoilt and underrated countryside, of black-and-white and red-brick villages and of the assertive south Shropshire Hills; it is ideal for those who like to make their own discoveries. To the west it adjoins the even lesser-known, and much less populated Welsh Marches, or borderlands. Only the highly satisfying market town of Ludlow and Ironbridge Gorge, birthplace of the Industrial Revolution, are firmly on the tourist trail; Shrewsbury, Hereford and numerous smaller towns and villages such as Much Wenlock and Ledbury make rewarding objectives. Walkers may like to head for the hills around Church Stretton and for the Malvern Hills. The russet-earthed territory of rural Herefordshire, its pastures

grazed by docile Hereford cattle, is amiably sleepy, and has a wealth of half-timbered 'black and white' buildings as well as several outstanding churches, some tucked well away. Worcestershire has the cathedral city of Worcester for its centrepiece.

The Cotswolds and their fringes East of the fruit and vegetable heartlands of the Vale of Evesham, the buildings change hue dramatically towards the **Cotswolds** (mostly belonging to **Gloucestershire** and **Oxfordshire**). Its honey-yellow stone villages and towns have enchanted generations of visitors; the area is rich in both places to visit and accommodation of all types.

Non-Cotswold Gloucestershire includes Gloucester, Cheltenham and the lowlands abutting the Severn Estuary, the final stages of Britain's longest river; on a waterside site, the naturalist Peter Scott set up the celebrated wildfowl reserve at Slimbridge. The Forest of Dean was once a coal and charcoal producing area; the villages are not particularly attractive, but there are verdant walks, including the Sculpture Trail (west of Cinderford). The Lower Wye Valley (see page 152) is close at hand.

The fringes of the Cotswolds harbour some of the greatest visitor attractions of central England, including Oxford, Blenheim Palace and Shakespeare's Stratford-upon-Avon. These are close enough to London for day trips. Notable arrays of stately homes and manor houses open to the public are found in **Warwickshire** (Baddesley Clinton, Charlecote Park, Coughton Court, Farnborough Hall, Kenilworth Castle, Packwood House, Upton House, Warwick Castle) and **Buckinghamshire** (Chenies Manor, Chicheley Hall, Claydon House, Nancy Astor's Cliveden, Dorney Court, Disraeli's Hughenden Manor, Wycombe Park and above all the trio of Rothschilds' properties – Ascott House, Mentmore Towers and Waddesdon).

To the east lie the **Chiltern Hills**, whose gently rolling chalk hills and majestic beech woods have been carefully preserved by Green Belt legislation and whose villages look distinctly prosperous.

There are old musical instruments at Snowshill Manor as well as a collection of Japanese Samurai armour, toys and bicycles

REGION HIGHLIGHTS ◀◀◀◀◀

Only the wanderer
Knows England's graces,
Or can anew see clear
Familiar faces.

And who loves joy as he
That dwells in shadows?
Do not forget me quite
O Severn meadows.

Ivor Gurney, *Song* (on Gloucestershire), written in the World War I trenches

*Blenheim Palace,
Vanbrugh's vast,
stately edifice*

▶▶ Blenheim Palace 111A3

This is more of a gilded palace than a charming English country house, impersonal in scale but undeniably impressive for its sumptuous state rooms, furnishings, tapestries and door-cases carved by Grinling Gibbons. It is considered to be the finest true baroque house in Britain.

Blenheim was built to the design of John Vanbrugh for the 1st Duke of Marlborough, John Churchill, as a reward from Queen Anne in recognition of his crushing victory over the French at Blenheim in Bavaria in 1704. In 1874, it was the birthplace of Sir Winston Churchill, and the contents include some fascinating Churchilliana. He is buried in the churchyard at Bladon near by.

The palace stands in a great park laid out by Henry Wise, gardener to Queen Anne, and later modified by Capability Brown. Allocate an hour or two for exploring the numerous walks, beechwoods and formal features that include the Triumphal Way, Italian Garden maze, ornamental bridge, lake and Column of Victory.

Woodstock is the nearest town to Blenheim, with delightful houses and shops, and home to the Oxfordshire County Museum.

Bridgnorth's caves
Ethelward (died 924), grandson of Alfred the Great, is traditionally said to have lived in a cave in Bridgnorth, leading the life of a recluse, surrounded by his beloved books. The four rock chambers that he made his home can still be seen near the top of Hermitage Hill (close to the A454); reached by a footpath. Some former cave dwellings, inhabited up to 1856, can be found near the cliff railway.

▶ Bridgnorth 110C2

Bridgnorth's site is quite remarkable, astride a sandstone cliff above the River Severn; steep paths and winding lanes connect the high and low towns, together with a cliff railway. Much of the centre is a pleasing amalgam of half-timbering and plum-red brick, with the town hall

(1652) as its focal point (*Guided tours*) leave from the tourist office on Listley Street). Stroll along Castle Walk, which forms a clifftop esplanade, passing the alarmingly slanting bulk of a Norman castle ruin – blown up by the Parliamentarians in 1646 during the Civil War.

At Stanmore Hall, 3km (2 miles) east of Bridgnorth is the **Midland Motor Museum▶**, a collection of some 100 vintage vehicles, including 1920s and 1930s classic models.

The **Severn Valley Railway▶▶**, running between Bridgnorth and Kidderminster, successfully recaptures the style and flavour of long-distance travel of yesteryear. Steam locomotives pull old-fashioned carriages through the agreeable countryside of the Severn Valley, giving a 26km (16-mile) ride of just over an hour. The stations are particularly well preserved.

The railway runs through **Bewdley▶** and has helped put the town on the map. Bewdley's compact centre has a legacy of Georgian brick and older half-timbered buildings, similar to Bridgnorth. It is at its best in Load Street, which tapers outwards by the 18th-century church, sandstone guildhall and Old Shambles (which contains Bewdley Museum). At its far end, Thomas Telford's bridge (1798) spans the Severn. West of the town lies **Wyre Forest▶**, an extensive area of broadleaved woodland, designated a National Nature Reserve. The Forestry Commission Visitor Centre gives information on waymarked trails. **Harvington Hall▶**, near Kidderminster, is a moated Elizabethan manor house with an exceptional number of priest holes, or hiding places, including false chimneys and a false step in a staircase.

Stourport-on-Severn▶ is an industrial town, but one given considerable character by its heritage of 18th-century canalside architecture, including a fine warehouse with pristine wooden clocktower. The town stands at the confluence of the rivers Stour and Severn; waterway engineer James Brindley created the canal.

| ▶ | **Chiltern Hills** | *111A4* |

Stretching some 80km (50 miles) from the Thames Valley west of Reading to around Luton at their northern edge, the Chilterns are a modest protuberance of chalk downs northwest of London. Although the area is part of the City stockbroker belt, once you are clear of the large suburban developments you find yourself in deep countryside, with pretty brick-and-flint cottages, some fine manor houses and pleasant country pubs. The beechwoods that made the area an important furniture-making centre at one time are still a distinctive feature of the landscape.

The Ridgeway
The eastern half of the long distance Ridgeway Path follows the western escarpment of the Chilterns. Near Wendover it climbs over Coombe Hill, where a Boer War memorial marks the highest point in the Chilterns; close by you can glimpse Chequers, the country retreat of British prime ministers since 1921. Ivinghoe Beacon looks over the seemingly endless south Midlands plain. Walks here extend into the woodlands of the Ashridge Estate, past the monument to the 3rd Duke of Bridgewater, the 18th-century canal developer, and to the pretty village green at Aldbury.

More walks in the Chilterns
Between Luton and Whipsnade, the Dunstable Downs is a fine escarpment popular with walkers and kite-fliers; gliders and superb sunsets add further dimensions. Near Tring, off the Chilterns proper, the Tring Reservoir National Nature Reserve provides plenty of interest in the way of birdlife and canal scenes. Burnham Beeches is a glorious place for autumn colours (it is surprisingly easy to lose the way; look for the helpful maps). The Chess Valley has very attractive walks, with the pretty villages of Chenies, Latimer and Sarratt as focal points.

The Temple of Venus, one of several eye-catching follies in the grounds of West Wycombe Park

THE HEART OF ENGLAND

West Wycombe and the Dashwoods

The most notorious member of the Dashwood family was undoubtedly Sir Francis Dashwood, who set up the Hell Fire Club, a black-magic brotherhood more interested in drinking and whoring than satanic rites. Its meeting places included the West Wycombe Caves (*Open* to the public, just north of the village street), and the hollow gold ball on top of the Church of St Lawrence. The Dashwood memorials are within the curious roofless, hexagonal mausoleum (1764) next to the church.

Mapledurham Mill, the last working water-mill on the Thames, still uses wooden machinery and produces flour and bran

As one who long in
  populous city pent,
Where houses thick and
  sewers annoy the air,
Forth issuing on a
  summer's morn to
  breathe
Among the pleasant
  villages and farms
Adjoin'd, from each thing
  met conceives delight.
John Milton (1608–74),
  Paradise Lost

At **Mapledurham▶**, by the Thames, you can visit a working watermill and Elizabethan manor house (Mapledurham House), while the 18th-century brick façade of **Stonor House▶**, the home of the Stonors for 600 years, conceals a much earlier structure that incorporates a private chapel and a medieval solar. Almost all of **West Wycombe▶** village was purchased by the National Trust in 1929 to save it from a road-widening scheme; its main street, unfortunately busy with traffic, is predominantly of 17th- and 18th-century houses. Adjacent stands West Wycombe Park, a mansion built in 1765 for Sir John Dashwood (see panel); its interior has painted ceilings. Humphry Repton landscaped the park in 1803, adorning it with follies and classical temples.

Benjamin Disraeli, the 19th-century Conservative prime minister, lived at **Hughenden Manor▶** (NT) north of High Wycombe; his library and study have been carefully preserved, and his character is firmly imprinted on the Victorian house. **Beaconsfield, Princes Risborough, Berkhamsted** and **Wendover** are commuter towns, but each has an old and attractive centre.

In 1665 John Milton came to **Chalfont St Giles** as an old and blind man, escaping plague-ridden London to spend a year in a cottage (now a **museum▶**) where he completed *Paradise Lost* and began *Paradise Regained*. Close by, traditional Chiltern buildings can be seen at the Chiltern Open-Air Museum; the diverse structures include an Iron Age dwelling, a 19th-century farm and a 1940s prefab. In the Chess Valley, **Chenies** is a tiny 19th-century village built for estate workers at the medieval step-gabled brick **manor▶** (*Open* to the public) of the Russell family, the earls and dukes of Bedford.

Whipsnade Wild Animal Park▶▶, planned by the Zoological Society of London, is one of Europe's foremost animal collections, located in a spacious park; close by, **Whipsnade Tree Cathedral** was created by Edmund Kell Blyth in 1931 as a war memorial, with trees laid out in aisles, transepts and cloisters.

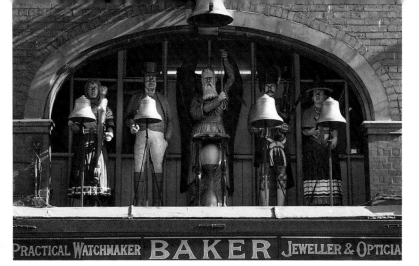

PRACTICAL WATCHMAKER **BAKER** JEWELLER & OPTICIA

▶ **Gloucester**

Gloucester's earthy redbrick textures contrast rudely with the dreamy golden hues of the nearby Cotswolds, but the city offers a tonic in its small but absorbing medieval centre and its revived 19th-century docks.

Just off the main historic axis of Westgate Street, with its **Folk Museum**, lie the dignified precincts of the **cathedral▶▶**. It became a place of pilgrimage after the installation of the tomb of Edward II, murdered at nearby Berkeley Castle in 1327. From the outside it is a pleasing medieval mishmash; within, its glory is the glass of the east window, one of England's largest, and the 14th-century fan-vaulting in the cloisters, England's earliest.

The **Beatrix Potter Museum** is in the house featured in the Beatrix Potter children's story, *The Tailor of Gloucester*.

Meanwhile, in the **docks**, the towering redbrick warehouses have been partly converted to offices, shops and cafés; you can take 40-minute trips around the site on an old Thames craft. Here the **National Waterways Museum▶** charts the development of Britain's canals; the entertaining **Robert Opie Collection of Advertising and Packaging▶** is an unashamed wallow in nostalgia; and the **Regiments of Gloucester Museum** details 300 years of regimental history.

Gloucester's neighbour, **Cheltenham▶** is an elegant Regency spa, with a pump room designed in the best 19th-century Greek Revival tradition. A mineral spring was discovered here in 1715, allegedly by observing the comings and goings of a healthy-looking pigeon population; pigeons feature on the town's crest. Cheltenham later received the royal approval of George III and acquired handsome terraces, wrought-iron balconies and leafy thoroughfares. Other attractions are the art gallery and museum; Holst's Birthplace Museum, where the composer of *The Planets* was born in 1874; the annual festivals of music (July) and literature (October); and the racecourse.

To the northwest, **Tewkesbury▶**, where the Avon and Severn meet, is a handsome town of high-medieval and later façades. The **abbey church▶** is one of England's finest examples of Norman ecclesiastical architecture.

These five figures form the 'Baker's bells'; a distinctive carillon in Gloucester's Southgate Street

Three Choirs Festival
This major music festival takes place in the last week of August and rotates in a three-year cycle between Gloucester, Worcester and Hereford cathedrals. Its origins date to the early 18th century; from the 1890s three organist-conductors (one from each cathedral) were appointed and a distinguished list of works by some of the country's greatest composers were given their first performance, including *Fantasia on a Theme of Thomas Tallis* (1910) by Vaughan Williams, the *Colour Symphony* (1922) by Bliss, and the *Choral Fantasia* (1931) by Holst. Elgar directed his own music until his death in 1934.

■ **Perfect touring country, the Cotswolds is an area of beautiful honey-coloured limestone villages of carefully groomed charm, secretive manor houses, cottage gardens, russet-earth fields enclosed with drystone walls, and country roads which lead to nowhere in particular.** ■

South Cotswolds houses
Buscot Park (NT), near Faringdon, is an 18th-century house renowned for its paintings and porcelain. Also near Faringdon is *Great Coxwell Tithe Barn* (NT), built by the monks of Beaulieu and considered to be one of England's finest. An oddity is *Woodchester Mansion* (near Stroud), an unfinished Victorian country house.

118

Cotswold architecture: honey-hued limestone walls, stone-mullioned windows and stone lintels

South Cotswolds gardens
Among many outstanding gardens are the *Rococo Garden* outside Painswick, *Westonbirt Arboretum* (a Forestry Commission collection of over 17,000 trees), *Barnsley House Garden* (Georgian summerhouses, laburnum walk, herbaceous borders), *Batsford Park Arboretum* (rare trees) and *Miserden Park* (topiary, shrubs, borders and more, in a woodland setting).

The Cotswolds present timeless tableaux of rural England. The scenery is beautiful rather than dramatic, with the best views to be had from the western edges. There are plenty of hotels, some very high class indeed, and the area is rich with sights (with plenty for children). Wool was the key to the area's medieval prosperity. Almost every town and village seems to have a Sheep Street. The wealth it created is commemorated in a striking legacy of grand churches.

The area is described in two parts, one lying south of the A40, the other north.

The south The undoubted capital of the south Cotswolds, Cirencester►► is a handsome town with more bustle than most of its neighbours, and plenty of speciality shops. In Roman times, only London (*Londinium*) was bigger than Cirencester (*Corinium*) and these and later days are celebrated in the excellent Corinium Museum, which displays mosaic pavements and reconstructions of Roman domestic interiors.

Dominating the market square is the cathedral-like parish church, with its fan-vaulted porch and grand interior. One of the finest streets is Cecily Hill, its far end leading into Cirencester Park (pedestrians only), the grounds of Lord Bathurst's stately home.

At **Bibury**▶▶ a triple-arched footbridge over the Coln leads to Arlington Row, a group of former weavers' cottages. The former Arlington Mill houses the Cotswold Museum, while the rest of the village is full of unspoilt corners and pretty cottage gardens. The Victorian artist-craftsman William Morris, who with his pre-Raphaelite friends 'discovered' the Cotswolds and in 1871 came to live at nearby Kelmscott, declared Bibury to be the most beautiful village in England. More low-key, sleepy charm is found in abundance in the **Colns** (Coln St Aldwyn, Coln Rogers and Coln St Dennis) and the **Duntisbournes** (Duntisbourne Abbots, Duntisbourne Leer and Duntisbourne Rouse, the latter having a little Saxon church). **Fairford**▶ prides itself on its splendid 'wool church', famed for its late 15th-century stained glass.

Painswick▶▶ has an appealing, sloping knot of central lanes and greystone walls; grand houses jostle cheek by jowl with tiny cottages. Best of all is the churchyard, dominated by 99 yews; an explanatory leaflet describes the fine 16th- to 19th-century tombstones. The surrounding area is lush and deep-set, with numerous viewpoints, including **Painswick Beacon** and **Haresfield Beacon**. **Slad** is the village of writer Laurie Lee, who captured the pre-motor car age so evocatively in *Cider with Rosie*. **Stroud** is not particularly attractive, but the atmospherically derelict **Thames and Severn Canal** is worth exploring near Sapperton. Further south are some finely sited towns and villages, including **Wotton-under-Edge** and **Dursley**, snug beneath the escarpment, as well as **Minchinhampton**, on a breezy hilltop site.

Chedworth Roman Villa▶ (NT), excavated 1864–6, stands alone in the woods near Chedworth and gives an excellent insight into the high living of the period with the discovery of mosaic floors and hypocaust and bath systems. Uley Bury (EH), known as **Hetty Pegler's Tump**, after the wife of its 17th-century owner, is a neolithic burial mound with stone slabs still in place. You can enter by obtaining a key from the neighbouring house.

Drystone walls are the main type of field boundary in the Cotswolds

Family attractions (south)
South of Burford, the *Cotswold Wildlife Park* features white rhinos, tigers and more. At *Prinknash Abbey*, a living community of Benedictine monks, there is a bird sanctuary and pottery. At Northleach are two absorbing attractions, *Keith Harding's World of Mechanical Music* (antique mechanical instruments) and the *Cotswold Countryside Collection* (exhibits from yesteryear housed in a former prison). Further afield, the *Wildfowl and Wetlands Trust* at Slimbridge, on the Severn Estuary, has a huge collection of wildfowl, and *Berkeley Castle* is famous for the dungeon in which Edward II was gruesomely murdered in 1327.

The Cotswolds

Family attractions (north)
The *Gloucestershire–
Warwickshire Railway*
operates steam trains
between Toddington and
Winchcombe, while the
Cotswold Farm Park (west
of Stow-on-the-Wold) is
home to rare animal
breeds. Just outside
Witney, the *Cogges Manor
Farm Museum* offers a look
at rural Edwardian life in
Oxfordshire, with craft and
farming demonstrations.

*Angular gables,
stone roofs and trim
lawns typical of
many Cotswold
manor houses*

North Cotswolds houses
Stanway House is a good
example of Jacobean
architecture, while
Broughton Castle, near
Banbury, is a moated
medieval manor, and
Snowshill (NT) contains a
collection of bicycles, and
dummies of Samurai
warriors. By contrast,
Sezincote was remodelled
in the 1800s as an Indian
fantasy; the Prince Regent
paid a visit in 1807 and
found in it inspiration for
his Royal Pavilion in
Brighton (see page 90).
Sudeley Castle, an
imposing part-ruined
stately home outside
Winchcombe, was the
home of Henry VIII's sixth
wife, Catherine Parr,
the lucky one who
survived him.

North Cotswolds gardens
The magically secretive
gardens of *Hidcote Manor*,
north of Chipping
Campden, are pure joy; a
20th-century creation of a
series of 'rooms' bounded
by hedges and walls. Close
by, *Kiftsgate Court
Gardens* have rare shrubs
and a fine rose collection.

The north In the far north, **Chipping Campden▶▶**
should not be missed for its showpiece main street, primitive open-sided market hall, the 11-room Woolstaplers
Hall Museum, and a fine church with Gloucestershire's
largest memorial brass. The great manor house of
Campden has gone, but its Jacobean lodges and gateway
remain. The pace is unhurried and its charms have been
preserved without being commercialised. By contrast,
Broadway▶ is a tourist honeypot, its elegant (but traffic-
ridden) main street well kitted out with gift shops and tearooms. It lies beneath the Cotswold escarpment on the
brink of the Vale of Evesham, a major fruit-growing area
with roadside stalls selling produce in season; the abrupt
transition from Cotswold stone to Midland red brick is
quite striking.

Other quieter villages near by have charm in plenty,
including **Buckland** and **Stanton**. Within the town centre
of **Winchcombe▶** you can find a much-gargoyled church

(look for the splendid weathercock) and an old-fashioned
ambience; attractions include **Sudeley Castle▶**, the home
of Catherine Parr (see panel), a folk and police museum,
and a museum of railway memorabilia. Just out of town by
the B4632, **Cleeve Hill▶** is a blustery highland (only 317m/
1,040ft but it feels higher), a place for strolls, kite-flying
and enjoying the view west to the Malvern Hills (see page
125). **Hailes Abbey▶** (EH) is a ruin of a 13th-century
Cistercian foundation with a small museum.

Stow-on-the-Wold and **Chipping Norton** are conveniently placed market towns, the latter with a superb
19th-century tweed mill. With its series of tiny bridges
spanning the Windrush, **Bourton-on-the-Water** is so
pretty it is almost twee. It is the most commercialised
village in the Cotswolds, drawing crowds to its model
village, perfumery exhibition, model railway, Birdland
aviary, Motor Museum and Village Life Exhibition. Neighbouring **Lower Slaughter▶**, on the other hand, is an
unspoilt delight, with cottages and an old mill overlooking
a brook. **Burford** has an impressive church and a distinguished main street lined with shops and inns, sloping
down to an ancient stone bridge. Close to Witney is
Minster Lovell▶ (EH), with a spooky, 15th-century hall.

THE COTSWOLDS

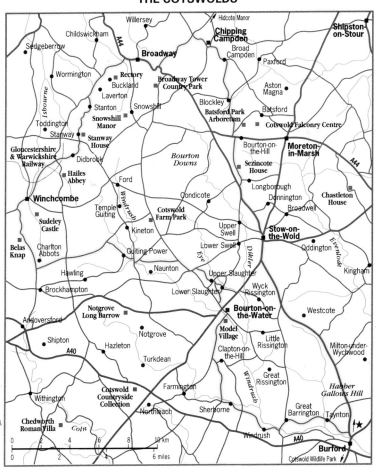

Drive The Cotswolds

This tour promises golden stone-built villages, dignified manor houses and fine views (approx. 90km/55 miles).

Start from **Burford►**, descending the main street, and carry on past **Stow-on-the-Wold** to branch off, past **Sezincote House►►** and **Blockley**, which still has a few of its old silk-throwing mills. Continue to **Chipping Campden►►**; head southwest to the A44 where you turn right (Broadway Tower, a famous viewpoint, is soon off left) to **Broadway►**. Take the

B4632 to skirt peaceful **Buckland►**; branch off left through **Stanton►** and **Stanway►** and rejoin the B4632 close to the turning to **Hailes Abbey►**.

Continue into **Winchcombe►**, stopping off for **Sudeley Castle►**. Pass **Belas Knap** prehistoric burial mound and **Guiting Power**. The villages of **Upper Slaughter** and **Lower Slaughter►** make an agreeable prelude to busy **Bourton-on-the-Water**. Finish by exploring the quiet countryside around **Great Barrington**.

Cider in Herefordshire

This alcoholic apple drink has a venerable tradition in the county; in former days, many farms produced cider specially for farm labourers. True farmhouse 'scrumpy' cider is now a rarity, but cider in general has enjoyed a revival in recent years. Bulmer's Cider, one of the largest operations, produces in Hereford (there is a factory shop; tours by appointment, tel: 01432 352000). A Cider Museum (not part of Bulmer's) displays cider-making methods ancient and modern. Near Pembridge, a village on the Black and White Villages Trail, Dunkerton's Cider is an engagingly rustic outfit, operating from a barn, and Weston's, a much larger company, produces at Much Marcle.

The astonishing 900-year-old carving on the south doorway of Kilpeck church features serpentine monsters climbing its shafts, dragons and other beasts real and mythichal

► **Hereford** *110B1*

The capital of the county of Herefordshire, renowned for its eponymous cattle breed and for cider making, stands pleasantly by the River Wye. There are some good medieval (and later) streets. The highlight is the sandstone **cathedral►►** (begun 1107) with its library of over 1,400 chained books and its priceless *Mappa Mundi*, a 13th-century map of the world.

Southwest of the town is **Abbey Dore►**. Only a portion of what was once a huge Cistercian abbey church remains, but it echoes its heyday impressively; the Early English work, immense stone altar and 17th-century glass linger in the memory.

Nearby **Kilpeck Church►►** is a perfect Norman building, breathtakingly embellished inside and out with virtuoso carvings of birds, mythical beasts and angels. Prudish Victorians removed many of the more salacious, but look for the ones they missed.

The **Black and White Villages Trail►►** is a well signposted car tour west of Hereford through some beautiful,

unspoilt half-timbered villages, including **Weobley**, **Pembridge**, **Eardisland** and **Lyonshall**.

At **Shobdon►** the stonework of the old church, which may well have been of the same hand that sculpted Kilpeck, was turned into a garden ornament in the mid-18th century for a nearby house; the 'new' church built in its place reveals an interior of wedding-cake 'Strawberry Hill Gothick', a style of architecture named after the one used in writer Horace Walpole's 1747 house at Strawberry Hill in Twickenham, near London. Further north, **Croft Castle►** (NT) is a fascinating mix of medievalism and Georgian Gothic. Walks in the adjacent National Trust estate include the ascent of Croft Ambrey, a finely sited Iron Age hillfort with visible ramparts.

► **Lichfield** *111C3*

The trio of sandstone spires of the **cathedral►** dominates a gracious close of 17th- to 19th-century buildings. There is much Early English and Decorated work. The west front has 113 statues, including 24 English kings. The city's most famous son was the man of letters Dr Johnson (1709–84), subject of Boswell's biography.

Ironbridge Gorge

■ A tranquil area today, the wooded gorge of the River Severn cradled the birth of the Industrial Revolution. What happened at Ironbridge signalled the emergence of Britain as the first industrial nation, and was the catalyst for a dramatic change in the face of the country as the Midlands and northern England became a great industrial heartland. ■

Here in 1709 Abraham Darby first smelted iron ore with coke instead of charcoal, enabling mass-production of iron for the first time. The gorge soon filled with industrial activity. Today it is a pretty, semi-rural spectacle and you have to imagine the noise and smoke of the great ironworks and other industries, but the first-rate **Ironbridge Gorge Museum**, spread over six sites, skilfully brings it all alive. Ironbridge is just south of Telford.

What to see The Iron Bridge itself was the world's earliest iron structure of its kind (built in 1779). **Blists Hill Open-Air Museum▶▶▶**, the largest site, is a working Victorian town re-created in 17ha (42 acres) of woodland. There are iron furnaces, a toll-house, period shops, a colliery, a sawmill and an inclined railway once used for linking two canals. Staff are dressed in period costumes to further enhance the atmosphere of a Victorian village. **Jackfield Tile Museum▶▶** is housed in a huge Victorian tile factory that had lain abandoned; today it has been re-opened and tiles are put on display. The **Coalport China Museum▶▶** marks the original site of the Coalport china works, based here from the 1790s until the 1920s; today there is a stunning display of china as well as some early brick beehive kilns. You have to wear a hard hat to enter the gloomy **Tar Tunnel▶**, where bitumen was once extracted. At **Coalbrookdale Furnace and Museum of Iron▶▶▶** you are indeed in hallowed territory, the very spot where Darby sparked the industrialisation of Britain.

History today: the daily round at Blists Hill

123

Don't miss
There is too much to see in one day in the gorge; if you have only a short time, concentrate on Blists Hill, the Iron Bridge and Coalbrookdale. You can buy separate tickets for each site, or a 'passport' which allows return visits on different occasions. Buses run between the sites.

The Iron Bridge gives its name to Ironbridge town, which rises steeply on the hill behind

The keep of Ludlow Castle, from which Roger Mortimer effectively ruled the country after wresting power from Edward II in 1326

English Heritage
Stokesay Castle is just one of hundreds of historic properties that are in the guardianship of the government organisation, English Heritage. Its sister organisations are Cadw in Wales (Welsh Historic Monuments); Historic Scotland; and Manx National Heritage on the Isle of Man. Properties include prehistoric and Roman remains, medieval castles and abbeys and working industrial monuments, as well as some stately homes. Membership of any one of these bodies provides free admission to the historic sites protected by all four organisations.

▶▶▶ Ludlow   110C1

This is often acclaimed as England's most perfect country town – and it is easy to see why. On its hilltop site its streets spread elegantly out from the ancient butter cross and market place, on which is found the absorbing **museum** of local history. Just behind the Butter Cross stands the cathedral-like **Church of St Laurence▶▶**. Within its soaring interior, the patron saint's life and miracles are celebrated in the great east window, and there is a renowned set of 15th-century carved misericords. Poet A E Housman of *Shropshire Lad* fame (see page 130) is buried in the churchyard.

Broad Street is Ludlow's most celebrated thoroughfare, with its timber-framed Tudor buildings and 17th- to 19th-century brick façades combining happily along the gentle slope to a gateway at the bottom end. The **Feathers Hotel**, a riot of half-timbering, is an outstanding house of its period. **Ludlow Castle▶▶**, founded by Roger Montgomery, Earl of Shrewsbury, in 1085, was built to withstand both Welsh and Norman incursions; its long list of distinguished visitors includes Sir Philip Sidney, Edward IV and Catherine of Aragon. A Norman chapel within the castle has an unusual circular nave. During the Ludlow Festival in June and July, outdoor performances of Shakespeare plays are held in the inner bailey, attracting large audiences.

Ludlow is splendidly situated for exploring the Welsh Marches, and the South Shropshire Hills (see page 130) are within close reach. **Stokesay Castle▶▶** (EH), near Craven Arms, is an outstandingly well-preserved example of a 13th-century fortified manor house; it was designed with windows unusually large for those lawless times. The adjacent church dates mostly from the 17th century, but has a Norman doorway.

The Feathers, one of the finest examples of 17th-century half-timbering in Britain

▶▶ Malvern Hills   110B2

The jagged Malvern ridge rises between the low plains of Herefordshire and the Vale of Evesham. From a distance it looks like a mountain range; close up it reveals itself as a friendly upland stripe offering superlative views from the easily accessible paths along its spine.

Its advantages as a defensive site were exploited by Iron Age man: Worcestershire Beacon (the highest point, 425m/1,381ft), and Herefordshire Beacon are both well-preserved hillforts. To the west there are views of Eastnor Castle, a 19th-century mock medieval extravaganza designed by Robert Smirke and A W N Pugin in the Gothic Revival style inspired by medieval architecture. In the further distance are the hills of the Welsh Marches; to the east is the Cotswold escarpment.

Worcester▶ is the home of Royal Worcester porcelain (*factory tours available on weekdays*), and Worcestershire Sauce. It was an important centre during the Civil War, as is explained by the exhibition in the Commandery in Sidbury Road, Charles II's headquarters during the Battle of Worcester. The city is a mix of the sublime and the mundane with a fine **cathedral▶▶** (look for the monuments, crypt, cloister garden and marble pulpit), but unattractive postwar development. The county cricket ground, set by the Severn with a magnificent view of the cathedral, is a perfect place for watching the game.

Just west of Worcester, **Lower Broadheath▶** was the birthplace, on 2 June 1857, of composer Sir Edward Elgar (see panel). The modest cottage commemorates his life with scores, photographs and concert programmes.

Malvern Wells and **Great Malvern▶** lie right under the Malvern Hills. Malvern Water put the area on the map as a spa after a Dr Wall wrote in 1756 of the medicinal efficacy of the waters. Within a modest stone pavilion is St Ann's Well, the original source of the water. The priory church, the glory of Great Malvern, has magnificent 15th-century stained glass.

Southwest is **Ledbury▶**. The town's broad high street focuses on John Abel's 16th-century half-timbered market house. Pretty Church Lane leads to the church, with its 'gold vane surveying half the shire', in the words of locally born John Masefield, former Poet Laureate.

A Royal Worcester vase

125

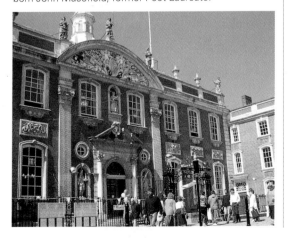

Sir Edward Elgar (1857–1934)
Elgar's musical education was derived mainly from his experience as a violin player, as a singer at the church where his father was organist, and from browsing the scores in his father's music shop in Worcester. For a long time he felt the musical world was set against him, yet the fact that he was mainly self-taught probably gave him a freshness of vision. Elgar's early works were recognised only locally, but his international reputation was assured when Richard Strauss acclaimed the ever-popular *Enigma Variations* (1899). *The Dream of Gerontius* (1900) enjoyed success in the Three Choirs Festival (see panel, page 117) in 1902. The *First Symphony* (1908) and the *Pomp and Circumstance Marches* (1901–30) won widespread popularity.

Worcester's spectacular Guildhall, dated 1722

Christ1 Church College
Tom Quad, the main quadrangle, is so called because of Tom Tower, designed by Sir Christopher Wren and named after the bell, Great Tom, which strikes the hour. Ever since 1682, at 9.05pm it has rung 101 times, recalling the original number of students; this signalled the time for students to be back in college. The 16th-century college hall has portraits of some of the college's distinguished former members, including William Gladstone, Lewis Carroll, John Ruskin and W H Auden.

Oxford versus Cambridge
The two universities maintain an ancient rivalry, most obviously displayed in the University Boat Race, rowed on the Thames in west London every spring, and in the Varsity rugby match, played at Twickenham in the autumn.

'Oxbridge' subtleties
Oxford and Cambridge universities are referred to jointly as 'Oxbridge'.
● When 'punting' on the river in Oxford, you stand inside the boat; in Cambridge you stand on its platform (and are more likely to end up in the river).
● Only at Oxford does formal academic dress feature a mortar board as well as a gown.
● In Cambridge, colleges have courtyards, in Oxford they are known as quadrangles (or quads).
● At Cambridge, students' academic work is charted by directors of studies; at Oxford the terminology is tutors.
● There are more colleges at Oxford, but they mostly have fewer students than their Cambridge counterparts.

▶ ▶ ▶   **Oxford**   *111A3*

What is immediately striking about this, the home of one of the great universities of the world, is its stunning heritage of historic buildings, the number of students milling about, and the co-existence of a bustling city with large swathes of green along the Cherwell and Thames (or Isis) at Christ Church Meadow. As with Cambridge, there is no campus in Oxford: instead the colleges are set in cloistered seclusion behind high walls; most are open to visitors in the afternoon.

Most notable among the university buildings are the circular **Sheldonian Theatre**, built in 1664 as a ceremonial assembly hall, and the **Radcliffe Camera**, a great domed building, now a reading room for the **Bodleian Library**, which contains well over 5½ million volumes. The Bodleian is one of five 'copyright' libraries in the United Kingdom, entitled to receive a copy of every book published in the country. The view from the tower of **St Mary the Virgin**, the university church, on the High Street, extends over the city centre.

Christ Church▶▶, founded as Cardinal College by Cardinal Wolsey in 1525, is the largest college, has the biggest quadrangle, and its chapel (which predates the college) is England's smallest cathedral; the college picture gallery contains works by Dürer and Michelangelo. **Magdalen College▶▶** (pronounced 'mawdlin') has its own deer park. **All Souls College** has a highly scholarly reputation and admits only post-graduate students, while **St John's College** is the wealthiest of all, with luscious gardens. **New College▶** (founded 1379) has a splendid chapel with a statue of Lazarus by Jacob Epstein. Also seek out **Oriel▶**, **Merton▶▶**, **Queen's▶** and **Keble▶** colleges, the buildings of the latter now recognised as masterpieces of Victorian architecture.

Of Oxford's museums, the outstanding attraction is the **Ashmolean▶▶▶**, a treasure-house of art and antiquities whose exhibits include a 9th-century brooch. The city's history is illustrated in the **Museum of Oxford**, on St Aldates, while a more populist approach is provided by the **Oxford Story**, on Broad Street, where you sit at moving desks on a voyage through the city's past.

Sightseeing **buses** tour the centre at frequent intervals; they can be joined at the railway station and other points.

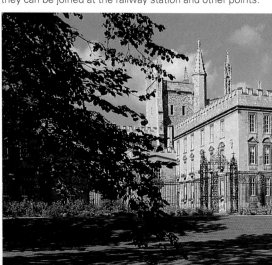

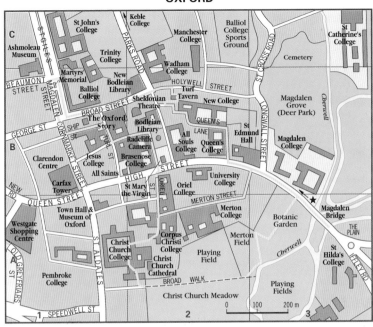

OXFORD

Walk Magdalen Bridge to the Botanic Garden

Start from Magdalen Bridge, pass **Magdalen College►►** and turn right into Queen's Lane, which weaves past **St Edmund's Hall►** (founded 1220) and **New College►** (1379). Just before the Bridge of Sighs

View of Oxford New College from its grounds

(which spans the street), take an alley on the right, passing the Turf Tavern, an old pub with an appealing court-yard. Turn left along Holywell Street and continue past the **Sheldonian Theatre**, with its array of sculpted heads of Roman emperors, and along Broad Street to the **Martyrs' Memorial**, where three bishops were burnt for their Protestant beliefs in the 1550s. Diagonally opposite is the **Ashmolean Museum►►**. Double back along The Broad and turn right down Turl Street to the **Radcliffe Camera** and **Bodleian Library**. Cross the High Street, taking Oriel Street, on its south side, to enter **Christ Church►►** by the gate near the col-lege's picture gallery (if closed, con-tinue along Merton Street to the start of the walk), crossing Tom Quad and leaving by the turnstile at the south side of the college to follow Broad Walk along **Christ Church Meadow**. The **Botanic Garden►** is the oldest of its kind in the country.

■ **There are few more pleasant ways to explore Britain's scenery, wildlife and history than an easygoing passage along the inland waterways. The slow, unhurried pace of a narrowboat gives the rare opportunity to take a long look at the world. Canals run through towns as well as countryside, and supply delightful and unexpected perspectives. Spectacular flights of locks, aqueducts, tunnels and bridges, warehouses and workshops, pleasant pubs and inns are the legacy of a time when the canal system seemed to hold the future of Britain's inland transport.** ■

Waterways holidays
Britain's canals are now used primarily for leisure – boating holidays, horse-drawn barge trips, angling, and towpath walks. For information about waterways holidays, apply to: Customer Services, British Waterways, Willow Grange, Church Road, Watford, Hertfordshire WD1 3QA (tel: 01923 226422).

Canal art
During the 19th century, a rich tradition of canal art developed. Boat owners covered the boats and their interiors and utensils with a riot of roses and castles, daisies and marigolds in simple patterns and vivid primary colours – a popular art form similar to the one which developed during the same period in travelling fairs.

Some 3,200km (2,000 miles) of navigable inland waterways have been described as the British holiday trade's best-kept secret. From prehistoric times to the 18th century, travel by river was generally faster, safer and more comfortable than travel by road. Rivers like the Severn, the Thames and the Trent bustled with boats carrying goods and people, and towns along their banks prospered as inland ports.

The Canal Age dawns The trouble with rivers is that they do not always go where you want them to, they silt up, water levels vary and shallows cause problems with navigation, as do periodic floods. Attempts to control and improve rivers were made from early times, and artificial cuts were made to shorten routes, straighten bends and evade shallows. The Canal Age in the 18th and 19th centuries brought much more radical action. A network of artificial rivers was constructed to mesh with the natural waterways and create an efficient system covering much of the country. The canals were the principal arteries of the first stage of the Industrial Revolution.

The first canal of this period was begun in Lancashire in the 1750s to link St Helens with the Mersey, but much more excitement was aroused in the 1760s when the **Duke of Bridgewater** ordered the construction of a canal to carry coal mined on his estates at Worsley a distance of 12km (7½ miles) into Manchester. The duke's engineer was an illiterate genius from Derbyshire named **James Brindley**. The Bridgewater Canal was soon extended to the Mersey, linking Manchester with Liverpool. (The Manchester end is now part of the Castlefield urban heritage area.)

Not only did the duke's canal halve the price of coal in Manchester, but the spectacle of canal boats crossing the River Irwell at Barton on an aqueduct, above the barges on the river, fired the public imagination. A bold plan was swiftly hatched to build a canal joining the Trent and the Mersey – Josiah Wedgwood, the great potter, was one of its keenest promoters – from which other canals would run to the Thames and the Severn. This would link Britain's four most important rivers and provide an inland waterway connection between London, Birmingham, Hull, Liverpool and Bristol. Brindley was the engineer for the Trent and Mersey, which was completed in 1777, five years after his death, and the other components of the plan soon followed.

The heyday The success of the early ventures set off 'canal mania', a frenzy that saw subscribers flocking to meetings all over the country to invest their money in new waterways. It reached its peak in 1793, when parliament passed 24 canal construction acts in one year. One politician of the time said he hoped his grandchildren would be born with webbed feet as no dry land would be left in England for them to walk on.

A total of 275km (170 miles) of canal in 1770 grew to 2,575km (1,600 miles) by the end of the century and 6,840km (4,250 miles) in the 1850s as armies of 'navvies' (navigators) – tough, brawling, hard-drinking labourers – drove the new waterways across country on giant embankments and through cuttings and tunnels. The earliest tunnels had no towpaths and the boats had to be 'legged' through by the crew, lying on their backs or sides, walking along the brickwork.

The canals' brief heyday was ended by the arrival of the railways from the 1830s on, and the development of motor transport almost finished them off. Even so, some 4 million tonnes of goods are still carried on the waterways every year, though they are used far more today for recreation. There could be a further revival: an ambitious scheme now being put forward is a huge commercial waterway across the neck of northern England.

Narrowboats in the sky
Among the most spectacular engineering feats of the canal engineers were flights of locks and aqueducts. The most famous staircase of locks is probably the Bingley Five Rise on the Leeds and Liverpool Canal, which climbs 18.2m (20 yds). The most sensational of aqueducts is Pontcysyllte near Llangollen in North Wales, designed by the great Scots engineer Thomas Telford in the 1790s. The canal is carried across the aqueduct for 307m (336 yds) in an iron trough almost 3.6m (4 yds) wide, with an iron towpath set above it. Boats still go across and visitors can also walk across.

The Rochdale Canal at Hebden Bridge: boats were once pulled by horses plodding along the towpath

Shrewsbury Castle has Norman origins, but was rebuilt in the 13th century and then converted into a private house by Thomas Telford in the 1790s

Decorative quatrefoils in the Square, Shrewsbury

▶ **Shrewsbury**   *110C1*

Shrewsbury has a natural defensive site, within a tight loop of the meandering River Severn, with a castle to guard the land-linked neck of land. Shrewsbury's charms are less obvious than those of nearby Ludlow, but its legacy of Tudor half-timbering and redbrick Georgian architecture, reminders of prosperity brought by the wool trade, is remarkable. Look for example for **Owen's Mansion** and **Ireland's Mansion** (both near the arcaded old market hall), and **Council House Court**: the timber-framing includes decorative cable-moulding and quatrefoils.

Finds from the Roman city of Wroxeter (*Uriconium*), a short way out of town, are displayed in Shrewsbury's **Rowley House Museum**. Robert, Lord Clive (of India) was the local MP in the 1760s; you can visit his house (**Clive House**). **Bear Steps**, a tiny alley, looks medieval, with a hall founded in 1389 as a guild for wool merchants. **Shrewsbury Quest**, in Abbey Foregate, is a hands-on recreation of monastic life, where you can try out the crafts and chores carried out by medieval monks. The Benedictine **abbey** has Norman features and a statue of Edward III on its tower.

Street names in Shrewsbury are bemusing. Butcher Row is self-explanatory (although the butchers are not in evidence), and Grope Lane suggests a variety of possibilities, but Wyle Cop, where Henry VII had a house, may baffle you – it means 'hilltop'. The provenance of Dog Pole is uncertain: perhaps a low gate or 'ducken poll'.

The **Shropshire Hills▶▶▶** are south of Shrewsbury, the heartland of the territory immortalised in A E Housman's 1896 collection of poems *A Shropshire Lad*. **Church Stretton** is the jumping-off point for the **Long Mynd** area, a massif of bracken- and bilberry-clad hills deeply cut by valleys such as Ashes Hollow and Carding Mill Valley; these and nearby Caer Caradoc, itself best reached by walking from Hope Bowdler, offer magnificent walking. The **Stiperstones** are a series of quartzite rocks on a breezy ridge close to **Snailbeach**, a village with numerous relics of a lead mining industry that flourished in the 18th and 19th centuries.

►► Stratford-upon-Avon *111B3*

Long since celebrated as the birth- and deathplace of William Shakespeare, Stratford is usually swamped with visitors. The Shakespeare connection looms large at every turn with souvenir shops stocked with miniature ceramic models of Anne Hathaway's cottage, and a shopping mall called Bard's Walk. For devotees of the Bard the town is a must. The attractions can be divided into three categories: the hallowed Shakespeare sites, the town itself, and the ancillary attractions tacked on for visitors who wonder why they have come here. The town is agreeable enough, with plenty of half-timbered buildings and a pleasant boating scene on the River Avon; look in Holy Trinity Church for a famous memorial to Shakespeare, quill pen in hand.

An open-topped bus tours the sites at 15-minute intervals (board at any point on its route). The places in town can be easily reached on foot, but the bus is handy if you want to take in Anne Hathaway's Cottage (see page 132) and Mary Arden's House (see page 132); a ticket (valid for one day) allows its holder discount entry to Shakespeare properties. You can get round them all in one full day if you start early.

*Foremost among the sites maintained by the Shakespeare Birthplace Trust is obviously **Shakespeare's Birthplace**►► itself. Entrance is through a visitor centre and the cottage's garden. Inside, an auction notice describes the property ('a truly heart-stirring relic') when it came up for sale in 1847 and was purchased, for £3,000, as a national memorial. A miscellany of Shakespearean bits and pieces makes up the exhibits.

Shakespeare's daughter Susanna and her husband Dr John Hall lived at **Hall's Croft►**, a rather grander house, now furnished with Tudor trappings and home to an exhibition about medicine in Shakespeare's day as well as the career of Dr Hall.

Shakespeare died in New Place, a house adjacent to **Nash's House►**; New Place is no longer, but an Elizabethan-style knot garden marks the site, and Nash's House itself houses Tudor furniture and exhibits relating to Stratford's past. Shakespeare was baptised and buried at **Holy Trinity Church**.

A national treasure
Before the auction in 1847, Shakespeare's Birthplace had been in the keeping of two widowed ladies, who had made a good thing out of showing such relics as 'the identical lantern with which Friar Laurence discovered Romeo and Juliet at the tomb'. The house was a mess but, spurred by a rumour that a wealthy American planned to ship the house across the Atlantic, the people of Stratford determined to buy the property. The place was restored and a shilling (about 5p) was charged for admission.

131

Britain's most hallowed literary shrine: Shakespeare's Birthplace

I know a bank whereon the
  wild thyme blows.
Where oxlips and the nod-
  ding violet grows
Quite over-canopied with
  luscious woodbine,
With sweet musk-roses,
  and with eglantine:
There sleeps Titania some
  time of the night,
Lull'd in these flowers with
  dances and delight;
And there the snake
  throws her enamell'd
  skin,
Weed wide enough to
  wrap a fairy in.
William Shakespeare,
*A Midsummer Night 's
Dream*

Out of town at the village of Shottery, **Anne Hathaway's Cottage**▶ was the home of Shakespeare's wife Anne before her marriage; it is a picturesque thatched timber building that gets very crowded at peak times (you may have to queue to get in). Nevertheless the old-world atmosphere has been kept intact, thanks to the Trust's foresight in purchasing the cottage back in 1892. Less hectic, but equally good an example of domestic Tudor architecture (minus the thatch) is **Mary Arden's House**▶, the farmhouse childhood home of Shakespeare's mother, at the village of Wilmcote. This has been set up as a farm and countryside museum, with falconry flying demonstrations, rare farm breeds and exhibits evoking rural life in the last century.

Shakespeare productions are performed at the **Royal Shakespeare Theatre** by the Royal Shakespeare Company (for details tel: 01789 269191); the **RSC Collection**▶ exhibits over 1,000 props and costumes used for past performances. The company also has a London base at the Barbican (see page 46). There is a fascinating **backstage tour**▶▶ of the Royal Shakespeare and Swan theatres.

The **World of Shakespeare** gives a fizzed-up history show of the sights and sounds of Shakespearian England in a 25-minute presentation, while the **Butterfly Farm and Jungle Safari** re-creates a jungle environment as a setting for some 1,000 exotic butterfly species. Stratford is home to the **National Teddy Bear Museum**.

Shall I compare thee to a
summer's day?
Thou art more lovely and
more temperate:
Rough winds do shake the
darling buds of May,
And summer's lease hath
all too short a date: ...

But thy eternal summer
shall not fade,
Nor lose possession of
that fair thou ow'st
Nor shall death brag thou
wander'st in his shade,
When in eternal lines to
time thou grow'st; ...

William Shakespeare,
Sonnet XVIII

The Royal Shakespeare Theatre, one of the venues used by the Royal Shakespeare Company

▶▶   **Waddesdon Manor**   *111A4*

Ferdinand de Rothschild had this French renaissance-style château built in the Buckinghamshire countryside in the 1870s and 1880s, with no expense spared. It is breathtaking in its opulence – the contents as much as the house itself. Harkening back to the golden days of collecting, the treasures include clocks, Sèvres porcelain, lace and paintings. Within the grounds, designed by a French landscape gardener, are two grand fountains and an aviary. Waddesdon, in the care of the National Trust, is the grandest of a trio of local Rothschild mansions (*Open* to the public): the others are **Mentmore Towers**▶ and **Ascott**▶ (NT).

▶▶ Warwick *111B3*

Warwick is a pleasant country town with a magnificent castle that has become one of Britain's most visited stately homes.

The centre of town was rebuilt after a fire in 1694; a walk around **High Street** and **Northgate Street** takes in some of the finest buildings, including Court House and Landor House. The **County Museum** (*Admission free*) in the market square is a good place to bring children, with displays including natural history, a model of old Warwick and the historic Sheldon tapestry map of Warwickshire; its **Doll Museum**, on a separate site, displays antique toys and games.

Two of Warwick's medieval town **gateways** survive, complete with chapels. Of these, Westgate Chapel forms part of **Leycester's Hospital**▶, a spectacularly tottering half-timbered range enclosing a pretty courtyard. Since 1571 the building has been used as a hospice for retired soldiers, and part of the interior houses the Queen's Own Hussars regimental museum. Pre-fire features of the collegiate **Church of St Mary**▶ include the fan-vaulted Beauchamp Chapel, with an outstanding collection of Warwick tombs, and a Norman crypt (complete with a tumbrel, part of a medieval ducking stool).

Warwick Castle▶▶ looks at its very best from Castle Bridge, where the 14th-century walls are reflected in the waters of the Avon. There is a walk along the ramparts and, inside, a tour of the palatial mansion takes you from the grim austerity of the original dungeons to the gloomy but sumptuous opulence of rooms later adapted for comfortable living. There are waxworks of a royal weekend party and much to explore within the grounds, including a re-created Victorian rose garden, the formal Peacock Gardens and an expanse of open parkland, landscaped by Capability Brown from 1753 onwards.

Warwick Castle rises sheer from the River Avon

Kenilworth Castle
On the western edge of Kenilworth, this huge sandstone castle (EH) is the venue for events featuring medieval pageantry, drama and music. The castle was built as a fortress in Norman times but was much adapted by the Earl of Leicester, Queen Elizabeth Is favourite, whose neglected wife Amy Robsart died near by in mysterious circumstances (it was never discovered whether her fall down stairs was murder, accident or suicide). The Virgin Queen was compelled by the resulting controversy to distance herself from Leicester, whom she eventually had executed for treason.

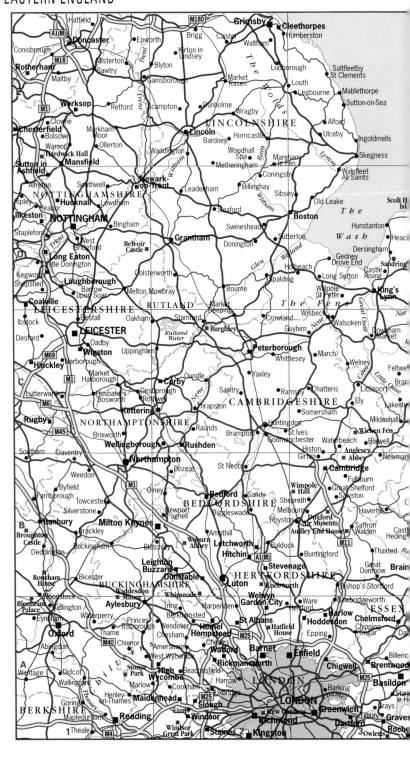

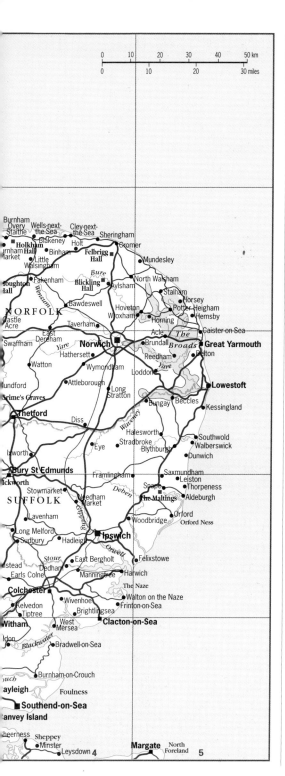

Map labels:

0 10 20 30 40 50 km	
0 10 20 30 miles	

Burnham Overy Staithe, Wells-next-the-Sea, Cley-next-the-Sea, Sheringham, Holkham, Blakeney, Holt, Cromer, Binham, Felbrigg Hall, Mundesley, Little Walsingham, North Walsham, Fakenham, Blickling Hall, Aylsham, Stalham, Horsey, Houghton Hall, Bawdeswell, Hoveton, Potter Heigham, Wroxham, Hemsby, NORFOLK, Castle Acre, Taverham, Horning, Caister on Sea, East Dereham, Acle, The Broads, Great Yarmouth, Swaffham, Norwich, Brundall, Belton, Hathersett, Reedham, Watton, Wymondham, Yare, Loddon, Lowestoft, Attleborough, Long Stratton, Bungay, Beccles, Kessingland, Thetford, Diss, Waveney, Halesworth, Southwold, Stradbroke, Walberswick, Eye, Blythburgh, Dunwich, Bury St Edmunds, Saxmundham, Framlingham, Leiston, Snape, Thorpeness, Stowmarket, Needham Market, The Maltings, Aldeburgh, SUFFOLK, Deben, Lavenham, Woodbridge, Orford, Orford Ness, Long Melford, Hadleigh, Ipswich, Sudbury, Orwell, East Bergholt, Felixstowe, Dedham, Manningtree, Harwich, Earls Colne, The Naze, Colchester, Walton on the Naze, Wivenhoe, Frinton-on-Sea, Kelvedon, Brightlingsea, Tiptree, West Mersea, Clacton-on-Sea, Witham, Blackwater, Bradwell-on-Sea, Burnham-on-Crouch, Rayleigh, Foulness, Southend-on-Sea, Canvey Island, Sheerness, Sheppey, Minster, Leysdown, Margate, North Foreland

EASTERN ENGLAND

135

REGION HIGHLIGHTS ◄◄◄◄

CAMBRIDGE *see pages 138–9*

ELY *see page 140*

LINCOLN *see page 141*

BLICKLING HALL *see page 142*

NORTH NORFOLK COAST *see page 142*

AUDLEY END HOUSE *see page 143*

NORWICH *see page 143*

HATFIELD HOUSE *see page 146*

SOUTHWOLD AND AREA *see page 146*

WOBURN ABBEY *see page 147*

The River Ant near How Hill is typical of the waterscapes of the Norfolk Broads

Eastern England This region extends from the northern edge of London to the brink of Humberside. There are no uplands: the rural landscape is of flat or gently undulating agricultural country, with only the Lincolnshire Wolds, Bedfordshire's Dunstable Downs and Leicestershire's Charnwood Forest rising to any appreciable height. Fields are often prairie-like in scale. It pays to be selective as to where you travel.

East Anglia The most consistently picturesque area of eastern England lies within East Anglia, the collective term for **Norfolk**, **Suffolk**, northern **Essex** and eastern **Cambridgeshire**. Here, above all, the prosperity brought about by the medieval wool trade left a noble legacy of church architecture and villages and towns of handsome timber-framed and plaster-fronted cottages. A speciality of the countryside immortalised by the paintings of Constable on the Essex/Suffolk border is pastel-coloured plasterwork ornately decorated with relief patterns known as 'pargetting'. In **Norfolk**, flint walls and Dutch gable ends, reflecting former trading links with the Low Countries, are a common sight. Windmills are ubiquitous, the skies are vast and the light effects subtle.

Scenically, the coast is the most appealing part: south Essex is unimpressively built-up around the Thames Estuary, but east of Ipswich, the **Suffolk** coast has much of interest to the walker and naturalist, although the presence of Sizewell Nuclear Power Station is unfortunate. The **Norfolk Broads National Park** is excellent for a sail-it-yourself boating holiday – out of peak times.

More beauty can be found along the unspoilt north Norfolk coast. North of Cambridge lie the **Fens**, a vast expanse of fertile, flat, black-soil farmland, formerly beneath water but since drained by cuts and sluices; much of the landscape transformation was begun by the Dutch engineer, Cornelius Vermuyden, in the 17th century. Wicken Fen near Ely gives an idea of what the Fens were like before this great agricultural upgrading.

On a still day, the light can have the delicate outlines of a Japanese picture. On a stormy day, even in summer, the grey sea batters itself against the shelf [of pebbles], dragging the shingle down with a scrunching, grating, slithering sound. To anyone born on the Suffolk coast, this sound has always meant home.
Imogen Holst, *Britten,* in the 'Great Composers' series (1966)

The inland shires The interest here lies in pockets. Hertfordshire has some fine country houses and oases of rural charm such as Ayot St Lawrence and Benington, but Hertford, Hemel Hempstead and others are commuter satellites. **Bedfordshire** has grand houses such as Luton Hoo and Woburn Abbey, but the former hat-making centre of Luton and Bedford itself are uninteresting. Northampton is famed for shoe-making, but not for the quality of the countryside in **Northamptonshire**; however, the ironstone villages of Badby and Everdon, and around Rockingham Forest, make for pleasant walking and touring country, and there is an appealing canal scene and canal museum at Stoke Bruerne. Milton Keynes is the newest of Britain's new towns, loosely based on Frank Lloyd Wright's scheme for Broadacre City in the USA, with a low population density and much thought given to landscaping and separating pedestrians and traffic.

Leicestershire is endowed with some large country estates and rolling countryside on its eastern side, but further west many of its towns belong to the industrial east Midlands; Leicester, the county town, is an industrial centre, but it does have an excavated Roman site within the Jewry Wall Museum and a good Museum of Technology. Belvoir Castle, home of the Duke of Rutland, is one of the grandest 19th-century statements of wealth and social standing.

Nottinghamshire is the county of Robin Hood, although what is left of Sherwood Forest is inevitably smaller and tamer than in the famous outlaw's day; the great country estates known collectively as the Dukeries include Newstead Abbey and others, while Clumber Park is a popular strolling-ground. The writer D H Lawrence lived at Eastwood, in the Nottinghamshire coalfield, and his house is open as a museum. Nottingham has an attractive lace market and an excellent crop of museums.

Cambridge and the cathedral cities Visitors come above all to the university city of **Cambridge**, whose colleges and river combine in perfect composition. Former alumni include Oliver Cromwell, John Milton, Isaac Newton, Lord Byron and Charles Darwin. **Ely, Norwich, Peterborough, St Albans, Southwell** and **Lincoln** each have splendid cathedrals, abbeys or minsters. Of these places, Norwich and Lincoln are less well known because of their relative isolation than many of England's other great cathedral cities and deserve a longer look.

137

St Albans Abbey and parkland contain remains of the Roman city of Verulamium

The collegiate system
Colleges are the life and soul of the university of Cambridge, just as they are at Oxford (see page 126). The colleges are where most students live, eat and have their supervisions (in which small groups of students discuss their work with teachers). Lectures, examinations and societies are organised on a university basis, but there are comparatively few 'university' buildings as such.

Excursions from Cambridge
Wimpole Hall (NT) is Cambridgeshire's grandest house, a formal Georgian composition. It has restored Victorian stables and a large park with lots of walks. Rare breeds of domestic animals and a barn display of two centuries of farm machinery may be seen at adjacent Home Farm.
Anglesey Abbey (NT), built in about 1600, has impressive grounds laid out this century.
Duxford Air Museum, part of the London-based Imperial War Museum, claims to hold Europe's largest collection of historic military aircraft.

The 19th-century entrance hall of the Fitzwilliam Museum assumes the baroque grandeur of an Italian palazzo

▶▶▶ **Cambridge**   134B3

The home of one of the world's oldest and greatest universities is a city ideal for casual wandering. It is a place of cloistered tranquillity, students on bicycles and riverside beauty, as well as a bustling market town. Many of the best bits are not obvious at first sight; look for obscure entrances into secretive courts and gardens. Respect 'Private' notices, but otherwise you may wander at will. (*Guided tours* from the tourist information centre on Wheeler Street; some colleges close to visitors Apr–Jun).

The university comprises about 30 colleges scattered around the city, of which 16 have medieval origins. **King's College** has the most famous building; its **chapel**▶▶▶, a symphony of fan-vaulting and magnificent stained glass, is regarded as the finest example of the Perpendicular (15th-century Gothic) style. Near by, **Clare College**▶ is a formal composition, like a Renaissance palace. The grand Palladian **Senate House** is used for formal functions, including graduation ceremonies. **Trinity College**▶▶ has the largest court in Oxford or Cambridge, and Christopher Wren's famous library (*Open* to the public) in Nevile Court. **St John's College**▶▶ has two Tudor courts: beyond them the Bridge of Sighs leads into 19th-century Gothic New Court. More modest in scale is **Queens' College**▶, with its half-timbered court and painted hall. The Mathematical Bridge here is a wooden structure, constructed without using any bolts – until curious engineers dismantled it and were unable to reassemble it as it was!

The river Behind Trinity and King's, the River Cam slices through a delectable swathe of greenery, fringed by neat gardens and lawns; this area is known as The Backs. Punts (boats originally designed for gathering reeds for thatching) can be hired near Silver Street Bridge. Walk south through watermeadows for 3km (2 miles) to Grantchester, or head north from Magdalene Street Bridge to watch college rowing crews training.

The **Fitzwilliam Museum**▶▶▶ (*Admission free*) is a major collection of art, medieval manuscripts, armour and more. The **Cambridge and County Folk Museum**▶ is packed with local memorabilia and **Kettle's Yard**▶ is an idiosyncratic private house and modern art gallery.

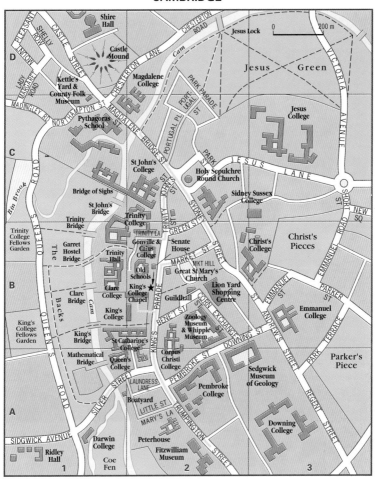

CAMBRIDGE

Walk The best of the colleges, the river and the streets

With the **Church of Great St Mary's** (fine view from **tower▶**) on your left, follow King's Parade (which becomes Trumpington Street). On the right is **King's College** with its superb chapel**▶▶▶**. Pass **Corpus Christi** (its Old Court is hidden at the back) and **Pembroke** (chapel by Wren); further on are **Peterhouse** (founded 1284, the oldest college) and the **Fitzwilliam Museum▶▶▶**. Enter Little St Mary's Lane, turn right by river (punts for hire). Pass Mill Inn, cross Silver Street

Bridge to pass **Queens' College▶**. Take a path on right across grass for classic views from **the Backs**. Garret Hostel Lane leads over river to Trinity Lane. Turn left past **Trinity Hall▶**. Enter **Trinity▶▶** and St John's**▶▶** colleges from Trinity Street; at river, take walkway on right to a footbridge by **Jesus Lock** and turn sharp right across Jesus Green to enter Portugal Street. Return to the start past the Norman **Round Church▶** and **Sidney Sussex College** in Sidney Street.

Grime's Graves
A major centre of
England's neolithic flint
industry occupies a site in
Thetford Warren, the
conifer forest on the low-
lying sandy tracts of the
Breckland (east of Ely).
Over 400 shafts have been
discovered, down which
neolithic man climbed to
work in cramped tunnels,
chipping away the flint for
use in tools and weapons.
One shaft has been opened
to the public.

*Ely was dependant
on the River Ouse
as a waterway for
centuries*

▶▶ Ely *134C3*

The little town is dwarfed by its great cathedral, occupying a slightly elevated site and dominating the pancake-
flat Fenland plain for far around. The region is still called
the Isle of Ely – a reminder of the days when the town
was more or less an island in the undrained marsh. There
is surprisingly little to see in town, but the **cathedral▶▶▶**
ranks among the greats.

Part of the building shows Norman work, including the
west front and tower, but restoration was soon needed:
in 1250 the east end was rebuilt in Purbeck marble. In
1321 Alan of Walsingham supervised the building of the
Lady Chapel; when the central tower collapsed the next
year he created the wonderful octagonal lantern, lodged
on eight oak pillars, that graces the building today (divine
intervention must have prevented a further collapse: the
structure has alarmingly little to support it). Attached to
the cathedral are a stained-glass museum and a brass-
rubbing centre. Around the precincts are the houses of
the King's School, an eminent public school founded by
Henry VIII.

▶ King's Lynn *134D3*

Once a member of the Hanseatic League, a powerful
commercial association of towns in northern Germany
formed in the 14th century, King's Lynn still has a slightly
continental look in its darkened redbrick buildings. It traded with northern Europe for many centuries and its docks
and industrial area are still very much functional. St
George's Guildhall (1420) is the oldest guildhall in
England, and has a splendid beamed roof; this and twin-
towered St Margaret's Church (Norman, with fine memorial brasses) justify a visit to the town. Bygone lifestyles
are evoked within **True's Yard**, where a pair of fishermen's cottages house a museum.

The villages of **Castle Rising** and **Castle Acre▶**, respectively 6km (4 miles) north and 20km (13 miles) east of
King's Lynn, both have an impressive Norman castle. West
of Castle Acre, the priory church of a Cluniac foundation survives almost intact. Castle Rising has jousting contests in
summer.

Fenland churches▶▶ Among the finest are **Walpole
St Peter**, with superb benches, font and pulpit, and
Walsoken, a Norman church with a magnificent roof and a
16th-century wall-painting of the Judgement of Solomon.

Wicken Fen
Britain's oldest nature
reserve, located south of
Ely and now owned by the
National Trust, gives an
idea of what the fens were
like before they were
drained. Villagers left the
fen undrained to preserve
its supply of reeds for
thatching; it is in parts
wooded, wetland and
meadow, with waterways
enclosing the site. A nature
trail takes you past a re-
erected pumping mill,
some bog oaks (logs sub-
merged for thousands of
years under the fen and
recently unearthed) and
the birdwatchers' hide,
from the top of which Ely
Cathedral can just be seen.

Museums in Lincoln
Lincoln's indoor attractions include the *Museum of Lincolnshire Life*, with a sizeable collection of horse-drawn vehicles, and domestic and agricultural bygones; the *Incredibly Fantastic Old Toy Show*, with bygone toys and old pier amusements; and the *Usher Hall Gallery*, which exhibits applied arts, including a noted collection of watches, memorabilia relating to poet Alfred, Lord Tennyson (born at Somersby in the Lincolnshire Wolds) and paintings by Lincolnshire watercolourist Peter de Wint.

▶▶▶ Lincoln   134E2

The massive towers of Lincoln's superlative cathedral soar high from a hilltop site. The cathedral, castle, museums and historic streets provide enough of interest for a full-day visit. However, outside the small historic core much of the city is quite undistinguished.

The cathedral▶▶▶, one of England's finest, was largely rebuilt in the 13th and 14th centuries after an earthquake in 1185 destroyed an earlier structure. Features to look out for are the elaborate west façade, the carved choir stalls and the stained-glass rose windows, the Dean's Eye and the Bishop's Eye. High up, the Lincolnshire Imp steals the show; the story goes that he got too close to the angels and was turned to stone for his sins. Steps lead up the central tower to a viewing point.

Minster Yard, the cathedral close, has Georgian and medieval houses. Near the cathedral's east end, the **Bishop's Old Palace** dates from the 12th to 15th centuries. **Steep Hill** lives up to its name, climbing from the River Witham, past the Jew's House, inhabited from Norman times, and continuing beyond the cathedral as **Bailgate**. The street is spanned by Newport Arch, a Roman gateway into the city. Opposite the cathedral's west façade, **Exchequergate** leads to **Lincoln Castle▶** which dates from Norman times and has curtain walls, gateways, towers and a 19th-century prisoners' chapel.

▶ Norfolk Broads   135C5

Ever popular with boat enthusiasts and birdwatchers, the Broads is an area of reedy lakes (called 'broads'), waterways and fertile fens formed from flooded peat-diggings; windmills, erected to pump water to drain the farmland and now mostly defunct, proliferate. The broads themselves are difficult to see except from a boat; one of the best waterside walks is in the vicinity of Horsey, where the pumping mill is open to the public. The National Trust owns the broad of Horsey Mere; marsh harriers, bitterns and otters make up part of the local population. Other strolling grounds include the banks of the rivers Bure, Thurne and Yare.

Numerous boatyards cater for visitors; boats can be hired at Wroxham and Hoveton.

Spalding
A major bulb-growing centre in the Fens, Spalding holds a Flower Parade every May. It is one of the great free shows of eastern England, where often as many as three million tulips are used to decorate the floats in a procession accompanied by bands and general bonhomie. Springfield Gardens, a tulip and rose grower, hosts the parade and has fine shows of hyacinths, tulips and narcissi.

■ **The virtue and joy of this little-explored corner of picturesque English coastline is its isolation. The area also has a tremendous sense of place and history, and is of great interest to the naturalist. Dutch gables, flints, huge medieval 'wool' churches, and weather-beaten coastal villages supply the manmade elements – saltmarshes (Europe's largest expanse), vast sandy beaches, prolific birdlife and dramatic skyscapes are among the natural attractions.** ■

Great Norfolk houses
Blickling Hall (NT) is a lovely red-brick 17th-century house, famed for the Jacobean plasterwork in its Long Gallery.
Holkham Hall is a neat Palladian mansion built for Thomas Coke, 18th-century agricultural pioneer.
Felbrigg (NT), a tall-chimneyed, 17th-century pile in a wooded park, has Georgian furnishings and a fine 18th-century library.
Houghton Hall exudes Palladian elegance and was the seat of Sir Robert Walpole, the first English prime minister.
Sandringham (*Open* when the Royal Family is not in residence, park and drives always open) was built in the 19th century as a country home for the Prince of Wales, the future Edward VII.

A shrimping boat at Wells-next-the-sea

The villages Cromer, famed for its crabs, and Sheringham are demure Edwardian resorts atop crumbly cliffs; from the latter a private steam railway heads towards Holt. Inland lies Norfolk's highest land (heathy protuberances rather than fully fledged hills). **Cley▶** has a much-photographed windmill (*Open* periodically), while **Blakeney** is a yachting centre, where mast-stays flap in the wind and a shingle bank leads to Blakeney Point (still building up westwards). Inland, **Binham▶** has a superb 13th-century priory church, beside the ruins of an 11th-century Benedictine priory.

Wells-next-the-sea produces 80 per cent of English whelks; the appealing port looks out over wide saltmarshes. A walk westwards brings you to **Holkham Gap**, where Corsican pines stabilise the dunes, flanking an immense beach. Another privately operated steam railway connects Wells with **Little Walsingham▶**, a pilgrimage centre for 900 years with both Roman Catholic and (very high-church, incense-filled) Anglican shrines to Our Lady of Walsingham; it is of interest even to non-pilgrims.

The 'seven Burnhams' are a scattering of hamlets and villages whose names are prefixed Burnham. **Burnham Overy Staithe▶** broods over saltmarshes with a fetching harbour scene – close by are a tower windmill and pretty watermill. **Burnham Thorpe** is famed as Admiral Lord Nelson's birthplace – every other pub hereabouts seems to be called the Nelson or the Hero. The nation's greatest sailor died on board HMS *Victory* (see page 104) after defeating the French and Spanish at Trafalgar in 1805; he was buried in St Paul's Cathedral in London but there are memorials in Burnham Thorpe Church. **Burnham Market** is an attractive village set around a spacious green. **Hunstanton** is an uneventful resort with chalk cliffs, the setting for L P Hartley's trilogy *Eustace and Hilda*.

The wildlife Among the best places for observing Norfolk's wildlife are the reserves at **Holme-next-the-sea**, at **Cley**, a site with reedbeds and shallow lagoons, and **Blakeney Point**, reached by boat from Morston or by a long coastal walk over sand and shingle from Blakeney. The coast supports a huge population of waders, with wood and curlew sandpipers in summer; great tern colonies exist at Scolt Head island, common and grey seals breed here, and there are sizeable numbers of autumn migrants and wintering birds.

▶▶▶ Norwich 135C4

Tucked well away from the tourist mainstream in the northeast corner of East Anglia, Norwich is considerably less overrun by the tourist industry than most other great cathedral cities in England. It is the major commercial centre for the region and a university city, too, which gives it a workaday bustle. For the visitor there is enough to fill a weekend, and you can escape to the Norfolk Broads for peace and space (see page 141). The market place (one of England's grandest), antique showrooms and speciality shops (including the Colman's Mustard shop) make for fascinating browsing, and there is a fair range of theatres. The medieval centre has a mishmash of good streets – the finest being **Elm Hill**, **Bridewell Alley** and **Colegate** – a number of eye-catching ancient buildings (head for the **Guildhall** and **Pull's Ferry**), and a multitude of outstanding medieval churches, notably **St Peter Mancroft** (Perpendicular) and **St Peter Hungate**, which has a fine hammerbeam roof, a museum of church art, and a brass-rubbing centre. Top of the sights is the **cathedral▶▶** (founded 1096), surrounded by a sweet close of houses and boasting some remarkable detailing in the roof-bosses, misericord carvings, glass and stone vaulting; the Norman cloister is the largest in the country. More prominent is the **castle▶**, sited on a commanding mound; guided tours take you around the Norman keep, battlements and dungeons.

Museums in Norwich
Bridewell Museum, Bridewell Alley, shows the trades and industries of Norwich over two centuries, in a former prison. *Castle Museum,* Castle Meadow, displays a celebrated collection of paintings by the Norwich school; ceramics (including hundreds of teapots), archaeology and natural history (Norfolk's last pair of great bustards are here, alas in stuffed form). *Sainsbury Centre for Visual Arts,* University of East Anglia campus (western edge of the city), has an outstanding art collection, admirably and innovatively displayed. In King Street, *Dragon Hall* is a medieval merchant's hall with a fine roof and vaulted undercroft.

143

Pull's Ferry, a 15th-century watergate on the River Wensum at Norwich

▶ Saffron Walden 134B3

From medieval times until the 18th century this was a centre for the saffron crocus industry. The legacy of its wealth is a knot of historic streets around the largest parish church in Essex which is largely in the Perpendicular Gothic style, and has notable carvings, roofs and memorial brasses. The former Sun Inn in Church Street is outstanding among many examples of the East Anglian craft of pargetting (decorative external plasterwork). On the Common is an enigmatic turf maze; Bridge End Gardens has a more conventional hedge maze.

Just west of the town is **Audley End House▶▶** (EH). Although only a fraction of its original size, it represents Jacobean architecture on its grandest scale. Vanbrugh and Robert Adam were responsible for early 18th-century alterations; Capability Brown landscaped the park.

■ **That fragile national asset, the British countryside, is adored for its infinite variety. Yet the landscapes of Hardy and Constable have been transformed in the name of progress. With environmental awareness on the increase in recent years, public attitudes have greened, but is it too late?** ■

144

A conservation Who's Who English Nature, the Countryside Council for Wales and Scottish Natural Heritage are the official bodies responsible for the conservation of flora, fauna, and geological and physiographical features; they manage National Nature Reserves. Local Nature Reserves are managed by local authorities in consultation with the above-named national bodies. In addition, numerous conservation trusts and wildlife trusts own reserves.
The Countryside Commission is the official adviser to the government on matters concerning the rural environment; it is responsible for the establishment of National Trails ('official' long distance footpaths).

Britain's footpaths need a constant watch to ensure they are in usable condition

The protection of birdlife The Wildfowl and Wetlands Trust at Slimbridge in Gloucestershire is dedicated to the protection of wetland sites and has wildfowl collections at eight centres in the UK. The Royal Society for the Protection of Birds (RSPB) is the principal body concerned with wild birds and their environment and has 120 reserves in the UK.

The shaping of the landscape The countryside is made by a combination of human and natural activity; patches of the primeval tree-cover that once cloaked much of the country exist here and there; but slash and burn led to a legacy of barren moorland, nature and farming produced a patchwork of hedge-lined fields, and wealthy landowners created great estates and hunting grounds. Yet so embedded in Britain's national culture has the landscape become that this unique blend of elements has become 'nature' in the public imagination. No value can be placed on landscape amenity, but the populace tends to expect it to be available for its enjoyment.

Agricultural revolutions Pressures for change have intensified. There are many contentious issues: agricultural improvements creating larger and more 'efficient' fields, the use of chemical fertilisers and pesticides that adversely affect the water table, the construction of factory-like barns and farms, the removal of small woodlands and the introduction of alien conifer plantations (environmentalists argue they can be deserts for wildlife), to name a few. The statistics make sobering reading: since 1945 the British countryside has lost 40 per cent of its traditional woodlands, 60 per cent of its heathlands, 80 per cent of its chalk downland pastures and 95 per cent of

its herb-rich hay meadows. Many hedgerows are extremely ancient and harbour diverse wildlife; an estimated 200,000km (125,000 miles) of hedgerows have been ploughed out. (However, in 1997 a campaigner won a court case which held that an ancient enclosure act protecting hedgerows is still in force.)

Whose countryside is it anyway? Farmers, estate owners and institutions such as company pension funds legally own much of the country's farmland and forests, and no value can be put on the public's enjoyment of the great outdoors. Access to the countryside has increased greatly in the past 30 years, and with it an awareness of the threats that loom large. As a proportion of the total population, the number of people employed in farming and forestry is not large, but the agri-business lobby is very strong.

Pressures on land Road-building, housing and industrial development, cable-bearing pylons and mineral extraction have marred many corners of Britain. In a small island, pressure to exploit the countryside is inevitably strong, and it would take courage for a government to resist growth. But the balance between environmental and economic interests is getting increasingly tricky to achieve.

Helping hands? The National Trust, a charitable body (see panel page 102), holds much of Britain's finest land for public enjoyment in perpetuity: it has been responsible for safeguarding large areas of coast, downland, upland and forest. Hundreds of important wildlife sites have been acquired by local and national nature trusts as nature reserves; many others are designated Sites of Special Scientific Interest (SSSIs) – but that status by no means guarantees a safe haven in the planning jungle. The 11 National Parks and 85 Areas of Outstanding Natural Beauty may have stricter planning guidelines but often they face another problem – how to manage the sheer number of visitors.

Tax concessions on planting forests have recently disappeared, but many areas of upland Britain (particularly the Scottish Highlands) are already blanketed with conifer plantations. Perversely, the presence of the Army on training land has preserved the wildness of some areas, notably the Brecklands in Norfolk and parts of Dorset, but there is a strong feeling that the Ministry of Defence should move out to allow more public access.

Investing in the environment The planning system restricted urban growth in the post-war years, and public inquiries in the face of objections to road-building and other construction schemes have led to amendments; 'green belts' around major cities have halted the creeping suburbanisation of some revered tracts, including the Weald and Chilterns. But agricultural changes (including erection of farm buildings) have until recently been outside the scope of the system. The creation of Environmentally Sensitive Areas (ESAs) means that farmers within them are entitled to grants to maintain traditional farming practices, and subsidies are given to hill farmers. Sensibly targeted government and EU-initiated schemes could save the day.

The campaigners
The Council for the Preservation of Rural England (CPRE), the Council for National Parks and the Friends of the Earth are among the leading conservation campaigners. The National Trust (NT) is Britain's largest owner of amenity countryside; the catalyst for its formation was the unsuccessful battle to save Thirlmere, in the Lake District, from conversion into a reservoir in the 1870s. The Ramblers' Association and the Open Spaces Society are pacesetters for the campaigns for public access to the countryside.

145

Voluntary work
The British Trust for Conservation Volunteers (36 St Mary's Street, Wallingford, Oxfordshire OX10 0EU, tel: 01491 839766; fax 01491 839646) runs over 500 conservation working holidays and many one-day projects (footpath maintenance, drystone walling and so on); participants pay a small amount towards food and accommodation.

Nature on the Suffolk coast
Walberswick, a scattered hamlet, abuts reedbeds, mudflats and heath, a habitat for bearded tits, reed warblers, bitterns, water rails and marshland plants. Much of the former port of Dunwich has disappeared beneath the sea; Dunwich and Westleton heaths are near by, and Minsmere is a freshwater lake owned by the Royal Society for the Protection of Birds (over 280 bird species have been recorded locally, including bearded tits, nightjars, woodpeckers and nightingales). Access to Minsmere reserve is tightly controlled but birdwatchers' hides are open to the public.

Southwold: choose from today's catch at the harbour

▶ **St Albans** *134A2*

Less than 30km (19 miles) from London, St Albans has preserved its provincial character surprisingly well. Its **abbey church**▶ is a medieval foundation built on the site where Alban, the first British martyr, was executed in the 4th century. Its brick-and-flint fabric dates from the 11th century and has been added to in every century since. The Roman city of **Verulamium**▶ lies in a nearby park; excavations include a semi-circular amphitheatre, part of the city walls, foundations of houses and a temple. Site finds are well displayed in the Verulamium Museum.

The **Gardens of the Rose**▶, the Royal National Rose Society's home at Chiswell Green, on the southwest edge of St Albans, have some 30,000 bushes, at their heady best in July. Some 8km (5 miles) east of St Albans, Jacobean **Hatfield House**▶▶ has been in the same family since it was built for Robert Cecil in 1611. It has sumptuous state rooms and formal knot and scented gardens.

▶ **Southwell** *134D1*

The medieval minster in this small Nottinghamshire town is not England's best-known, but the chapter house (begun in 1292) boasts some of the country's most breathtakingly intricate carving: a celebration of Sherwood Forest's foliage in stone, featuring oak, maple, vine and ivy leaves. Two of the three Norman towers were rebuilt after a fire in 1711, but the nave, crossing and transept display characteristic Norman simplicity.

▶▶ **Southwold** *135C5*

A bewitchingly old-fashioned seaside town, Southwold is a centre for exploring the best of Suffolk's coast. The former home town of essayist and novelist George Orwell (Eric Blair), it was largely replanned after a fire in 1659 around a series of greens edged by flint, brick and colour-washed cottages. The great Perpendicular church has a superb interior, a white lighthouse gleams behind the Sole Bay Inn, and the town museum and Sailors' Reading Room have displays on local maritime life. Just south of town, the River Blyth has an attractive boating scene. Around Southwold lie numerous marshlands, some unspoilt low-lying coast and much heathy grassland – the traditional sandlings, or sheepwalks, on which Suffolk's economy depended in the wool-prosperous Middle Ages – making an area of exceptional interest for naturalists.

Southwards 25km (16 miles), **Aldeburgh**▶ is a small coastal town, the birthplace of George Crabbe, an 18th-century poet. His poem *The Borough* was adapted by Benjamin Britten for his opera *Peter Grimes,* the brilliant evocation of life on this coast premièred in 1945. Britten (1913–76) is buried in the churchyard of St Peter and St Paul; a memorial window was designed by John Piper. Britten co-founded Aldeburgh's esteemed June music festival, which is centred on the old maltings at Snape.

Just north of Aldeburgh is **Thorpeness**▶, a seaside resort village planned in the early 20th century as a weatherboarded and half-timbered 'olde-English' haven. Beside the Meare, the village's artificial lake, stands a former corn windmill, moved here to pump water to the adjacent extraordinarily tall former water tower, known as the House in the Clouds.

▶▶ Stamford 134C2

An eye-opening oasis of mellow, Cotswold-like limestone buildings, Stamford scarcely has an out-of-place building. Its clutch of medieval churches includes **St Martin's**, a complete Perpendicular church with a notable 16th-century alabaster monument to Lord Burghley, while **St Mary's** has a gold-star-embellished 15th-century chapel of the 'golden choir'. Of Stamford's inns **The George** is the most conspicuous, with its 'gallows' inn-sign spanning the street, and has a grandiose interior. Look for two good examples of almshouses, 15th-century **Browne's Hospital** and Elizabethan **Lord Burghley's Hospital**.

Capability Brown's landscaped park at **Burghley House▶** laps the brink of Stamford. The palatial mansion was built by one William Cecil, chief minister to Elizabeth I. The Elizabethan exterior belies an interior refurbished 100 years later, full of baroque flourishes, including a dazzling array of Italian plasterwork and painted ceilings in the 'Heaven' and 'Hell' rooms. **Rutland Water**, to the west, is a huge reservoir and major recreation area. Further afield, 22km (14 miles) southeast of Stamford, **Peterborough** is sprawling and industrial but worth a visit for its pleasant market place and Georgian streets, and above all a Norman cathedral that boasts a superb, painted wooden ceiling – Europe's largest.

▶▶ Woburn Abbey 134B2

Britain's largest animal safari park forms part of the grounds of this stately home, the seat of the Russells, the dukes of Bedford, since 1550. Despite its abbey origins – a Cistercian foundation prior to the Reformation – the house is an 18th-century Palladian composition set in a deer park landscaped by Humphry Repton. Within it is the finest set of Canaletto paintings to be found anywhere. The long family connection with the house (which claims to be the birthplace of afternoon tea), is readily apparent, with portraits and accumulated possessions spanning many centuries.

George Bernard Shaw
The great Anglo-Irish dramatist George Bernard Shaw lived at Shaw's Corner (NT), in the village of Ayot St Lawrence near Welwyn, from 1906 until his death in 1950. Numbered among his most famous plays are *Arms and the Man*, *Saint Joan* and *Heartbreak House*. Shaw's Corner epitomises his plain living and high thinking; his hats, glasses, pen, desk and exercise machine are there, as if he has just stepped outside the door. He died in the dining room and his ashes were scattered in the garden.

147

A windmill stands among the tranquil marshes flanking the Blyth Estuary near Southwold

CONSTABLE COUNTRY

[Map of Constable Country showing locations including Haverhill, Clare, Lavenham, Sudbury, Hadleigh, Thaxted, Halstead, Castle Hedingham, Manningtree, Flatford Mill & Lock, Dedham, and surrounding area with the River Stour]

Drive Constable Country

As pretty as a picture: the candy colours of local plasterwork, the village greens and the great medieval churches, built on the prosperity of the wool trade, have changed little since Constable's day. The countryside is mild and agreeable if unspectacular: it is the towns and villages – well endowed with tearooms, craft and antique shops – that have most appeal (approx. 140km/90 miles).

Start at **Sudbury**, where Thomas Gainsborough's birthplace is now a museum. The route follows the River Stour, along the B1508 to **Bures** then eastwards through **Stoke-by-Nayland►**, where the church tower (a familiar feature in Constable's paintings) presides over the Maltings and Guildhall. **Dedham►** has an

Gainsborough's House, Sudbury

attractively broad main street and the building of Constable's school survives; the artist Alfred Munnings lived here and his works are displayed in his former house. Near **East Bergholt**, Constable's birthplace, is **Flatford Mill►** (also reached by a pretty 2km/1¼ miles river path or by boats hired from Dedham); Willy Lott's Cottage by the millpond is still recognisable as the setting for Constable's *The Haywain*.

Turn northwest along the B1070 through **Hadleigh►**, a handsome town by the River Brett with a fine church and half-timbered Guildhall. Detour through **Kersey►**, a single-street charmer, and join the A1141 to **Lavenham►►**, with its resplendent half-timbering, a huddle of inns and an outstanding church. Westwards, **Long Melford►** has antique shops, another magnificent church, and two fine stately homes adjacent.

The A1092 heads past **Cavendish**, a confection of pink rendering and thatch around the green, and **Clare**, with its market place and flint-built church noted for its woodcarving. Seek out the church, windmill and Recorders' House at **Thaxted►►**. Eastwards lies **Finchingfield►** with a delightful green and windmill. **Castle Hedingham►►** has a mighty Norman keep.

East Anglia's artists

■ The landscape of East Anglia has long held a special fascination for painters. Gainsborough and Constable both came from Suffolk, and Gainsborough's birthplace in Sudbury is now a museum. Constable was born at East Bergholt, and works such as *The Haywain* and *Flatford Mill* made the winding valley of the Stour 'Constable country' even during his own lifetime. ■

While **Constable** and **Gainsborough** are the two biggest names, many other distinguished artists recorded the East Anglian scene. **Philip Wilson Steer** painted the Suffolk coast in the 1880s. **Sir Alfred Munnings**, who painted all over his native East Anglia, settled at Dedham after World War I and his house is now a museum. **John Nash**, one of

this century's major landscape artists, lived and worked in Essex for years before his death in 1977.

The Norwich School Norwich's Castle Museum has a splendid collection of paintings by the Norwich School of painters, which began in 1803. Its chief figures were **John Crome** and **John Sell Cotman**. Crome, shrewd and boozy, was much more successful, to the anguished jealousy of Cotman, who is now regarded as the greater painter, admired for his ability to impose simple and satisfying patterns on the natural scene. The work of the Norwich School echoes the Dutch school of landscape painting – a flat landscape studded by windmills and grazed by cattle beneath an immense sky of towering cloudscapes.

The wealth and the comparatively isolated position of Norwich in the early 19th century meant that most of its painters worked and were known only locally. The local gentry wanted representations of the scenes they knew – the tranquil Norfolk landscape, picturesquely dilapidated cottages, ruined towers and crumbling abbeys, cattle and sheep, river and coastal views. The Norwich School painted the rural scene as it was in the last days before the Industrial Revolution changed the face of Britain.

Above: from Wood scene *by John Crome, 1810*

Fishing boats off Yarmouth *by John Sell Cotman*

East Anglian art on show
In addition to Gainsborough's House in Sudbury, there are notable collections of works by East Anglian artists at the Castle Museum and the Sainsbury Centre, both in Norwich, the Fitzwilliam Museum in Cambridge, and at theTate Gallery and the National Gallery in London – the latter displays Constable's *The Haywain*.

How much real delight have I had with the study of Landscape this summer. Either I am myself much improved in 'the Art of seeing Nature' (which Sir Joshua Reynolds calls painting) or Nature has unveiled her beauties to me with a less fastidious hand – perhaps there may be something of both so we will divide these fine compliments between us ...
John Constable, to his future wife (1812)

WALES

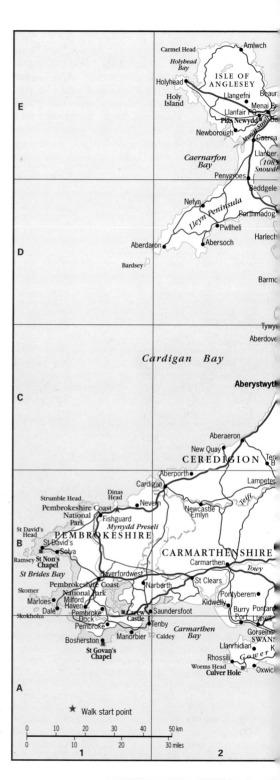

E

Carmel Head • Amlwch
Holyhead Bay
ISLE OF ANGLESEY
Holyhead •
Llangefni • Beaur.
Holy Island
Menai Br
Llanfair PG
Plas Newydd
Newborough
Caerna
Caernarfon Bay
Llanber.
(108
Snowd
Penygroes

D

Beddgele
Nefyn •
Lleyn Peninsula
Porthmadog
Pwllheli •
Harlech
Aberdaron •
Abersoch •
Bardsey
Barmo

Tywy
Aberdove

Cardigan Bay

C

Aberystwyt

Aberaeron •
New Quay •
CEREDIGION
Ten
B
Aberporth •
Lampeter
Cardigan •
Teifi
Strumble Head
Dinas Head
Nevern •
Pembrokeshire Coast National Park
Fishguard
Newcastle Emlyn
St David's Head
Mynydd Preseli
PEMBROKESHIRE
CARMARTHENSHIRE

B

St David's •
Solva
Carmarthen •
Towy
Ramsey St Non's Chapel
Haverfordwest
St Brides Bay
Narberth
St Clears
Skomer
Pembrokeshire Coast National Park
Pontyberem
Marloes •
Milford Haven
Kidwelly
Burry Pontard
Skokholm
Dale
Saundersfoot
Port
Llanelli
Pembroke Dock
Carew Castle
Gorseins
Pembroke
Tenby
SWANS
Manorbier
Caldy
Carmarthen Bay
Bosherston •
Llanrhidian
St Govan's Chapel
Rhossili •
Gower
K
Worms Head
Oxwic
Culver Hole

A

★ Walk start point

0 10 20 30 40 50 km
0 10 20 30 miles

1   **2**

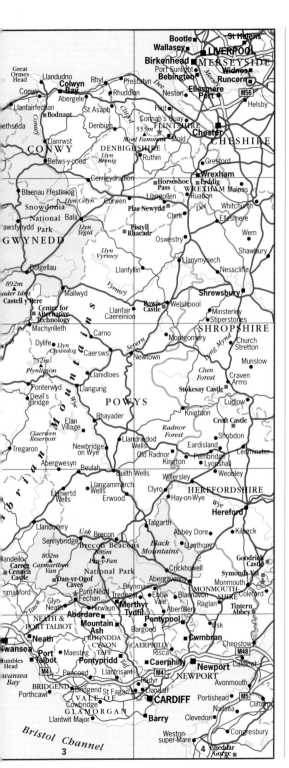

WALES

151

Tourism is now Wales' largest industry and Welsh woollen goods are popular as souvenirs

The fishing industry has seen decline – but there is always activity in a harbour

Wales Constitutionally Wales is closer to England than is Scotland; there is no separate legal system, and the two principalities have been unified since 1535. Yet the Welsh are proudly independent in culture and outlook; the Welsh language, impenetrable to an outsider, is very much alive (much more so than Gaelic in Scotland) and is taught in schools. Welsh is the first language of many, particularly in North and West Wales; signs ('dim parcio/no parking', 'croeso i Gymru/welcome to Wales') are predominantly bilingual; roughly one in five of its inhabitants is a Welsh speaker. Plaid Cymru, the Welsh Nationalist Party, has returned Members of Parliament since 1966 and devolution is very much a current talking point: in September 1997, the Welsh people voted by a narrow margin to establish a Welsh Assembly in Cardiff, which will manage the budget previously administered by the Welsh Office.

There are strong traditions of choral singing and of Nonconformism, virtually every village having at least one chapel. The Welsh love of music, literature and art manifests itself in the numerous *eisteddfods*, in which music, poetry, drama and fine arts feature. Welsh vernacular architecture on the other hand is humble – typically sturdy stone-built farmsteads and houses beneath slate roofs; the railway age added red and yellow brick façades. Grand houses are a rarity, but there are plenty of medieval castles to visit. Wales also prides itself on its educational system; it has the highest teacher/pupil ratios in the UK, and a higher proportion of 16-year-olds go on to higher education than in England.

South Wales For all its proximity to central and northwest England, Wales is strikingly remote. Cross into South or Mid Wales from the English border and the hills rise immediately. The southern borderland (the border country often being termed as the Marches) is defined precisely by the gorge of the **Lower Wye**, whose scenic reaches are punctuated by features such as Tintern Abbey, Chepstow Castle and Symonds Yat rock. Crisscrossing the English border from the South Wales coast to its northern one, the exhilarating and extremely hilly 285km (177-mile) **Offa's Dyke Path** roughly follows the line of a 9th-century boundary dyke built by Offa, King of Mercia. Further into South Wales lie the coalfields and the declining industrial heartlands of the **mining valleys**, which, though hardly picturesque, have a particular fascination; **Cardiff**, the Welsh capital, is the administrative and cultural capital. The coast becomes increasingly seductive as you proceed westwards; Nash Point near Llantwit Major on the Vale of Glamorgan coast displays extraordinary candy-striped rocks, while the **Gower Peninsula** has magnificent bays and cliffs, and is a pleasant relief from industrial Swansea.

Pembrokeshire, too distant for day-tripping on a major scale, is a favourite destination for seaside holidays without the host of commercialised trappings found in so many English resorts.

Mid Wales This nebulous term is applied to a relatively unknown region, sparsely populated except by sheep, which are encountered everywhere (one-quarter of the EU's sheep population is here). The **Brecon Beacons National Park** offers the grandest scenery, with the best-known tracts on its eastern side, including the Black Mountains, the Brecon Beacons and the second-hand bookshop town of Hay-on-Wye.

Further west, the **Cambrian Mountains** are scarcely inhabited and largely impenetrable by car, except by a handful of spectacularly lonely mountain roads which are former routes used by drovers taking sheep to market in the pre-petrol era. Aberystwyth is the principal seaside town of Ceredigian (or Cardigan), whose coast – while it cannot compete with that of Pembrokeshire for scenic variety – does have a few pleasant places, such as Llangranog, New Quay and Aberaeron.

North Wales Along the north coast stretches a line of resorts, undistinguished with the notable exception of Llandudno in Conwy. But more significantly, North Wales contains **Snowdonia National Park**; here are the highest mountains in England and Wales, and a good range of attractions, including castles, mines and steam railways. This can be a frustrating area for motorists: roads are confined to the valleys and the scenery slips by; but there are outstanding walks from easy forest strolls to tough scrambles up scree-covered mountain slopes.

153

Rounding up sheep the Welsh way – but sheep dogs normally do the precision work

WALES

Stained-glass window in the secular setting of Anglesey Sea Zoo, near Llangeinwen

▶ **Anglesey, Isle of**   150E2

Wales' largest island is flat and fertile, and it is its shores that provide most of interest to visitors. Good beaches include **Newborough Warren**, which offers distant views of Snowdonia, and **Amlwch Bay**.

Pioneering neolithic man built an amazing number of chamber tombs on Anglesey, the most notable being Bryn celli ddu and Barcloddiad y Gawres. The island's geographical position en route to Ireland and its gold and copper inevitably attracted the Celts too; a great hoard of Iron Age chariot fittings and weapons was found at Llyn Cerrig Bach. In medieval times, when the island's productive farmland provided valuable supplies for granaries in England, Anglesey was held by the English. Edward I built a stronghold in the 1290s at **Beaumaris**▶▶; the castle (Cadw) was never attacked and the moated shell survives to this day. The town's former prison houses a museum where you can find ghoulish delights such as the treadmill, the condemned cell and the route to the scaffold.

Between Anglesey and the mainland is the Menai Strait, spanned by Thomas Telford's suspension bridge, the longest such structure in the world when constructed (1826) and one of the Scottish engineer's greatest achievements. Overlooking the strait is **Plas Newydd**▶ (NT), the Pagets' 18th- and 19th-century family home; it has a remarkable *trompe l'oeil* mural in the dining room, painted by Rex Whistler in the 1930s. **Holy Island**, attached to the rest of Anglesey by a 1km (½ mile) causeway, is good for birdwatching and, although the industrial port of Holyhead is disappointing, there are exhilarating walks on Holyhead Mountain, the island's highest point, which has the remains of a Roman watch-tower and traces of 3rd- and 4th-century hut circles. Ferries leave from Holyhead for Dublin in Ireland.

The druids of Anglesey
The religious leaders of the Celts were the Druids and Anglesey was famed far and wide as a druidic centre. Tacitus, the Roman historian writing in the 1st century AD, speaks of Anglesey as the place where youths aspiring to the priesthood were sent to be schooled in philosophy, religion and poetry; in more sinister mode, he also speaks of human blood being smeared on the Druids' altars and human entrails being used for prophesies.

Porth Dafarch, on Anglesey's Holy Island, is a popular beach for divers and canoeists

▶▶ Brecon Beacons National Park   151B3

The Park is an east–west upland of four distinct areas, the Black Mountains, Fforest Fawr, the Brecon Beacons themselves and (confusingly) the Black Mountain. It is less rugged than Snowdonia but has some fine moments and excellent walking; it also attracts fewer visitors.

The eastern flanks comprise the **Black Mountains**, a series of ridges enclosing deep sheep-grazed valleys. Drive up from **Hay-on-Wye▶**, a small town crowded around its castle and a mecca for second-hand bookshop browsers. Above Hay the **Gospel Pass▶▶** is perhaps the most scenic drive in the Park, with easy access to the summit of Hay Bluff. The road dips into a valley, past the ruins of 13th-century **Llanthony Abbey▶**. Up an obscure side valley **Patrishow Church▶** boasts a rare musicians' gallery and an eerie mural of a skeleton bearing a shovel, scythe and hour-glass. Further west, the A479 skirts the massif between the attractive towns of **Crickhowell** and **Talgarth** before passing through **Tretower▶**, with its fortified medieval manor (Cadw) by the ruin of an earlier castle.

The **Brecon Beacons** are really a sandstone ridge culminating in Pen y Fan 886m (2,906ft), the highest point in Wales outside Snowdonia. The graceful M shape of the twin summits is seen from far around. To the south is the little **Brecon Mountain Railway**. Brecon itself is an amiable market town with a small cathedral and a military museum. Out of town, the **Brecon Beacons Mountain Centre** is the main National Park information outlet.

Predominantly grassy upland, **Fforest Fawr** includes, near Pont Nedd Fechan, the superlative '**waterfall country**'▶▶ of the wooded Nedd, Hepste and Mellte gorges (see Walks, page 158). **Dan-yr-ogof Caves▶** near by are part of Britain's largest known cave system; one has a re-creation of a Bronze Age dwelling, another presents a history of caving in a *son et lumière*.

To the west, the **Black Mountain** is an expanse of moors and forests dominated by the craggy ridge of **Carmarthen Fan**. Much of it is for the serious walker only, but **Carreg Cennen Castle▶▶** (Cadw), a majestically placed ruin in a valley close to Llandeilo, merits a detour.

The National Park includes the highest land in South Wales

Love-spoons
Throughout rural Wales during the 17th, 18th and 19th centuries, young men would spend many long, dark evenings carving ornamental wooden 'love-spoons'. These would be presented as tokens to the girls or women they courted; if accepted it was a sign that courtship would lead to marriage. They are still produced as souvenirs; the Brecknock Museum in Brecon and the Welsh Folk Museum at St Fagans (see page 157) have fine collections of this genre of folk art.

■ **The industrial valleys of South Wales present a startling transition from the lonely wilds of the Brecon Beacons to the north. Here, stretching from Pontypool in the east (close to the English border) to Llanelli in the west, is one of the most strongly characterised industrial regions throughout all of Britain.** ■

'Nye' and the NHS
Aneurin Bevan, or Nye as he was fondly called, was born the son of a miner in 1897. As a boy he was himself a miner and had early trade union experience in the South Wales Miners Federation. In 1929 he was elected MP for Ebbw Vale and held the seat until he died in 1960. One of parliament's greatest orators, he has gone down in history as the minister who in 1948 introduced the National Health Service providing the people of Britain with a comprehensive medical, dental and welfare service funded largely by general taxation.

An old pit head

How green was my valley Between narrow fingers of abruptly rising ridges runs a series of deep dales grooved with houses built in long terraces in the heyday of the industrial prosperity of the Valleys.

Towards the end of the 18th century, the Industrial Revolution heralded a new dawn; peasants from rural areas migrated *en masse* into the Valleys as ironmasters established works at Aberdare, Dowlais, Hirwaun and Merthyr Tydfil. In 1804 Richard Trevithick signalled the birth of the railway age with his steam railway from Merthyr to Abercynon. The Merthyr ironworks supplied cannon for the British forces in the Napoleonic wars and rails for railways across the globe.

Coal, choirs and rugby Later, iron production ceased and the Valleys specialised in coal extraction; the coalfield witnessed a great influx of new population. Work was hard, and often dangerous, but community life brought its rewards – passions for rugby union and choral singing; the Valleys choirs still carry away the honours at the International Eisteddfod (see panels, pages 160 and 163). Numerous leading socialists were born and bred here, including Aneurin Bevan, son of a miner who was to be the instigator of the National Health Service (see panel), and Neil Kinnock, former leader of the Labour Party.

Facing the future Now most of the collieries have gone, the coal seams exploited beyond the point of satisfactory economic return. The smoke has cleared from the air, and vegetation has returned; conifer plantations cloak the upper slopes. Tower Colliery at Hirwaun, the last of the the nationally owned pits, has recently been privatised; but open-cast mining continues and some 90 private mines are operated, providing employment for some 850 people. Unemployment overall, however, is running high and houses stand empty.

Service industries are alive, and the area has awakened to its tourist potential. At Pontypool there is the Valleys Inheritance Centre, which chronicles the story of a typical mining valley. The major heritage museum is the Big Pit Mining Museum in Blaenavon, where former miners, well-stocked with anecdotes, show visitors the pit-head showers, winding machine and the depths of the mine. There are *guided tours*, too, round the casting sheds of the nearby Blaenavon Ironworks, whose blast furnaces date from the 18th century.

There is a limit, however, to the number of such attractions that can be opened up for visitors.

► **Cardiff** 151A4

Although it is located in the industrial heartland of Wales, Cardiff is a surprisingly clean and liveable place. Despite its status as Welsh capital and as home of Welsh rugby union and of the (much-acclaimed) Welsh National Opera, Cardiff is not a particularly Welsh city. Bute Park cuts a swathe by the banks of the Taff, close to the civic centre, a gleaming group in Portland stone begun in the 1890s. **Cardiff Castle►►** dates from Norman times but had money poured into it in the 1860s and onwards by the fabulously wealthy 2nd Marquess of Bute (who built the city's docks and made Cardiff the world's prime coal port); the result was a mock-medieval fantasy of Ludwig II proportions, designed by William Burges.

Cardiff has a fine array of **museums►►**. At the wide-ranging **National Museum of Wales**, collections include a group of paintings by French impressionists as well as silver, ceramics, fossils, dinosaur skeletons and shells. Cardiff Bay, where the harbour and docklands are being revived through ambitious new development, now has numerous attractions: engines, early locos and boats are on show at the **Welsh Industrial and Maritime Museum**, while a three-dimensional model of the bay can be seen in the futuristic **Cardiff Bay Visitor Centre**, and **Techniquest** is one of the largest hands-on science cen-

157

Castell Coch
Another fairy-tale concoction of William Burges was Castell Coch (Cadw), on the edge of Cardiff, designed for the 3rd Marquess of Bute. It was never completed, but there are hints at what might have been in the breath-taking splendour of the giltwork, painting, tiles, statues and carvings. Murals of Aesop's fables decorate the drawing room, while the ceiling of Lady Bute's bedroom is painted with the story of Sleeping Beauty.

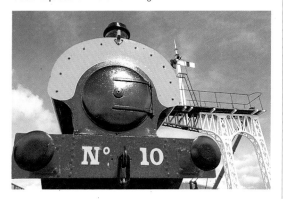

A locomotive on show at the Welsh Industrial and Maritime Museum; other galleries display trams, shipping, cars and industrial engines

tres in the country, a 'wonderland of science and technology' for all age and experience levels.

The medieval **Llandaff Cathedral►** is dominated by the figure of 'Christ in Majesty' by Jacob Epstein, an impressive if not totally likeable creation in concrete. The **Welsh Folk Museum►►►** at nearby **St Fagans** has a collection of rural dwellings from all over Wales, including a farmhouse, a terrace from the mining valleys, a Unitarian chapel and domestic bygones.

A little north of Cardiff, double-moated **Caerphilly Castle►►** (Cadw), dating from the 13th and 14th centuries, is the largest castle in England and Wales after Windsor. South of Abergavenny, **Big Pit Mining Museum**, in Blaenavon►►, is the best attraction in the industrial Valleys, successfully capturing the atmosphere of a working mine (see opposite page).

Walks

Dinas Island, Pembrokeshire *150B1*
Coast National Park, Pembrokeshire

Off the A487 east of Fishguard; car park near 'Sailors' Safety Inn'. The 'island' is in fact a peninsula, ideal for an exhilarating circular walk of 1 to 1½ hours along the clifftop path, passing Dinas Head, the highest point, and Needle Rock, with its large birdlife population. A well-trodden public foot-path cuts across the narrow neck of land to complete the circuit.

Llyn Idwal, Snowdonia *150E2*
National Park, Gwynedd

Car park by Idwal Cottage Youth Hostel on the A5. The nature trail around Llyn (lake) Idwal gives straightforward access to supremely dramatic scenery, passing the crags of the Devil's Kitchen beneath Glyder Fawr (1½ hours). The slopes support a rare flora, including alpine species, and the area is a designated National Nature Reserve. Trail leaflet available on site.

Moel Fammau, Denbighshire *151E4*

Car park and picnic site on the B5429 between Llanbedr-Dyffryn-Clwyd and Llandyrnog. The walk up from the road to the partly collapsed Jubilee Tower gives views westwards to Snowdonia and eastwards to the Peak District. Start from the picnic site and walk through the forest (following blue or red markers); return along the open ridge to drop to the road, then turn left to the starting point. (1½ hours)

The Nedd, Hepste and *151B3*
Mellte waterfalls, Brecon
Beacons National Park, Powys

Car park at Pontneddfechan, east of Glyn Neath. These mighty waterfalls crash their way along wooded gorges in the southern fringes of the National Park. The Hepste and Mellte Falls can be reached by a woodland path from Craig y Ddinas car park at the east end of Pontneddfechan or from Porth yr Ogof to the north; the highlight is Sgwd yr Ira, where you can walk behind the curtain of the fall. (1 to 2 hours)

Symonds Yat, Lower *151B4*
Wye Valley, Herefordshire border

Car park at end of the B4432, north of Coleford. This renowned viewpoint over the Wye gives access to one of the prettiest parts of the gorge. Descend to the west, past a refresh-ment kiosk and on a waymarked path to the riverside Saracen's Head Inn, where a chain ferry takes you across. Turn left on the far bank to the wire suspension bridge (it will bounce as you cross); return on the old railway track on the east bank. (1½ hours)

Pennygarreg Reservoir Dam, Elan

►► **Elan Valley and the Cambrian Mountains** *151C3*

One of the best places for spotting the rare red kite, the **Elan Valley** is a chain of reservoirs gracing the great unpopulated wilds of the Cambrian Mountains. The lakes supply water to Birmingham, and both the dams and Elan village, built for the reservoir workers, are in characteristically solid Edwardian waterworks style. The Elan Valley Visitor Centre in Elan village has details of walks; the trackbed of an old railway used in construction of the reservoirs makes for enjoyable lakeside strolls. An exciting **mountain road►►** climbs the Cambrian range, leaving Rhayader for the Elan Valley and continuing past abandoned lead and zinc mines to **Devil's Bridge►**, where three bridges, stacked one upon the other, span a gorge. A narrow-gauge **steam railway►** with quaint carriages runs from here to **Aberystwyth**, the main seaside resort for Cardigan Bay. The bay-windowed Victorian guesthouses on the seafront overlook a shingle beach, hemmed in by the bulky bluff of Constitution Hill from where you can see Snowdonia and the Preseli Hills. A cliff railway makes an effortless ascent to the top and a camera obscura enhances the panorama on sunny days.

►► **Erddig** *151D4*

Although not a particularly distinguished house architecturally, Erddig (NT), 3km (2 miles) south of Wrexham, is an excellent introduction to life below stairs in a country mansion. The National Trust rescued the house when mining subsidence threatened the structure; all the service buildings and most of the contents had survived intact and it is now preserved as a fascinating picture of the workings of a country estate in the 18th and 19th centuries. The Yorke family, who lived here from 1733 to 1973, treated its servants kindly and as a visitor you see the house somewhat through a servant's eyes, entering not by the main door but through the servants' quarters, where portraits and photographs of generations of domestic staff hang on the walls.

Devil's Bridge
The oldest of the three bridges here dates back at least as far as the 12th century and was used by Cistercian monks from nearby Strata Florida. Legend has it that the Devil built it to assist a woman whose cow was stranded on the far side of the river; the Devil in return was to have the first living creature to go across. However, the woman threw a piece of meat over and a mangy dog crossed the bridge to get it. The other bridges were built in 1753 and 1901.

Far left: the family bicycle collection at Erddig

■ **Look at any holiday brochure or tourist poster for Wales and you are likely to come across the same well-worn images: male voice choirs; young girls in chimneypot Welsh hats playing the harp; mist-shrouded mountains and lakes; and rugged mining valleys. Like all clichés, they convey only a superficial picture. The reality is far more varied and vital: a combination of sentimental reverence for the past and passionate concern for the future. One element links all the many strands of politics and culture in Wales: a fervent sense of Welsh identity.** ■

The National Eisteddfod
Welsh-language culture is seen at its most robust at an eisteddfod. All over the country, local eisteddfodau (literally 'sittings') are set up in schools and chapels and singers, dancers, musicians, actors, artists and writers of all ages compete to reach the next level in the categories of Awdl (a complex, ancient form of Welsh poetry) and Pryddest (free verse). The nationwide contest culminates, in the first week of August, in the National Eisteddfod, presided over by the Gorsedd of Bards in their druidic robes.

Lloyd George (1863–1945), Wales' finest statesman

Dylan Thomas summed up the eccentricity and claustrophobia of small-town Welsh life in his play *Under Milk Wood*. The action is set in Llareggub, a mythical fishing community whose name should be read backwards for full impact, and one of its residents, the Reverend Eli Jenkins, captures the emotional exuberance of Welsh culture with his cry 'Praise the Lord! We are a musical nation!' Music and poetry have an influence which is recognised and nurtured in Wales. The famous male voice choirs, some of which now perform and record all over the world, are still rooted in the close mining communities of South Wales and the farming and slate-mining areas of the north; and the Eisteddfod (presided over by Bards chosen for their contributions to Welsh life) is a well-known celebration of Welsh culture and an important focus for the 500,000 or so Welsh-speakers remaining in Wales (see panel).

The Welsh language The survival of this ancient Celtic language – one of Europe's oldest – does much to explain the defensive pride of the Welsh. Banned from use in official channels by Henry VIII, one of the Welsh Tudor dynasty, the language lived on in the home and in the arts. Fluency in English became essential for anyone wishing to get on in life, and many parents with ambitions for their children favoured and encouraged its use. But Welsh continued to be the language of worship, and as Nonconformist chapels sprang up in the wake of religious revival, it survived as the linchpin of many communities.

Political issues With new generations came new attitudes, and the 20th century saw a battle to re-establish Welsh education. Plaid Cymru, the Welsh Nationalist Party (which now has several MPs in Westminster), began in the 1920s calling for a return to the agrarian, Welsh-speaking way of life – a call not welcomed by the struggling industrial communities of South Wales, where socialism still has a firm hold.

In the 1960s and '70s, nationalism took a more radical turn, as young members of Cymdeithas yr Iaith Gymraeg (the Welsh Language Society) kept the 'language issue' in the headlines with campaigns such as the painting out of Anglicised placenames on road signs. In recent years the

language has enjoyed a revival – it is included in the statutory school curriculum, a Welsh TV channel has been established and a lively pop culture has developed, willing to absorb the dreaded Anglo-American influence. Today you will hear Welsh spoken by children and their elders in much of north and west Wales particularly, and Welsh is taught in schools.

The current 'hot' political issue in Wales is immigration and the decline of Welsh communities. A small minority of activists have attracted publicity and hostility by setting fire to a series of empty second homes. Meanwhile English 'incomers' living on the northern Lleyn peninsula have been issued with threats and deadlines for leaving the country. Most Welsh people are quick to condemn these acts, which veil the very real fears of communities whose younger generations are leaving in search of work, while cottages are sold at unaffordable prices to absent landlords and stand empty for half the year, turning once vibrant areas into sad and ghostly places.

Conflict in the field For a glimpse of the whole Welsh nation at its sentimental and raucous best, try and get hold of a ticket for one of the international rugby matches at Cardiff Arms Park – preferably Wales vs England, when rivalry is keen and emotions are high. Hearing a stadium full of fans singing the Welsh anthem before watching what they regard as their national game is enough to bring a lump to the throat – whatever the final result might be.

As part of the Eisteddfod druid ceremony, a hand-maiden makes her offering to the crown bard

The 'Welsh Not'
In 1847, education commissioners preparing a report for the government visited schools in Wales, where they heard children using Welsh, which they attacked as immoral and backward. Thus a campaign to stamp out the use of Welsh was rigorously pursued – often by the Welsh themselves. Pupils slipping into the language were forced to wear wooden boards around their necks bearing the words 'Welsh Not'. The report, bound between blue covers, was never really forgiven and has passed into Welsh history as the Treason of the Blue Books.

WALES

162

A Norman stronghold
Like southern Pembrokeshire, the Gower has been a 'little England beyond Wales', with a long history of English-speaking. In the 12th century the Normans held the Gower and built a chain of castles, of which remains exist at Oxwich, Oystermouth, Pennard, Penrice and Weobley.

Taking the waters
Llandrindod Wells, Builth Wells, Llangammarch Wells and Llanwrtyd Wells constitute the spa towns of Mid Wales. In 1732, Revd Theophilus Evans tried the highly sulphurous waters and found a cure for his skin ailment. Chalybeate and saline springs were discovered close by and the area became known as a place for taking the waters. A Mrs Jenkins found a sulphur source in 1736 at Llandrindod, and by the 1830s Llangammarch was offering barium chloride as a remedy for heart conditions.

Llandrindod Wells: its hotels recall its heyday as a spa

▶▶　　Gower Peninsula　　　　150A2

The Gower peninsula stretches out west of Swansea. The residential and industrial outskirts of that city abruptly give way to green countryside, rolling commons and a coast that, on its southern seaboard, is the rival in miniature of Pembrokeshire (see pages 165–6). It has great limestone cliffs and superb sandy beaches, followed for their length by a coast path, while the north seaboard is low-lying and marshy. There is some resort development, but generally the Gower is rural and unspoilt.

The western tip is the best part of all: here **Rhossili Down**, a moorland ridge with views of the entire peninsula, dips to a sublime and seemingly endless beach; westwards stretches **Worms Head**, a high-tide island accessible on foot by those courageous enough. Near by, **Mewslade Bay** shows rock strata tilted and folded, just like a geography textbook. Further east are more good beaches at **Oxwich Bay** and at tiny **Brandy Cove**. Gower oddities include **Llanrhidian village**, with a mysteriously carved leper stone in the church and a village green dominated by a pair of gigantic stones.

▶　　Llandrindod Wells　　　　151C3

A rare instance of a spa town whose traditions are still alive. A few years ago Llandrindod's Victorian pump-room was semi-derelict; today it stands proudly in restored state and you can sample the rusty-tasting waters spurting from a nearby fountain. Grand redbrick terraces and spa hotels, ornate wrought-iron arcades and balconies and spacious tree-lined streets suggest something larger than a town of under 5,000 in the heart of Mid Wales sheep country. Somehow it has kept its period character, and it deserves the success of its Victorian Festival – held in late August or early September – when barrel organs and civic pomp return to the streets, and half the town wears period dress for the occasion.

Cefnllys▶ is an Iron Age hillfort finely sited above the River Ithon by a lone church and the (now robust) Shaky Bridge. There is a nature trail along the river.

The **Beulah to Abergwesyn road▶▶**, an old drovers' road to the southwest of the town, takes a spectacular course over the wilderness of the Cambrian Mountains.

Towards New Radnor, the interestingly named **Water-break-its-neck▶** waterfall is to be found north of the A44

in Radnor Forest, a lonely massif of rounded hills and steep-sided valleys. **Old Radnor Church►** is arguably the finest parish church in Wales, with a lovely medieval screen, Britain's oldest organ case and a font hewn from a prehistoric monolith.

►► Llangollen, Vale of 150D4

This deep valley, hemmed in by natural terraces of limestone crags, is a landmark on the A5. From it the A542 rises up the hairpin bends of the **Horseshoe Pass**, engineered by Thomas Telford. **Llangollen** itself, venue for the world-famous international musical eisteddfod (see panel), is of little intrinsic interest but is a busy tourist centre, convenient for a number of attractions. On the valley floor stand the picturesque ruins of **Valle Crucis Abbey►** (Cadw), a Cistercian foundation of 1201; notable features are the Early English west façade and the vaulted 14th-century chapter house. An outstanding timber roof installed in St Gollen's in Llangollen is said to have been taken from here. On the edge of Llangollen, horse-drawn barge trips operate along the **Llangollen Canal**; the canal's proudest moment occurs further east as it crosses the valley on the Pontcysyllte Aqueduct, 38m (126ft) above the valley and built by Telford in 1805. Above town is the **Panorama Walk**, really a small road but quite panoramic. Even better views, extending towards the Berwyn hills, are had by making the steep climb up to the spectacularly placed ruins of **Castell Dinas Bran►►**, built about 1236.

The view from Castell Dinas Bran towards the Vale of Llangollen

The Llangollen International Eisteddfod
Established in 1947, this eisteddfod (see panel, page 160) has become a major international musical competition, now attracting competitors from 30 countries. The hugely popular event takes place in the first week of July. During this time, informal performances by groups of musicians and dancers take place on the Dee Bridge. Llangollen is also home of the European Centre for Traditional and Regional Cultures.

A wind turbine at the Centre for Alternative Technology

164

The Centre for Alternative Technology

The centre was established in 1974 as a place for promoting environmentally friendly technologies. A water-powered cliff railway whisks you up to the site entrance and a trail takes you around an informative exhibition which includes an energy-efficient house, ecologically oriented gardens and displays of solar heating and other alternative energy sources. Although obviously an idealist set-up, the centre is a great place for talking to people (several workers live on site), and learning how to cut your energy bills, improve your garden and give a greener tinge to your lifestyle. Plenty of appeal for children.

Just south of town, **Plas Newydd**▶▶ is a remarkable mock-Tudor inspiration, home for half a century from 1780 to eccentric recluses, Lady Eleanor Butler and Miss Sarah Ponsonby, the 'Ladies of Llangollen'. They transformed a cottage into this eye-catching half-timbered house, where they entertained a distinguished line of guests, including Sir Walter Scott and the Duke of Wellington. The house is whimsical in the extreme and full of personal touches.

Pistyll Rhayader▶, Wales' tallest waterfall, is at the head of a remote valley south of Llangollen. The fall has been engineered to give the water a twist as it tumbles, but the effect is pleasing. There is easy access by road.

Pistyll Rhayader, Wales' most spectacular waterfall

Machynlleth   151C3

A market town centred on a clocktower (of a design that seems to be mandatory for Welsh towns), Machynlleth sits comfortably in the peaceful hills south of the Snowdonia National Park. It is an uneventful place in a pleasant kind of way. The town's hinterland is partly inhabited by a significant hippy population. Topping the bill of local attractions is the excellent **Centre for Alternative Technology**▶ (see panel).

The road to Dylife▶ is a scenic drive over the shoulder of Plynlimon, a boggy upland from which rise the Wye and the Severn, the two great rivers of Wales. At Dylife a stream plummets into a gorge via Ffrwd Fawr, a splendid waterfall. A memorial viewpoint (view indicator) at a curve in the road takes in Cader Idris, the major summit in southern Snowdonia.

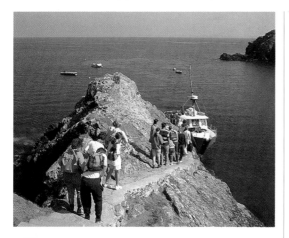

A boat trip leaves Martin's Haven for Skomer Island

Island hops
Skokholm and Skomer are major bird sanctuaries, supporting the largest concentration of Manx shearwaters in Britain. Puffins abound on Skomer, and Skokholm has a population of storm petrels. Boat trips start from Martin's Haven. Ramsey Island harbours numerous grey seals, which can be seen off the mainland too, and cliff-nesting birds including choughs; boat trips begin from Whitesands Bay and St Justinian. Caldey Island, reached by boat from Tenby, is home to a community of Cistercian monks.

165

▶▶▶ Pembrokeshire Coast National Park   *150B1*

As its name implies, the National Park is largely confined to a coastal strip. Here are magnificent cliffs, sandy coves (many excellent for swimming if you can bear the chilly water), complex natural harbours and a diversity of wildlife which ranks on a par with the best of Cornwall. The south and north parts of the park are strikingly different: a wave-cut platform, now raised high above sea level, leaves the southern cliffs mostly level-topped, while further north the scene is more dramatic, with assertive bluffs, soaring headlands and exciting changes in height. Southern Pembrokeshire was for a long time a 'little England beyond Wales', owned by the English, who left a legacy of English placenames and Norman castles for keeping watch over the unruly Welsh. Regrettably, the Army's foothold on the south coast in the vicinity of Castlemartin means restricted access. Walking is the main draw of the north, which is less populated and consequently less busy in season. Scenic drives are very few as the roads generally keep too far inland; a much better bet is to take in some of the coastal path, which snakes around the intricate seaboard for some 290km (180 miles). A car will, however, get you into the wilds of the Preseli Hills (see panel, page 166).

Towns and villages Most famous is undoubtedly **St David's▶▶▶**. Scarcely more than a large village of craft shops, galleries and cafés, it keeps its great Norman cathedral half-hidden in a valley, alongside the considerable ruins of a 14th-century bishop's palace (Cadw). Allegedly, relics of St David, patron saint of Wales, lie beneath the altar. Of the coastal towns, **Tenby▶▶** is perhaps the most seductive, with its maze of narrow streets, a harbour surrounded by tiers of colour-washed Georgian and Tudor merchants' houses, a castle up the rise and a five-arched gate in the town wall. It is very pretty – and suffers for it in summer, with bumper-to-bumper traffic. **Pembroke▶** is less important than one somehow expects, a one-street market town completely dominated by an exceptional Norman castle, occasionally the venue for public medieval banquets. **Fishguard** is split in two by the lie of the land, with the lower town crowded around the

St David's Cathedral: 39 steps (or 'Articles') lead down to its door

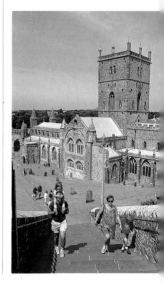

WALES

The inland hills
The Pembrokeshire Coast National Park also encompasses the Preseli Hills, a tract of remote upland near Fishguard that is scattered with the burial mounds and hillforts of early settlers. It was from here that the bluestone rocks were transported to Wiltshire for the construction of Stonehenge (see page 84), a feat that has baffled archaeologists. The rocks may have been moved by raft: this is technically feasible but more plausible perhaps is the theory that they were naturally moved closer to Stonehenge by glaciers during the last ice age, possibly to the Somerset Mendips.

The Welshpool and Llanfair Railway
The privately operated steam railway operates along 13km (8 miles) of track between Welshpool and Llanfair Caereinion. Its chief distinguishing features are the narrow (76cm/30in) gauge and the antique wooden carriages from the Zillertal in Austria.

Tiny St Govan's Chapel, tucked in the cliffs, can be reached on foot by taking the coastal path from Bosherston Lily Ponds

harbour, and the upper town grouped around sloping streets. Ferries depart from nearby Goodwick to Rosslare in Ireland; day trips to Dublin are possible. The village of Solva▶ is a boating centre and one-time port prettily set at the end of a narrow and steep-sided bay.

The best of the coast In the south, the indented headlands and traceried bays around **Dale** and **Milford Haven** (itself an industrial port adjacent to oil refineries, but worth seeing for its natural harbour site) have constantly changing views, while **Wooltack Point▶▶** near Marloes gives views across to Skomer and Skokholm islands. At **Bosherston** a series of **lily ponds▶** makes a popular walk which can be tagged on to a visit to a fine beach. On the margins of some luscious estuarine landscape east of Milford Haven is **Carew Castle**, adjacent to a tide mill and a superb 11th-century Celtic cross. Perched among Pembrokeshire's cliffs are three primitive hermitage chapels, **St Govan's**, just west of St Govan's Head, **St Justinian's** and **St Non's** (both near St David's). **St David's Head▶▶** and **Strumble Head▶** have rugged grandeur; it is sometimes possible to see the Wicklow Mountains in Ireland from these. Among the most popular bathing beaches are **St Bride's Bay**, **Tenby**, **Saundersfoot** and **Whitesands Bay**, but there are numerous smaller ones offering greater privacy.

▶▶ Powis Castle   151D4
A great border stronghold, owned by the Herbert family from 1587 to 1952, Powis (NT) stands just outside Welshpool. It is memorable for its superb gardens (terraced in the 18th century), its remarkable architectural continuity, and its lavish state apartments with fine panelling and plaster work.

Montgomery▶ More English than Welsh in character, the tiny town centre is focused upon a gracious square with an 18th-century town hall and a pleasing assemblage of plum-red brick façades that date from Elizabethan times. The castle mound above town was the stronghold of Roger de Montgomery, who in the 13th century launched assaults on the Welsh.

▶▶▶ **Snowdonia National Park** *151D3*

Snowdonia is unsurpassed among the national parks of England and Wales for the wild drama of its scenery. Ideal for walking, rock-climbing and horse-riding, it has a fair offering of scenic drives, although these tend to be confined to valley routes and are limited in scope.

The main mountain group is quite compact, centred on Snowdon, the highest point in England and Wales. Perhaps the hallmark of Snowdonia is the individuality of each of the main summits: each has its distinctive shape and visitors soon find their personal favourites.

Snowdonia's coast is disappointing, ribboned as it is by main roads and with no cliffs to speak of. Sightseeing interest on the other hand is particularly rich, with a host of nostalgic railways, old mines, and medieval castles.

The main centres In northern Snowdonia **Betws-y-coed** (pronounced 'bettus-ee coe-ed') is a touristy village of Victorian hotels and craft shops. It has grand scenery on its doorstep and walks along the Llugwy River and the Swallow Falls, and a series of attractive reservoirs close by to the west; the big mountains keep hidden, however. Also central and with a touch more charm, the Victorian mountain resort village of **Beddgelert▶** lies close to the Aberglaslyn Gorge, Moel Hebog and Snowdon. A much-publicised but probably bogus attraction here is Gelert's Grave, Gelert being the noble 13th-century Prince Llywelyn's dog. An absorbing tour can be taken round **Sygun Copper Mine▶▶** (but be prepared for crouching, climbing 100 steps and smoky explosions). **Bala** too gets busy in high season; Wales' largest lake adjoins it, but the scenery is not quite so stupendous.

Of the north coast seaside resorts **Llandudno▶** is by far the most attractive. It is one of Britain's best-preserved Victorian seaside towns, with its elegant curving bay, its pier, Punch and Judy shows on the sands and a mountain tram up to Great Ormes Head. **Conwy▶▶▶**, also on the coast but a historic walled town, is the most rewarding town for casual wandering, with a splendid castle and what is reputed to be Britain's smallest house. **Caernarfon▶▶▶**, too, boasts a great castle and is a place everyone should try to visit (although for some it may be too far out to appeal as a base). **Harlech▶▶** straddles a slope above marshland, one of the few portions of this coast not to be followed by a main road; good beaches lie to the south. The castle is the spectacular attraction.

Mountains of slate-spoil surround **Blaenau Ffestiniog**, at the heart of the Snowdonia slate industry. A town of slate roofs upon sturdy terraced houses, it is not pretty but has curiosity value and is right in the centre; it is establishing itself as a tourist venue now that the old **Llechwedd Slate Caverns▶▶** have been opened to the public. At **Llanberis** is the **Welsh Slate Museum▶** and a branch of the National Museum of Wales, **Dinorwic Discovery▶** which offers trips to Dinorwig underground hydroelectric storage station. There are also tours at the **Gloddfa Ganol Slate Mine** and the hydroelectric power station nearby at Tanygrisiau.

Dolgellau▶, the only town inside the national park, is a place of grey-stone houses and narrow streets; life revolves around its market place. It makes a good base for

Great little trains of Snowdonia
The *Snowdon Mountain Railway* climbs 1,000m (3,281ft) from Llanberis to the summit: many people walk back down. *Ffestiniog Railway*, built for the slate industry and now one of the most scenic of all Britain's private railways, runs from Porthmadog to Blaenau Ffestiniog. *Bala Lake* and *Llanberis Lake* railways run alongside the lakes from which they take their names. The shorter *Welsh Highland Railway* starts from Porthmadog.

Cadw season tickets
Most of the great castles of Wales – including Conwy, Caernarvon, Harlech, Beaumaris and Dolbadarn – and other ancient monuments are in the care of Cadw, the Welsh Historic Monuments Commission. Cadw (tel: 01222 500200) offers 3-day, weekly, and annual passes to its properties.

WALES

touring southern Snowdonia and has some excellent easier walks on its doorstep, including Cregennan Lakes at the foot of Cader Idris, and the Precipice Walk (hair-raising for those with tiny children) above the Mawddach Gorge. Further west, near the seaside resort of Barmouth, the railway bridge across the Mawddach carries a footpath that makes a highly memorable walk in its own right.

The major peaks The king of them all, **Snowdon** (Yr Wddfa in Welsh) rises high and majestic to 1,085m (3,307ft), five ridges (known collectively as Eryri, 'abode of eagles') radiating from its central pyramid. Not surprisingly, it is the most popular mountain ascent, not just because it is the highest, but also because of the views both on the way up and from the top.

Paths approach from all directions, or you can cheat and use the Snowdon Mountain Railway (see page 167); the route from Llanberis, parallel to the railway, is the easiest but least interesting path, while the Horseshoe Route (along knife-edge ridges) is the most enthralling and demanding.

The first half of the Miners' Track from Pen y Pass (see page 170) takes you into the wilds, rising past lakes and abandoned copper mines to a splendid corrie beneath the summit and main ascent – this initial stage provides an unchallenging way of sampling a great mountain route.

Classic, post-glacial scenery – this is the towering form of Y Garn, seen across Llyn (lake) Ogwen

Almost as high as Snowdon, and just as spectacular, are **Glyder Fawr** (999m/3,278ft) and **Glyder Fach** (994m/3,264ft), two peaks on a great ridge with rock pinnacles and precipitous drops, the **Carneddau group** and (lower but with good views) **Moel Siabod** (872m/2,861ft). The southern giant is **Cader Idris** (893m/2,930ft), a complex sprawling mass with gentle slopes but huge panoramas.

Houses, castles and gardens Penrhyn Castle►► is an imposing mock-Norman pile built by slate magnate Lord Penrhyn in the mid-19th century; architect Thomas Hopper gave it battlements and turrets, and a grandiose interior which epitomises high living of the period. Genuine castles abound in Snowdonia. Most famous of all is **Caernarfon Castle►►►** (Cadw), begun in 1283 after Edward I's conquest of Wales. It was the setting in 1969 for the investiture of the Prince of Wales; his investiture robes are on show here, together with a display of the dynasty of the Welsh princes. **Harlech Castle►►►** (Cadw), also founded in 1283, has a fine site above the coast; although seemingly impregnable it was taken by Owain Glyndwr in 1404. **Conwy Castle►►►** (Cadw), another of Edward I's foundations, is sited in the town wall (which you can walk around); it has 21 semi-circular towers and overlooks a castellated suspension bridge, one of some 1,200 bridges designed by Thomas Telford between 1792 and his death in 1834. Much less substantial, but beautifully set among the hills, are the castles of **Dolwyddelan►** (Cadw) (near Blaenau Ffestiniog) and **Castell y Bere►** (Cadw) (near Abergynolwyn).

Bodnant Gardens►►, near Llanrwst, rate among Britain's finest horticultural creations. Try to visit **Portmeirion►►**, an Italianate *trompe l'oeil* fantasy village created in this century (see Accommodation, page 279). It was used as a film set for the TV series *The Prisoner*, and Noel Coward wrote *Blithe Spirit* here.

Caernarfon Castle, where the eldest royal son receives the title of Prince of Wales

The Canal Terrace at Bodnant Gardens

SNOWDONIA NATIONAL PARK

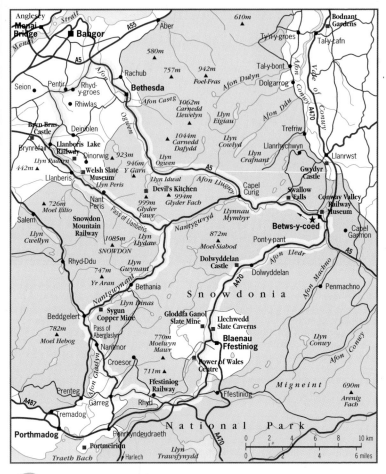

Drive **Snowdonia National Park**

A circuit of the grandest uplands in Wales (approx. 100km/65 miles).

Start at **Betws-y-coed** and take the A5 past the entrance to the spectacular **Swallow Falls▶** to Capel Curig. Continue past Llyn (lake) Ogwen; from the car park at its far end, a short path leads to **Llyn Idwal▶▶**, beneath the vast crags of the Devil's Kitchen (see Walks, page 158). Beyond the mining town of **Bethesda** take the B4409 then the A4086 past **Llanberis,** base station for the

Snowdon Mountain Railway▶. At the top of the **Llanberis Pass**, the Miners' Track and Pyg Track leave for an exciting ascent of **Snowdon**. Continue on the A498 past **Beddgelert▶** and along the **Pass of Aberglaslyn**. Take the B4410 and A496 to **Blaenau Ffestiniog**, passing **Ffestiniog Hydro-electric Station▶**, **Gloddfa Ganol Slate Mine▶** and **Llechwedd Slate Caverns▶▶**. **Dolwyddelan Castle▶**, further up the valley (A470), is supposedly the birthplace of Prince Llywelyn the Great.

The River Wye, as seen from Symonds Yat, near the end of its journey from its source on Plynlimon in Mid Wales to the Severn Estuary

►► Wye Valley 151B4

The River Wye defines the English/Welsh border for its glorious finale, as it enters a sandstone gorge whose slopes are cloaked with woodlands that display breathtaking autumn colours. Once the gorge was a hive of industrial activity, the trees supplying charcoal for iron-smelting; brass was invented here in 1568. The valley established a name for itself during the late 18th-century Romantic movement that sought a deepened appreciation of the beauties of nature. **Ross-on-Wye**, though not in the gorge proper, has a mock-Gothic town wall built in the 1830s at the time of this 'picturesque discovery'. Its much-photographed arcaded market house is two centuries older. **Symonds Yat►**, a rock reached by a stairway, overlooks a meander of the Wye; paths lead steeply down to the river, which is crossed by chain ferry (see Walk, page 158). **Goodrich Castle►** is an impressive 12th-century sandstone bulk, intact until a Parliamentary siege in the Civil War.

The Monnow flows into the Wye at **Monmouth►**, the Monnow spanned by a medieval bridge with a fortified gateway incorporated into it. Above the town, a rustic folly commemorating admirals of the Napoleonic wars caps **Kymin Hill►**, a good viewpoint. Turner painted and Wordsworth revered the ruins of **Tintern Abbey►►** (Cadw), in a setting on the valley floor that illustrates the Cistercian eye for a fine site. This is one of the great medieval abbey ruins, roofless but standing to its original height. Its exquisite tracery includes an impressive east window.

Chepstow has a formidable Norman **castle►►** (Cadw) with keep and mighty curtain wall. The main street rises up to a gateway in the Port Walls, the town wall. Above the east bank, **Wintour's Leap** is a quarried cliff-face by the road with a dizzy drop to the river, while the **Wynd Cliff►**, on the west bank, offers a wider view.

One of the world's first iron bridges – the Regency bridge over the Wye, at Chepstow

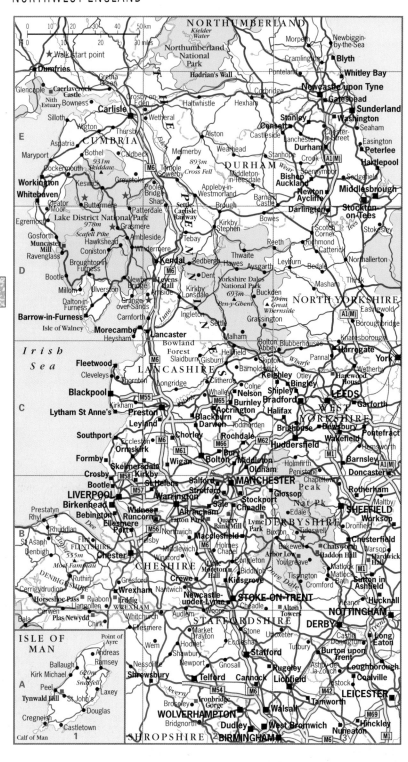

Northwest England This strip covers the region from the industrial northern Midlands to the Scottish border. The most hallowed feature is doubtless the **Lake District**, within the northerly county of Cumbria.

Lake District delights Here the lakes, high fells, pastures and woodlands offer constantly changing vistas of unrivalled scenic beauty. It is all at a perfect scale for exploration on foot, as equally suited for those wanting a gentle saunter with the mountains as a backdrop as for aspiring rock-climbers; boat trips on the lakes add a further option. Roads and car parks get annoyingly busy in peak periods, but out of season driving is a delight. Public transport is a feasible option (Ambleside and Keswick would make good bases) but it restricts what can be visited. The Lake District scores highly for quantity and quality of accommodation, for the range of sights suitable for those all-too-frequent rainy days and for the scope of other outdoor activities, which include sailing, mountain biking, horse-riding and angling (swimming in the lakes is discouraged because of undercurrents). As a general rule, the western Lake District is more remote and has more spectacle, the east is milder, more crowded and has more indoor sights.

The rest of Cumbria Outside the Lake District, the rest of Cumbria offers a long and not especially beautiful coastline, but an interesting one: along it are the early industrial town of Whitehaven, well worth a visit, St Bees Head (ideal for birdwatching) and the free visitor centre at Sellafield nuclear reprocessing plant, set up to woo support for the nuclear industry. Northern Cumbria is fairly flat; views across the Solway Firth to southern Scotland and the bits-and-pieces historic city of Carlisle are redeeming features. Southern Cumbria is fringed by the great expanse of Morecambe Bay, an important site for wading birds and the setting for Britain's fastest incoming tides; tourist offices have details of guided walks over the bay (follow routes precisely to avoid the quicksands).

Lancashire, Merseyside and Greater Manchester The more built-up parts of Morecambe Bay lie within **Lancashire** – Blackpool, Morecambe and Southport were developed as resorts to serve the cotton-mill towns which in the 19th century changed the face of the county

Below (left): Dove Dale, the best-known limestone valley in the Peak District, needs time to be savoured in full

*Bakewell's livestock
market, one of the
busiest in Northern
England*

and heralded a major phase in the industrialisation of Great Britain. The mills have closed or changed to other uses but these urban landscapes, immortalised by the paintings of L S Lowry (see panel, page 183), still exist, the straight lines of millworkers' terraced houses being a particularly striking feature: Burnley and Accrington are examples. Manchester and Liverpool were the great cities created by this expansion; today Manchester is distinctly more prosperous, but Liverpool wins on museums and general atmosphere. The Forest of Bowland in northern Lancashire is, despite its name, a tract of high, open country; access is limited but there are exhilarating views.

Cheshire, Derbyshire and Staffordshire Cheshire extends from the Welsh border to the brink of the Peak National Park; between lies a fertile plain, pockmarked by tiny lakes and ponds called meres. Black and white half-timbering and red brick are predominant building materials, seen to best advantage in Chester, remarkable for its intact city walls. Cheshire, Staffordshire, Derbyshire and South Yorkshire share the **Peak District**, a very accessible and much-visited national park; although it cannot quite match the Lake District for scenic quality, it has lovely limestone dales, austere gritstone moors, caverns, the strongly contrasting houses of Chatsworth and Haddon Hall, and some charming villages, many of which indulge in the ancient annual custom of well dressing. Other houses in **Derbyshire** include Calke Abbey and Hardwick Hall. Although undistinguished visually, Derby has a clutch of good museums; Derby porcelain is on show at the Derby Museum and at Royal Crown Derby. Stoke-on-Trent (**Staffordshire**) is the china-making capital, part of the 'six towns' of the Potteries area.

Walks

Arnside Knott, Cumbria   *172D2*
Car park by seafront at Arnside. The wooded limestone hill is laced with paths to its summit, where a view opens out over the southern Lake District and Morecambe Bay, one of Europe's most important sites for waterbirds of the wader family. The quickest way up is southwards through the village, up residential roads that give way to paths. (Allow 1 hour.)

Buttermere, Lake District National Park, Cumbria   *172E1*
Car park at Buttermere village. A well-trodden path leads to Buttermere. The path round the lake is straightforward and level, but is graced with a fine mountain backdrop; the path weaves out of forest, through a section of tunnel and along the water's edge (1½ hours). Optional add-ons include the ascent of Haystacks, the jagged, dark-topped fell to the south.

Grasmere and Rydal Water, Lake District National Park, Cumbria   *172D1*
Car parks at Grasmere village. Seek out the path along the south side of these two lakes: walk past Grasmere Church on your right, take the left fork of roads to reach the lakeside path, which leaves the road near a boathouse. After a short wooded section, climb up to the level path along Loughrigg Terrace on your right for grandstand views of Wordsworth's valley. Continue on around Rydal Water or head back by dropping through woods, over a bridge and the A591 to take a minor road to Wordsworth's Dove Cottage at the edge of Grasmere village. (1½ hours)

Monsal Dale and Chee Dale, Peak National Park, Derbyshire   *172B3*
Car park at Miller's Dale (old station). Turn left along the railway track (Monsal Trail) to enter Miller's Dale; the trail is diverted from the railway as it passes through a tunnel. You pass the Wye's old textile mills, rejoin the railway and cross Monsal viaduct (2½ hours). In the other direction from the car park, the trail shortly leaves the railway track for an exciting stepping-stone route along the Wye as it enters a gorge beneath Chee Tor, a popular haunt of rock-climbers. (2 hours.)

Ullswater, Lake District National Park, Cumbria   *172D1*
Car park at Glenridding. Begin by taking the lake steamer from Glenridding to Howtown, and follow the well-trodden lakeside path back (allow 4 hours); it undulates delightfully and ducks in and out of woods with sudden vistas. An optional add-on is to climb Hallin Fell, close by Howtown, by a path up its southern side.

A Lake District scene between Rydal Water and Grasmere

175

Blackpool: roller-coaster by night

The Isle of Man
Ruled by Queen Elizabeth II, but not part of the UK (it has its own parliament) the Isle of Man has curiosity value. Its residents are called Manx, as is its almost extinct Celtic language. Manx cats are a tailless variety. Placed in the Irish Sea, the island does not enjoy the best climate and its resorts are a bit faded. Fish and chips is the rule, haute cuisine the exception. Yet to some the isle's charms are irresistible: its coastline, particularly around the fishing port of Peel and the folk museum village of Cregneish, is of high, unspoilt cliffs, while inland the hills reach surprising heights. A splendid legacy of historic railways has been preserved. and the T T Races, an annual motorcycle event since 1907, draws large crowds. Reach the island by ferry from Liverpool, Heysham and Fleetwood, or by air.

The Citadel, a prominent landmark at the centre of Carlisle

Blackpool 172C1

In Victorian times, Blackpool was the traditional day-out treat for millworkers in the Lancashire cotton towns; it is still the liveliest and brashest seaside resort in the north: it offers unsophisticated fairground fun, nightlife, pleasure gardens and views of Morecambe Bay and the Lakeland fells from Blackpool Tower. Trams travel up the seafront to Fleetwood, giving the best view of the Illuminations (August to November). The beach has had a bad record in recent years for pollution.

► Carlisle 172E1

Cumbria's largest town has recently smartened itself up as a regional shopping centre. This does not rank among the great cathedral cities, but there is enough here for an absorbing half-day in the compact historic centre.

For centuries, Carlisle was plagued by border skirmishes and the **castle►►**, dating from 1092, was much attacked and repeatedly rebuilt (the view from its walls is a real stomach-churner). The keep is 12th-century; inside, the story of the Border Regiment is told with spectacular uniforms and weapons. Don't miss the haunting graffiti carved by captives in the prison.

The castle is today rather ignominiously chopped off from the rest of the old city by a busy road. Over the way are some good Georgian and earlier streets, the medieval **cathedral►**, one of Britain's smallest, notable above all for its east window with its 14th-century glass, and an outstandingly lively city museum in **Tullie House►**.

Settle–Carlisle line►► Part of the national railway network, this most scenic line was saved in recent years by a volunteer-led campaign. From Settle, in the Yorkshire Dales, the route crosses the high Pennines in spectacular fashion, over the Ribblehead Viaduct in the shadow of

Whernside and along the Eden Valley. Special steam trains sometimes run on the route. The most dramatic landscape is between Settle and Appleby-in-Westmorland, which has a fine castle. The Appleby Horse Fair,. Britain's largest gypsy gathering, takes place in June, and features racing and fortune-telling.

▶▶▶ Chester   172B1

Founded as the Roman city of Deva, Chester was a major port until the River Dee silted up in medieval times. Its fortunes then slumped until a revival in the 18th century. Today, it has plenty to show for these three periods.

Foremost is the **city wall▶▶▶**, one of the finest in the country, which provides a fascinating 3km (2-mile) walk, raised above street level for much of the way. A number of its gateways are still *in situ* and Roman masonry can be seen here and there within it, although much of its fabric is medieval. Roman finds are exhibited at the **Grosvenor Museum▶** (*admission free*). By **Newgate**, on the east side, part of the **Roman amphitheatre** (Britain's largest) can be seen near a park that also has remains of a Roman central heating system and some re-erected columns. The staggered crossroads of the city centre, where often a picturesquely attired town crier bellows out public announcements, have Roman origins.

Of medieval Chester, the most famous feature is **The Rows**, which has an upper tier of shops above street level. Nobody quite knows why it developed this way, but its success lives on as a thriving shopping area. The central streets harbour a pleasing amalgam of half-timbered Tudor, redbrick Georgian, and exuberantly elaborate 19th-century fake black-and-white buildings. Chester's Victoriana also includes a Gothic **town hall**, where the Council Chamber and Assembly Rooms are open to the public, in Northgate Street. The red sandstone **cathedral▶▶** was restored in the 19th century, but its superbly carved 14th-century choir stalls are unaltered. Many of the abbey buildings were retained after the Reformation in the 16th century, including the chapter house and cloisters.

Chester Zoo▶ is 5km (3 miles) north up the A41. Animals roam in enclosures that simulate natural environments.

A walk along Chester's walls: Part 1
From Grosvenor Bridge (the largest single span in the world when erected in 1832), take an anti-clockwise tour of the walls, crossing Bridgegate with a pleasant boating scene a little east (boat hire available). The walls now turn north, past Newgate and the Roman amphitheatre, over Eastgate with its ornamental clock of 1897.

A walk along Chester's walls: Part 2
Skirt the cathedral precincts (Abbey Square); the northeast tower is known as the King Charles Tower since that king watched from here the defeat of his army by the Parliamentarians on Rowton Heath in 1645. By Northgate the drop on the canal side plummets spectacularly; on the south side is the Bluecoat Hospital (1717) and the sideless Bridge of Sighs, which condemned felons had to cross on their way to prison. From the Water Tower (1322) are views of the Welsh hills. The west side of the walls (where you must follow the road) has less of interest.

The principal routes of Chester's Roman gridplan meet at the Cross, the haunt of the Town Crier as well as of impromptu buskers

■ **The Lake District National Park – Lakeland, the English Lakes or just the Lakes – is a microcosm of breathtaking variety and scenic perfection that captivates the adventurous traveller. Its elusive character wavers between windswept mountainous upland and drystone-walled, sheep-nibbled lowland pastures. It is outstanding for outdoor pursuits, particularly walking, climbing and sailing, but the climate is fickle: benign-looking summer days have a habit of deteriorating alarmingly suddenly. Fortunately the area has plenty of indoor attractions, especially for literary pilgrims.** ■

178

William Wordsworth
Wordsworth was born in Cockermouth in 1770 and a happy childhood there was to influence his poetry in later life. His favourite home was Dove Cottage, in Grasmere, where he lived from 1799 to 1808, following a lifestyle of plain living and high thinking, with his wife, Mary, and sister, Dorothy. He loved the place deeply and walked over, mused upon and wrote about every corner of the vicinity; aptly, he is buried in Grasmere churchyard. Wordsworth spent the last years of his life, less happily, at Rydal Mount, dying in 1850.

Literary Lakeland
The Wordsworths were the centre of a group of friends, among them poets Samuel Taylor Coleridge and Robert Southey. Tennyson reputedly wrote *Idylls of the King* at Mirehouse, near Keswick and, later, poet Matthew Arnold and critic John Ruskin both made their homes here. In this century, Beatrix Potter wrote and illustrated her enchanting children's stories at Hill Top in Near Sawrey, while Arthur Ransome set his *Swallows and Amazons* in the Lakes.

The north and west Keswick▶, the major centre for the northern lakes, is a grey-slate Victorian town, full of walkers, tourists, and bed-and-breakfast signs. Here are the Fitzpark Museum (with its 'piano' of Cumberland slates), a unique pencil museum, and Beatrix Potter's Lake District – an audiovisual show explaining Potter's role in preserving much of Lakeland. Just east is the prehistoric **Castlerigg Stone Circle▶**. **Derwent Water▶▶▶** is breathtakingly beautiful; a boat service circuits the lake. **Lingholm Gardens▶** on its western shores look their best when the rhododendrons and azaleas are at their prime in early summer.

Borrowdale appealed to early discoverers of the 'picturesque'; Castle Crag is an excellent viewpoint. The main road heads over **Honister Pass** to skirt **Buttermere▶▶▶**, magnificently sited and looking like a miniature Scottish loch. **Cockermouth▶**, outside the Park, is a likeable market town of colourwashed terraces and odd corners.

North of Keswick, the fells flatten and the crowds disappear, but the moors have a quiet beauty of their own. **Hesket Newmarket**, with its green and its old market cross, is the prettiest village hereabouts. Southeast of Keswick, **Thirlmere▶**, a lake enlarged into a reservoir, is the most popular starting point for walks up Helvellyn (950m/3,117ft). **Ullswater▶▶▶** twists its way south from Pooley Bridge, the scenery getting better all the while; a steamer plies the length of the lake. By the A592, **Aira Force▶▶** is a popular waterfall, tumbling into a shady chasm at the side of Gowbarrow Park, the hill where Wordsworth spied that famous host of golden daffodils. East of Ullswater, **Askham▶** is a trim village of stone cottages.

The Lake District's western tracts are less accessible and have considerable escapist appeal. **Wast Water▶▶▶** is one of the great sights, looking to the heights of Great Gable, and Scafell Pike is the highest peak in England at 978m (3,207 feet). **Eskdale▶** is mellow and broad; the narrow-gauge Ravenglass and Eskdale Railway runs along the valley to the tiny village of Boot with its restored corn mill. At the dale's east end, the **Hardknott Pass▶▶▶** is the great scenic drive of Lakeland, rather like taking your car for a fell walk; the Isle of Man may be visible from the remains of a Roman fort at the top. Motorists can continue along **Wrynose Pass** or into the **Duddon Valley (Dunnerdale)**.

The south and east Windermere, England's longest lake, has wooded shores sprinkled with villas built by 19th-century industrialists; steamers ply the length of the lake and from Lakeside, at the southern end, a steam railway runs on to Haverthwaite. **Bowness** is a tourist trap, clogged with traffic in summer; **Windermere town**, away from the lake, is mere railway-age suburbia. **Ambleside**, at the lake's northern end, is more attractive, particularly up the hill. On Windermere's shores are a number of gardens (**Holehird▶**, **Stagshaw▶** and **Graythwaite▶**), the **Brockhole National Park Visitor Centre▶** and the absorbing **Windermere Steamboat Museum▶**. For good views, it is an easy walk up **Orrest Head** from Windermere, or further south, **Gummer's How** .

West of Windermere, the landscape rolls gently, heavily cloaked in trees; in **Grizedale Forest** woodland paths are enhanced by modern sculptures. **Stott Park Bobbin Mill▶** demonstrates the process of bobbin making. Visit the pretty village of **Hawkshead▶▶** out of season – or queue for the car park and join the crowds in its quaint little streets; it has craft shops, tearooms, a Beatrix Potter gallery and Wordsworth's former school. Just out of the village, **Tarn Hows▶** is a pretty, if over-visited, pair of tarns artificially merged into one as a landscape feature. Above the village of **Coniston,** beneath the Old Man of Coniston, are spectacular relics of its bygone copper-mining industry. Glide silently over **Coniston Water** on the National Trust's antique steam yacht, *Gondola*▶▶.

North of Ambleside, the A591 enters more mountainous terrain; **Grasmere▶▶** and surroundings are immortalised by the works of Wordsworth (see panel, page 178). Today the village is a busy resort with several good shops. Westwards loom the craggy-looking **Langdale Pikes**.

Further south, **Cartmel▶▶** is a handsome village, less overrun than Hawkshead, with a fine priory church and a pretty square. For views over Morecambe Bay, walk up **Hampsfield Fell** from Grange over Sands. **Kendal▶** (just outside the National Park) deserves special mention for its Art Gallery and Museum of Lakeland Life and Industry.

Far left: exhibits at the Windermere Steamboat Museum

Know your Lakeland terms
Small lakes are called *tarns*, mountains are always *fells* (from the Nordic fjaell), streams are known as *becks*, spotted black-faced sheep are *Herdwicks*, white-faced ones are *Swaledales*, loose stones created by freeze-thaw weathering are termed *scree*. *Force* means waterfall. Bassenthwaite Lake is the only lake in Lakeland termed as such: all the others are *meres* or *waters*. 'Lake Windermere' is a useful term to avoid confusion with Windermere, the town, although Lake District purists will shudder if you use it!

179

Grasmere, beloved of William Wordsworth

Drive **The Lakes**

A succinct cross-section of the best of the Lakes (approx. 125km/80 miles), taking in Wordsworth's Grasmere, spectacular high passes and the less-visited western areas.

From **Keswick** the route heads south along the A591 past **Thirlmere▶**, beneath the shadow of Helvellyn, and past the Wordsworths' former houses, Dove Cottage at **Grasmere▶▶** and Rydal Mount, **Rydal**. Turning west at the resort town of **Ambleside**, you shortly enter **Langdale**, passing beneath the impressive forms of Langdale Pikes, whose slopes were once home to a neolithic axe factory. A minor road loops around the end of the dale, above Blea Tarn, to turn right on to the **Wrynose Pass**. This leads into the magnificent **Hardknott Pass▶▶▶**, passing the substantial remains of a Roman fort on the right after the summit; drop into **Eskdale**, with glimpses of its narrow-gauge railway. Fork right to **Santon Bridge** (from where you can detour to majestic **Wast Water▶▶▶**) and continue to **Gosforth**, with its renowned **Celtic cross▶** in the churchyard. Take the A595 to **Calder Bridge**, then fork right to **Ennerdale Bridge** via a high-level road with views of the coast and **Sellafield nuclear reprocessing plant** (its visitor centre is now a major draw). Beyond **Lamplugh** bear right and right again on minor roads to **Loweswater** and the B5289, where you turn right for a superb finale past **Buttermere▶▶▶**, up the **Honister Pass**, along **Borrowdale** and beside **Derwent Water▶▶▶**.

❏ Houses open to the public:
Brantwood, east side of Coniston Water: home of critic, artist John Ruskin.
Dalemain, near Penrith: Norman pele tower, Elizabethan rooms, priest's hole.
Dove Cottage, Grasmere: Wordsworth's home for his most productive period.
Hill Top (NT), Near Sawrey: Beatrix Potter's farmhouse.
Holker Hall, near Cartmel: flamboyant Victorian house in Elizabethan style.
Levens Hall, near Levens: Elizabethan manor, gardens. Steam attractions. ❏

THE LAKE DISTRICT

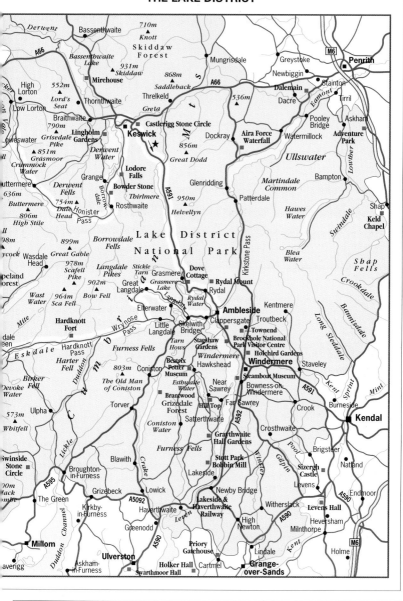

❑ Houses open to the public (continued):
Mirehouse, near Keswick: manuscripts of Tennyson, Wordsworth etc.
Muncaster Castle, Eskdale: built around pele tower; bear menagerie, owls etc.
Rydal Mount, Rydal: Wordsworth's last house; grander than Dove Cottage.
Sizergh Castle (NT), near Levens: Elizabethan panelling, carvings; gardens.
Townend (NT), Troutbeck: traditional Cumbrian farmhouse.
Wordsworth House (NT), Cockermouth: birthplace of William Wordsworth ❑

In the rejuvenated docklands

Museums and galleries in Albert Dock

Beatles Story The Fab Four, who immortalised Penny Lane and the Cavern Club, are the focus for this sight-and-sound experience of the music of the 1960s.
Merseyside Maritime Museum An ambitious museum tracing the history of the port in a restored complex surrounding the Canning Half-Tide Basin: piermaster's house, pilotage building, boat hall, ship-building and an excellent display on European emigrants.
Tate Gallery (Admission free) A branch of the great London establishment, concentrating on modern art.

Other museums and galleries in Liverpool

Liverpool Football Club Visitors Centre, Anfield Road: trophies, memorabilia, video moments and a look into the ground.
Liverpool Museum and Planetarium, William Brown Street (*Admission free* to museum): science and natural history.
Museum of Liverpool Life, William Brown Street: social history of the city: housing, education, work and industry.
Sudley, Mossley Hill Road: former house owned by shipping magnates, the Holts, with a distinguished art collection (Turner, Gainsborough, Reynolds) and fine furniture by George Bullock.
Walker Art Gallery, William Brown Street (*Admission free*): among Britain's finest provincial art galleries: Italian, Dutch and pre-Raphaelite paintings, modern art and sculpture.

▶▶ **Liverpool** 172B1

Industrial activity on Merseyside has declined and the city's population has dwindled this century; out of the centre, run-down streetscapes are testimony to some of the worst urban problem areas in Britain. Yet despite tangible signs of a long economic slump, Liverpool has an exhilarating sense of place, recalling its 19th-century heyday as England's second greatest port. After the silting up of Chester's port, Liverpool took over; it flourished in the late 18th century in its trade with the West Indies.

The ocean-going liners of the 19th and early 20th centuries have gone – to get a hint of what it was like to arrive from sea you should take the humbler **ferry** to Birkenhead and back. The **Royal Liver Building** (1911) and **Cunard Building** (1917) stand sentinel by the Mersey waterfront. Architecture in the city centre displays a legacy of wealth and civic pride, seen at its best around **Dale Street**, **Water Street** and **William Brown Street**, and around classical **St George's Hall** (1854). Now revamped, **Albert Dock**▶▶ (1846) has shops, cafés and a branch of the Tate Gallery installed in the rejuvenated warehouses.

At either end of the plum-brick Georgian terraces of **Hope Street** stand the city's cathedrals. The **Anglican cathedral**▶▶, the largest of its denomination in the world, is a mightily proportioned Gothic edifice, built between 1906 and 1980 to the design of 21-year-old Giles Gilbert Scott. To make the most of its hillside setting, the conventional east–west orientation was not used. A lift, followed by a flight of more than 100 steps, will take you to the top of the tower for a superb view. By contrast, the **Metropolitan Roman Catholic Cathedral of Christ the King**▶ is a squat, tent-like affair set beneath a pinnacled lantern. This design by Frederick Gibberd was adopted after it became apparent that the original plan of Sir Edwin Lutyens was far too costly. Of Lutyens's vast building the foundation stone (1933) and the crypt exist.

▶ Manchester 172B2

Manchester was the great commercial centre for the Lancashire cotton industry. It has suffered some dreary post-war development, but there are several moments of impressive 19th-century grandeur and some enjoyable museums. The **town hall▶** (*Guided tours* Mon–Fri at 10am and 2.30pm) is a cavernous Gothic creation, with an astonishing marble interior designed by Alfred Waterhouse, which fills one side of Albert Square. Just north are the classical **Royal Exchange**, with its excellent lunar-module style theatre, **Barton Square**, a splendid Victorian shopping arcade of iron and glass, and at the city's heart the **cathedral** (originally a medieval church).

Further south around **Peter Street** imposing buildings include the Athenaeum (1837), the Theatre Royal (1845) and the Free Trade Hall (1856); just behind, in the former Central Station, is the modern G-Mex exhibition centre. In Deansgate is the Gothic Revival **Rylands Library**, with its richly ornamental façade, while just off **St John Street** is the finest Georgian street in the city. Pre-Raphaelite paintings are the pick of the works at the **City Art Gallery▶** (*Admission free*) in Deansgate.

The recently revived area of Castlefield includes a reconstruction of a Roman fort that once stood here. The canal basin, where the Bridgewater and Rochdale canals meet, has atmosphere; the walk along the Rochdale Canal passes huge Victorian warehouses. The outstanding **Museum**

Trams have made a comeback to the city's streets

183

of Science and Industry▶▶ occupies the world's oldest passenger railway station; displays include stationary steam engines and a 'hands-on' science centre. A major draw to the city is the **Granada Studios tour▶**, with exhibitions on TV and cinema, including the set used in the TV soap *Coronation Street*. The ambitious **Gallery of English Costume▶▶** in Platt Hall exhibits 400 years of fashion.

Manchester boasts a successful new light rail 'tram' system that runs right across the city, the MetroLink.

L S Lowry (1887–1976)
Manchester-born Laurence Stephen Lowry studied art in Manchester and Salford, and around 1916 developed an interest in painting the bleak landscapes of industrial Lancashire mill towns. The naïve style of the matchstick men figures has been much copied, but at the time his choice of subject was quite apart from the mainstream; many of his works had touches of darkness and satire, and an element of the grotesque. A selection of his work is on display at the Salford Museum and Art Gallery.

■ **The largest cities in Britain today were once its great manufacturing, engineering and trading hubs. Their centres are packed with historical interest and cultural attractions. Yet with the demise of their original industries, many of their inner areas have become run down, presenting huge policy challenges for governments since at least 1945. Many of the problems are now being tackled anew.** ■

Sketches by Boz

'The peculiar character of these streets, and the close resemblance each one bears to its neighbour, by no means tends to decrease the bewilderment in which the unexperienced wayfarer through 'the Dials' finds himself involved. He traverses streets of dirty, straggling houses, with now and then an unexpected court composed of buildings as ill-proportioned and deformed as the half-naked children that wallow in the kennels. Brokers' shops, which would seem to have been established by humane individuals as refuges for destitute bugs … are its cheerful accompaniments.'
Description of Seven Dials, London, from *Sketches* by *Boz* (1850) by **Charles Dickens**

There are some appalling scenes of dereliction …

184

For many centuries, a town was virtually all centre. With its houses and churches, shops and inns huddled tightly together, the typical town was snugly protected from the outside world by its surrounding wall. The Industrial Revolution caused towns to swell out over the neighbouring countryside and many became cities, their centres transformed by grandiose public buildings endowed by proud and philanthropic local entrepreneurs.

Community spirit Despite this vast expansion, the areas around a city's core still enjoyed a strong sense of identity: people lived near to their work and often close to their extended families. The tiny back-to-back houses sheltered large families, who shared a water tap and latrine at the end of the terrace with neighbours, but community spirit was strong even in the most notoriously overcrowded streets.

No-go areas With the decline of heavy industry and the migration outwards to the suburbs, some of these 'inner city' areas became deprived pockets of high unemployment and poor housing, isolated from the country's trend of increasing affluence. A wave of riots in the summer of 1981 – in Brixton, Toxteth, and Bristol – led to them being portrayed by the media as 'no-go areas', and caused the government to look urgently at making inner city areas better places in which to live, work and do business.

Sustainable development The 1990s has seen widespread recognition that the countryside cannot accommodate everyone who would like to live there without becoming irrevocably 'suburbanised'. Reclaiming derelict inner city sites is now preferred on environmental grounds to building out from the edge of the city.

Mistaken visions But the planners have much to atone for. Typically inner city areas include much high-rise housing, put up by the local councils, with all the best intentions, in the 1950s and 1960s. The modern movement in architecture at that time believed in austerely functional highrise buildings to provide decent, modern accommodation on the minimum of land. Unfortunately, neither the building materials nor the concepts weathered well in the British climate: the ubiquitous concrete soon looked depressingly grey and drab; pedestrian walkways became havens for muggers; and many residents were unhappy at having no 'defensible space' around their homes.

New opportunities Crescent-shaped 1960s blocks in the Hulme district of Manchester became notorious as some of Britain's worst public housing. In 1992 a £37½ million City Challenge project began to redevelop the area: new brick-built dwellings with pitched roofs and gables have now appeared on the site, and are much more in keeping with the taste and aspirations of most inner city residents. Meanwhile, inner city communities don't just need buildings, but a whole range of education and training, transport, health and social services to help transform themselves. Many small- and large-scale projects are under way. In central Liverpool, a mixture of government, EU and private sector funding has helped Sir Paul McCartney (of Beatles fame) to turn his derelict old school into the world-class Liverpool School of the Performing Arts.

Prosperity and pride Environmental pressure on the countryside and congestion in the suburbs may well entice more people and businesses to move to the inner city, with its facilities, good public transport, and an often vibrant cultural mix. But the love affair of the British with their cars and their private gardens, and the economic dominance of the southeast, may pull them in the other direction. Even London's Docklands, an up-and-coming area of the 1980s and only a few miles from the thriving financial centre of the City, has had difficulty maintaining its development in the more depressed economic climate of the 1990s.

Yet much has improved in the centres of Britain's great cities; there has been large-scale rebuilding as well as imaginative restoration of existing buildings in Birmingham, Manchester, Glasgow and Cardiff. It is in their smartly cleaned-up stone buildings, new concert halls and stylishly refurbished shopping arcades that future visitors to Britain will feel a reviving sense of civic pride.

Demonstrating a new spirit of enterprise: Manchester's MetroLink trams

The second Blitz
Prince Charles once remarked that far more damage had been inflicted on London by planners and developers after World War II than the entire might of the Luftwaffe during it. The same is true of too many other British cities and towns, devastated by a postwar alliance of property developers and architects too fond of concrete. Whole areas were torn down, often against the wishes of their inhabitants, rebuilt in concrete and pierced by high-speed roads. The only mercy is that the destruction was eventually halted by public resentment and professional misgivings.

... but initiatives are being taken to improve things

185

Monsal Dale: the old viaduct now carries a footpath

▶▶ Peak National Park *172B3*

Britain's first National Park, created in 1951, is encircled by large industrial cities. Though there are no major peaks as such – the district is essentially one of rolling hillscapes – the feeling of escape is exhilarating. The Peak forms the southern part of the Pennine chain that forms the backbone of northern England.

The White Peak Most of the southern park comprises the limestone landscapes of the White Peak, where rivers groove deep-cut gorges, or 'dales', beneath a plateau of drystone-walled farmland. Most spectacular of all are **Dove Dale**▶▶ and its continuation, **Beresford Dale** (despite the crowds), **Monsal Dale**▶▶ (with its famous viaduct), the **Manifold Valley**▶ just below Wetton, and wooded **Lathkill Dale**▶ near Youlgreave. Rewarding villages include **Winster, Alstonefield, Tideswell, Ilam, Ashford in the Water** and **Eyam**▶, whose villagers were ravaged by the plague in 1665 when, following their vicar's lead, they gallantly confined themselves to their village after an infected box of cloth arrived from London. **Tissington**▶ has perhaps the loveliest of all Peak village streets, with wide grass verges and a Jacobean hall. Equally absorbing is **Cromford**▶, an early industrial village where Richard Arkwright set up the world's first water-powered cotton mill in 1771 (now a museum). The Peak's finest prehistoric monument is **Arbor Low**▶, south of Monyash, a 2,000-year-old stone circle. **Castleton**▶▶ is the nub of the Peak's caving district (see panel): north of the village, a ridge ends at Mam Tor, known as 'Shivering Mountain' because of frequent landslips; Cave Dale looks up to the Norman keep of Peveril Castle, holding its head high above the village.

The National Park boundary excludes all the local towns except **Bakewell**, home of Bakewell Puddings (way superior to the mass-produced Bakewell tarts). The centre is marred by traffic, but it is more pleasant up the hill around

Above: Richard Arkwright
Below: on the High Peak Trail

the church and the commendable Old House Museum of bygones. Out of town are the Peak's two great houses: **Haddon Hall►►** is a wonderfully preserved medieval house with a panelled gallery, a chapel and walled garden; palatial **Chatsworth House►►►**, home of the dukes of Devonshire, has a breathtaking collection of art and furniture. Its grounds were landscaped by Capability Brown and Joseph Paxton (see page 17); Paxton also designed the quaint estate workers' village, **Edensor**.

Buxton►►, an elegant former spa, is the *de facto* Peak capital. Its classically inspired 18th-century Crescent, an Opera House, pavilion gardens and town hall all contribute to a distinguished ambience. An excellent town museum features a Wonders of the Peak exhibition. **Matlock Bath**, a former spa, occupies an extraordinary site in the Derwent Gorge. Cable cars make it an easy climb up to the **Heights of Abraham**, a park with woodland walks, views and caves. Near by at Crich is the wonderful **National Tramway Museum►►**, which offers tram rides and a host of exhibits related to this mode of transport.

The Dark Peak Millstone grit is the underlying rock in the northern Peak. The moors and grassland really are dark; the scenery is bleaker and more rugged. Millstones, for grinding grain, were once a major industry – workings litter abandoned quarries and the stone discs now stand on plinths to mark the National Park boundary. The one-street village of **Edale** lies below the massive peat-bog plateau of Kinder Scout, the highest terrain in the Peak (636m/

2,807ft). The A57 heads over the **Snake Pass**, giving a good picture of the austerity of the northern moors, while the **Derwent Reservoirs►** near Hope are the most attractive of many manmade lakes. Old cotton-mill towns have a 19th-century workaday character: **New Mills** is one of the most rewarding, with a gorge cutting through its centre. **Lyme Hall►** has a fine Palladian hall with Grinling Gibbons woodcarving; its park has gentle walks. The gritstone edges such as **Stanage Edge** provide dramatic level tops, with easy paths and challenging rock climbs.

Caves
Of the five limestone caverns near Castleton that are open to the public, Treak Cliff has some fine stalactites and displays of Blue John (a crystalline fluorspar, worked into jewellery and souvenirs, and sold locally), Speedwell Cavern features an underground boat trip along a tunnel that forms part of an old lead mine, and Bagshawe Cavern near Bradwell may appeal to those wanting to experience adventure caving. Peak Cavern on the edge of Castleton has a magnificent entrance and is the largest cave in England. Blue John Cavern has Blue John but no stalactites. On the edge of Buxton, Poole's Cavern has the finest formations.

187

Bakewell Pudding started life at the White Horse Inn, where the cook attempted to make strawberry tart, but put the jam in first and poured the egg mixture over the top

Lead mining
Lead mining was big in the White Peak until the last century – the Manifold Valley and Lathkill Dale have traces of past mining activity, Magpie Mine near Sheldon is the most conspicuous relic. Many villages expanded for the purpose; today these stone-built settlements are surprisingly rural and merge into the scenery along with their agricultural neighbours. At Matlock Bath, a mining museum is close to the re-opened Temple Mine, which nonclaustrophobics may like to walk around.

■ **This most famous of factory-workers' villages looked forward to a new age of cities: of greenery, clean air and sanitation. A place in which, in the words of its founder, the inhabitants 'will be able to know more about the science of life than they can in a back slum, and in which they will learn that there is more in life than the mere going to and returning from work, and looking forward to Saturday night to draw their wages'.** ■

Village trail
The Port Sunlight Heritage Centre tells the story of Port Sunlight and a village trail leads visitors round the garden village, taking in the Lady Lever Art Gallery. Set up by Lever after the death of his wife, the gallery contains a surprising wealth of art, including pre-Raphaelite paintings and Wedgwood ceramics.

WELCOME TO PORT SUNLIGHT VILLAGE
*
UML Limited

Fair deals for the workers Port Sunlight was in fact one of several 19th-century innovations in the Wirral. In 1842 Joseph Paxton's Birkenhead Park had been Britain's first public park and in 1853 Prices Patent Candle Company had created Bromborough Pool Village for its workers.

The soap king The industrialist William Hesketh Lever, the first Viscount Leverhulme, was a Liberal Member of Parliament and philanthropist, with an interest in the arts and landscape design. He co-owned a soap factory in Warrington; the success of Sunlight Soap spiralled and in 1887 he came to the Wirral, the peninsula that juts out between the Mersey and Liverpool on one side and the Dee and Wales on the other, to set up a new factory. He acquired Thornton Manor and transformed Thornton Hough into a mock-Tudor village for his estate workers.

A vision of the future The factory village of Port Sunlight was to be a haven of peace and cleanliness. Cottages were built to a high standard in half-timbered Tudor and bricky Queen Anne and Elizabethan styles (no two groups of cottages are the same); gardens and parks were liberally provided. The village's visionary design was a predecessor of the garden cities of Ebenezer Howard, which in turn influenced the growth of the garden suburb and of the first New Towns.

►► Quarry Bank Mill   *172B2*

The centrepiece of Styal Country Park, a swathe of green on the fringes of Manchester, is this water-powered cotton mill, built in the 18th century and now maintained by the National Trust. It gives an excellent idea of the working of a weaving mill, complete with the authentically deafening clatter of the looms. Exhibits explain cotton processing, the role of water as an energy source, the working conditions of the time and the role of the Gregs (who established the mill) as pioneers of the factory system. Spinning and weaving demonstrations take place. Visitors can also see inside the original Apprentice House, and glimpse the living conditions of the 1830s.

►► Stoke-on-Trent (The Potteries)   *172B2*

Stoke is a conurbation of six towns – Burslem, Fenton, Hanley, Longton, Stoke and Tunstall – but only locals know where one ends and the next begins. At first glance the industrial and residential sprawl is unappetising, but this is the heart of pottery country and anyone interested in the potter's craft should certainly make a visit. In summer, a 'China Service' coach from Stoke Station provides a convenient way of getting between the sites.

The **Gladstone Pottery Museum►►►** is a preserved 19th-century pottery with bottle-shaped brick kilns (once a common feature of Stoke-on-Trent, but now all but vanished). It has pottery demonstrations and a fine display of ceramics ranging from high-class ornaments to Victorian lavatories. The **Etruria Industrial Museum►** features the last steam-powered potter's mill in Britain, while the **City Museum and Art Gallery►** has a huge collection of Staffordshire pottery. Also open to the public are the **Minton Museum►**, the **Sir Henry Doulton Gallery►** and the **Wedgwood Visitor Centre►** at Barlaston, 9km (6 miles) south of Stoke.

Huddled around a courtyard and built in the 15th and 16th centuries, **Little Moreton Hall►►** (NT), 14km (9 miles) north of Stoke-on-Trent, is the best example of the Cheshire half-timbered vernacular, with a wainscoted gallery, great hall, chapel and knot garden.

About 24km (15 miles) east of Stoke-on-Trent is **Alton Towers**, where the parkland that surrounds the ruined home of the 15th Earl of Shrewsbury reverberates to the sounds of rollercoasters and joyous children in Britain's most famous theme park.

Staffordshire figurines
Simple figure models in earthenware or salt-glazed stoneware were first made in Staffordshire in the mid-18th century. These included the so-called 'pew' groups of figures seated on a high-backed settle, and the famous soldiers on horse-back associated with John Astbury. At the end of the century the range of production greatly expanded and potters such as the Wood family produced classically inspired figures along with busts of contemporary celebrities such as Napoleon. The early Victorian period saw the emergence of the flat-back portrait figure, simply moulded representations of royalty, politicians, preachers, actors, literary and sporting characters. Also from this period are the perenially popular, and much reproduced, Staffordshire dogs.

189

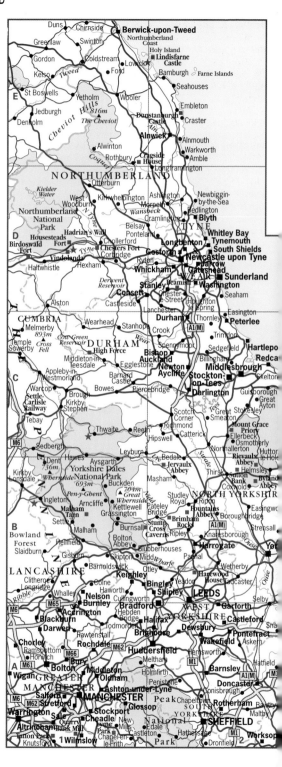

Northeast England This region includes most of the **Pennines**, the chain of hills that forms the backbone of upland England, from the Peak District in the south to the Scottish borders in the north. It also encompasses **Yorkshire**, the largest county in Britain, divided into North, West and South for administrative purposes. It has a reputation for friendliness, and possesses the finest of Britain's medieval cities in York itself and a magnificent heritage of abbey ruins and ecclesiastical architecture.

Industrial Yorkshire The industrial parts of **West Yorkshire** should not be overlooked: the moorland and the scenically sited, 19th-century stone-built mill towns around Calderdale have a strong and unique personality; there are canals and hills to explore and there is Brontë country at Haworth. Industrial heritage is the big theme here. Leeds recalls its mill days in the Armley Mills

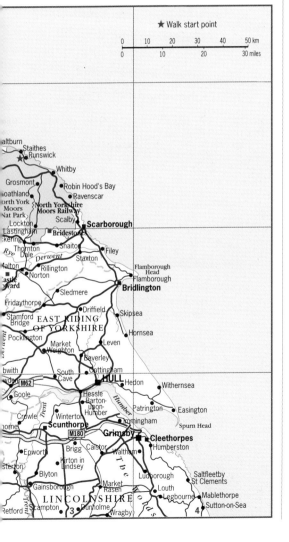

★ Walk start point

The black-and-white faced Swaledale tup: a Yorkshire Dales National Park emblem

SHORTLIST: WHERE TO GO
HISTORIC TOWNS AND
CITIES
County Durham : Barnard Castle, Durham.
East Riding of Yorkshire: Beverley.
North Yorkshire: Harrogate, Helmsley, Knaresborough, Middleham, Richmond, Ripon, Scarborough, York.
Northumberland: Alnwick, Hexham.
Tyne and Wear: Newcastle-upon-Tyne.
INDUSTRIAL HERITAGE
Abbeydale Industrial Hamlet, Beamish, Bradford, Halifax, Hebden Bridge, Hull, Saltaire.
SCENERY
North York Moors, Northumberland, South Pennines (Calderdale and Haworth areas), Yorkshire Dales.
COASTAL TOWNS
AND VILLAGES
North Yorkshire: Robin Hood's Bay, Runswick Bay, Staithes, Whitby.
Northumberland: Bamburgh, Berwick-upon-Tweed.
HISTORIC SITES
AND REMAINS
Fountains Abbey, Hadrian's Wall, Holy Island, Rievaulx Abbey.

Museum and at Thwaite Mills; and it has some handsome Victorian and Edwardian shopping arcades. Bradford impresses for its legacy of the past and for its vibrant museums. Sheffield, in **South Yorkshire**, has cultural attractions and Abbeydale Industrial Hamlet is a fitting memento to the city's steel manufacturing days.

The Dales, the Moors and the Vale of York The **Yorkshire Dales** are for lovers of the great outdoors – an excellent area for car-touring, walking and caving.

East of the Pennines, in the **Vale of York** are York itself, the elegant spa town of Harrogate and the enchanting ruins of Fountains Abbey. Southeast Yorkshire is less visited: the flat agricultural scenery may be humdrum but Selby and Beverley (the latter in the **East Riding of Yorkshire**) each have splendid churches; Hull has a range of sights, including the Town Docks Museum which celebrates its nautical past; a huge suspension bridge spans the Humber.

The **North York Moors** are detached from the Pennine chain and have a quite different character. The coast, with its high cliffs and fishing villages, is a joy. Further south along the coast are the scalloped chalk cliffs of **Flamborough Head** and the narrow spit of **Spurn Head**.

County Durham, Tyne and Wear, Northumberland The **Pennine** landscape becomes bleaker and more lonesome as one proceeds, towards Scotland, through Teesdale, in County Durham, and the Cheviots, in Northumberland. Elsewhere much of **County Durham** has an industrial face, and, like Middlesbrough (in North Yorkshire) is economically depressed. The open-air museum at Beamish is a re-creation of an early 20th-century industrial village, while Durham has a great Norman cathedral. **Tyne and Wear** incorporates a conurbation centred on Newcastle-upon-Tyne; locals here are nicknamed Geordies and are known for their quickfire humour and guttural accent. It is not a prosperous region economically, but the place has considerable verve. On its back doorstep, **Northumberland** has wide open spaces, the great Roman structure of Hadrian's Wall, and a long and quiet coastline.

Walks

Hadrian's Wall,   190D1
Northumberland National Park

Nearly all the interest is along the Wall itself, with its host of Roman features. There is little point in contriving circular routes – simply walking along the Wall is a great experience, with views from the ridge of the Great Whin Sill across lonely Northumberland. For a sample, start at Housesteads fort and walk west, past Craig Lough to Twice Brewed youth hostel and back (2½ hours). In summer you can use a bus service along the B6318 to take you back.

Holy Island,   190E2
Northumberland

Use main car park in village (note tide times). The island's best circular walk is three-quarters coastal, all of it level. Follow Sandham Lane north (turn left and left again out of the car park), turn right beyond the dunes and follow the coast round, past Emanuel Head, where an obelisk looks along the coast into Scotland. Pass Lindisfarne Castle to finish by Lindisfarne Priory in the village. (1½ hours)

Ingleton Waterfalls,   190B1
Yorkshire Dales National Park

Car park by main entrance to falls. Also known as Ingleton Glen, this splendid gorge is well worth the entrance fee. A circular trail takes in a series of falls of considerable indi-

Lindisfarne Castle on Holy Island

viduality; the most dramatic are the first two , Pecka Fall and Thornton Force. Beyond lies a handily placed refreshment kiosk, then the path leads into more open country with views of surrounding hills before a finale along the Doe Gorge (2 hours). A booklet available locally explains the geology.

Runswick Bay and Staithes,   191C3
North York Moors National Park

Park just above Runswick Bay village. This walk along the clifftops (part of the Cleveland Way) links two captivating coastal villages. From Runswick Bay village, walk up the road; at the top follow the Cleveland Way as it leaves on the right, soon reaching the clifftop for an easy walk past Port Mulgrave and reaching Staithes harbour. Return the same way. (2½ hours)

Upper Swaledale, Yorkshire   190C1
Dales National Park

Roadside parking, Muker village. This walk from Muker enjoys a magnificent steep-sided section of the dale. Walk into the village, and find a path out of its north end that leads to a bridge over the Swale; continue north up the dale for 3km (1¾ miles) to the next bridge (close by Keld). Cross and turn left on the Pennine Way (fork left soon for a short detour to Kisdon Force waterfall). The Way rises slightly, offering fine views. Finally leave it for a farmtrack that drops to Muker. (2½ hours)

Misericords

The folding seats in the choirstalls of many cathedrals and major churches have a carved under-bracket known as a misericord. When the seats were turned up, the misericords made ledges for the monks to rest on during the long periods of standing in their services. Frequently carved in fanciful designs, the misericords were deliberately made so narrow that there was no chance of dozing off.

Take a ride on the open-top omnibus at Beamish

Saltaire

This famous example of a 'factory village' dates from the 1850s, when Titus Salt, an enlightened industrialist of liberal views and temperance ideals, decided to house his workforce in this garden village of parks and spacious streets, free from Bradford's smog. The place has scarcely changed, though the houses are now mostly privately owned. The mill itself is used for a variety of purposes. Paintings by local artist David Hockney are on show in a gallery and there is a museum of harmoniums and reed organs. Other sections are leased for commercial use.

▶▶ **Beamish: North of England Open Air Museum**   *190D2*

Life in northern England in the early 1900s is evocatively created in meticulous detail at this ambitious museum. It is divided into five sections: the colliery village, the town with its shops and houses, the manor house, the railway, and the home farm. Costumed actors play out roles within the museum.

▶▶ **Beverley**   *191B3*

Beverley is a delightful town. It has pleasing Georgian brickwork, the North Bar (the only survivor of five town gates), an animated Saturday market and, above all, two gems of church architecture. Begun in Norman times, the **Minster**▶▶ is famed for the quality of its Gothic stone-carving, its 68 misericords (see panel) made by the Ripon school of woodcarvers, and its fine-towered west front. **St Mary's Church**▶ has a 15th-century west façade and a panelled chancel ceiling depicting early kings, all cloaked and crowned against a gold background.

▶ **Bradford**   *190A2*

A patchily impressive Victorian city (knocked about by postwar planning), Bradford is the fruit of the textile-mill age; the Gothic Revival **town hall** and the spectacular tombs of **Undercliffe Cemetery**▶ are monuments of past achievement. In recent days, the hugely entertaining **National Museum of Photography, Film and Television**▶▶▶ (*Admission free*) has put Bradford on the map: here you can see yourself read the news, watch a Victorian magic lantern show or 1950s TV advertisements; the place is usually full of children. The museum is annexed to a cinema with Britain's only 'IMAX' screen, as high as a five-storey building; film shows feature balloon flights or hair-raising journeys into the Grand Canyon.

The **Colour Museum**▶ explores the use of colour-chemistry, and the **Bradford Industrial Museum**▶, with rebuilt back-to-back houses, has a tour through the world of textile production.

▶▶ Calderdale   *190A1*

A former textile valley in the heart of the Pennines, Calderdale is thick with local colour. Sturdy terraces of stone cottages and the geometry of drystone-walled fields stripe the sides of the valley. The largest settlement, **Halifax**▶ is unjustifiably ignored by many visitors; in fact it is the best preserved of West Yorkshire's industrial towns, with the splendid galleried Piece Hall, the former cloth market built around a great courtyard, and some handsome stone civic buildings. The town hall was designed by Charles Barry (one of the architects of the Houses of Parliament, London). Calderdale Industrial Museum covers the stories of mining, local textiles, the Halifax Building Society and toffee. **Eureka!**, in Discovery Road, is a lively 'hands-on' museum for children.

Hebden Bridge▶, near the site of the last clog mill in England, is magnificently set at the meeting of two valleys, its grey houses rising terrace by terrace up the hillside. From the original Hepton Bridge a cobbled path rises steeply to the hilltop village of **Heptonstall**▶▶, a fascinating place with cobbled streets, a ruined church and the oldest Methodist chapel in the world in continuous use (since 1764). The village was a busy hand-loom centre until eclipsed by the mills in Hebden Bridge.

▶▶ Castle Howard   *191B3*

In the gentle Howardian Hills, this enchanting early 18th-century house stands surrounded by a vast park adorned with ornamental lakes, a colonnaded mausoleum and a 'temple' designed by Vanbrugh. He is commonly attributed with the design of the house itself, yet he was then a man of no architectural experience; it seems likely that his clerk of works, the great architect Nicholas Hawksmoor, had more than a helping hand. The house has portraits by Holbein and others, statues, tapestries, porcelain, furniture and a costume collection. It was the setting for the TV dramatisation of *Brideshead Revisited*.

Walks in Calderdale
Calderdale is an excellent centre for walking, with the Pennine Way and Calderdale Way striding over open moors and a dense network of public footpaths. From Hebden Bridge, walk along the Rochdale Canal towpath in either direction for glimpses of typical Pennine features such as back-to-back cottages and old mills. This can be combined with a walk up to Heptonstall, which abuts the top of a dramatic gorge (Colden Clough). The area north of Hebden Bridge is a popular beauty spot with strolls through woods, along the river or up to Hardcastle Crags themselves.

The mill at Saltaire (see panel opposite)

Cathedral firsts
Durham Cathedral represents the highest achievement of the Norman style. In addition to the characteristic use of rounded arches, the building has what are thought to be the earliest transverse Gothic-style pointed arches in English architecture: since the cathedral was built largely over a single period, this represents a transition in building techniques. The sense of scale is created by the hitherto unprecedented use of rib-vaulting, which creates space between load-bearing columns.

Durham Cathedral stands high above the River Wear, on a site where monks from Lindisfarne Abbey built a wooden church in AD 955

St Cuthbert
The Chapel of the Nine Altars in the cathedral contains the relics of St Cuthbert, brought here by Lindisfarne monks who escaped from Holy Island (see page 199) when Danish raiders arrived in 875. Cuthbert was a shepherd boy from the Lammermuir Hills who decided to dedicate his life to God, living on Holy Island and later the Farne Islands. He remained a lover of all animals.

▶▶▶ **Durham** *190C2*

Few places in Britain can rival the drama of Durham's setting, its majestic cathedral soaring over sandstone cliffs and woodlands ribboning the route of the River Wear. The historic centre is compact and largely traffic-free, and walking around it is pleasant. The **Heritage Centre** in St Mary-le-Bow church chronicles the city's history.

The nave, chancel and transepts of the **cathedral▶▶▶** were built over a single period (1070–1140). The sense of balanced might and soaring space is enthralling – this is Britain's finest Norman church architecture. In the cathedral precincts is College Green, the most complete example of a Benedictine monastery in England. Durham was until 1836 a 'palatinate', enjoying royal rights and ruled by prince bishops, who were thus lay and religious leaders.

The main entrance to the cathedral is via **Palace Green**, where the other buildings belong to the **university**, England's third oldest. The **castle▶▶** (*Guided tours*), erected to serve as the palace of the prince bishops for almost 800 years, dates from the 1070s. The university rebuilt the octagonal keep in 1840 but several earlier features survive, including the Great Hall (1284) and the Black Staircase (1662).

For the best views, follow the **riverside path▶▶**, cross over **Prebends Bridge**, beside weirs and old mills (one houses an **archaeological museum**), and go up to **South Street**. **North Bailey** and **South Bailey** are particularly attractive streets, leading past **Durham Heritage Centre**.

The **Oriental Museum▶** in Elvet Hall (part of the university) has jade and ancient Egyptian collections.

►►► Fountains Abbey and Studley Royal   *190B2*

Fountains Abbey

In medieval times, **Fountains Abbey** (NT) had grange farms and lands across much of northern England and was a major wool producer. Its former prosperity is evident in what are widely regarded as the greatest of Britain's abbey ruins. Founded for 12 Benedictine monks who later embraced Cistercian rule, the abbey still has a 12th-century nave and transepts, a tower completed shortly before the Dissolution, and buildings where the monks lived and worked.

Adjacent lies the **Studley Royal** estate; its 18th-century park has follies, a water garden, deer park and delicious vistas of the abbey. St Mary's Church (EH) is a remarkable mock-medieval creation with a painted roof and walls of Egyptian alabaster, built 1871–8 by William Burges.

Ripon► is an appealing town with a fine cathedral notable for its west front, misericords and Saxon crypt. Since 886 the nightwatch horn has been blown in the market square at 9pm to guard the town in darkness.

►►   Harewood House   *190B2*

The seat of the earls of Harewood is a supremely stately composition, completed in 1771, with an impressive list of credits: interiors and furniture by Robert Adam, exterior by John Carr, murals by Angelica Kauffman, formal gardens by Charles Barry, and parkland landscaped by Capability Brown.

Painted ceilings, Sèvres and Chinese porcelain, and intricate plasterwork further grace the building, and there is an aviary of exotic birds.

►   Haworth   *190B1*

The Brontë Parsonage Museum (see page 198) as well as the walk taking in the Brontë Waterfalls and Top Withins justify a literary pilgrimage to this extremely popular Pennine village.

The village is a stop on the private **Worth Valley Railway►**, which steams from Keighley to Oxenhope.

Ripon's saint
St Wilfred was the abbot of the monastery of Ripon in the 7th century and later became Bishop of York. On the Saturday before the first Monday in August, a procession with floats is headed by a man dressed as St Wilfred, complete with mitre and crook, riding a horse; the dean greets him at the west door and a service of thanksgiving follows.

■ **Charlotte (1816–55), Emily (1818–48) and Anne (1820–49) Brontë** were the daughters of an Irish clergyman. The Brontë's lives were constantly beset by ill health and unfortunate circumstance. Charlotte had an unhappy love affair in Brussels, Emily had no close friends and Anne had a tendency towards religious melancholy. Meanwhile, their brother Branwell, disillusioned with his attempts to be a writer and artist, took to drink and opium. ■

My sister Emily loved the moors. Flowers brighter than the rose bloomed in the blackest heath for her; out of a sullen hollow in a livid hillside her mind would make an Eden. She found in the bleak solitude many and dear delights; and not the least and best loved was – liberty.
Charlotte Brontë
(1816–55)

Haworth's cobbled main street is today lined with gift shops

The Brontë name
The family name was originally Brunty or Prunty but the form Brontë was adopted after Lord Nelson was given the title Duke of Brontë by the King of Naples after the Battle of the Nile in 1798.

The Brontës lived in the bleak parsonage (now a museum) in Haworth, overlooking a graveyard which polluted the water supply, severely reducing villagers' life expectancy. The girls consequently escaped into fantasy worlds. It was Charlotte's determination that got the Brontës into print, after she had chanced upon some secret poetry of Emily's and had been convinced of its worth; the three contributed works to a volume published in 1846 under the pen-names of Acton (Anne), Currer (Charlotte) and Ellis (Emily) Bell; the sales were dismal (two books in the first month), but with Charlotte's drive, the sisters each submitted novels. Emily's *Wuthering Heights*, probably set in the now-ruined farmhouse of Top Withins, and Anne's *Agnes Grey* were published in 1847. Charlotte failed to get *The Professor* published, but the constructive comments of one publisher gave her encouragement: she completed *Jane Eyre* soon after and it won immediate acclaim – Thackeray read it in a single sitting.

Hard times But the sisters had to spend much time nursing their brother Branwell, and the money from the books went to paying off his debts; after his death in September 1848, Emily contracted consumption and went to her grave three months later. Anne too fell ill and died the next year at Scarborough, after writing *The Tenant of Wildfell Hall*.

Charlotte was brought to London as a literary celebrity and it was here that she made friends with the successful novelist Mrs Gaskell, who later wrote her biography. Meanwhile, Charlotte worked on *Villette*, based on her time in Brussels, and married Arthur Bell Nicholls after two years of opposition by her father. She died nine months later in pregnancy.

IN MEMORY OF
EMILY JANE BRONTË
WHO DIED DEC. 19TH 1848,
AGED 30 YEARS.
AND OF
CHARLOTTE BRONTË
[...] APRIL 21[...] 1816
[...] MARCH 31[...] 185[...]

▶▶ **Northumberland Coast** *190E2*

England's northeasternmost seaboard is low-lying and virtually unspoilt, characterised by expansive beaches, profuse birdlife, quiet resorts with golf courses and sands, and wind-haunted castle ruins. The immediate hinterland is flat, uneventful farmland.

Berwick-upon-Tweed▶▶ changed hands 13 times between England and Scotland during the period 1100–1510; the Tweed, a famous salmon river which runs just south beneath a trio of bridges (including 17th-century Berwick Bridge with its 15 arches) seems the natural border but the town has been English since 1482. You can take an excellent walk following the 16th-century walls, the best-preserved fortification of its date in Britain, which encircle the town; you will pass the restored quay, Berwick Barracks (1717, the first purpose-built barracks in the country, now housing a regimental museum and a branch of the Burrell art collection) and a rare church built at the time of the Commonwealth (1652).

Berwick bits and pieces
● Although the town of Berwick is English, the old county of Berwickshire was in Scotland and Berwick Rangers play as a Scottish football club.
● With the coming of the railway, Berwick's castle was pulled down to make way for the station.
● There is a local story that the town is still at war with Germany.
● There's nothing fishy about Berwick cockles – they are an old-fashioned peppermint.

199

Holy Island▶▶, accessible by car at low tide (at times posted) via a causeway, is excellent for walks (see page 193) and has great historic interest as the cradle of Christianity in England (see panel). Lindisfarne Castle, lone by the shore, was converted in the 1900s by architect Sir Edwin Lutyens and is open to the public. **Bamburgh▶** close by has a Norman castle, revamped in the 18th and 19th centuries, with porcelain and armour collections. The Grace Darling Museum pays tribute to the woman who helped rescue nine shipwrecked marines in a gale in 1838. **Dunstanburgh Castle▶** (EH) is an eerie ruin, the largest of the Northumbrian coastal strongholds, begun in 1313. It is an easy walk along the coast from the port of **Craster**, which has a workaday harbour and kipper smokeries. Inland lies **Alnwick▶**, a dignified stone-built market town and a pleasant base for exploring the area. **Alnwick Castle▶** dates from Norman times, but has a sumptuous Renaissance-style interior, fine Meissen

The Farne Islands

Holy Island
In 635, at the request of the king of Northumbria, Aidan, a missionary, founded the now ruined Lindisfarne Priory (EH) on what is today known as 'Holy Island'. This became a Benedictine monastery in 1082, and Christianity spread from here across northern England. A museum tells the story. *The Lindisfarne Gospels*, an illuminated manuscript of *c*700, is now kept in the British Museum in London.

Lindisfarne nature reserve
Home to wildfowl and waders; a major site for wigeon and the only British wintering ground for pale-bellied Brent geese, the nature reserve includes mudflats and dunes around Holy Island, and the further-flung Farne Islands. The latter are an important habitat for seals and seabirds; from Easter to October cruises depart from Seahouses – it is an exciting boat ride that offers really close-up encounters with the surprisingly tame wild birds.

china and paintings by Reynolds and Titian; the Victorian architect Salvin was responsible for much of the building, and a century earlier Capability Brown landscaped the parkland. Adjacent Hulne Park is open for walks at weekends; there is a Carmelite Priory and an 18th-century folly tower. At the mouth of the River Coquet, **Warkworth▶** has the dual attraction of a medieval castle and a 14th-century hermitage chapel (EH) gouged out of the cliffs, with the hermit's living quarters still intact (walk along the river and take a ferry across).

By complete contrast, **Newcastle-upon-Tyne▶** is a sprawling industrial conurbation, fairly knocked about and definitely not pretty at first sight, but with plenty of atmosphere. Its six great river bridges include Robert Stephenson's double-decker road and rail bridge of the 1840s. A cluster of medieval quayside buildings, the 17th-century guildhall and the castle are pre-industrial survivals, while Grey Street and Eldon Square are fine examples of early 19th-century townscaping. Among Newcastle's many museums are the Laing Art Gallery (paintings by the extraordinary religious visionary John Martin), the 'interactive' Newcastle Discovery (with sections on fashion, photography, life in the armed forces, and the city's history) and the Hancock Museum (natural history). The local beer, Newcastle Brown, is just as famous as the local 'Geordie' accent.

▶▶ Northumberland National Park   190D1

Because of its remote location and lack of facilities, this is one of the least visited national parks. Villages are modest and scattered, the grassy hills are quiet and strikingly empty – even at the height of summer you often have only Cheviot sheep for company. It is excellent for solitary walks, although the variety is not immense. Vast Kielder Forest spreads its seemingly endless conifer plantations, home to red squirrels and deer, over western Northumberland. Kielder Water and the forest trails offer a

Manmade beauty: the huge Kielder Water amid the conifers of Kielder Forest

The ruins of Housesteads Roman Fort, on Hadrian's Wall

retreat from the elements, and there is a 19km (12-mile) forest drive; boats and canoes can be hired.

The **Cheviot Hills** reach to the Scottish border; the best of the walks involve treks along solitary sheep-drovers' roads, now quiet grassy tracks, to the ridge which forms the border, taking in the summits of Windy Gyle (619m/2,031ft) and The Cheviot (816m/2,677ft). Scenic drives tend to be of the there-and-back variety; notable among these is the road along **Coquetdale** from Rothbury, past the craggy Simonside Hills, to Alwinton and beyond.

Rothbury itself is an attractive sandstone town with a sloping green and a spacious main street; **Cragside▶** (NT) on the edge of town was built by the 19th-century architect Norman Shaw and was the first house in the world to be lit by hydro-electric means. The wooded grounds are laced with trails and have lakes, a formal garden and a fine show of rhododendrons. **Chillingham Castle** has for more than 700 years been home to Wild White cattle, a breed kept by ancient Britons. **Ford** is a model estate village for Ford Castle and has craft workshops.

The southern part of the national park holds the finest surviving stretch of **Hadrian's Wall▶▶▶**, the largest Roman monument in Britain (see panel). Of its 118km (74-mile) length, remains can be seen along 16km (10 miles), the best sections being between points north of Haltwhistle and Hexham. Walkers may like to make use of a summer bus service which runs along the main road parallel to the Wall.

Housesteads Fort, which still has a hospital and latrines, and Chesters, a cavalry fort, are particularly well preserved. At Vindolanda Fort a section of wall is reconstructed as it would have been at the time of the Roman occupation, while at Corbridge are the remains of the garrison town of Corstopitum and a museum of finds.

Also try to take in Birdoswald Fort, over the border in Cumbria, and the National Park information centre at Once Brewed.

Hexham▶ makes an attractive base. It has a superb priory church; both its crypt and bishop's throne are Saxon – before destruction by Danish marauders in 875 it was the largest church in northern Europe. Local history features at the Border History Museum.

Hadrian's Wall
This great fortification at the northernmost point of the Roman empire was planned in AD 122 by Emperor Hadrian from Newcastle to the Solway Firth on the Cumbrian coast. The natural feature of the Great Whin Sill, a ridge of hard rock, made an ideal base to the construction for much of its length. To the north lay wilderness and the Picts, and it still feels primevally wild on the wall today. Milecastles were placed at intervals of Roman miles; the Vallum, or southern rampart, was below the wall and is visible in places. Seventeen forts, housing 13,000 infantrymen and 5,500 cavalrymen, were connected by a military road. The best preserved is Housesteads (NT, EH).

More North Yorkshire priories and abbeys
Byland Abbey (EH), near Coxwold, had the largest priory church in England – the shattered rose window gives a scant idea of its glory. Mount Grace Priory (EH), near the attractive village of Osmotherley, was a Carthusian house; the lifestyle was austere, with vows of silence and prison-like confinement; one cell has been reconstructed. Guisborough Priory (EH), an Augustinian foundation at the edge of Guisborough in Cleveland, is now largely rased but retains a huge east window. The substantial ruins of Whitby Abbey (EH) overlook the sea; an inscription on a stone cross commemorates the Creation Hymn, the first poem in the English language, penned by Caedmon, an Anglo-Saxon herdsman.

The ruins of Rievaulx Abbey (pronounced 'reevo'), desolate and still in sheltered Ryedale

Rievaulx Abbey
Before Henry VIII started his dissolution of the monasteries in 1536 there were more monasteries in Yorkshire than in any other county in England. In North Yorkshire Rievaulx Abbey (EH), is the undoubted star. Founded in 1131, it became very prosperous, rich in sheep, and by the 1160s there were 140 monks and 500 lay brothers. By the Dissolution numbers had dropped to 22. The ruins occupy a site of remote beauty in Ryedale.

►► **North York Moors National Park** *191C3*

This distinctive massif, tucked into Yorkshire's northeast corner, is England's largest tract of heather moor, a plateau dotted with ancient stone crosses (former way-marks), and interrupted by sharply contrasting green dales scattered with red-roofed, yellow-stone farms and hamlets. The most dramatic scenic moments are at the point where the high terrain dips abruptly to the plain and along a sublime stretch of coast well supplied with sights, absorbing villages, beaches and walks along the east coast's highest cliffs. This variety of moods is perhaps the key to the area's enduring appeal.

The moors and dales Farndale, celebrated for its wild daffodils, and **Rosedale**, formerly an ironstone-mining centre, typify the contrasts of moorland plateau and lush vales.

Helmsley► is a cheery, small market town with craft-shops and bookshops, and a handsome market square; close by are the huge east tower of the Norman castle (EH) and Duncombe Park, a revamped Palladian mansion memorable for its fine classical entrance hall and panelled saloon, and for its grass terrace complete with temples.

The village street of **Coxwold►** is without blemish, all trim grass verges and stone cottages; Laurence Sterne lived and wrote *The Life and Times of Tristram Shandy* at what is now known as Shandy Hall (house open).

Lonely St Gregory's Minster in **Kirkdale** has a remarkably preserved Anglo-Saxon sundial from 1060.

Hutton-le-Hole►►, with its sloping, sheep-nibbled green, is home to the Ryedale Folk Museum, where rural buildings have been re-erected to give an insight into life of yesteryear.

Lastingham Church► is built over a remarkable Norman crypt, and the touristy village of **Thornton Dale►** has some pretty corners by its brook.

Captain James Cook
The great explorer was born in 1728 at Marton (now part of Middlesbrough, Cleveland), where a museum charts his life and travels. The site of the Cooks' house at Great Ayton is marked by an obelisk and the school James attended is a modest museum. After being a shop apprentice in Staithes, he was apprenticed to a Quaker shipowner in Whitby (the house where he lived with his master is a museum of Cook's life). From 1768 onwards he undertook his voyages of discovery to New Zealand, the east coast of Australia and the Pacific Isles. He was murdered by natives in Hawaii in 1799.

203

The area's major tourist attraction, the **North Yorkshire Moors Railway**►► (journey takes about an hour), runs from Pickering to Grosmont along unspoilt dale scenery. **Pickering**► itself is a bustling market town with a lively local museum and remains of a Norman castle; look in the church for the set of 15th-century murals, one of the most complete in England. **Goathland** has a long green and sheep everywhere; from the Mallyan Spout Hotel a path drops down to **Mallyan Spout**, a waterfall, while south of the village you can walk along a section of Roman road, **Wade's Causeway**►. At **Grosmont** you can peer into the loco shed or take a British Rail train into **Eskdale**.

Much of the eastern moors is dominated by commercial forestry, including **Dalby Forest**, laid out with trails, picnic sites and a drive; it abuts **Bridestones Nature Reserve**, where strange mushroom-shaped rocks are clustered on the moor. The western and northern escarpments, followed by the long distance **Cleveland Way** footpath, offer grandstand views towards the Pennines and over industrial Teesside respectively; **Sutton Bank**►, by the A170, is an inland cliff with a dizzying view across the Vale of York to the Pennines; at its southern end is the White Horse, a 96m (314ft) tall hill carving created by local school children and their teacher in 1857.

Along the coast A footpath (the finale of the Cleveland Way) follows the coast continuously; roads reach the coast in only a few places. **Staithes**►► is still an authentic-looking fishing village, not too prettified; **Runswick Bay**► is smaller and neater, picturesquely huddled beneath the cliff. **Whitby**►► was once a famous whaling centre, hence the whalebone arch above town from which you look across to the ruined abbey and St Mary's Church. The town has expanded as a resort but has kept its character in a maze of old streets around the harbour; a few shops still specialise in Whitby jet ornaments. The densely stocked Whitby Museum displays some astonishing local fossils. A beach extends north to Sandsend.

Red-roofed **Robin Hood's Bay**►►, one of the most famous of all English fishing villages, clings to steep slopes that drop to the shore, where low tide reveals rock-pools and fossils; tales of smuggling haunt the quaint hotchpotch of lanes. **Scarborough**►, just outside the Park, is both a Regency spa and a Victorian resort with sandy bays. It is an exhilarating blend of the brash and genteel. Wood End Museum displays natural history and has a section on the ultra-literary Sitwell family who used to live in this house.

The Laurel Inn, Robin Hood's Bay

York Minister, one of the wonders of Gothic architecture, as seen from the north corner of the city wall

 ►►► **York** 190B2

York is England's unrivalled showpiece cathedral city: nowhere else has quite such a concentration of medieval and other historic treasures. There are far more museums than can be visited in a single day (see page 206): the Castle Museum, the National Railway Museum and the Jorvik Viking Centre are the top three. Around every corner are outstanding examples of buildings of every period including a host of medieval churches and such time-warp streets as The Shambles, with its overhanging upper floors. Shoppers, sightseers and buskers throng the city centre, but much of it is pedestrianised and a pleasure to explore on foot. The York Mystery Plays, a 14th-century cycle of 48 plays covering man's fall and redemption, are performed every four years (next performance 2000).

The city wall►►► The Romans built the original defensive wall around the settlement of Eboracum, at the confluence of the rivers Ouse and Foss; in Viking times the city was known as Jorvik, later corrupted to 'York'. Today the fabric of the wall is largely medieval. It can be followed along its top for much of its 4.5km (2¾-mile) length and provides a splendid city overview (see Walk, page 205); west of the river, the wall skirts a largely railway-age residential area. The wall's gateways are known as bars; on Micklegate Bar during the Wars of the Roses, the heads of enemies would be exhibited on spikes.

The Minster►►► Built 1220–1475, this is the largest medieval cathedral in Great Britain and the city's crowning glory. Its magnificent glass dates from 1150 – look for the depictions of 'Genesis' and 'Revelation' in the east window, as well as the 'five sisters' windows within a quintet of lancets. Look too for the rich interior of the chapter house, the painted roof of the nave, the carved rood screen, the undercroft display and the Treasury.

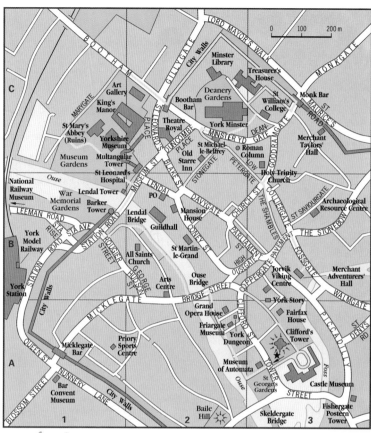

YORK

Walk City highlights

Outside **Castle Museum▶▶▶**, face **Clifford's Tower▶**, turn left to take a path to the near side of the tower; beyond Ouse Bridge view the city from the north river bank; recross by Lendal Bridge. Enter the **Museum Gardens**, pass fragments of medieval **St Leonard's Hospital**, **Multangular Tower**, a Roman relic beside a section of Roman wall, and ruins of **St Mary's Abbey**. The **Yorkshire Museum▶** is also in this park. Find a gate into Marygate and go to **Bootham Bar**; join the walkway along the top of the wall, with superb views of the Minster. Leave the wall at Monk Bar; the

Treasurer's House▶ (NT) is filled with period décor, while **St William's College** has an exhibition on the Minster. Skirt the **Minster▶▶▶** to its main entrance. Pass **St Michael-le-Belfrey Church** (fine 15th- and 16th-century glass), detour into Stonegate for its shopfronts; go on along Low Petergate, detour left into Goodramgate for unspoilt **Holy Trinity Church▶**. Find **The Shambles▶▶** York's most famous street. From Fossgate you can visit the **Merchant Adventurers' Hall▶▶**; beyond Coppergate are the **Jorvik Viking Centre▶▶▶**, **Fairfax House▶** and the **York Story**.

*The Shambles,
originally a street of
butcher's shops*

York's museums

ARC St Saviourgate: 'hands-on' archaeology for all: learn how to solve the enigmas of the past.

Bar Convent Blossom Street: still a convent, but housing a museum on early Christianity in northern England.

Castle Museum►►► Eye of York: this alone justifies a visit to York. Collections include a full-scale cobbled street of shops, re-creations of domestic interiors over the centuries and a working watermill by the river.

City Art Gallery Exhibition Square: includes nudes by local artist William Etty.

Clifford's Tower► (EH) Tower Street: a neat 14th-century quatrefoil castle on a Norman site, with a good view from the top. Scene in 1190 of the mass suicide of 1,250 Jews to escape slaughter by their Christian debtors.

Fairfax House► Castlegate: a Georgian town house offering an insight into life in the mid-18th century: furniture, clocks and paintings, mostly from Joseph Terry, the Quaker confectionery magnate.

Friargate Museum Lower Friargate: over 60 life-sized wax models in tableaux depicting moments in history.

Guildhall St Helen's Square: a painstaking re-creation of the original 15th-century building, destroyed in an air raid.

Jorvik Viking Centre►►► Coppergate: entertaining and realistic time-travel journey into 10th-century Viking York. Go early or late when the queues are shorter.

Merchant Adventurers' Hall►► Fossgate: the most impressive timber-framed building in the city; the 14th-century hall of a city merchants' guild, still in use.

Museum of Automata► Tower Street: entertaining exhibition of gadgetry past and present, including a history of robots and a host of objects to try out.

National Railway Museum►► Leeman Road: Britain's finest selection of historic locos and carriages (including the royal carriage used by Queen Victoria). Timetabled working demonstrations.

Richard III Museum Monk Bar: the medieval monarch on trial – guilty or not guilty?

York Dungeon Clifford Street: a chilling glimpse into a world of punishment and death.

The York Story Castlegate: a model of the city illustrates York's long history.

Yorkshire Museum► Museum Gardens: Roman, Saxon and Viking artefacts; statuary and part of a Viking ship.

*The Castle Museum's
re-created cobbled
street, Kirkgate, takes
its name from Dr
John Kirk who
started the museum*

Drive **The Yorkshire Dales** (see also pages 208–9)

This tour (approx. 90km/55 miles) captures the essence of the Dales, taking in waterfalls, Castle Bolton, unspoilt dales and lonely moors.

From the busy little town of **Hawes** at the heart of Wensleydale, take the A684 Sedbergh road, turning off very soon for an unclassified road sign-posted to Kettlewell, to enter the northern end of **Wharfedale** at **Hubberholme** (with its charming church). The B6160 leads over into Bishopdale and **West Burton▶**, with its long village green. Proceed past the **Aysgarth Falls**, taking the road rising up to the formidable fortress of **Castle Bolton▶▶**. Beyond this, the road rises on to Redmire Moor; pause for views at the top and drop down into **Swaledale** at **Grinton**; the odd castellated structure on the right as you descend is a former shooting lodge and now a youth hostel. Grinton Church, grandiosely dubbed 'cathedral of the dales', merits a short pause, while **Reeth▶**, with its inns ranged around a sloping green, makes a good halfway stopping-point. The route goes along bleak **Arkengarthdale**, rising to the astonishingly remote **Tan Hill Inn**, England's highest pub, near the meeting of Cumbria, North Yorkshire and County Durham. Re-enter **Swaledale** at **Keld**; beyond **Thwaite** the road to Hawes is known as the **Buttertubs Pass**, so-called because of the natural limestone 'sinks' into which farmers used to place their butter to cool on long journeys.

Other good routes to explore by car include the valley routes along Wharfedale, Ribblesdale, Wensleydale, Swaledale and Garsdale.

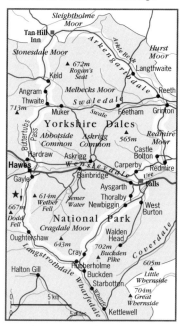

Grassington, in Wharfedale

Nidderdale and Teesdale
Although outside the National Park, Nidderdale's scenery matches the best of the Dales; but access is limited by grouse shooting and reservoirs. How Stean Gorge has small cliffs; near Pateley Bridge (commendable folk museum) are Brimham Rocks, a weird, naturally sculpted landscape of tors. Stump Cross Caverns are a tour-it-yourself showcave. North of the Park, within County Durham, lies Teesdale, in the midst of the wildest and emptiest tracts of the Pennines. High Force is the mightiest waterfall in England. With its harsh climate and unusual soils, the designated nature reserve harbours arctic and alpine species, including the rare Teesdale Violet.

▶▶▶   **Yorkshire Dales National Park**   *190B1*

The great Pennine mass that forms the backbone of England has its proudest moments here, in the limestone dales and gritstone moors of the Yorkshire Dales National Park, where villages and field walls are almost universally grey stone. Spend a few days in the area and you will see the subtle differences between one dale and another.

Wharfedale This is a long dale, with several moods. Around **Bolton Abbey▶**, all is pastel-shaded and gentle, graced by the ruined Augustinian priory and the functioning priory church; upriver the Wharfe swirls through a chasm in Strid Wood. **Burnsall**, with its old bridge and green, and **Arncliffe** are two idyllic villages; **Grassington** is larger and busier, with a range of shops and places to eat around its central square. Looming over the dale is **Kilnsey Crag**, England's largest overhang, quite a challenge for rock climbers. Like many Dales places, **Buckden** and **Kettlewell** grew up around the lead-mining industry; relics litter the moors. Tiny **Hubberholme** has a gem of a church, with a rare musicians' gallery of 1558.

Airedale England's most famous limestone scenery is concentrated in the area **around Malham▶▶▶**, where the subterranean River Aire reappears at the base of Malham Cove, a great inland cliff topped by limestone pavements; a short walk away, formidable Gordale Scar waterfall impressed the early Romantics. Other local rambles include those to Janet's Foss (waterfall) and Malham Tarn, with its rich plant and bird life. Downstream lies **Skipton**, a market town with a rewarding castle restored by the indefatigable Lady Anne Clifford after Civil War damage; a steam railway heads into Wharfedale.

Swaledale Stone barns, abandoned lead mines (notably in Gunnerside Gill) and Swaledale sheep are features of the landscape along with the fast-flowing Swale itself. **Reeth▶**, ranged around a spacious green, is an alluring village. Enchanting **Richmond▶▶▶** crowns a hilltop site, its mighty Norman castle (EH) staring down to the Swale and over the large market place. There are two absorbing museums (the Richmondshire Museum and the Green

A traditional landscape: Swaledale has 750 stone barns and numerous drystone walls

One of the deep lime-stone shafts on Buttertubs Pass; a high route between Swaledale and Wensleydale

Howards regimental museum) and the streets are full of interest, but there is nothing self-conscious about the town. Even its theatre (1788), the oldest in its original form in England, is concealed by a barn-like exterior. Walk by the Swale, through Hudswell Woods or to the ruins of Easby Abbey.

Wensleydale The dale's cheese-making heritage is illustrated in the folk museum in **Hawes** and shops sell the flaky Wensleydale cheese. This town is conveniently located, but villages such as **Askrigg**, **Bainbridge** and **West Burton▶** have more appeal; **Middleham▶▶** has a pretty central square (around which stable hands parade horses from nearby racing stables) and a 12th-century castle (EH) (the former home of Richard III). Of the dale's many waterfalls, **Aysgarth Falls** are the best known; close at hand are a museum of antique carriages and Aysgarth Church, with its superb screen brought from **Jervaulx Abbey▶**, whose lichen-encrusted ruins can be seen further east. **Hardraw Force▶**, the tallest waterfall in England, is reached through the pub at Hardraw. **Castle Bolton▶▶** is an impregnable-looking bulk, little altered since the 14th century; here Mary, Queen of Scots was kept prisoner, in some comfort, between 1568 and 1569. **Masham▶** has plenty of local colour around its large cobbled market place.

Ribblesdale and Dentdale Settle is a likeable market town, if a bit noisy with quarry traffic; the train journey to Carlisle gives great views (see page 176). The 'Three Peaks' – **Whernside** (737m/2,414ft), **Ingleborough** (723m/2,372ft) and **Pen-y-ghent** (693m/2,277ft) are near by; a popular challenge walk, often started from Horton-in-Ribblesdale, takes in all three. Ingleborough is dotted with pot-holes and caves, including **Ingleborough▶** and **White Scar▶** caverns (both have public access), and Gaping Gill, big enough to hold London's St Paul's. **Ingleton** is the base for walks into **Ingleton Glen▶▶** (see page 193). Dentdale, in Cumbria, lies below Whernside; don't miss **Dent▶▶** with its cobbled streets, the epitome of the rural Pennines.

Barnard Castle
Just beyond the Park's northeastern boundary, in County Durham, is the town of Barnard Castle, whose namesake castle perches above the Tees. The Bowes Museum here, built in opulent French château style, houses a splendid collection of fine arts. Try to time your visit to catch the 'performance' by the automaton silver swan in the entrance hall (12.30 and 4pm).

209

Limestone pavement above Malham Cove

SOUTHERN SCOTLAND

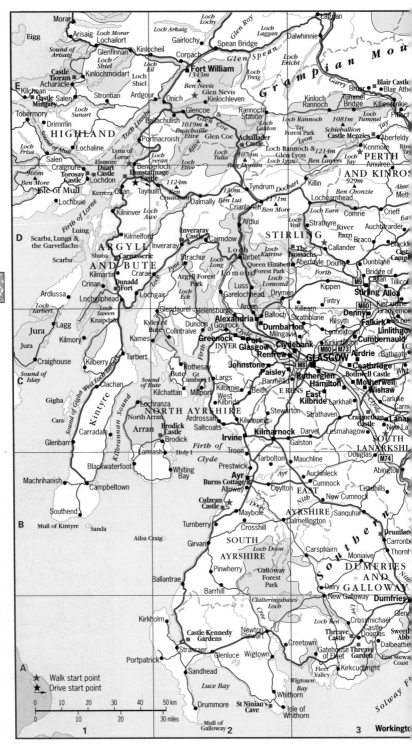

Map labels

Morar, Eigg, Arisaig, Lochailort, Loch Morar, Glenfinnan, Kinlocheil, Loch Arkaig, Gairlochy, Loch Lochy, Glen Roy, Spean Bridge, Loch Laggan, Laggan, Dalwhinnie

Kilchman, Castle Tioram, Acharacle, Kinlochmoidart, Loch Shiel, Loch Eil, Corpach, Fort William 1343m, Glen Spean, Loch Ericht, Grampian Mou

Salen, Mingary, Strontian, Ardgour, Onich, Ben Nevis, Glen Nevis, Kinlochleven, Rannoch Station, Kinloch Rannoch, Tummel Bridge, Killiecrankie, Blair Atholl, Blair Ath

Tobermory, Drimmin, Lochaline, Ballachulish, Glencoe, 1019m, Glen Coe, Buachaille Etive, Loch Laidon, Loch Rannoch, Tay Forest Park, Schiehallion 1081m, Castle Menzies, Loch Tummel, Aberfeldy, Riv

Loch Frisa, Salen, Portnacroish, 1074m, Loch Rannoch & Glen Lyon, 1214m, Glen Lyon, Ben Lawers, Loch Tay, Kenmore, PERTH AND KINRO

HIGHLAND, Loch Sunart, Sound of Mull, Lismore, Lynn of Lorne, Loch Creran, Loch Etive, Ben Dorain, Amulree

966m, Ben More, Craignure, Torosay Castle, Duart Castle, Benderloch, Dunstaffnage Castle, Lochdon, 1124m, Tyndrum, Dochart, Killin, 929m, Ben Chonzie, Crieff, AND KINRO

Isle of Mull, Lochbuie, Kerrera, Oban, Taynuilt, Ben Cruachan, Dalmally, 130m, Ben Lui, 171m, Ben More, Crianlarich, Lochearnhead, Comrie, Meth

Luing, Kilninver, Loch Awe, Ardlui, Loch Voil, Strathyre, River Earn, Auchterarder, Ea

Scarba, Lunga & the Garvellachs, Kilmelford, INVERARAY, Inveraray Castle, Cairndow, STIRLING, Loch Earn, Callander, Braco, Blackf, Camp

Shuna, ARGYLL AND BUTE, Carnasserie Castle, Inveraray, Strachur, Loch Long, Loch Katrine, The Trossachs, Aberfoyle, Doune, Dunblane, Cast

Crarae, Argyll Forest Park, Tarbet, Queen Elizabeth Forest Park, Forth, Bridge of Allan, Tillico

Crinan, Dunadd Fort, Lochgair, Loch Eck, Luss, Loch Lomond, Drymen, Kippen, Fintry, STIRLING, Alloa, Kincar

Ardlussa, Lochgilphead, Glendaruel, Helensburgh, Arden, Balloch, Killearn, Denny, Grange, M9, M80

Jura, Lagg, Knapdale, Kyles of Bute, Dunoon, Colintraive, ALEXANDRIA, Gourock, Strathblane, Milngavie, Kilsyth, Lennoxtown, Kirkintilloch, Falkirk, Linlithgo, Cumbernauld, Airdrie, Bathgate

Kilmory, Kames, Rothesay, GREENOCK, Port GLASGOW, INVER, Clyde, Clydebank, GLASGOW, M80, M73, Coatbridge, Whit

Craighouse, Tarbert, Bute, Gt Cumbrae I, Millport, West Kilbride, Largs, Johnstone, Paisley, M8, Rutherglen, Hamilton, Motherwell, Wishaw, Carluke

Gigha, Cara, Carradale, North Arran, Ardrossan, Saltcoats, Kilwinning, NORTH AYRSHIRE, Beith, Barrhead, E RENS, East Kilbride, Larkhall, Craignethan Castle, SOUTH LANARKSHI, New La

Glenbarr, Brodick Castle, Brodick, Lamlash, Holy I, Firth of Clyde, Troon, Irvine, KILMARNOCK, Galston, Darvel, Strathaven, Lesmahagow, M74, Douglas, Abington

Blackwaterfoot, Whiting Bay, Prestwick, Tarbolton, Mauchline, Auchinleck, Cumnock, Leadhills

Machrihanish, Campbeltown, Sanda, AYR, Burns Cottage, Alloway, Coylton, EAST AYRSHIRE, New Cumnock, Nith

Southend, Mull of Kintyre, Culzean Castle, Maybole, Dalmellington, Sanquhar, Drumlan, Carronb

Ailsa Craig, Turnberry, SOUTH AYRSHIRE, Crosshill, Loch Doon, Carsphairn, Moniaive, Thornt

Girvan, Pinwherry, Galloway Forest Park, DUMFRIES AND GALLOWAY

Ballantrae, Barrhill, Clatteringshaws Loch, Cree, Dalry, New Galloway, Dumfries

Kirkcolm, Castle Kennedy Gardens, Newton Stewart, Creetown, Loch Ken, Crossmichael, Castle Douglas, Glen, Sweet Abb

Stranraer, Glenluce, Wigtown, Gatehouse of Fleet, Threave Castle, Threave Garden, Dalbeattie

Portpatrick, Sandhead, Fleet Valley, Kirkcudbright, East Stewa coast

Luce Bay, Wigtown Bay, Whithorn, Isle of Whithorn, Solway F

Drummore, St Ninian's Cave, Mull of Galloway, Workingto

Legend

★ Walk start point
★ Drive start point

0   10   20   30   40   50 km
0   10   20   30 miles

1   2   3

Braemar
Balmoral Castle
Linn O'Dee
t a i n s
1154m
Lochnagar
Strachan
Stonehaven
Deeside & Lochnagar
Clova
Fettercairn
Inverbervie
Spittal of Glenshee
North Esk
Laurencekirk
Johnshaven
Kirkmichael
Edzell Castle
ANGUS
Brechin
Aberlemno
Montrose
Bridge of Cally
Kirriemuir
South Esk
Forfar
Friockheim
Inverkeilor
Blairgowrie
Alyth
Isla
Glamis
Glamis Castle
Arbroath
Dunkeld
Birnam
Coupar Angus
Capath
Stanley
Muirhead
Dundee
Carnoustie
Balbeggie
Monifieth
Scone Palace
Firth of Tay
Newport-on-Tay
Perth
M85
Glencarse
Leuchars
Elcho Castle
Newburgh
St Andrews
Cupar
Craigtoun
Auchtermuchty
Eden
Ceres
Fife Ness
Falkland
Ladybank
Crail
M90
Falkland Palace
FIFE
Pittenweem
Anstruther
Glenrothes
Leven
Elie
Kinross
Loch Leven
Buckhaven
Earlsferry
Cowdenbeath
Kirkcaldy
Dunfermline
Firth of Forth
Burntisland
North Berwick
Inverkeithing
South Queensferry
Gullane
Dunbar
Hopetoun House
EDINBURGH
East Linton
Haddington
Cockburnspath
M9
St Abb's Head
Dalmeny
Musselburgh
EAST LOTHIAN
Grantshouse
St Abbs
Livingston
Dalkeith
Gifford
Eyemouth
Loanhead
Bonnyrigg
Newtongrange
Chirnside
Penicuik
MIDLOTHIAN
Lammermuir Hills
Berwick-upon-Tweed
West Linton
Duns
Dolphinton
Eddleston
Lauder
Greenlaw
Swinton
Peebles
Tweed
Eildon & Leaderfoot
Gordon
Coldstream
Lowick
Biggar
Traquair House
Galashiels
Kelso
Tweed
Ford
Drumelzier
Abbotsford House
Melrose
Upper Tweeddale
Selkirk
St Boswells
Yetholm
Wooler
Tweedsmuir
BORDERS (SCOTTISH)
Jedburgh
Cheviot Hills
816m
Grey Mare's Tail
Denholm
The Cheviot
Hawick
Alwinton
Moffat
Rothbury
Beattock
Teviothead
Coquet
Eskdalemuir
Hermitage
NORTHUMBERLAND
Otterburn
Kielder Water
West Woodburn
Lochmaben
Langholm
Border Forest Park
Kirkwhelpington
Lockerbie
Northumberland National Park
Caerlaverock Castle
Gretna Green
Housesteads Fort
Hadrian's Wall
Chollerford
Bowness
Birdoswald Fort
Vindolanda
Chesters Fort
Annan
Brampton
Haltwhistle
Hexham
Corbridge
Carlisle
Crosby-on-Eden
Wetheral
Silloth
Wigton
Thursby
Alston
Castleside
Aspatria
CUMBRIA
M6
Lazonby
Stanhope
Maryport
Bothel
Caldbeck
Melmerby
Wearhead
Derwent
Bassenthwaite
931m
Skiddaw
Greystoke
Penrith
Cross Fell 893m
DURHAM
Cockermouth
Langwathby
Cow Green Reservoir
High Force

SOUTHERN SCOTLAND

The miniature Highland scenery of the Trossachs was put on the tourist map by Sir Walter Scott's The Lady of the Lake

The Scottish nation Scotland is now part of the UK, but has a long history as an independent state. After having fought hard to maintain its sovereignty, Scotland surrendered its independence in an act of Parliamentary Union with England and Wales in 1707. Scotland's parliament was abolished and since then it has been ruled from London by a British parliament. However, it was allowed to keep its church, legal and educational systems distinctive and separate. In 1997, the Scots voted to have their own parliament once again. This comes into operation in the year 2000, and will control most aspects of Scotland's home affairs. Scotland will remain part of the UK, but at the time of writing it is not clear how the relationship between the new Scottish parliament and the British government will work.

Southern Scotland Those who know southern Scotland through its books already know the country well; Robert Burns and Sir Walter Scott have familiarised the whole world with its language, people, rivers and hills and in this century novelist John Buchan has exemplified the local character to millions more: strength, self-reliance and doughty self-confidence.

The lie of the land Southern Scotland is composed of the Central Lowlands and the Southern Uplands, a wide band of hills that stretches from coast to coast. In the west this latter area is known as **Dumfries and Galloway** while the eastern part is known as the **Scottish Borders**, though in fact both parts have acted since time immemorial as a war-torn border country, a self governing shield between England and Scotland. The Lowlands occupy a rift valley, comprising the westward flowing River Clyde and the long eastern intrusion of the Firth of Forth. This is the heart of Scotland, studded with ancient Christian sanctuaries, sturdy medieval burghs, royal palaces, baronial seats, thickly populated manufacturing towns and its great rival cities of Glasgow and Edinburgh. The Central Lowlands, encompassing **Argyll** and **Bute**; **West, Mid-**

TAMDHU
SINGLE MALT SCOTCH WHISKY
YEARS **10** OLD
PRODUCT OF SCOTLAND 100% SCOTCH WHISKY
DISTILLED AT
TAMDHU DISTILLERY

and East Lothian; Stirling; Fife and part of the **Perth and Kinross and Angus** regions, are by no means uniformly low-lying. The handsome capital city of **Edinburgh** is perched among volcanic hills, Glasgow is overlooked by the Campsie Fells, Dundee is fringed by the Sidlaw Hills and the Kingdom of Fife is given a backbone by the Ochil hills. The northern frontier of the Lowlands is the Highland Boundary Fault, which divides the island of Arran in half, continues northeast through Helensburgh to Loch Lomond, skirts through old market towns such as Crieff and Dunkeld to reach Stonehaven on the east coast.

The heritage Most of the great prehistoric monuments of Scotland are found in the north, but there are good collections of Pictish and early Christian carved stones to be seen in Angus and St Andrews. Viking invasions in the 9th century destroyed much of the evidence of Celtic Christianity except for the distinctive round towers at Brechin in Angus and Abernethy in Perth and Kinross. Dunfermline Abbey and the famous Norman church in Leuchars, near St Andrews in Fife, are good examples of the Romanesque influence, which came to Scotland in the late 11th century. This was followed by the Gothic period, represented by the ruined Border abbeys as well as the surviving cathedrals of Dunblane and Glasgow. The 15th century is the most distinctively Scottish period, with the development of the simpler collegiate church with battlemented towers and stone-slabbed roofs and spires. This period also saw the birth of the tower house with its thick, vertical stone walls, a concept gradually enriched by combining towers into L, T and Z plans; the roofs budded a playful array of corner turrets, crow-stepped gable ends and balconies. The neat burghs, or market towns, are dominated by a broad high street, typically with a mercat cross and the Tolbooth, which served as both jail and town hall. The 16th-century royal palaces at Linlithgow, Falkirk and Stirling reveal the influence of the Renaissance but it was not before the more peaceful politics of the late 17th century that Scotland produced a truly classical style. Sir William Bruce ushered in this period, dominated by William and Robert Adam, who gave the term Adamesque to their palladian vision of 18th-century Britain. Mellerstain, Culzean and the New Town of Edinburgh are their great works. In the early 19th century, the Romantic movement encouraged a return to an indigenous spirit, which led to the Gothic-Baronial style of the high Victorian era that still dominates the land. The crudity of some of this work is exposed by the scholarship of architects such as Sir Robert Lorimer and Charles Rennie Mackintosh.

O Caledonia! stern and wild,
Meet nurse for a poetic child!
Land of brown heath and shaggy wood,
Land of the mountain and the flood,
Land of my sires! what mortal hand
Can e'er untie the filial band
That knits me to thy rugged strand?
Sir Walter Scott,
The Lay of the Last Minstrel (1805)

213

Auld Lang Syne
Should auld acquaintance be forgot,
And never brought to mind?
Should auld acquaintance be forgot,
And auld lang syne!

For auld lang syne, my jo,
For auld lang syne,
We'll tak a cup o' kindness yet
For auld lang syne

From *Auld Lang Syne* by **Robert Burns**, sung all over Britain on the stroke of midnight on New Year's Eve. Hogmanay, as the New Year holiday is called, is a time of great celebration in Scotland.

Walks

Callander Crags, Stirling   210D3
Car park on west side of Callander. A signposted path from Tulipan Crescent, by the tennis courts, leads into woods. A steep climb is eventually rewarded by splendid views of the Trossachs from the top of the Crags, which form the edge of an abrupt escarpment. (1½ hours)

Culzean Country Park,   210B2
South Ayrshire
Car park by Culzean Castle. The park is laced with trails; a detailed map is available on site. Aim to take in the castle, Happy Valley (with its exotic trees), the walled garden and Swan Pond. Maidens village to the south is an alternative starting point, with a walk along the beach until the estate gates are reached. (1 to 2 hours)

Grey Mare's Tail,   211B4
Dumfries and Galloway
Car park by A708 between Selkirk and Moffat. A fine waterfall, visible from the road, but worth taking either of the waymarked trails for close-up views. The longer trail climbs to the top of the fall and heads for lonely Loch Skeen. (1 to 2½ hours)

St Abb's Head: the view of the cliffs at White Heugh, where guillemot and kittiwake may be seen

New Lanark,   210C3
South Lanarkshire
Car park in New Lanark. This remarkable industrial 'model' village provides the starting point for walks along the Clyde Gorge, with its dramatic waterfalls. Walk south, parallel with the river, through the village, then fork right on to a track and right again on to a path above the river. Cross the river at a sluice bridge and turn right for further views to ruined Corra Castle. Return the same way. (2 hours)

St Abb's Head,   211C5
(Scottish) Borders
Car park by nature reserve visitor centre just west of St Abb's village. A short path leads towards the village, then turns north parallel with the coast for bracing cliff views, to the lighthouse at St Abb's Head, where there are nesting sites for 50,000 birds, including puffins. Either return along the cliffs, or take the easier lighthouse access road, with spectacular views of the coast. (1 hour)

► **Angus** *211E5*

The county of Angus extends westwards from the North Sea across prosperous farmland (renowned for its black cattle) to the Grampians. The best scenery is to be found in the 'Braes of Angus' – beautiful glens such as Glen Isla, Glen Prosen, Glen Clova and Glen Esk – and on the wild rocky coast between **Montrose►** and **Arbroath►**. Montrose is a delightful summer resort whose Flemish-style architecture reflects centuries of prosperous trading with the Low Countries. The fishing and market town of Arbroath, too, has something of a resort air in the summer. Its most famous monument is the great 12th-century, red stone abbey – a picturesque ruin which is surrounded by tombstones. Immediately north is the hamlet of **St Vigeans**, where a museum houses over 40 locally carved stones from the Pictish period (5th to 9th centuries) on.

Inland, and north of Arbroath by 22km (14 miles) is **Brechin**, a red stone market town on the banks of the South Esk River. Standing proud beside the small cathedral is Scotland's finest **round tower►** (HS). Only three such tall, slender towers, dating from the 10th century and used as the refuge and watchtower of the independent monasteries of the Celtic Church, are known outside Ireland. At **Aberlemno**, 8km (5 miles) southwest along the back road to Forfar, are some fine carved Pictish stones.

Due north of Brechin is **Edzell►►** (HS). The ruins of its castle are handsome enough but it is the walled garden, the Pleasance, laid out by the scholar Sir David Lindsay in 1604 that makes the place quite exceptional. Sculptural reliefs decorate the walls.

In the fertile Vale of Strathmore, a little southwest of Forfar, is **Glamis Castle►►** (as in Shakespeare's *Macbeth*), its brooding bulk standing quiet and solemn in the spacious acres of its deer park. Near the castle, a row of stone-roofed cottages houses the Angus Folk Museum (NTS) of reconstructed interiors and domestic bygones.

►► **Arran** *210C1–C2*

The largest of the Clyde Islands, Arran is a traditional holiday island, easily and quickly reached from Glasgow. Sheltered by the Kintyre peninsula, it enjoys unusually warm weather and has dramatic mountains (Goat Fell rises to 874m/2,867ft), deep valleys, and sandy and rocky bays. As you approach the island on the ferry from Ardrossan, **Brodick Castle►** (NTS), an ancient stronghold of the Hamilton family, dominates the shoreline. Its spectacular gardens include one of the finest rhododendron collections in Scotland. Arran is studded with prehistoric stones and is a paradise both for hill-walkers and birdwatchers, and for geologists, who come by the busload because virtually every rock type is represented on the island.

North lies the flatter, fertile island of **Bute**. Another important Clyde resort, the capital town of Rothesay is reached by ferry from Wemyss Bay. Ruined Rothesay Castle, like Arran's, was once the personal property of the Stuart kings. Cromwell destroyed it in the 17th century. By following a minor road to the southern end of the island and then a footpath across a field, you can walk among the scant ruins of St Blane's monastery; it is a lovely spot, with good views of the Firth of Clyde.

Angus info
● The Angus market towns proudly boast more fish and chip shops per head of population than anywhere else in the world.
● Arbroath has its own, separate culinary status as the home of 'Arbroath Smokies', split smoked haddock on the skin.
● In 1885 Arbroath fielded a team in the Scottish Cup that recorded the highest score in British football. They beat Bon Accord 36:0. Seven further goals were disallowed for offside. The score might have been even greater: much time was spent retrieving the ball when a goal was scored, as the goalposts then had no nets. The Arbroath goalkeeper was said to have smoked a pipe throughout the match.
● The Declaration of Arbroath was an open letter presented by the abbot of Arbroath in 1320, signed by all the dignitaries of the land and addressed to the pope. It summarised the case for an independent Scotland.

215

Brodick Castle and Garden, Isle of Arran

▶ Ayr *210B2*

Admirers of Scotland's national poet, Robert Burns, will need no encouragement to visit **Alloway▶** on the southern outskirts of the seaside resort of Ayr. It was the birthplace of one of the few European poets to rival Shakespeare for wit and vigour. Burns spent his first seven years at the humble cottage next to what is now the Burns Museum. Close by, the **Tam o'Shanter Experience** is an audio-visual show recounting his famous poem.

High on a clifftop 19km (12 miles) down the coast road from Ayr, **Culzean Castle▶▶▶** (NTS), built 1772–90 and ancient seat of the Kennedys, secretes behind its battlemented exterior a supremely elegant classical interior by Scottish architect Robert Adam, arguably his finest. The celebrated oval staircase rises through three tiers of columns to an exceptional first floor salon.

Culzean Country Park (see Walks, page 214), with its walled summer garden, woodland walks, lake and camellia glasshouses, is the most popular of the National Trust for Scotland's properties.

Laid out on the dunes a little south of Culzean is the famous **Turnberry Golf Course**.

More Burns sites
Near the birthplace and Burns Museum in Alloway are the Brig o'Doon and 17th-century Alloway Kirk; both feature in Burns' poem *Tam o'Shanter*, and Burns was baptised in the Kirk. The imposing Burns Monument was erected in 1823 and bears figures (added five years later) of Tam o'Shanter and his drinking companion, Souter Johnny.

Robert Burns
Often described as Scotland's ploughman poet, Robert Burns (1759–96) was well educated for his time. Though his amorous exploits have gained notoriety, his contribution to literature was through poetry which shrewdly observes the foibles of his fellow men. He also wrote numerous sentimental, lyrical and narrative pieces and was an avid 'improver' of Scottish traditional songs. A major theme running through his work was a belief in the universal brotherhood of man.

Culzean Castle, Robert Adam's supreme creation

THE (SCOTTISH) BORDERS

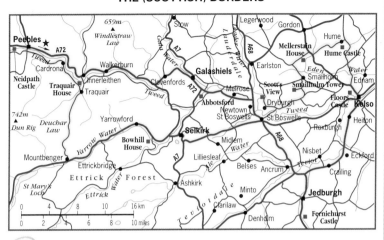

Drive **The (Scottish) Borders towns, abbeys and houses to visit**

A 160km (100-mile) tour of the best of the (Scottish) Borders towns, abbeys and uplands. See also pages 218–9.

Start from **Peebles** and take the A72 east, following the Tweed, to **Traquair House**►► outside Innerleithen. Carry along the A72 (passing the Scottish Museum of Woollen Textiles in Walkerburn) to reach Galashiels. Here look out for the turning to Walter Scott's house, **Abbotsford**►. From Abbotsford join the A72 but turn off into **Melrose** to look at the ruined **abbey**►► (HS). Head back on to the A72 then the A68 for St Boswells and **Dryburgh Abbey**►► (HS). Detour north on the B6356 to Scott's View. Take the B6404 for a look at **Smailholm Tower** (HS) on your way north to **Mellerstain House**►►. From here cross to **Hume Castle** and join the B6364 to Kelso to see its ruined abbey and, to the west of town, **Floors Castle**►►.

Follow the A698 south along the Teviot Valley to **Jedburgh** with its ruined **abbey**►► (HS), Jail Museum and Mary, Queen of Scots House. You can detour south of the town to Ferniehurst Castle Centre and the Capon Tree. From Jedburgh take the A68 north to St Boswells and turn west on to the A699 to **Bowhill House**. Follow Yarrow Water upstream, along the A708, turning north at Mountbenger on to the B709 for the lonely crossing of Deuchar Law to Traquair House. From here a small road on the south bank of the Tweed passes **Kailzie Gardens,** near Cardrona, on the return to Peebles.

Dryburgh Abbey, founded in 1150

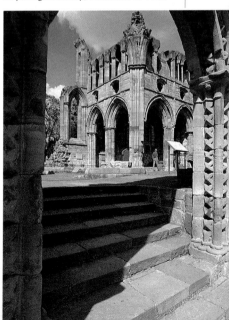

SOUTHERN SCOTLAND

Young Walter Scott, in Smailholm Tower

The Eildon Hills and Walter Scott

Legend has it that these pink hills that rise prominently out of the valley near Melrose were cleft in three one night by the 13th-century wizard Michael Scott (Michele Scot in Dante's *Inferno*), to settle a dispute with the devil (the wizard's spell-book is said to be buried in Melrose Abbey). Mundanely, geologists insist they are the relics of old volcanoes. Either way, they make excellent walking territory for those staying in Melrose and were a favourite of Sir Walter Scott. Visit Scott's View, beside the B6356 north of St Boswells, for the view of them he so enjoyed.

Children's playthings on display in Traquair House

▶▶▶ The (Scottish) Borders — 211B4

As famous for its salmon as for its tweed, the Scottish Borders is a land scarred by centuries of turbulence. Fought over since the days of the Romans, it has many sites that bear silent testimony to this past – tower houses built to ward off border raiders, skeletons of abbeys vengefully destroyed by England's Henry VIII. It is also Sir Walter Scott country, the countryside that inspired Scotland's most celebrated novelist. There is nowhere else quite like it in Scotland – no big mountains, but lonely, rounded hills, good for bracing moorland walks, and a pleasant coast. Even in the holiday season, there is space.

The town of **Jedburgh▶** is best known for its **abbey▶** (HS) and anyone planning to visit the four great Scottish Borders abbeys – Jedburgh, Dryburgh, Melrose and Kelso – should visit the Abbey Visitor Centre here, which admirably explains their role. Jedburgh Abbey holds the record for border raids, destroyed and rebuilt eight times in its 400-year working life. Its finest features are the two late Norman doorways and the excellent tracery window in the north transept. Also in the town are Mary, Queen of Scots House and the Castle Jail Museum.

Selkirk is a tweed-manufacturing town and a good base. **Bowhill House** is 6km (4 miles) west, set in the high ground between two tributaries of the Tweed. Its many magnificent works of art include the last Leonardo da Vinci in private hands in Britain. The house is surrounded by beautiful grounds; hidden in the woods is an adventure playground no child will forget.

Just outside Innerleithen, 10km (6 miles) east of Peebles, is **Traquair House▶▶**, one of Scotland's oldest inhabited houses. Its forbidding outline is softened by the pale harling of its walls but it remains dark and chillsome inside. In the gardens is an excellent maze that children will love. The house includes an 18th-century brewery which brews the excellent Traquair House beers. **Peebles**, a pleasant town set on the River Tweed, was the home of the writer John Buchan (1875–1940), most famous for his tales of spy-hunter Richard Hannay.

Between Galashiels and Melrose is **Abbotsford▶**, the imposing turreted mansion that the great novelist Sir

Walter Scott built himself on the banks of the Tweed. It is still inhabited by his descendants and houses his extraordinary collection of assorted Scottish curiosities.

Melrose is an appealing town. Close by the compact main square stands **Melrose Abbey▶** (HS), its remains being the finest there are of the golden age of Scottish ecclesiastical architecture. Its soft pink stone is warm, forgiving and kind, a magical atmosphere pervades the site. Robert the Bruce's heart is said to be buried here. From the town there are delightful walks up to the Eildon Hills (see panel, page 218) and along the River Tweed.

Dryburgh Abbey▶▶ (HS), set peacefully in an exquisite bend of the graceful River Tweed near St Boswells, is the most moving of the four Borders abbeys. Large sections stand astonishingly well preserved, especially the cloisters. If you walk nowhere else, walk here; it makes all the difference to your enjoyment of the peace and tranquillity of Scotland's serenest ruin.

A little way northeast is **Smailholm Tower▶** (HS), a classic pele tower (see panel), with a display of dolls and costumed figures. **Mellerstain House▶▶** is found 9km (6 miles) northwest of Kelso. This breathtaking Georgian house, built by William and Robert Adam in the mid-18th century (see panel page 51), is the perfect example of the

Adam's skill in combining stateliness with domestic ease and comfort. Inside, the large, wide and light rooms, in their pale Adam colours, are as perfect as the day they were finished. A little museum contains a wonderful portrait of Bonnie Prince Charlie disguised as Flora MacDonald's Irish maid, Betty Burke (see page 246).

Kelso is a proud town but the abbey ruins are the least captivating of the Scottish Borders abbeys, the formidable square tower strongly resembling a fortress. To the west of Kelso stands **Floors Castle▶▶**, its Adam and Playfair exterior one of the stateliest of all the Border palaces. On a sunny day its pinnacled façade gleams above its terraced riverside grounds. Only the hall retains its original Adam interior but in the state rooms are many treasures. The 19th-century Gothick bird room is a popular curiosity.

The coast at **St Abb's Head▶** (see Walks, page 214) is a prime site for naturalists and birdwatchers.

Pele towers
The word 'pele' or 'peel' is derived from the Latin 'palus' or palisade and was the name given to the tower houses built around the Scotland–England border against the raiding enemy. Smailholm Tower, near St Boswells, is a well-preserved example from the 16th century. Then it housed a continuous day and night watch; now it stands square and stern and stark on a moorland crag, overhanging a sullen pool. The 15th-century towerhouse at Cranshaws in the Lammermuir Hills features in Scott's *The Bride of Lammermuir*.

Founded by French monks in the 12th century, Jedburgh Abbey was in use as a place of worship until 1875, although its role as an abbey had ended 330 years previously

Common ridings
These ceremonies take place annually in several Borders towns in recollection of the violent battles of the past. Horseriders in Selkirk, for instance, carrying symbols of the independence of their town, gallop over the moors to commemorate the Battle of Flodden Field.

The Falls of Clyde run through a gorge just below New Lanark

Mary, Queen of Scots' lover
James Hepburn, Earl of Bothwell, is one of history's more exciting characters. He was the lover of Mary, Queen of Scots, the possible father of James VI and certainly the murderer of Darnley, the queen's second husband, whose body was found strangled outside the bombed-out house of Kirk O'Field. He then divorced his wife and rushed the queen out to a secret marriage at Dunbar Castle in 1567. Hounded by their enemies, the lovers were, however, forced to part and Bothwell was eventually imprisoned in the Danish Castle of Dragsholm, where he died insane.

►   **The Clyde Valley**   *210C3*

Deep in the wooded Clyde Valley near Lanark (see Walks, page 214) is the 18th-century model mill town of **New Lanark►►**. It is linked with such key figures of the Industrial Revolution as the inventor Richard Arkwright and Robert Owen (1771–1858), the social reformer, who attempted through enlightened programmes to create a co-operative industrial community here; Owen believed that such ideas would one day replace private ownership. His Nursery building, the Institute for the Formation of Character, the school and flats housing the workers have all been restored and a thriving community is living here again. One of the mill buildings houses an award-winning visitor centre which runs a history 'ride' with special effects, specifically tailored for children.

Some 8km (5 miles) west of Lanark, **Craignethan Castle►►** (HS) is a fine example of a 16th-century stronghold. The most exciting feature – thought to be the earliest example in Britain – is the caponier, a large vaulted gallery built on to the floor of the moat providing efficient protection from artillery fire (though it nearly suffocated the defenders in gunpowder smoke).

Bothwell►►, just southeast of Glasgow, boasts a pretty 14th-century church and a monument, by the bridge, that commemorates the defeat of the Covenanters (see panel) at the battle of 1679. However, the town is chiefly renowned for its 13th-century castle. Set high above the Clyde, its redstone curtain walls studded with round towers, it always held a strategic role. It was much damaged in the Wars of Independence.

► **Dumfries and Galloway** *210B3*

The western hills are a bit wilder and more expansive than the better known Scottish Borders District to the east. The character of the region is also more solemn but it is enlivened by some interesting archaeological sites, some haunting ruins and some splendid castles. While much of the countryside inland is humdrum, the southern coast makes for pleasant pottering, with the occasional surprising view of the English Lake District (best from the top of Criffel, south of Dumfries). The area is never crowded; some of the wildest parts of the Southern Uplands are in Galloway Forest Park (parts of which are tediously blanketed in conifer plantations) and some of the Lowlands' most beautiful countryside is in the hills and valleys of the Rivers Nith, Annan and Esk, to the north and east of the grey stone town of Dumfries.

Standing beside the Solway Firth 14km (9 miles) south of Dumfries is **Caerlaverock Castle**►► (HS). Its unusual triangular plan, its full moat and the pleasing green serenity of its site make this, 'the lark's nest' castle, one of the most memorable in the country. It has been much fought over and the outer walls were put to the test of a siege by King Edward I in 1300 less than a decade after the foundations had been laid. The interior bears a very fine Renaissance façade added by the enlightened Lord Nithsdale, head of the Maxwell clan, in the 17th century. Not far away, at Ruthwell is the particularly fine carved Anglo-Saxon **Ruthwell Cross**►. Over 5m (16ft) high and dated to the 7th century, it is one of the most important monuments of the Dark Ages.

Threave Castle (HS) and **Threave Gardens** (NTS)►►, a grim castle and a delightful garden, lie a few miles apart near Castle Douglas, 16km (10 miles) northeast of Kirkcudbright. The castle was built by Archibald the Grim who boasted how the awful gallows' knob that sticks out over the entrance 'never wanted a tassel'. The castle was a 14th-century stronghold of the notorious Black Douglases, so called because of their merciless pillaging, and was besieged unsuccessfully by the royal forces of James II in 1455. To the south of the ruined castle is the Threave Wildfowl Refuge, where wintering birds include wild geese and teal.

Curling
For at least 350 years this team game, something like bowls played on ice, has been enjoyed all over Scotland. The curling stones are made from granite and have handles let into the top. The object is to slide the stones along the ice into a tee, the team with the most stones at the centre of the tee being the winner. The best stones are reputed to be from Ailsa Craig, a 335m (1,100ft) high volcanic plug of a rock 16km (10 miles) off Girvan that persistently pops up into view as you drive around the Ayrshire coast.

221

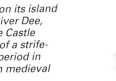

Lonely on its island in the River Dee, Threave Castle speaks of a strife-ridden period in Scottish medieval history

SOUTHERN SCOTLAND

Dulce Cor

The beautiful ruined red walls of Sweetheart Abbey (HS), south of Dumfries on the A710, have a romantic tale to tell. The abbey was founded in 1273 by Lady Dervorgilla after her husband John Balliol was killed by Robert the Bruce (she also founded Balliol College, Oxford, in his memory). She kept her husband's embalmed heart close to her until her death at the age of 90. Both were then interred in the church, which became known as Dulce Cor ('sweet heart').

The nearby (but separately administered) Threave Gardens are where the National Trust for Scotland trains its budding young gardeners. Every type of terrain and condition they are likely to encounter is re-created here, from rose to heather garden, from rock to wood, and there are herbaceous borders, a walled garden and fabulous glasshouses in which grow exotic flowers and fruits. In spring there is a display of some 200 types of daffodil.

The town of **Kirkcudbright▶** is set sweetly on the River Dee around MacLellan's Castle (HS). With its typical pastel-painted housefronts, it has long been beloved of Scottish artists ; E A Hornel was a member of the artists' colony founded in the early years of this century. There are several art galleries in the town today. It is a tranquil place to spend a day wandering around. Visit the ancient tollbooth, with its curious and beautiful spire, or the Stewartry Museum with its many local antiquities and curios; a display explains the strange and ancient Scottish pastime of curling (see panel, page 221). In Gatehouse of Fleet, 13km (8 miles) northwest, is the **Mill on the Fleet▶▶**, a visitor centre based on a restored 18th-century cotton mill that portrays the town's industrial past.

Whithorn, 29km (18 miles) south of Newton Stewart, is one of the oldest Christian centres in Britain; here, in 397, St Ninian built the first Christian church in Scotland, although the present ruin dates from the 13th century. The Whithorn Museum (HS) has finds related to the saint.

The most southwestern corner of this region is the strange spit of land known as the Rhinns of Galloway (from which there are views of the Mourne Mountains in Northern Ireland). Here is the **Logan Botanic Garden▶**, where plants from the temperate regions of the southern hemisphere thrive in a walled garden. **Castle Kennedy Gardens▶**, near Stranraer, were laid out on a grand scale by the 18th-century Earl of Stair, with ruins, lakes and wooded walks. It is at its most majestic when the rhododendrons and azaleas are in bloom in early summer.

In the northern part of Dumfries and Galloway, set beside the River Nith near Thornhill, is **Drumlanrig▶▶**. No building looks more solid or more imposingly rooted in Scotland than this pink 17th-century palace. Within its massive walls are the region's finest collections of old masters, including a Rembrandt, and exquisite French furniture of the 18th century. Rural craftsmen, with work for sale, operate in the grounds.

Drumlanrig Castle, ringed by forests and hills

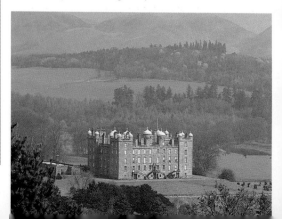

▶▶▶ Edinburgh

211C4

The capital of Scotland is an outstanding city. It is rich in open spaces, museums, beautiful buildings and elegant streets, all lit by the piercingly clear Lothian light. The dark courts, cobbled streets and steep steps of the medieval Old Town contrast with the gracious squares, circuses and crescents of the Georgian New Town. Edinburgh is at its most exhilarating during the renowned International Festival and Festival Fringe in August.

The Royal Mile▶▶ is the original and chief street of the city. At its western end is the castle▶▶, on the site of an ancient fortress and home to the Scottish Crown Jewels; at the other end, the Abbey and Palace of Holyroodhouse▶, the official Scottish residence of the Queen (open to the public when the royal family is not here). The Royal Mile is the heart of the Old Town; many of the city's most historic landmarks are on it and there are numerous museums and houses to visit (see panel).

St Giles' Cathedral▶, the High Kirk of Edinburgh, was originally built in the traditional shape of a cross though later additions have given it an unusual square design. Canongate Kirk▶ is a dignified example of a Presbyterian church, with typical white-painted walls and wooden box pews. The Royal Museum of Scotland▶▶ in Chambers Street has decorative art and archaeology galleries, a natural history section, a geology department and (most popular with the young) technology galleries. In the churchyard of Greyfriars Kirk▶ is the flat tomb on which the National Covenant was signed in 1638 (see page 220) amid such excitement that when the ink ran out men wrote their names in blood. The Grassmarket▶▶ is for many the pleasantest part of the Old Town with its plentiful antique shops and bistros.

The Mound is a causeway between the Old and New Towns. There are views across to chilly Calton Hill▶▶ on which stands the National Monument▶, modelled on the Parthenon in Greece to commemorate the Scots who fell in the Napoleonic wars. It was never completed, but recalls the 18th-century claim that Edinburgh had become

Princes Street and Edinburgh Castle, dramatically perched on a volcanic crag, as seen from Calton Hill

The Royal Mile: museums and houses to visit
The Camera Obscura, near the castle in the Outlook Tower, gives a beautiful 'living image' of the city projected via lenses (best on a bright day). Opposite, *The Scotch Whisky Heritage Centre* tells all there is to know about whisky and whisky-making. *Gladstone's Land* (NTS), in the Lawnmarket, is a re-creation of a typical Old Town, six-storey tenement house. *Lady Stair's House* contains memorabilia of Scottish writers, Robert Burns, Sir Walter Scott and Robert Louis Stevenson. *The People's Story* tells the story of ordinary folk from the 18th century on. *John Knox House* displays interesting artefacts from the life of this pivotal figure of the Scottish Reformation. Opposite is the absorbing *Museum of Childhood*. *Huntly House*, a striking 16th-century mansion, houses the city's excellent museum of its own history.

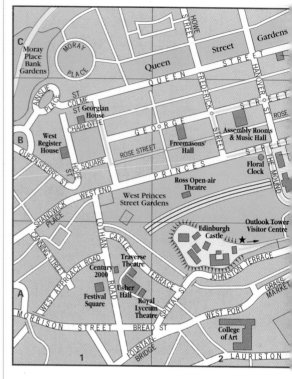

the Athens of the North. Beside the Mound is the **National Gallery of Scotland►►►**, a classical building which houses the national art collection (see panel).

Princes Street► is the principal shopping street. Running along one side are Princes Street Gardens; the **Scott Monument** is the most striking, if endearingly over-the-top, landmark, covered with statuettes depicting characters from Sir Walter Scott's novels and poems.

In Queen Street, in the New Town, a distinctive redbrick Venetian palace houses two exceptional museums, the **Scottish National Portrait Gallery►** and the **Museum of Antiquities►**. There is not one second-rate picture in the portrait gallery, and no shortage of famous subjects. Especially striking is the wonderful Allan Ramsay portrait of the great 18th-century Edinburgh philosopher David Hume. The antiquities gallery houses major prehistoric, Viking and Roman collections. In 1791 Robert Adam was commissioned to design one superb square to enhance the quality of the New Town. Grand, spacious and elegant, his **Charlotte Square►** is the quintessence of the New Town. Number 7, the **Georgian House** (NTS), has been restored as a typical Georgian New Town home, giving a glimpse of an interior from about 1800.

The **Royal Botanic Garden►**, beyond the New Town, has superb tropical houses. Good walks are to be had on **Arthur's Seat**, a volcanic hill in Holyrood Park, and along the **Water of Leith**, to the west of the New Town.

EDINBURGH

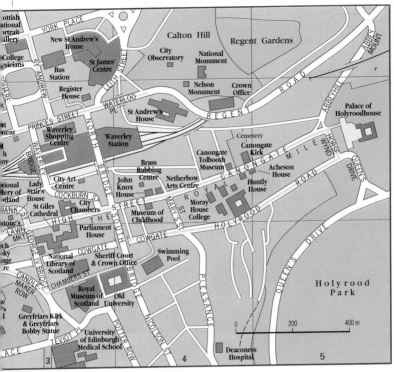

Walk From the Castle to Charlotte Square

Start at the **Castle**►►, then enter the **Royal Mile**►► at Lawnmarket to visit the **Scotch Whisky Heritage Centre**►, **Camera Obscura**►, and **Gladstone's Land**► (NTS). Continue along High Street past Parliament House, the Tron Kirk, the **High Kirk of St Giles**► and the City Chambers. Then go on past the **Museum of Childhood**► and **John Knox House** along Canongate, to the **People's Story Museum**►, Huntly House, the **Canongate Kirk**► and its graveyard, to the **Palace of Holyroodhouse**►.

Return up Holyrood Road and into the Cowgate to pass the University, the **Royal Museum of Scotland**►►, **Greyfriars Church**► (and statue of the loyal little dog, Greyfriars Bobby) and into **the Grassmarket**►►. Turn up Victoria Street, left down Bank Street

to Lady Stair's House► and then down The Mound to the **Scottish National Gallery**►►► and the **Royal Scottish Academy**, with views towards the National Monument on Calton Hill. Turn right into **Princes Street**► to the **Scott Monument**, across and into St Andrew Square and Queen Street for the **Scottish National Portrait Gallery**► and **Museum of Antiquities**►.

Follow George Street as far as Frederick Street, turn left then right into Rose Street and into Robert Adam's **Charlotte Square**► to visit the **Georgian House** (NTS).

The Cramond ferry leaving the Dalmeny side of the river

End of an era
With the opening of the Forth road bridge, the villages that stand on either side of the Firth and are known as South Queensferry and North Queensferry lost the ferry that had served them for 900 years. Among the earliest travellers here was Queen Margaret, wife of Malcolm Canmore, who used this route in the 11th century between her palace and her abbey near Dunfermline – hence the 'queens's ferry'.

The Forth bridges
The Forth rail bridge, built between 1882 and 1889 and illuminated since its centenary, still wins the admiration of young engineers. For most of its life it was the longest bridge in the world. A little west is the fabulous modern suspension road bridge (1964), much lighter and a superb feat of modern engineering. A visitor centre at South Queensferry explains the structures.

▶▶ **The Firth of Forth**   211D4

The Firth of Forth is a wide tidal inlet that bites deep into the east coast of the country. From a first glance at a map it appears to have almost severed Scotland into two. It has served much more as trading canal than as frontier moat. The long tidal shores are dotted with merchant towns whose markets and privileges are established in ancient royal charters. The old local adage that a farm by the Forth is better than an earldom in the north expresses the realities of this land which formed the heartland of the medieval kingdom of Scotland.

Hopetoun House▶, 6km (4 miles) west of the Forth rail and road bridges is the beautiful stately home of the Marquis of Linlithgow. Begun in 1699 by Sir William Bruce and completed by William Adam and his sons, it houses a sumptuous collection of paintings, tapestry and furniture. An equal distance east of the bridges, near South Queensferry, is **Dalmeny▶**, a large 19th-century house set in a fine park that is home to one of Britain's outstanding Rothschild Mentmore collections of 17th-century French furniture, tapestry and Sèvres porcelain. Dalmeny can be reached on foot along the estuary from Cramond, a lovely walk. **Cramond▶** is a pretty village of whitewashed cottages and old mills at the mouth of the River Almond, on the outskirts of Edinburgh. A little ferry takes you across to the Dalmeny estates and there are delightful walks up the riverbank.

Further west, still on the southern side of the Firth, **Linlithgow Palace▶▶** (HS) stands above the town of Linlithgow. At the time of Mary, Queen of Scots' birth here in 1542 it was a magnificent structure but a fire in 1746 left it a ruin. Its enormous roofless red body survives and there is a fine octagonal fountain in the courtyard, a vast Great Hall and a swathe of turf around the outer walls on which to picnic.

Across the Firth, on the western edge of Fife, the small coastal town of **Culross▶▶▶** (pronounced *Coo*-ross) is set in an unpromising landscape of coal mines with a

226

distant prospect of Grangemouth refinery. Persevere, however, for Culross is one of the jewels of the Scottish National Trust, a perfectly preserved example of an early 17th-century trading burgh. It made its way in the world by digging coal from under the Forth, smelting iron to be hammered out into girdles and boiling up sea water to extract salt. The cobbled streets are lined with traditional corbelled houses, roofed with the distinctive terracotta pantiles of Fife. You can inspect three period interiors: start at the town's Tolbooth where free video shows on local history are put on alongside the jail chamber in the basement. Next door is the restored palace of Sir George Bruce, the local entrepreneurial landowner, with its painted ceilings, tiled kitchen and panelled rooms. Bishop Leighton's Study, also carefully restored, is the traditional name for the tall corbelled townhouse that overlooks the Mercat Cross. From there a short walk up steep Kirk Street leads to the slight ruins of a Cistercian monastery standing immediately beside the old abbey chapel which has functioned, with later additions, as the parish church since the Reformation.

Dunfermline Abbey►► (HS) stands above the wooded glen of Pittencrieff Park in Dunfermline. The abbey was founded as a Benedictine house in the 11th century. Its tower and eastern end were rebuilt in the 19th century to serve as a parish church. It is the sturdy 12th-century nave with its solid pale stone columns, strong round arches and the zigzag chevrons so characteristic of the Romanesque that excites the greatest interest. The visitor centre has a good range of display material.

A more recent attration at North Queensferry is **Deep Sea World►**, one of the country's top aquarium attractions, with a viewing tunnel as long as a soccer pitch. In summer, boat trips can be taken from South Queensferry, by the Forth bridges, to Inchcolm Island, to see the well-preserved abbey and a colony of seals.

See page 230 for the Firth of Forth fishing villages of the East Neuk of Fife.

Dunfermline Abbey, burial place of King Robert the Bruce

227

The Forth rail bridge, which requires continuous repainting on a four-year cycle

Royal Tennis
The 16th-century Falkland Palace (NTS), inland from Kirkcaldy, was a favourite hunting seat of the Scottish kings until James VI died in 1625. The royal tennis court was built in 1539 and is still in use. Sir Walter Scott used the palace as the setting for part of his novel *The Fair Maid of Perth*. which was made into an opera by Bizet.

▶▶▶ Glasgow 210C3

Glasgow's skyline of chimneys, factories and tower blocks offers a prospect of almost grotesque beauty. These industrial outskirts are a potent reminder of Scotland's 19th-century industrial core but the middle of Glasgow is today a place of captivating charm and a vibrant, entertaining centre. The city's merchant dynasties have bequeathed it an extraordinary legacy of art and architecture – and most of the museums and galleries are free. The grid plan of the streets makes it easy to explore.

The city has three distinct areas: the original medieval centre, the Merchant City and the West End. The **cathedral▶**, a dark-hued, heavy Gothic glory begun in the 13th century, is one of the two surviving buildings of the medieval town, on the eastern side of the city. St Mungo (or Kentigern) founded a missionary chapel here in the 6th century, around which the trading burgh of Glasgow later grew. Opposite the cathedral, the unique **St Mungo's Museum▶** explores the religions of the world. In High Street, is **Provand's Lordship**, built in 1471 for a canon of the cathedral and now displaying period artefacts and furnishings; it is the city's oldest house.

The Merchant City district has its origins in the heyday of the 'tobacco lords'. Glasgow was well placed for trade with the New World and the 18th century saw a period of glory as an international trading city. It was the tobacco lords who laid the foundations for later industrial development. By the 19th century Glasgow was one of the world's greatest ship-building centres and, in an expression of bursting civic pride, money was poured into the Merchant City district to create some of the best Victorian streets in Britain, with some of the most innovative architecture of the day. The great rectangular **George Square▶** is the centre of Glasgow today, flanked on one side by the splendidly overblown façade of the **City Chambers▶▶** (*Guided tours* free), built 1883–8. Immediately to the north is Queen Street Station; Central Station, with its even more impressive 19th-century interior, is just a few blocks west. **Trades House** with its Adam façade dates from 1791, while **Hutchesons' Hall** and **Stirling Library** are early 19th century. Glasgow Green is one of many city parks and here is the **People's Palace▶**, an excellent museum devoted to the social history of Glasgow, and its huge Winter Gardens conservatory. Near by is the old Templeton's carpet factory (1889), an amazing mock-up of the Doge's Palace in Venice.

In the leafy area of the West End, with its fine early 19th-century terraces around Glasgow University, is the **Art Gallery and Museum▶▶**, an enormous Victorian red sandstone building in Kelvingrove Park which holds works of art from neolithic weapons to Cubist paintings; there is a strong emphasis on 17th-century Dutch and Flemish works. In Kelvin Hall, opposite, is an exciting **Transport Museum▶▶**, with reconstructed subway stations and shops, old trams, cars and motorbikes. The **Hunterian Art Gallery▶▶** is renowned for its collection of works of James McNeill Whistler (1834–1903). Also strongly represented is 19th- and 20th-century Scottish art, including works of the Scottish colourists such as S J Peploe and of the 'Glasgow Boys', a group of painters led by W McGregor who advocated realism in art instead of

The great shipbuilding yards on the Clyde were born in the 19th-century steam era, when Clyde-built vessels acquired a high reputation worldwide

The interior of the City Chambers, an astonishing statement of 19th-century municipal confidence

Charles Rennie Mackintosh (1868–1928)
Mackintosh was prominent in the Arts and Crafts Movement and was the first Scottish architect since the 18th century to achieve international fame. While his stained glass and metalwork used the art nouveau motifs of inter-twining tendrils, his buildings have a taut quality of austere, geometric simplicity; his furniture design is typified by the tall, starkly simple ladder-chair. The Glasgow School of Art (1896–1909) is his master-piece, designed when he was only 28; other notable buildings in Glasgow include the Scotland Street School and the Willow Tea Rooms (now serving tea again).

229

Victorian romanticism. The Mackintosh Wing is an elegant re-creation of the nearby house (now demolished) occupied and furnished by Glasgow architect Charles Rennie Mackintosh (see panel). Within the Botanic Gardens is a beautiful 19th-century glasshouse, **Kibble Palace**▶▶, where tree ferns grow amid white statuary.

The **Glasgow School of Art**▶▶ (*Guided tours* daily), in Renfrew Street, is the finest completed example of Mackintosh's vision. It houses a comprehensive collection of his paintings and his designs for furniture, metalwork, light fittings, and stained glass. **The Tenement House**▶▶ (NTS) on nearby Buccleuch Street is the ordinary workaday flat of a Miss Agnes Toward, preserved as she left it in 1965, having changed virtually nothing in more than half a century. The simple dignity of the four-roomed flat and her belongings tell a visitor more about the realities of a Scottish life than two dozen ducal palaces.

A short drive but a million miles in atmosphere from the city centre, a fantastically light, glass-walled building constructed in 1983 in the grounds of Pollock House houses the extraordinary art collection of shipping magnate Sir William Burrell. The **Burrell Collection**▶▶▶ is a vast one, but one that you will want to visit and revisit. Everything is of the very best, be it the Egyptian alabaster, the Chinese ceramics or jade, the Persian rugs, the medieval illuminated manuscripts, stained glass or carved doorways.

The old Templeton's carpet factory, to be seen from Glasgow Green

SOUTHERN SCOTLAND

*St Andrews –
Scotland's first
university town
(1410) seen from St
Rule's Tower*

The St Andrews martyrs
The year 1546 was a heady
one packed full of events
that are still commemorated in the town of St
Andrews. It started with
the trial and burning of two
leading Protestant reform-
ers, George Wishart and
Patrick Hamilton, by
Cardinal Beaton, the all-
powerful regent and firm
ally of France. He was
assassinated in revenge
and the castle was seized
by a body of Protestant
zealots who held out in
a year-long siege, with
such reforming luminaries
as John Knox among
their ranks.

▶▶▶ St Andrews   211D4

Scotland's oldest university, its first golf course and the
ruins of its principal pre-Reformation cathedral mingle
with the everyday business of a old Fife market town and
summer resort. It was already a holy place for the southern Picts when a shrine to St Andrew, patron saint of
Scotland, was established on the eastern clifftops in the
8th century. Within a century St Andrews had become
the administrative centre of Christianity in Scotland. The
top of 12th-century St Rule's church tower gives a bird's
eye view over the enormous ruined nave of the adjoining
14th-century **cathedral**▶▶ (HS) and of the town's little
harbour with its long mole. Westwards along the coast
are the ruins of the bishop's **castle**▶ (HS) with its bottle
dungeon, from which no one ever escaped, and 16th-cen-
tury mine and counter mine. A visitor centre inter-
prets its role. Below the Martyrs' Memorial, the
handsome **Royal and Ancient Club House** (home of
the ruling body for golf the world over) overlooks the
oldest course in the world and the British Golf
Museum. Near by a Sea Life Centre stands by the long
West Sands. In the three converging streets that comprise the 'auld grey toun' are lesser but impressive buildings such as the university's 15th- and 16th-century
colleges and the West Port gate, all among elegant town-
houses and secretive 'wynds', or alleyways.

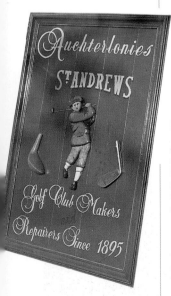

The East Neuk A road south leads to **Anstruther**▶, one
of several pretty old fishing villages dotted along the
southern coast of Fife's East Neuk. Here is the Scottish
Fisheries Museum and an aquarium. Boat trips go out in
summer to the Isle of May. Fishermen's cottages in
Crail▶▶ are now home to artists and holidaymakers. To
see a fishing fleet in action go to the harbour at
Pittenweem▶; here St Fillan, a 7th-century missionary,
lived in a cave that is still used for the occasional church
service. Flemish gables reflect former trading links with
the Low Countries. Inland is **Kellie Castle**▶▶ (NTS), a
good example of the 16th-century round tower houses
typical of the Lowlands; another is **Scotstarvit Tower**▶
(NTS), near Ceres. Also in the vicinity is the **Hill of Tarvit
Mansion House** (NTS), rebuilt by Sir Robert Lorimer in
1906 to house the art collection of a jute magnate.

▶▶ Stirling

210D3

Stirling Castle▶▶ (HS) stands in a strategically commanding position on a volcanic crag, the symbolic key to Scotland. For centuries the Old Bridge was the only 'gateway to the Highlands', and even today Stirling is still at the geographical and historical centre of the country.

The **Wallace Monument▶▶** and its visitor centre, on the northeastern edge of the town, commemorate Scotland's first freedom fighter, William Wallace; Wallace rose from obscurity to lead the national resistance to the advances of the English king, Edward I, winning a major victory at the Battle of Stirling in 1297. On the other side of town, the Bannockburn Heritage Centre tells the story of the most famous battle in Scottish history (see panel). Midway between them on the banks of the Forth are the restored Gothic ruins of Cambuskenneth Priory. Walk up to the old town to see the Church of Holy Rood where in 1543 Mary, Queen of Scots was crowned at the age of nine months. The Guildhall, the shell of Mar's Wark (HS) – built in 1570 as the town house of the 1st Earl of Mar, Regent of Scotland – as well as Argyll's Lodging, are all notable buildings in this vicinity. Within the grey castle walls are 18th-century artillery batteries, gardens, a royal chapel and the Renaissance palace of the Stewart kings. Also here is the Argyll and Sutherland Highlanders regimental museum. In summer, pageants and plays recapture bygone splendours.

Dunblane▶ is a small residential town beside the meandering Allan River. Although its name is now indelibly associated with the 1996 primary school tragedy, Dunblane does have one of Scotland's finer Gothic cathedrals; the tower is 12th-century but the splendid interior, one long soaring 63m nave, is mid-13th century. The town is also a good centre for touring the Ochil Hills to the east. At the foot of the Ochils near Dollar, 16km (10 miles) east of Stirling, **Castle Campbell▶** (HS, NTS), built at the end of the 15th century, stands perched on a huge crag. Do take the short trail around its base through Dollar Glen, part of it hewn out of rock, over catwalks and past cascades and drippy ferns. A little west of Dunblane, **Doune** is worth a visit for a fine 14th-century royal **fortress▶** (HS) and motor museum.

Robert the Bruce
The Battle of Bannockburn was one of the most decisive in Scottish history. For several years Robert the Bruce (1274–1329) had been successfully waging a guerilla war against the English – and those of the Scottish nobility whom he had alienated – when in 1314 he was forced into a pitched battle over the vital control of Stirling Castle. With a mere 5,000 men but great cunning, he destroyed an English force of some 20,000. Stirling surrendered and Edward II fled to Dunbar; Scotland later won independence for 400 years and Bruce was acknowledged as king of Scotland.

231

Castle Campbell towers above the Burn of Sorrow and the Burn of Care

SOUTHERN SCOTLAND

▶▶   **The Trossachs**   *210D2*

The Trossachs is an area of rugged hills, tumbling burns (or streams) and picturesque lochs. It may lack the drama of the true Highlands but its accessibility from central Scotland has made it popular and it is well geared to visitors. Strictly speaking, the Trossachs is a narrow strip of country between **Loch Katrine** and **Loch Achray**, but in effect it is considered to stretch west from the busy resort town of **Callander** to the shores of Loch Lomond, with the somewhat commercialised **Aberfoyle** as its heart. It is undeniably beautiful but is also one of the most visited areas in Scotland and in summer has just too many coaches and tourists for those who prefer more lonesome parts.

The area became fashionable with the 18th-century Romantics in their cult of the picturesque – it was wild, but not too wild, and it was also easy to reach. Sir Walter Scott further popularised the area, using the Trossachs as the setting for his poem *Lady of the Lake* and his novel *Rob Roy*. For this was the territory of Rob Roy's Clan Gregor, a near criminal caste touched by a spirit of romantic lawlessness (see panel). The Trossachs was also the favourite sketching ground of the Glasgow Boys (see page 228).

The 37km (23-mile) long **Loch Lomond▶**, Scotland's largest inland loch (in terms of surface area), stretches from the suburbs of Glasgow to the fringes of the Highlands. It is overlooked by a dramatic variety of empty hills, rocky shores and wooded farmland. However, it is the nearest Highland loch to the Clydeside conurbation and traffic along the road up its western shore is sometimes so busy that it is hard to enjoy its beauty.

There are several pleasant summer **boat trips** (but get there early, to avoid queues): along the length of Loch Katrine on the SS *Walter Scott*; on Loch Lomond from Balloch, Ardlui and Tarbet, on the western shore, and from Balmaha or the Inversnaid Hotel pier on the quieter eastern shore; a more modest excursion goes out to the ruins of Inchmahome Priory on an island in the Lake of Menteith. Activities such as pony trekking, cycling, fishing and golf are well catered for, while walkers can choose between numerous forest trails or ambitious hill walks. The area's scenic drives can easily be combined with short strolls from the road, to beauty spots such as the Falls of Leny, off the A84 northwest of Callander, and the Trossachs viewpoint at the top of the A821 north of Aberfoyle.

Trossachs walks
The area's most energetic hikes are the main peaks such as Ben Ledi, Ben Lomond and Ben Venue, but numerous lesser summits have fine views, among them Ben An (climb up from the Trossachs Hotel north of Loch Achray on the A821) and Conic Hill, near the southeast corner of Loch Lomond. For lower-level walks try the forest around David Marshal Lodge near Aberfoyle, where there is an old tramway to explore, or the wooded glen north of Rob Roy's Grave at Balquhidder. (See also the Callander Crags walk on page 214.)

Rob Roy MacGregor
Robert MacGregor, known for his red hair as Rob Roy (Red Robert), was a colourful and free-booting cattle thief whose exploits frequently involved robbing the rich for the benefit of the poor. He was forced to become an outlaw in about 1712, but having successfully outwitted all attempts to bring him to heel, he gradually returned to living openly among his own people. In 1725 he was given a formal pardon. The full story of this Scottish folk hero is told at the Rob Roy and Trossachs Visitor Centre in Callander.

Still waters: Loch Ard

Clans and tartans

■ **The Highland clans in their 15th-century heyday formed a tribal system strong enough to threaten the authority of the Stewart monarchs. The aftermath of the last Jacobite rebellion of 1745 brought about the final dismantling of their distinctive way of life. However, the dress and tartan of the Highlands of former times then became fashionable – and the scene was set for the once outlawed cloth of a tribal minority to become the most potent symbol for the whole of Scotland. ■**

Life beyond the Highland Line

In Gaelic the word 'clann' means family. By the 13th century, clans had evolved into self-governing tribal units at whose head was a chief or 'father' to whom lesser chieftains and ordinary clansmen gave allegiance. The clan, at least in earlier times, counted its wealth in cattle. Consequently, cattle-raiding was common, as were territorial disputes. However, not all of the clan's preoccupations were warlike. The more powerful chiefs kept extensive retinues, an important member being the clan bard, who was official record keeper as well as composer. By the 18th century, better communications meant that the clans came more into contact with southern or Saxon – hence 'sasunnach' – ways. Some chiefs even sent their children to school in the Lowlands and developed a taste for fine wines or fashionable clothes. Thus the system was already in decline before the shock of Culloden.

The dress of the clans

The idea of a 'clan tartan' was essentially a marketing device of 19th-century textile manufacturers. Tartan was banned after Culloden, though the Highland regiments of the British army were still permitted to wear it. Later, the fashion industry used the military as a source of inspiration and tartan became very fashionable. Then the visit of King George IV to Scotland in 1822 created an excuse for the new landowners and clan chiefs of Scotland to play act and dress up in tartan costumes. The cloth has remained popular ever since, creating its own mythology and conventions.

How to recognise a fellow clansman

Contemporary evidence from the Battle of Culloden indicates a wide variety of tartans worn even by members of the same clan. The government forces were identifiable by the red or yellow tied badges on their bonnets, while the Jacobites had their famous 'white cockades', inspired by the wild white rose said to have been plucked by Charles as a symbol for the campaign. In fact, the British army was the first to define uniform tartans in the 18th century.

The Black Watch

One of General Wade's ways of policing the Highlands (see page 244) was to recruit local Highlanders. Six independent companies first enlisted in 1725 and from these was formed the 43rd, later the 42nd or Black Watch Regiment. By creating fighting units of this type, the martial spirit of the Highlands was harnessed for Britain's imperial wars of the 19th century.

NORTHERN SCOTLAND

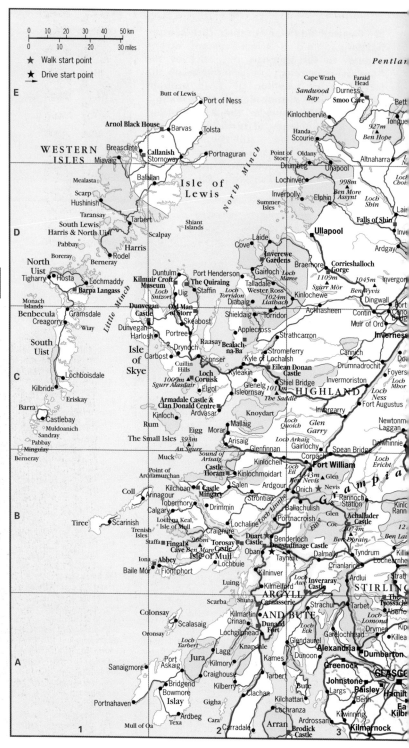

★ Walk start point
★ Drive start point

0 10 20 30 40 50 km
0   10   20   30 miles

Pentlar

WESTERN ISLES

Butt of Lewis
Port of Ness
Arnol Black House
Barvas   Tolsta
Breasclete   Portnaguran
Miavaig   **Callanish**
Stornoway
Balallan
Mealasta   Isle of Lewis
Scarp   Lewis
Hushinish   Shiant Islands
Taransay
South Lewis, Harris & North Uist
Scalpay
Pabbay   **Harris**   Rodel
Boreray   Berneray
North Uist   Tigharry   Hosta   Lochmaddy
Barpa Langass
Monach Islands   Gramsdale
Benbecula   Creagorry   Wiay
South Uist   Harlosh
Lochboisdale
Kilbride   Eriskay
Barra
Castlebay
Muldoanich   Sandray
Pabbay
Mingulay
Berneray

Cape Wrath   Faraid Head
Sandwood Bay   Durness   **Smoo Cave**
Kinlochbervie   Bett
Handa   927m   Tongue
Scourie   Ben Hope
Point of   Oldany
Stoer   Drumbeg   Ullapool
Lochinver   998m
Inverpolly   Ben More   Loch
Summer   Assynt   Shin
Isles   Elphin
Lair
Falls of Shin

Laide
Cove
Inverewe Gardens   Braemore   **Corrieshalloch Gorge**
Port Henderson   Gairloch   Loch   Invergor
Duntulm   Maree   1109m   1045m
Kilmuir Croft Museum   Talladale   Sgurr Mòr   Ben Wyvis
The Quiraing   Staffin   Wester Ross
Uig   Loch   Kinlochewe   Dingwall
Dunvegan   Snizort   Diabaig   1024m   Achnasheen   Contin
Castle   **Old Man of Storr**   Liathach   Muir of Ord
Skeabost   Shieldaig   Torridon
Dunvegan   Portree   Applecross   Strathcarron   Cannich
Raasay   **Bealach na-Ba**   Stromeferry   Drumnadrochit
Dryoch   Carbost   Sconser   Kyle of Lochalsh   **Eilean Donan**
Isle of Skye   Cuillin   **Loch**   Kyleakin   **Castle**   Invermoriston
Hills   **Coruisk**   Glenelg   Shiel Bridge
1009m   Elgol   Isleornsay   1011m   Loch
Sgurr Alasdair   **Armadale Castle &**   The Saddle   **HIGHLAND**   Ness
Clan Donald Centre   Knoydart   Invergarry   Fort Augustus
Kinloch   Ardvasar
Rum   Mallaig   Morar   Loch   Glen   Newtonm
Eigg   Arisaig   Quoich   Garry   Laggan
The Small Isles   An Sgurr   Gairlochy   Spean Bridge   Dalwhinnie
Muck   393m   Glenfinnan   Corpach
Sound of   Kinlocheil   Loch   **Fort William**   Loch
Arisaig   **Castle**   Ell   Ben Nevis   Ericht
Point of   **Tioram**   Kinlochmoidart   343m   Glen
Ardnamurchan   Salen   Ardgour   Onich   Nevis   Rannoch   Kinlo
Kilchoan   **Castle**   Strontian   Glen   Station   Rann
Arinagour   **Mingary**   Lochaline   Ballachulish   Coe   **Achallader**   12.
Coll   Tobermory   Drimmin   Portnacroish   Glen   **Castle**   Ben Lat
Calgary   1074m
Loch na Keal,   Lochaline   Portnacroish   Ben Dorain
Tiree   Scarinish   Isle of Mull   Creagure   Benderloch   Dalmally   Tyndrum   Lochearnhe
Trenish   Craignure   **Duart**   **Dunstaffnage Castle**   Crianlarich
Isles   Staffa   966m   **Castle**   Taynuilt   Ardlui   Strath
Fingal's   Torosay   Oban   Loch   **Inveraray**
Cave   Ben More   **Castle**   Kilninver   Awe   **Castle**   **STIRLING**
Iona   **Abbey**   Isle of Mull   Lochbuie   Kilmelford   Ardlui
Baile Mór   Fionnphort   Luing   Kilmartin   **Carnasserie**   **INVERARAY**   Strachur   Tarbet   The Tsossach
Scarba   Shuna   **Dunadd**   Loch   Garelochhead   Aber
Colonsay   Kilmartin   **ARGYLL**   **Fort**   Eck   Killea
Scalasaig   **AND BUTE**   Loch   Glendaruel   Drymen   Kip
Oronsay   Crinan   Lochgilphead   Tarbert   Kames   Dunoon   Alexandria
Loch   Knapdale   Colintraive
Tarbert   Lagg   Kilmory   Dunoon   **Dumbarton**
Port   Kilberry   **Greenock**
Sanaigmore   Askaig   Tarbert   Bute   Largs   **GLASGO**
Jura   Bridgend   Kilberry   Clachan   Johnstone   **Paisley**   Hamil
Bowmore   Gigha   Kilchattan   **Beith**   Ea
Portnahaven   **Islay**   Cara   Lochranza   Kilwinning   Kilbr
Ardbeg   Texa   Ardrossan
Mull of Oa   Carradale   **Arran**   **Brodick**   **Kilmarnock**
Castle

Inverness
Invermoriston
Inverness

Ardgay
Loch
Chot

Loch
N

Port
Cano
Brid
Do

Foyers
Loch
Mbor

SHETLAND

Muckle Flugga
Haroldswick
Unst
Gutcher
Uyeasound
West Sandwick
Fetlar
Isbister
Yell
Burravoe
Hillswick
Toft
Out Skerries
Sullom Voe
Muckle Roe
Brae
Whalsay
Papa Stour
Sandness
Voe
Mainland
Walls
Catfirth
Vaila
Lerwick
Scalloway
Isle of Noss
Bressay
West Burra
Shetland
Sandwick
Mousa
Tolob
Jarlshof
Sumburgh Head

ORKNEY

Stromness
Mainland
Houton
Hoy
Old Man of Hoy
Lyness
irth
Burwick
Dunnet Head
Duncansby Head
Strathy Point
Scrabster
John O'Groats
Thurso
Melvich
Wick
Grey Cairns of Camster
Hill O'Many Stones
Kinbrace
Latheron
Helmsdale
unrobin Castle
Brora
onoch
Tarbat Ness
Portmahomack
Tain
Balintore
Burghead
Lossiemouth
romarty
Findhorn
Rosehearty
Fraserburgh
Nairn
Forres
Elgin
Cullen
Portsoy
Macduff
Buckie
Banff
Rattray Head
Ardersier
Pluscarden Abbey
Keith
Aberchirder
New Pitsligo
Cawdor Castle
Ferness
Rothes
Turriff
Mintlaw
Peterhead
Culloden Battlefield
Aberlour
Dufftown
Huntly
Lochindorb
Dava
Cruden Bay
Tomatin
Grantown-on-Spey
Cabrach
Rhynie
Oldmeldrum
Ellon
Landmark Visitor Centre
MORAY
Tomintoul
Mossat
Inverurie
Newburgh
viemore
Strathspey Steam Railway
Strathdon
Glenbuchat
ABERDEENSHIRE
Dyce
Loch an Eilan
Coylumbridge
Kildrummy
Kintore
Aberdeen
Highland Wildlife Park
Corgarff
Craigievar Castle
Lumphanan
Kingussie
uthven arracks
Balmoral Castle
Aboyne
Banchory
Peterculter
Drum Castle
Braemar
Ballater
Dee
Crathes Castle
Linn O'Dee
Strachan
Stonehaven
M o u n t a i n s
Deeside & Lochnagar
Fettercairn
Inverbervie
Clova
ruar
Blair Castle
Spittal of Glenshee
Edzell Castle
Laurencekirk
Killiecrankie
Kirkmichael
ANGUS
Brechin
Castle Menzies
Pitlochry
Kirriemuir
Montrose
PERTH
Aberfeldy
Alyth
Forfar
Friockheim
Kenmore
Blairgowrie
Glamis Castle
Inverkeilor
ch Tay
Dunkeld
Coupar Angus
Arbroath
Amulree
Caputh
Muirhead
Carnoustie
AND KINROSS
Dundee
omrie
Methven
Newport-on-Tay
Crieff
Scone Palace
Leuchars
Perth
M85
Auchterarder
Bridge of Earn
Elcho Castle
Gleneagles Hotel
Castle Campbell
Falkland Palace
Dunblane
M90
FIFE
M9
Alloa
Loch Leven
Dunfermline
tirling
M80
alkirk
M9
EDINBURGH
Cumbernauld
M8
Livingston
Coatbridge
Penicuik
otherwell
West Linton
Wishaw
Dolphinton
M74
Lanark
Peebles

ORKNEY

Papa Westray
North Ronaldsay
Westray
The North Sound
Westray Firth
Rapness
Sanday
Rousay
Eday
Kettletoft
Birsay
Backaland
Stronsay
Mainland
Redland
Whitehall
Auskerry
Skara Brae
Finstown
Shapinsay
Maes Howe
Kirkwall
Ring of Brogar
Stromness
St Mary's
Old Man of Hoy
Houton
Burray
Hoy
Lyness
St Margaret's Hope
South Ronaldsay
Burwick 5

Northern Scotland The Highlands and Islands, with their awesome mountain and coastal scenery, have contributed much of what is now considered typical of Scotland. Malt whisky, bagpipes, tartans, clans, kilts and Highland flings were all distinctive aspects of Highland culture that today are considered essentially Scottish. This would have amazed any 17th-century native, for one of the key facts of Scottish history was the marked division between the northern Highlands and the main body of Scotland. The Highlands and the Lowlands were as different as chalk and cheese, and held each other in mutual scorn.

The water of life – pure single malt Scotch whisky

The great divide Though they might have traded cattle for corn at market towns, Highlanders and Lowlanders otherwise kept their distance. The Highlanders were Gaelic-speaking with a highly developed oral culture of bards, oaths and undying loyalty to kinship groups, while the Lowlanders were English-speaking, literate and litigious. The Highlanders were mobile pastoralists who counted their wealth in cattle and shunned towns, whereas the Lowlanders were firmly rooted agriculturalists dwelling in the well-established burghs that were evenly scattered over the coastal plains. The Highland Boundary Fault, running from southwest straight across to northeast Scotland, was not merely a geological divide: it was a linguistic, social, military, legal and economic boundary.

A war-torn territory The Highlands brought limited rewards back to the central government in Edinburgh but provided a vital resource in times of danger. The mountain valleys could be relied upon to produce hardened troops for any military adventure that offered loot. The region also served as a bulwark against foreign conquest, most graphically in the 14th century when the English occupied the Lowland towns for a generation but could make no effective headway into the Highlands. Even after the Act of Union between England and Scotland in 1707, the Highlands continued to supply manpower for Britain's imperial adventures, and to this day there is a tradition of military service.

The Jacobite rebellions of 1715 and 1719 were part of a long history of dissidence but there were to be new initiatives from the south. General Wade was commissioned to build and design a string of strategic forts and fortified barracks for the military occupation of the Highlands, all linked by roads and elegant bridges. Several examples survive in the old county of Inverness-shire, in what is now known as **Highland** region. The Jacobite rising led by Bonnie Prince Charlie in 1745 (see page 246) had catastrophic effects, for the Hanoverian victory at Culloden Moor near **Inverness** was followed by the deliberate destruction of the military basis of Highland society. The legal powers of the clan chiefs were destroyed, the kilt and weapons were proscribed, and a series of ruthless judicial commissions brought the gallows to every glen. This was followed, a generation later, by an economic crisis which was resolved by the Clearances, the wholesale eviction of the tenant crofters to make space for sheep pastures (often run by English-speaking farmers from the Lowlands), particularly in **Sutherland** and the **Black Isle**, the **West Highlands** and the **Western Isles**. Today, the shells of single-storey cottages are the desolate reminders of more populous times.

The heritage The rude stone castles of the Highland chiefs decayed into romantic ruin while the turf and drystone round huts of the crofting tenantry were reduced to ubiquitous lumps in the pasture. They were replaced by neat stone farmhouses, crisp neo-classical manses for the influential clergy and the light spartan halls of their Presbyterian churches. Ironically, at the same time as the Highland crofters were being packed off in emigrant boats, the fashion for all things Highland got into full swing, intensified by Queen Victoria's patronage of **Deeside**. In the late 19th century, a series of enormous, exclusive sporting estates were created for the summer recreation of Britain's plutocracy, notably in **Angus, Perth and Kinross, Moray, Aberdeenshire, Sutherland** and **Wester Ross**. A series of wonderfully excessive Gothic Baronial lodges, hotels and palaces still provide the dominant architectural theme of the Highlands, softened by modern bungalows and the neater shape of the older, stone-built dormer-windowed house still seen all over the Highlands and Islands. The influx of English speakers helped put the Gaelic tongue into a slow decline and, though still widespread in the crofting population of the **Western Isles**, it is now rare on the mainland.

237

Quoth God to the Highlander, 'What will you do now?'
'I will down to the Lowland, Lord, and there steal a cow.'
Anon

THAD'S A DH'FHÀSAS FLÙR AIR MACHAIR MAIRIDH CLIÙ NA H-AINNIR CHAOIMH.

"THE PRESERVER OF PRINCE CHARLES EDWARD STUART WILL BE MENTIONED IN HISTORY AND IF COURAGE AND FIDELITY BE VIRTUES, MENTIONED WITH HONOUR"
JOHNSON

Walks

Beinn Lora, Argyll and Bute *234B2*
Forestry Commission car park just south of Benderloch village (north of Oban). Beinn Lora is a 308m (1,010ft) high hill with magnificent views of Loch Linnhe. Follow a path through the forest; follow signs and eventually skirt an area of boggy pools; the summit then comes into view. Return the same way. (2½ hours)

Findlater Castle, *235D4*
Aberdeenshire
From Cullen harbour (Moray) follow the shore-level road eastwards; this dwindles to a coastal path. On a clear day the Caithness and Sutherland coastline can be seen across the Firth. Carry on to the 15th-century ruins of Findlater Castle, perched on the cliff. Either return the same way or follow the coast on through the old fishing village of Sandend and then on to Portsoy, with its attractive harbour. Frequent buses return to Cullen from Sandend or Portsoy. (2½ to 4 hours)

Duncansby Head, Highland *235E4*
Car park at Duncansby Head lighthouse. From the very northeasternmost tip of the British mainland a fine coastal path heads south to the Stacks of Duncansby, a trio of natural pillars cut off from the mainland by marine erosion. Return the same way. (1½ hours)

Glen Nevis, Highland *234B3*
Car park at end of road in Glen Nevis, southeast of Fort William. There is a waterfall by the car park. The path goes into a splendid gorge before entering more open terrain, passing further waterfalls and reaching ruins at Steall. Return the same way. (2 hours)

Kenmore, Perth and Kinross *235B4*
Start in Kenmore village square (east end of Loch Tay). Take the road northwest, cross the River Tay then immediately take a riverside path on the right; later, turn right on a road, then left on a rising forest track, which soon levels out; 45 minutes' walking leads to a signposted viewpoint over the loch and over Taymouth Castle; return to the last track junction reached and turn right to drop to Kenmore. (2½ hours)

The stacks at Duncansby Head

In the tropical hot houses of Duthie Park

▶▶ Aberdeen 235C5

The 'Granite City' is the third largest in Scotland, but although the oil boom years of the 1970s have given rise to smart new buildings on the waterfront and huge oil-rig vessels in the harbour, the town has managed to retain its Georgian roots and its 19th-century dignity. A major port, it has long been a bustling centre of commerce, and the grand sweep of Union Street reflects the city's rich history. Elegant floral displays soften the imposing Victorian buildings and the silver granite squares and terraces.

St Machar's Cathedral▶ was founded in 1131; the main part was built in the mid-15th century. It dominates the part of the city known as **Old Aberdeen**, a calm haven of cobbled streets and houses that date from 1500. In this area too is **King's College**, founded 1500–5 and part of the university, the Cruickshank Botanic Gardens and Seaton Park. Further out, the **Brig O'Balgownie** across the River Don is the oldest medieval bridge in Scotland.

Central Aberdeen is more formal, with straight rows of granite terraces and spacious streets. Its numerous university buildings, markets and museums are dotted in and around Broad Street and Union Street. The **Tolbooth**, on the corner of Broad Street, is the town jail, built in 1627. You can tour the ancient cells by appointment.

Provost Ross's House (NTS) traces the city's history of fishing, ship-building and its North Sea oil and gas industry; **Provost Skene's House** is furnished in 17th-century style as a museum of local social life. **James Dun's House** has changing exhibitions of family appeal and **Satrosphere** is a 'hands-on' science and technology centre. The **city library**, St Mark's Church and **His Majesty's Theatre** are known collectively as 'Education, Salvation and Damnation'. The **Art Gallery and Museum**▶ has works by Romney, Reynolds, James McBey, Augustus John and Scottish impressionist William McTaggart among others. The **Duthie Park Winter Gardens** are the largest glassed gardens in Europe, a tropical paradise. Early risers can catch a glimpse of Aberdeen's **fish market and auction**, which begins at around 4.30am, when the fishermen unload their catch.

Haddo House▶ (NTS) is half an hour's drive north, near Pitmedden, a handsome house designed by William Adam in 1731 and still relatively undisturbed.

North Sea flier
Cruden Bay, north of Aberdeen, witnessed the take-off of the first flight across the North Sea when Tryggve Gran made a solo 480km (300-mile) flight in 1914 to Stavanger in Norway. With the advent of World War I, his achievement went almost unnoticed. There is a monument to Gran close to the sinister ruin of Slains Castle, which Bram Stoker saw on a visit in 1895, inspiring him to write *Dracula*.

The Buchan coast
Aberdeen is the gateway to some of the country's most unspoilt coastline. Northwards to Cruden Bay and on to the busy fishing ports of Peterhead (the biggest whitefish port in Western Europe) and Fraserburgh stretch glorious miles of untouched sandy beaches. Along the north-facing coast of this far corner of Scotland little fishing villages such as Pennan and Gardenstown, west of Rosehearty, hide under spectacular cliffs.

Highland Games
Athletes compete at these traditional Highland gatherings, held all over Scotland in summer, in events such as putting the stone and tossing the caber (Braemar's weighs in at 59.9 kilos (132lbs), claims to be the longest, at 6.02m (19¾ft) and has been thrown successfully – i.e., absolutely straight – and from end to end – fewer than five times); there are also bagpipe and dancing competitions. Tradition has it that the games originated in martial contests held by King Malcolm Canmore back in the 11th century, to find the toughest men to fight the Normans.

The River Dee near Braemar

Challenging summit
The summit of Morrone (859m/2,819ft) is the objective of the mountain race from Braemar during the Highland Games. For those not wishing to emulate the athletes (the record stands short of 25 minutes), it can be climbed from the village at a more leisurely pace in two hours. The lower slopes are cloaked by Morrone Birkwood, reckoned to be Britain's finest sub-alpine birchwood of a kind found more often in Norway. The wood is home to some 280 plant species and is a National Nature Reserve.

▶▶▶ **Deeside** *235C4*

The River Dee drains the eastern slopes of the Cairngorms and flows almost 130km (80 miles) due east to Aberdeen and the North Sea, passing on its way through a classic Scottish landscape of blue hills and purply heather moors, deep green woods of larch, juniper and birch, rocky riverbeds and rippling waters.

The village of **Braemar**, 330m (1,082ft) up and circled by layers of hills, is at the heart of the most beautiful stretch of the Dee and a popular summer holiday centre. It is famous for its round-towered, L-plan castle, built as a hunting lodge by the 2nd Earl of Mar in 1628 and buffeted by the Jacobites in 1689, and for the Braemar Gathering held on the first Saturday in September. The Royal Family usually pays a visit to these Highland Games (see panel), which accounts for crowds of around 50,000 people. Robert Louis Stevenson wrote *Treasure Island* while staying in Braemar in 1881. To the west of the village, at the head of the valley just beyond Inverey, is the **Linn o' Dee▶**, where the river waters cascade down into a series of rocky pools. The minor road from Braemar to this beauty spot, much reproduced in Victorian engravings and contemporary postcards, is an attractive drive and could be the starting point for some beautiful walks in the Mar Forest and the foothills of Ben Macdhui (1,311m/4,301ft).

Balmoral Castle, some 14km (9 miles) east of Braemar, was bought by Queen Victoria and her husband Prince Albert in 1852. The old castle was too small and today's mansion, typically Scottish Baronial in style, was commissioned by Prince Albert. The Royal Family still holiday here; the grounds and exhibitions are open to the public 1 May to 31 July. The peak of Lochnagar (1,154m/3,786ft) towers over Balmoral; it featured in Prince Charles' first book, *The Old Man of Lochnagar*, an illustrated children's story written to amuse his younger brothers. Across the main road is the granite Crathie Church, attended by members of the Royal Family when staying in Balmoral. Queen Victoria's favourite dram was Lochnagar malt whisky; the Royal Lochnagar Distillery today has a visitor centre and shop and offers visitors a tour of the distillery.

Continuing east along the banks of the boulder-strewn Dee the A93 passes through the granite village of **Ballater**, built at the end of the 18th century to accommodate visitors taking the spa waters of nearby Pannanich Wells. With its hotels and guesthouses, it makes a good base for walking the hills of Craigendarroch, Craig Coillich and Glen Muick.

The main road stays close to the river, pausing at **Aboyne**, a town neatly planned around a large level green where the Highland Gathering takes place in September. On then, with the valley opening out, to **Banchory**, where the Water of Feugh joins the Dee from the Forest of Birse. Watch the salmon leaping up the rapids from the Bridge of Feugh. Like most of these Deeside resorts, Banchory has a golf course.

North from Banchory about 24km (15 miles), near Kemnay, **Castle Fraser▶** (NTS) is a massive Z-plan castle. It is an excellent example of the Scottish baronial style, notable for its turrets,

East along the Dee from Banchory, **Crathes Castle▶▶** (NTS) is a celebrated L-shaped tower house dating to 1553, one of the finest Jacobean houses in the country. Inside, the Room of the Nine Nobles, the Room of the Muses and the Room of the Green Lady are renowned for their remarkable, highly decorative ceilings. The ghost of the Green Lady, carrying a baby and, of course, dressed in green, is thought to haunt certain rooms. The grounds too are special, a labyrinth of colour enclosed within the dark green walls of a 300-year-old yew hedge. Don't look at the plan, just be lured on by the skilfully contrived arches, avenues and enticing prospects.

About 10km (6 miles) down the glen, in the midst of a surviving parcel of the Caledonian Forest called the Old Wood of Drum, stands **Drum Castle▶** (NTS). A cold, solid 13th-century keep, thick-walled and 20m (65ft) high, adjoins a crow-stepped gabled Jacobean mansion. It houses a collection of portraits, silver and furniture and has fine grounds with a café and adventure playground.

Raising the Old Pretender's standard
It was the Highland chiefs who alone were able to raise the men needed to fight the cause of Britain's exiled Stuart kings and when George of Hanover became king of Britain in 1714, it was in Braemar, on the spot where the Invercauld Arms Hotel now stands, that the 6th Earl of Mar raised the standard in 1715 to launch the Jacobite Rising, proclaiming the Old Pretender, James VIII and III as king.

241

The Loch Ness monster
Mystery surrounds the Loch Ness monster, a supposedly dinosaur-like beast whose alleged appearances lend a hypnotic lure to the surface waters of the loch, making even hardened sceptics pause a little longer than planned – just in case. The Loch Ness Monster Exhibition at Drumnadrochit has photographs of 'Nessie', together with scientific explanations and demonstrations of the latest techniques being used to solve the mystery.

Loch Ness, seen near Drumnadrochit, lies in the Great Glen Fault that runs across the Highlands

Inverness
234C3

Now as ever the Capital of the Highlands, Inverness holds a strategic position, at the head of the Great Glen. Its full but often violent history has left it with few historic buildings. The city museum has a good, original collection.

Less than 10km (6 miles) out of town, the vast depressing Drummossie moor, renamed **Culloden**, witnessed the last battle fought on British soil, on 18 April 1746, the end of Prince Charles Edward Stuart's attempt to gain the throne from the Hanoverian George II (see page 246). There is a good visitor centre (NTS), which tells the story of that rainy day in which a thousand of Bonnie Prince Charlie's Highlanders met their deaths. A mile south stand the prehistoric **Clava Cairns** and standing stones.

Cawdor Castle►, a little east, was built by the Thanes of Cawdor in the 14th century. The original keep remains and inside are fine Jacobean rooms. At the entrance to the Inverness and Beauly Firth sits vast **Fort George►** (HS), built between 1748 and 1769 in graphic demonstration of government intent to keep the Jacobites at bay.

The largest loch in Scotland in terms of volume of water, **Loch Ness**'s reputation relies more on the 'Nessie' legend (see panel) than its beauty. Good views can be had from **Urquhart Castle** (HS), its ruins set on a rocky cliff (HS).

Visit **Beauly►** (HS) for the remains of its 13th-century priory and for Campbells, a good tweed, tartan and woollen shop. **Strathpeffer** is a Victorian spa town with several old hotels; walk from here to the Rogie Falls. The **Black Isle►** is in fact a broad, fertile peninsula whose shores are the haunt of wading birds. In Cromarty look at the old port, the lighthouse and **Cromarty Courthouse►**, a most illuminating visitor centre. In **Rosemarkie** see the Pictish stone in the churchyard and Groam House Museum. In nearby **Fortrose** visit the Gothic cathedral ruins (HS).

LOCH NESS AND THE BLACK ISLE

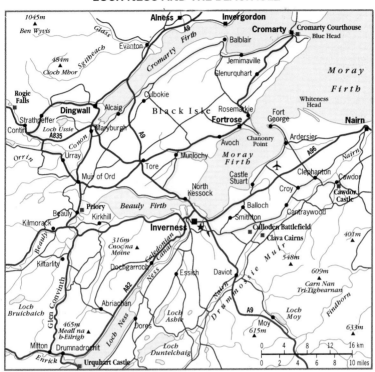

Drive **Loch Ness and the Black Isle**

A tour through varied mountain and coastal landscape (approx. 200km/130 miles).

Leave Inverness on the A9 southeast, turn on to the B9006 to see **Culloden battlefield** and visitor centre (NTS), and nearby **Clava Cairns** prehistoric stones. Continue to **Cawdor Castle▶**, scene of the murder of Duncan in Shakespeare's *Macbeth*. Turn back and take the narrow B9006 to **Fort George▶** (HS) with its regimental museum of the Queen's Own Highlanders. Follow the east coast of the **Moray Firth** into Inverness and out again on the A82 along the northern shore of **Loch Ness** to ruined **Urquhart Castle** (HS) and the Nessie Exhibition in **Drumnadrochit**.

From here take the road back north over the hills to the remains of **Beauly Priory** (HS). At Muir of Ord take the A832 northwest to reach **Strathpeffer**. Head east to **Dingwall** and follow the Black Isle shore to reach the old seaport of **Cromarty**. Go south along the A832 to the charming little resorts of **Rosemarkie** and nearby **Fortrose**. Continue southwest to rejoin the A9 and cross over Moray Firth on the new Kessock suspension bridge back into Inverness.

A sgian dubh, Gaelic dagger, in Inverness Museum and Art Gallery

Ben Nevis and Carn Mor Dearg

The Caledonian Canal

▶▶▶ Lochaber 234C3

This is the region once known as the West Highlands, an area of archetypal highland landscape – bleak moorlands set against soft valley meadows and the long reach of still lochs. It is the land of the Camerons and the Macdonnels, clans who provided the core support for the '45 Rebellion (see page 246) and who, a year later, tipped the Jacobite treasure into Loch Arkaig rather than see it in the hands of the Hanoverians.

At the southern end of Loch Ness (see page 242) the little town of **Fort Augustus** sits around the Caledonian Canal, a splendid waterway, with several staircase locks, designed by Thomas Telford. By linking the lochs of the Great Glen the canal joins Fort William at Loch Linnhe with Inverness on the Moray Firth. Fort Augustus has long since lost the fort built by General Wade (see panel); in its place is a Benedictine monastery and school.

The resort and aluminium smelting town of **Fort William** stands in the shadow of **Ben Nevis▶**, Britain's highest mountain at 1,347m (4,406ft). It is not the best in the Highlands for walking but if you do wish to climb it (and it looks deceptively small because it lacks a definitive peak) you should allow five hours to get to the top and three hours to pick your way back down. It is of course essential to be properly equipped and take all safety precautions. Low-level walks with superb views of the mountains include Glen Nevis (see Walk, page 238), the towpath of the Caledonian Canal, and Glen Leven (east of Kinlochleven), which threads its way up to the vast Blackwater Reservoir. Fort William is a modern, commercialised place, but makes a convenient base. Its story began in 1655 when General Monk built an earthwork fort here; this was replaced by General Wade's stone construction in the reign of William III; it was pulled down in the 19th century. The West Highland Museum in Cameron Square provides a good introduction to the region and its natural history.

South from Fort William the main road passes through **Glen Coe▶▶**, the scene, in the early hours of 13 February 1692, of Scotland's most infamous massacre. Acting under government orders, members of the Campbell militia who were billeted on members of the MacDonald clan,

The West Highland Line
The railway that runs from Glasgow to Mallaig can justly claim to be the most scenic rail route. The construction of the line between Fort William and Mallaig in particular involved some spectacular feats of engineering, with gradients of up to 1 in 48, numerous rock cuttings and dramatic bridges, viaducts and tunnels. Some services are steam-hauled.

245

turned on their hosts – breaking the strict code of hospitality that existed between clans – and indiscriminately massacred them. An act, so the government thought, that would dissuade anyone from harbouring doubts about the legitimacy of Queen Mary on the throne instead of her brother James VII (James II to the English). There is a visitor centre near the foot of the glen.

West of Fort William, at the head of Loch Shiel, the **Glenfinnan monument►** (NTS) marks the spot where the Young Pretender, Prince Charles Edward (see page 246), raised his standard on 19 August 1745 and launched the campaign to see his father recognised as rightful king.

The songwriter's 'Road to the Isles' from Fort William leads to **Arisaig and Mallaig►►** past the coral sandy beaches that featured in the film *Local Hero*. Inland are the dark waters of Loch Morar, the deepest freshwater stretch of water in Britain, with its own much neglected monster, Morag. On the wooded islands in the loch, the Jesuits maintained a secret seminary to keep the Roman Catholic faith alive. The busy fishing port of Mallaig is the departure point for ferries to the Inner Isles of Eigg, Muck, Rhum, Canna, Soay and Armadale on Skye (see pages 254–5). All the islands are easy day trips; only the Skye boat takes cars.

To the south is the untamed **Ardnamurchan** peninsula, whose far point is the westernmost part of the British mainland. Isolated on a tide-washed island in Loch Moidart stands the gaunt, empty keep of **Castle Tioram►**, last used by the MacDonald chief of Clan Ranald, who burnt it after the failure of the 1715 uprising rather than let the Campbells take possession. A short walk from the hotel bar in the village of Kilchoan, **Castle Mingary►** stands in one of the most impressive locations on the peninsula's southern shore, looking across the sound of Mull to Tobermory.

The small Highland village of **Lochaline►**, where ferries leave for Mull, sits on the picturesque Morvern peninsula, overlooking the tidal inlet of Loch Aline. The strong square keep of 14th-century Ardtornish Castle was one of the chief bases of the Lord of the Isles (see panel, page 254).

The monument to the '45 at Glenfinnan

The West Highland Way
This 152km (95-mile) long distance footpath starts from Milngavie, just north of Glasgow, and heads north of the eastern side of Loch Lomond, passing Rannoch Moor, Glen Coe, Lochaber and Ben Nevis to reach Fort William. As you get further north so does the scenery get more and more magnificent. It is never really steep but be prepared for plenty of up-and-down sections.

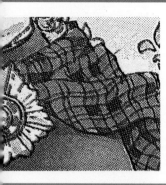

■ **Seen by contemporary opponents as a political and military threat to 18th-century Britain's stability, the Jacobites and their hopeless quest to restore a Catholic monarch to the British throne was soon turned into a romantic lost cause. At its head was the most romantic figure of all: Italian-born Prince Charles Edward Louis Philip Casimir Stuart, know variously as the Young Pretender, the Young Chevalier and, most familiarly, as Bonnie Prince Charlie. He was in Scotland for only 14 months.** ■

'Charles was the candle who lighted the bonfire, but they [his Highland supporters] were the timber that filled a dark sky with their splendid ardour.'
Eric Linklater,
The Prince In The Heather

246

'Over the sea to Skye'
'Carry the lad born to be King over the sea to Skye' is perhaps the best-known line from the corpus of Jacobite songs, and alludes to the perilous voyage from Benbecula to Skye which Charles took while disguised as Betty Burke, Flora MacDonald's maid. *The Skye Boat Song*, however, is a Victorian fake: its famous lyrics date from 1884 and most of the tune from 1879.

Charles set off from St Nazaire on his escapade with the blessing of a French government eager to see Britain de-stabilised. When the handsome young man landed on the island of Eriskay in the Western Isles, the local MacDonald chief told him to go home. Charles romantically replied that he had come home and, undaunted, went on to raise his standard at Glenfinnan in August 1745.

A persuasive personality The fatal charm of the Stuarts managed to persuade about one sixth of the estimated 30,000 fighting men in the Highlands of Scotland to take up arms in his cause. The campaign met with early successes but was finally halted on Culloden Moor in April 1746. There the Jacobites were blown away by the superior artillery of the British army. Charles went into hiding and the government forces (which comprised a number of Scottish regiments) went on to commit numerous atrocities in its efforts to destroy the Highland way of life. This policy was implemented by a far-off government in Westminster, who perceived the Highlands as a hotbed of potential Jacobites, where clan chiefs were able to call on, in effect, private armies.

The romance of a lost cause From these bare facts sprang the legend of an irresistibly handsome young man on a lost cause. With the real threat out of the way, the Jacobites were soon reinterpreted in song and story. Bonnie Prince Charlie became the figurehead of Jacobite mythology and has been on shortbread tins ever since. Flora MacDonald – whose dealings with the Prince covered only a few days and who had to be persuaded to have anything to do with the business at all – was quickly fêted as a romantic heroine. The notion that the Prince was never betrayed by a sympathetic Scottish people is a still current tale. In reality his supporters had to keep him well out of the way. But none of this matters. With Bonnie Prince Charlie, the romance is all.

▶▶ Mull
234B2

The beautiful 'isle-of-the-cool-high-bends', 38km (24 miles) long and 42km (26 miles) wide, has many aspects – fierce rocky cliffs, sheltered sandy beaches, quiet fishing coves, bleak moors, lone grey castles and lofty mountains – but is dominated by treeless green terraces of grazing land skilfully managed by crofts and small farms. Mull is served by ferries from Oban, Lochaline and, in summer, Kilchoan.

Duart Castle, perched above the narrow Sound of Mull 5km (3 miles) from Craignure, has its origins in the 13th-century. It has been restored as the summer home of the chief of Clan Maclean. **Torosay Castle**, just out-side Craignure, is a 19th-century baronial building (designed by David Bryce) with terraced grounds laid out by Sir Robert Lorimer. A narrow-gauge railway runs between the castle and Craignure. **Tobermory▶**, named after a holy well dedicated to Our Lady, is the island's main town, its arc of brightly painted houses encircling a bay popular with yacht owners.

The Holy Island of **Iona▶▶▶**, the 'Cradle of Christianity', is served by ferry from Fionnphort on the

Ancient burial place of kings
St Oran's Cemetery on Iona is the oldest Christian cemetery in Scotland. Here are buried 48 Scottish kings, including Kenneth MacAlpin, who first united the Scots and Picts in 843, and Duncan, murdered by Macbeth in 1040. Eight Norwegian kings also have graves here, a reflection of the several hundred years of Norse occupation of Scotland from the 9th century on.

A prehistoric standing stone on Ross of Mull

western tip of the Ross of Mull or by boat excursions from Oban. No cars are allowed on the island but all sights can be easily reached on foot. In AD 563 St Colomba and 12 companions landed here from Ireland and established a monastery as a base for numerous missionary journeys among the pagan Picts. It became the mother house of the Celtic church in Scotland and England. This era of great spiritual and creative achievement ended, however, with the Norse raid of 803 which killed 68 monks and persuaded those left alive to return to Ireland. Nothing of their monastery remains, but an astonishing collection of early Christian stone carvings recalls this heroic period. Apart from St Oran's Chapel of 1080, the existing abbey buildings all date from the second foundation in the early 13th century, when a Benedictine monastery and nunnery were established. In the 20th century, the abbey buildings were restored and are now the home of the Iona community. The island's sense of peace is for many visitors a source of spiritual refreshment.

Fingal's Cave, Staffa
The cathedral-like cave that inspired Felix Mendelssohn's *Hebrides Overture* is one of several on this tiny uninhabited island north of Iona. Smooth columns of black basalt, the result of volcanic action, rise out of the sea in what is known in Gaelic as 'An Uamh Ehinn' (the musical cave), because of the echoing sounds that the sea makes within it. Boat trips leave from Oban in summer.

▶▶ Oban and Argyll and Bute 234B2

Oban is a popular family holiday resort, accessible by bus and train from Glasgow. The harbour bustles with fishing vessels and ferries for the islands of Mull, Coll, Tiree, Colonsay and the Western Isles. Promenade along the seafront, browse in the woollen mills, then stroll along to Dunollie Castle where the Lords of Lorne used to preside. McCaig's Tower, an unfinished folly modelled on Rome's Colosseum, overlooks the town with fine views across to the Inner Hebrides. Oban is not known for reliable weather but there are a number of indoor attractions for when it rains, such as a glassworks, pottery, toy and model display and the distillery, best known for its 12-year-old malt whisky. Just east of the town is the Oban Rare Breeds Farm Park. The road north passes the 13th-century MacDougall fortress of Dunstaffnage (HS) on its way to the Sea Life Centre on the shore of Loch Creran.

Just north of the village of Taynuilt is the **Bonawe Iron Furnace**▶ (HS). Here you can see the restored remains of a charcoal furnace, founded in 1753, that used local wood for iron smelting. The village of Lochawe sits at the head of Loch Awe, the longest loch in Scotland, famous for its fishing. In summer the steamer *Lady Rowena* threads through the romantic burial islands of the MacNaughtons on Innis Fraoch and the MacArthurs on Innishail. The gaunt ruins of Kilchurn Castle, the original fortress home of the Campbells of Breadalbane, stands at the head of Kinloch Awe.

Inveraray▶▶, at the head of Loch Fyne, is a supremely elegant 18th-century town noted for its bridges, fishing harbour, gibbet pier, judges' lodgings and central double church. Its chief attraction is the Jail with its tableaux of jailers and wretched inmates. **Inveraray Castle**▶▶, home of the Campbell Dukes of Argyll, is a heavy grey stone castellated mansion, but it has delightful 18th-century interiors and is stuffed with Highland weapons, portraits and memorabilia. Walk through the grounds to the summit of Duniquaich for a panoramic view over the area.

Crinan▶ is a tiny place at the western end of the Crinan Canal (see panel), its handful of houses and a hotel overlooking the yachting activity in the old basin. The village of

The Crinan Canal

In 1793 work started on the construction of this short 14km (9-mile) canal that would link Loch Fyne with the Sound of Jura, saving ships the long, hazardous journey round the Mull of Kintyre. The chief engineer, Scotsman John Rennie, met with financial and engineering problems (Thomas Telford was also called upon for his expertise) and it was never a commercial success. However, it passes via 15 locks through a beautiful landscape of wooded mountains and its basin at Crinan is now popular with yachtsmen.

A 'Cal Mac' ferry arrives in Oban from the islands; above the town is the granite McCaig's Tower, a project to give work to unemployed masons

Kilmartin►► is surrounded by notable prehistoric sites, including the Nether Largie Linear Cemetery – an alignment of Bronze Age burial mounds, including one you can climb into by ladder – and the Temple Wood stone circles; in the churchyard is a fine collection of medieval carved stones and in the church itself a good Celtic cross. Dunadd Fort may have been the capital of the early Scots kingdom of Dalriada. On its rocky top are carved a footprint and a boar.

Across the Sound of Jura lies **Jura►**, the rugged, barely populated island, home of red deer, where George Orwell wrote *1984*. Next door, is the lovely, peaty isle of **Islay►►** (ferries from Kennacraig on the Kintyre peninsula), where no fewer than six distilleries operate. Islay's sights include the superb 9th-century Kidalton Cross and the local history museum at Port Charlotte.

The dazzling interior décor of Inveraray Castle

A carved stone at Kilmartin

The dawn of history
Grey recumbent tombs of the dead in desert places, Standing stones on the vacant wine-red moor, Hills of sheep, and the homes of the silent vanquished races, And winds, austere and pure.
From *Blows the wind today* by **R L Stevenson** (1850–94)

Drive Argyll and Bute (see map, page 234)

This tour takes in the beautiful sea loch of Loch Etive, the dramatic Pass of Brander and the shores of Loch Fyne, with its famous Inveraray Castle, before returning through an area studded with prehistoric remains on a road past many sea lochs with views of the Inner Hebridean islands (approx.160km/100 miles). There is an optional detour of approx. 60km (40 miles) down the Knapdale peninsula.

Leave **Oban►** going north on the A85 to pass Connel Bridge. Continue to Taynuilt for **Bonawe Iron Furnace►** (HS) and then on the A85 through a narrow treeless defile, the Pass of Brander, to **Lochawe**. Take the A819 south to **Inveraray►►** with its

splendid **castle►►** and then turn south on the A83, skirting the shores of Loch Fyne and passing Auchindrain open air museum and Crarae Glen woodland gardens. Reach the market town of **Lochgilphead** and turn north up the A816. A detour may be taken on the B841 to **Crinan►** at the end of the Crinan Canal and then south to Castle Sween and **Kilmory Knap** for its medieval carved stones.

Continue north on the A816 to **Dunadd Fort** and **Kilmartin►►**, centre for some absorbing prehistoric sites. Pass **Carnasserie Castle** at the west end of Loch Awe and, twisting in and out of view of the Firth of Lorne, return to Oban.

Wildlife

Both island groups are renowned for their seabird colonies, which are among the most important in the world. On Shetland, visit the Island of Noss, accessible by small ferry (weather permitting). Here and at Hermaness on the north of Unst you get wonderful views of puffins, gannets, guillemots, razorbills and many more species. As you explore the island, watch out for great skuas, arctic skuas and whimbrels, which nest on the moorland. On Orkney, visit Yesnaby Cliffs on Mainland, both for their seabirds and for the rare and miniature Scottish primrose.

The relentless pounding of the waves at Yesnaby, Orkney, has created a precarious pillar of rock now detached from the mainland

▶▶   **Orkney and Shetland**   *235A5/E5*

These two northern archipelagos have such a different cultural atmosphere from the rest of Scotland that many visitors feel they have arrived in another country. For 600 years they were under Norse rule and even when this domination officially ended, in the 15th century, it was another 200 years before the Scottish throne became strong enough to exert any real authority over these remote islands. Both groups of islands are astonishingly bleak and treeless and initially appear almost featureless, but both have splendid cliff and sea loch scenery and rare birdlife. Despite boasting what is arguably the finest collection of prehistoric sites in Britain they receive comparatively few visitors.

Orkney Islands In Kirkwall on Mainland the unaltered pre-Reformation **Cathedral of St Magnus▶▶** stands in proud dominance over the town. It was begun in the 12th century and the massive round pillars and arches of the arcades date from this time. In one of the pillars two skeletons were discovered early this century, one of which may be St Magnus himself. In the cathedral precincts are the ruins of the Bishop's Palace and Earl's Palace and **Tankerness House Museum**, a 16th-century town house that has been well fitted up as a museum of Orkney. Around the precincts wind streets of crow-stepped gabled houses, brightly painted.

   Skara Brae▶▶▶ (HS), also on Mainland, is an entire neolithic settlement that lay perfectly preserved in sand dunes for 4,000 years until a storm first uncovered a corner of it in 1850. Inside the houses are beds, hearths, dressers, cupboards, even fish tanks. The inhabitants left pots, jewellery, clothes and tools, which are displayed in the museum. **The Ring of Brodgar▶▶** (HS) is a wide circle of stones. When first constructed it was surely one of the most magnificent stone circles ever built by neolithic man. The scale is quite breathtaking and although only some of the stones remain the original majesty is well preserved. Many of the stones reach a height of 4.5m (15ft). Near by, **Maes Howe▶▶** (HS) is the finest chambered cairn, or burial chamber, in Europe, both for size and preservation. It was built around 2700 BC and so had been standing for at least a century before the first circle was marked out at Stonehenge in Wiltshire. It remained intact for nearly 4,000 years until the Vikings plundered it; their rude Norse inscriptions can still be seen on the walls.

A more modern curiosity is the **Italian Chapel**▶ at Lamb Holm, created from Nissen huts and scrap materials in 1943 by Italian prisoners of war who were building the Churchill Barriers in the bay of Scapa Flow. **The Pier Arts Centre**▶ is a delightful little gallery in the ferry port of Stromness. It has the best collection of modern British art in the north of Scotland. The masterpieces of Ben Nicholson and Barbara Hepworth admirably complement the island's ancient remains.

The famous **Old Man of Hoy**▶▶ is an enormous stack rearing a tremendous 135m (443ft) out of the sea off the island of Hoy. Like most of Orkney's cliff scenery, it is best seen from a boat (or the ferry from Scrabster).

Shetland Islands This is the most northerly part of Great Britain (Shetland is about 95km/60 miles north of Orkney) and the beauty of midsummer nights when there is little or no darkness has to be seen to be believed. The main industries are crofting, fishing and knitting. The fine wool of the Shetland sheep is knitted up in traditional, distinctive colours and patterns, often known as Fair Isle.

Some people travel to Shetland just to see **Mousa Broch**▶▶▶ (HS), on a little island to the southeast of Mainland. The Iron Age fortress tower still stands over 12m (39ft) high, all its distinctive features wonderfully preserved. Interestingly, when Shetland was covered with brochs (see panel) Mousa was acknowledged to be the smallest and meanest of them all. **Clickhimin**▶ (HS), near Lerwick, is another well-preserved broch.

On the southernmost tip of Mainland is **Jarlshof**▶▶▶ (HS), one of the most remarkable prehistoric sites in Europe. Impressive remains, standing several feet high, can be seen of the Bronze Age courtyard settlements, the Iron Age 'wheelhouses' (see panel) that succeeded them and the longhouses of the Viking settlers who followed on. There is also a 16th-century laird's house, home of Earl of Orkney Patrick Stewart and linked with Walter Scott's novel *The Pirate*. The same earl, renowned for his cruelty, built **Scalloway Castle** (HS). The **Shetland Museum** in Lerwick tells the islands' story.

Brochs and wheelhouses
Brochs are round towers, shaped like modern cooling towers, that are found only in the north of Scotland, the Outer Hebrides and Orkney and Shetland. Built by the Picts during the 1st and 2nd centuries BC as defensive structures, they typically have double, drystone walls with an inner staircase between, giving access to upper galleries. In the middle was a courtyard. Wheelhouses were a speciality of prehistoric Scotland, round buildings with a thick outer wall and a slab or corbelled roof. A number of inner walls ran in from the outer wall to a central area, like spokes of a wheel, forming 'rooms'.

251

This Iron Age wheelhouse is part of Jarlshof's legacy of 3,000 years of settlement

Loch Tay, one of Scotland's great salmon-fishing spots

The Stone of Scone

Also known as the Stone of Destiny, this is believed to be a druidic talisman, consecrated by St Columba at Iona, that was used in the investiture of the Dalriadic princes. It was brought here in the 9th century by Kenneth MacAlpin, the man who united Scotland after his defeat of the Picts at Scone. In 1296 it was removed by King Edward I of England and remained under the coronation chair in London's Westminster Abbey – except for a brief period in the 1950s when it was sensationally stolen and mysteriously reappeared in Arbroath Abbey. In 1996 the government announced that the Stone was to be returned to Scotland after 700 years.

▶▶ Perth and Kinross 235B4

More or less at the centre of Scotland and rich in historical associations, Perth and Kinross (formerly Perthshire) is a county of contrasts. As you travel north the lush farmland of the south is slowly transformed into the rounded heather-covered slopes of the Grampian Mountains. Cut through with great lochs, it is bound into one region by the silver waters of the Tay.

The town of **Perth**▶ enjoys a pleasant position beside the River Tay and its road and railway network makes it a good base. Despite its Tay bridges, its Georgian terraces and the Millais paintings in the city art gallery, it does not quite live up to the expectations set by its long history. Just above the town, Kinnoull Hill is graced with two 18th-century follies, imitations of Rhenish castles. **Branklyn Garden**▶ (NTS) is small but delightful collection of rhododendrons, shrubs and alpines. Balhousie Castle houses the regimental museum of the Black Watch. **Nearby attractions**▶▶ include the ruined pre-Reformation nave of Dunkeld Cathedral, the painted wooden ceilings of Huntingtower Castle (HS) (once known as Ruthven and scene of the kidnap of James VI by the earls of Mar and Gowrie), the 10th-century round tower at Abernethy and the world's highest beech hedge at Meikleour.

Situated just 3km (2 miles) upriver from Perth is **Scone Palace**▶▶▶ (pronounced 'skoon'), one of Scotland's great treasure houses. Scone was the coronation place of all the Scottish kings until the time of James I, the seat of Pictish government and the site of the famous Stone of Scone (see panel). The present palace was built over the foundations of the ancient abbey by Wyatt at the onset of the fashion for Gothick in the first decade of the 19th century. Its state rooms display the treasures from England and France assembled by the Earls of Mansfield, but it is chiefly loved for its lived-in, family atmosphere.

Pitlochry is a resort town, in a beautiful setting of loch, river, mountain and wood. It was the creation of the

Victorian era when the railway station and the Hydro, the large and originally strictly dry hotel, offered healthy walking breaks, away from the smog and sin of the big cities. It boasts a respected Festival Theatre with a broad summer programme. Local beauty spots include the Queen's View up Loch Tummel and Loch Rannoch, beneath volcano-shaped Schiehallion (1,064m/3,491ft). Just outside town is the site of the Battle of Killiecrankie (an early Jacobite victory) with its visitor centre (NTS).

To the northwest is **Blair Castle►►►**, its white walls and turrets surrounded by the rugged beauty of the Atholl Hills. The province of Atholl has been ruled from this towerhouse since the 13th century. The castle is famous as the seat of the only duke to be permitted a private army, the 100-strong Atholl Highlanders, who are recruited from tenants and neighbours. They parade on the last Sunday of May but the tunics, worn with a distinctive white bow tie, enliven many a Highland Ball throughout the year. The castle has many rooms open to the public, packed with treasures, including some rare surviving examples of 17th-century Scottish furniture. In the model 18th-century village outside the castle gates there is a local folk museum. A 5km (3-mile) track leads to the gorge, bridges and waterfall of Bruar.

Each loch in Scotland has its own marked character but **Loch Tay►►**, overlooked to its north by the 1,214m (3,983ft) summit of Ben Lawers, has a serenity totally out of keeping with the bloody clan feuds that went on around its shores. At its western end the village of **Killin** is noted for the **Falls of Dochart►**. Between the village and Loch Tay are the ruins of Finlarig, the murderous stronghold of Black Duncan of the Cowl, acquisitive chief of the local Campbells. His wealthy descendants built the elegant bridge and model village of **Kenmore**, at the east end of the loch. The market town of **Aberfeldy**, 11km (7 miles) east, with its monumental Wade bridge (see panel, page 244), is a popular base for summer visitors. You can walk to such nearby attractions as **Castle Menzies**, a classic 16th-century Z-plan tower house, the old **Kirk of Weem** with its pair of Celtic crosses, and the **Birks of Aberfeldy**, a sylvan glen made famous by Burns' poem.

Highland genealogy
Beware of trying to follow too closely the tangled web of Highland genealogies. Despite most fearsome blood feuds, practically all the great chiefs and nobles were, and are, inter-related. This allowed any one family to keep a finger in a number of pies and enabled it to survive the mercurial and murderous politics of Scotland. The Murrays are a fine example: during the '45 Rebellion John Murray, the 1st Duke of Atholl remained a fervent Hanoverian while his son George was in effective command of the Jacobite army.

Perth city's coat of arms, on a lamppost

Scone Palace: the bedroom used by Queen Victoria

▶▶▶ **Skye**   *234C2*

The most startlingly magnificent of the Hebridean islands, Skye is also the closest to the mainland. Since 1995, Skye has been joined by bridge from Kyle of Lochalsh to Kyleakin. It is an island of extremely irregular shape, a sort of smudged handprint some 80km (50 miles) from end to end and varying from 6 to 40km (4 to 25 miles) in width. It consists of a central nexus – on which are **Portree**, the bustling capital (and hub of the island's bus network), and the Cuillin Hills – and a number of long peninsular fingers intersected by sea lochs. The landscape changes with disorientating ease from Alpine peaks, to rolling farmland, bleak moorland, wooded valleys, coves of white coral sand and cliffs dotted with secretive caves.

Close to the ferry terminal at Armadale, the restored ruins of the 19th-century castellated mansion of Armadale now house the **Clan Donald Centre**▶. Displays and videos tell the story of the clan and its progenitor, Somerled, the first Lord of the Isles (see panel).

The central chain of mountain peaks, the **Cuillins**▶▶, their jagged silhouette seldom seen without at least a wisp of cloud, provides some of the most splendid scenery and demanding climbing in Britain. Rising to 1,009m (3,310ft), they enclose Loch Coruisk, a great pool of water locked in an amphitheatre of crags of the blackest gabbro – a scene of overpowering desolation and grandeur. It can be reached by boat trip from Elgol, or in a full day's walk from Elgol or Sligachan (not one, however, for the faint-hearted). An easier option is to walk the 6.5km (4 miles) along the coast from Elgol to Loch na Creitheach, on the threshold of the Cuillins.

The **Skye Heritage Centre**▶ tells the island's story from the point of view of the ordinary people rather than the landowners. At Skeabost, a little way northwest of Portree, are the ruins of the tiny **Columban Chapel**▶, one of a number of the earliest Celtic churches known to have been built here.

254

Lords of the Isles
The lordship of the Isles was an independent state that controlled the islands and much of the west coast of Scotland in the medieval period. The founder, and progenitor of clan MacDonald, was Somerled, who used the conflict between his Norse overlords and the Scots kings to establish a near autonomous state in the 12th century. Once Norse overlordship had ended, the MacDonald chiefs agreed to accept the rule of one of their number, Donald of Islay, as Lord of the Isles. Eventually James IV annexed the title in 1493 (one still borne by the heir apparent).

The path to Moonen bay and cliffs

Further west, **Dunvegan Castle▶▶** has been home to the MacLeods of Skye since the 12th century. Striking a magnificent attitude on this remote shore of the island, it contains treasures sacred to the clan such as the fairy flag, which when waved has the power to save the clan. Legend says it will work three times – it has already been used twice, with miraculous results. Close by is **Kilmuir Churchyard and Croft Museum▶**. In the churchyard lie the remains of Flora MacDonald, Hebridean heroine of the '45 Rebellion (see panel, page 246), beneath an imposing Celtic cross. The croft museum uses four thatched cottages to re-create aspects of the simple yet heroic self-sufficiency of the island's crofters.

North of Portree, the **Old Man of Storr▶** is another of the geological wonders of Skye – a precariously balanced rock needle. The scene of weird desolation is accentuated by the wind sobbing in the gullies. **The Quiraing▶▶▶** is one of the strangest and most fascinating hills in Scotland. Seldom seen without its raven guardians swirling around, it is a confused mass of cliffs, scree slopes and towering pinnacles.

On a wind-blown promontory at the northern end of the Trotternish peninsula stand the ruins of **Duntulm Castle▶**, a fortress built by the MacDonalds of Sleat when they were battling with the MacLeods of Dunvegan for the control of this region (see panel on page 254).

From Sconser a little ferry goes across to the tranquil island of **Raasay▶▶**. A track follows its long spine of hills to end at the silhouetted ruins of medieval Brochel Castle.

Across the Cuillin Sound south of Skye lie the **Inner Isles**, Rum, Eigg, Muck and Canna, served by ferries from Mallaig on the mainland and Armadale on Skye. Each has limited accommodation. **Rum▶▶** is the largest of the group and has a volcanic mountain cluster, the highest peak being Askival (810m/2,657ft). The haunt of red deer, wild goats, golden eagles and sea eagles, the island is a National Nature Reserve and has nature trails and a hotel owned by Scottish Natural Heritage.

Skye style: a traditional croft, with whitewashed stone walls, a central doorway and a roof of heather thatch secured by wire and held down with stones

Might is right?
The 1882 Battle of the Braes was a half-heroic, half-comical affair. A group of bailiffs who were attempting to evict crofters from the coastal strip just south of Portree were beaten off by a fierce band of Hebridean housewives armed with stone-weighted stockings. The English government, used to sending gunboats all over the world to force their way, promptly sent one up to Skye but backed down in the face of universal hostility. Instead they sent a Commission whose report paved the way for the enlightened Crofting Acts.

The valley of the River Spey near Newtonmore

► **Spey Valley** 235C4

One of the broad classifications of single malt whiskies is the Speyside malts which take their name from the River Spey. It rises in the Monadliath (literally 'the grey moors') and runs northeast, eventually spreading through the wildlife-rich Insh Marshes with the Cairngorms as a spectacular backdrop. Beyond Grantown-on-Spey it reaches the whisky distilling area stretching all the way to the Moray coast.

The typical Strathspey view features a pleasing mix of woods and farmlands backed by moorland slopes and, inevitably, a plume of white steam jetting up from yet another distillery tucked into the landscape. Visit Glenfiddich at Dufftown for a wide-ranging and entertaining interpretation of malt whisky, though there are plenty of other famous names, many of which have visitor centres, some on the signposted Malt Whisky Trail.

The resort town of **Aviemore** is a not particularly attractive creation of the 1960s but it is a popular centre for hill walking in the **Cairngorm Mountains►►** in summer and skiing on them in winter. Cairn Gorm itself rises to 1,245m (4,085ft); take the ski lift (it operates all year round) for a wonderful view. Other activities might include a visit to the osprey reserve at Loch Garten, a ride on the Strathspey Steam Railway from Aviemore to Boat of Garten (good walks at either end) or a visit to the Landmark Highland Heritage visitor centre. There are facilities for indoor sports, a swimming pool, ice-skating rink, cinema and discos. South along the A9 towards Kingussie is the Highland Wildlife Park.

Kingussie►, pronounced 'kinusie', is a pleasing town of just one main street. There are plenty of beautiful walks near by and if you visit only one highland history museum in Scotland, it should be the **Highland Folk Museum►►** here. It is divided into indoor and outdoor exhibitions and includes a 'black house' from the Outer Hebridean island of Lewis, a clack mill, a salmon smokehouse and fascinating exhibits from farming and domestic life. On a natural escarpment the other side of the Spey and the A9 stands the gaunt roofless ruin of the Ruthven Barracks (HS), a sister to the one in Glenelg (see page 258). They were built to police the main Highland trade routes after the suppression of the 1715 rebellion but a generation later, in 1746, were blown up by retreating Jacobites.

Elgin▶, the administrative centre of Moray, is the largest town in the favoured Laigh of Moray. (Laigh means a sheltered low-lying area and, in this case, refers to its position in the 'rain shadow' of the Grampians.) Elgin's cathedral (HS), 'the lantern of the North', founded in 1224, was burned in 1390 by the villainous Wolf of Badenoch. Though subsequently rebuilt, it is now a picturesque ruin. The local museum features a display on Britain's oldest dinosaurs, found nearby. East of the town is the attractive community of Fochabers, with plenty of antique shops to attract browsers, as well as another absorbing folk museum. On the coast, the otherwise rather workaday town of Buckie is enhanced by an interpretation of the development of the Northeast fishery, the Buckie Drifter. Summer boat trips from here give the opportunity to watch bottlenose dolphins.

Pluscarden Abbey▶ lies in a fertile valley about 9km (6mls) southwest of Elgin. Its atmosphere is potent, with Benedictine monks going to and fro amid the Gothic ruins. Originally founded by Alexander II in the early 13th century, the abbey was badly damaged by the endemic warfare of the region and fell into further decay after the Reformation. It was partly restored by the Marquis of Bute in the 19th century and in 1943 was bestowed by his son on a Benedictine community from Prinknash in Gloucestershire. The monks moved in five years later and are now rebuilding it.

The pretty coastal village of Findhorn▶, due north from Forres, made headline news in the early 1960s with tales of its hippy community. This developed into the Findhorn Foundation, a centre for mystic thought and learning with some 200 community members.

257

The copper stills at Glenfiddich Distillery; there are eight distilleries on the Malt Whisky Trail

The Speyside Way
The 75km (47-mile) long distance path starts at Spey Bay where the River Spey flows into the North Sea and offers fairly easy walking as far as Ballindalloch before tackling the more challenging section through the hills to Tomintoul. The countryside is varied and the path passes near several whisky distilleries.

NORTHERN SCOTLAND

The Sutherland Clearances
Dominating the skyline around the village of Golspie is a statue of the 1st Duke of Sutherland. He is the infamous Leviathan of Wealth who between 1810 and 1820 evicted 15,000 of his tenants from their self-sufficient crofts in order to turn their small plots into profitable sheep pasture.

The northernmost reach of mainland Scotland is often referred to as the last great wilderness of Europe. The eastern coast, a fertile strip backed by low brown moorland, could hardly be in greater contrast to the green-grey mountains that overlook the long, intruding sea lochs of the west coast of Ross.

In a remote and picturesque situation on the Sound of Sleat, **Glenelg▶** was once on the main cattle-droving route to Skye. Here are the two best-preserved brochs (see panel, page 251) in mainland Scotland, a handsome, ruined Hanoverian barrack block and Sandaig Bay, site of Gavin Maxwell's otter refuge of 'Camusfearna' so vividly described in *Ring of Bright Water*. In summer you can take a ferry across the surging Kylerhea tidal stream to Skye. A little north, across Loch Duich, the picturesque **Eilean**

Eilean Donan Castle, a Mackenzie fortress, was rebuilt earlier this century

Donan Castle▶▶ stands on an islet at the meeting of three lochs. On the northern shores of this peninsula are the stonebuilt houses and palm trees of the delightful little seaside village of **Plockton▶**. West of Lochcarron, the adventurous should take an exhilaratingly twisty road (certainly not one for timid drivers) over **Bealach Na Ba (The Pass of the Cattle)▶**. The glacier-scarred rocks on the summit of this pass offer a very fine view over Skye, especially at sunset. The road leads down to the remote coastal village of **Applecross**. Here a carved Celtic cross beside the kirk marks the site of the once influential 7th-century monastery of St Maelrubha.

Dornoch's claims to fame
Besides having the third oldest golf links in the world, considered as far back as 1630 to be superior to those of St Andrews, Dornoch also claims the best sunshine record in northern Scotland and the dubious distinction of being the last place in Scotland to burn a witch. The Witch's Stone by the 17th hole of the golf links commemorates the country's last judicial execution for witchcraft, in 1722.

Torridon▶▶ lies at the end of one of Wester Ross's wildest glens. The road along the southern shores of Upper Loch Torridon offers magnificent views of Beinn Alligin (985m/3,231ft). A National Trust for Scotland countryside centre in Torridon has a deer museum and an audiovisual presentation on local wildlife. Further north, in one of the most beautiful corners of the west coast, lies the spectacular, world famous **Inverewe Garden▶▶▶** (NTS), a collection of 2,500 species of tender and hardy shrubs and trees flourishing in the warmth of the Gulf Stream.

The port of **Ullapool**, placed amidst astounding scenery, doubles as a resort. The A835 eastwards heads down Loch Broom to the Falls of Measeach in the dizzying **Corrieshalloch Gorge▶▶**. To the north, the same road passes **Knockan Cliff▶** in the Inverpolly Nature Reserve

Osgood Mackenzie created Inverewe Garden in 1862, transforming a peaty wasteland into a lush spot where Himalayan lilies and other exotic species flourish

Generating power
Standing on the clifftops 16km (10 miles) west of Thurso, the giant golf ball of Dounreay nuclear power station can be seen for miles around. Elsewhere the waters of Scotland's mountains and reservoirs are harnessed in the production of electricity: the great pipes of the hydro-electric scheme at Kinlochleven can be seen on the hillsides south of Fort William and those of the Tay-Tummel system around Glen Affric. The pumped storage scheme at Ben Cruachan in Argyll has a visitor centre.

Wildlife
The flow or marsh country of Caithness and Sutherland is a vast stretch of plantations. It is home during the summer months to greenshanks, dunlins, golden plovers and other wading birds. Dunnet Bay, near Wick, is an excellent birdwatching spot in winter. Look for great northern divers, long-tailed ducks and scoters. The flora of the arctic species mingles with mountain species, almost at sea level. Handa Island, off Scourie, is another wonderful site for breeding seabirds. A private ferry often runs from Tarbert.

and Stac Pollaidh and Suilven, two of the most striking mountain shapes in Scotland. In the far north, you can take a ferry and minibus from Durness to **Cape Wrath**▶▶ to see some stupendous coastal scenery. Britain's highest mainland cliffs are nearby Clo Mor, east of Cape Wrath. Just outside Durness itself is the Smoo Cave, which is in fact three vast caves in the limestone cliffs, with a waterfall. A boat trip can be taken right into the second and third caves.

Few people who come this far north fail to visit **John O'Groats**, the most northeasterly point of the British mainland, named after the Dutchman Jan de Groot (Dunnet Head, near by, is actually the northernmost point). It is little more than an untidy collection of tourist shacks and disappointing to many visitors. Persevere instead to nearby Duncansby Head (see Walks, page 238): the three dramatic offshore stacks rise to over 60m (197ft), the wind blows off the wild North Sea in fiery gusts and the adventurous spirit feels true delight.

South of Wick, near the village of Lybster, are two impressive ancient relics, the **Hill O' Many Stones** and the **Grey Cairns of Camster**▶▶. The former is a curious and attractive arrangement of 22 rows of stones in a fan shape, the latter two excellently preserved neolithic burial chambers. If you do not mind the idea of crawling into someone's grave then enter one of the most handsome in the country, 60m (197ft) long and 18m (59ft) wide with separate chambers inside.

North of Dornoch the fairytale towers of **Dunrobin Castle**▶▶ stand on a coastal escarpment, the former seat of the earls and dukes of Sutherland, the largest landowners in Britain. Despite its fanciful 19th-century exterior, it is an ancient fortress with a medieval keep as its core. The collection of paintings inside includes a Reynolds and two Canalettos. **Dornoch**▶▶ is a secluded and ancient royal burgh, a pretty little sandstone town with miles of safe sandy beaches. The small cathedral of the Bishops of Caithness dates from the 12th century. The town is also renowned for its golf links.

Scarista Bay, Harris, typifies the majestic remoteness of the Western Isles

> A voice so thrilling ne'er
>   was heard,
> In spring time from the
>   cuckoo-bird,
> Breaking the silence of the
>   seas
> Amongst the farthest
>   Hebrides.
> **William Wordsworth**,
> *The Solitary Reaper*

The Lewis Chessmen
The chance discovery in the 19th century of the 12th-century chessmen on Lewis caused a storm of controversy. Their artistry was of a standard many found hard to attribute to the 12th century. Carved from walrus ivory, they are now divided between the British Museum in London and the Museum of Antiquities in Edinburgh. Replicas may be bought on Lewis.

▶▶▶   **The Western Isles**   *234D1*

Sail west across the Minch and you reach the Western Isles. For the most part the eastern side of the archipelago is barren, rocky and steep. Its west coast is all silver-white beaches, long and empty and backed by the 'machair', fertile peaty grassland enriched by white shell-sand – an almost unique habitat that supports a rich wildlife. Between the two lie watery, peaty and totally treeless moors.

The Western Isles change their religion with their latitude: strict Presbyterianism in Lewis, Harris, Berneray and North Uist, Roman Catholicism in South Uist, Eriskay and Barra, with Benbecula in between a mixture of the two. The difference is readily apparent: strict observation of the Sabbath in the northern islands means people go out only to attend church services and shops and bars are closed, whereas Sundays in the south are more lively and relaxed. Even the houses on the southern islands have a brighter look, often with coloured roofs and painted walls.

It is a perfect place to get away from it all. The people are exceptionally friendly and welcome visitors, but you will not find organised facilities. The few 'sights' are mostly archaeological; what visitors will remember is the empty beaches, the lochs, the hills, the wildlife, the pure quality of the light and the way of life.

Lewis and Harris Lewis and Harris are in fact one island, linked to the mainland and Skye by ferries from Stornoway and Tarbert. The world-famous Harris tweed is still produced here. The stone circle of **Callanish**▶▶▶ is one of the most haunting and eloquent places in Britain. An open-air temple of the Bronze Age that seems to have related particularly to the moon, it is tucked on to a broad peninsula on the west coast of Lewis that protrudes into the sheltered waters of Loch Roag. The inner circle of 13 stones surrounds a central 5m (16ft), 5-tonne menhir. In the central cairn, remains of a human cremation were discovered when the 1.5m (5ft)-high banks of peat were removed in 1860. At Arnol, the squat **Black House**▶ is now a museum (see panel, page 261); another museum evoking crofting life is found at nearby **Siabost**. **Rodel Church**▶▶, a bold attractive cruciform dating from 1500, stands on the southern tip of Harris. The cold bleak interior preserves a number of carvings.

North and South Uist On the road south from Lochmaddy is the finest chambered cairn in the Hebrides, **Barpa Langass▶**. A huge pile of stones sits on the side of the hill, Ben Langass; a little tunnel leads into the communal burial chamber built by Bronze Age Beaker people.

The northwest coast of North Uist has several beautiful coves and beaches; the one near Hosta is, on a clear day, the best place to see **St Kilda**, the most remote and evocative of the Hebrides 72km (45 miles) out in the Atlantic. Nearby **Balranald RSPB Reserve▶** harbours the rare corncrake and offers a nature trail across the flower- and bird-rich machair.

North Uist, Benbecula and South Uist are linked by a causeway. Near the top of South Uist the road passes Hew Lorimer's granite statue of Our Lady of the Isles serenely looking out to sea. At Milton a cairn stands on the site of the birthplace of Jacobite darling Flora MacDonald (1722). At the island's southern tip a ferry goes to tiny **Eriskay**, celebrated in the Gaelic melody, the Eriskay Love Lilt. It was here that Bonnie Prince Charlie first set foot in Scotland on his way from France and here that the whisky-laden SS *Politician* went down, inspiration for Compton Mackenzie's novel *Whisky Galore*.

Barra▶▶ is a microcosm of all the Western Isles with its rocky coastline on the east, sandy bays and machair on the west, where crofting is still the main occupation and Gaelic is still spoken. Ferries connect Castlebay with South Uist and the mainland.

Harris wool, here being sold locally; the tweed is sold worldwide

The standing stones at Callanish on the Isle of Lewis; at sunset during the spring and autumn equinoxes, the shadow from the central stone falls directly over the tomb entrance

Croft houses old and new
The Arnol Black House on the west coast of Lewis is a traditional crofter's house that gives a fascinating insight into the way of life that was common only 20 years ago. Inside the thick stone walls, a peat fire smoulders in the middle of the floor, the smoke filtering out through the oat straw thatch. Many of these old croft houses can still be seen, some left in ruin, some given new roofs. The modern houses that replace them are similarly low buildings, usually with dormer windows.

■ **Mountains, lochs and glens make a magnificent landscape but a harsh environment in which to live and work. Traditionally the Highlands supported a sophisticated, martial society with its own code of ethical conduct and unbreakable social responsibilities. This was wilfully destroyed in the mid-18th century and within a generation the infamous Clearances began, when the people were driven from the land. ■**

Prophet of doom
The 17th-century poet Brahan Seer, born on Lewis in the Outer Hebrides, described how the glens would be emptied of their people by sheep, how the sheep would in turn be displaced by deer before the coming of the black rain that would clear all life from the land. The 'black rain' has been widely identified with fall-out from a nuclear war or a disaster at the Dounreay nuclear reactor. Too many of his prophecies have been fulfilled for his dark vision of the future of the Highlands not to cast a chill of apprehension.

262

Mass evictions and emigrations have left the landscape dotted with ruined crofters' houses

The rule of the Highland chieftain Up until the defeat of the Jacobite clans at Culloden Moor in 1746, the Highlands were riven into small communities by the dramatic landscape of mountains and sealochs. It was primarily a cattle-breeding society that traded for grain grown in the Lowlands. The Highland cattle, small herds of sheep, goats and chickens were highly mobile and every community required a strongly motivated fighting force to protect its wealth from 'lifting'. This was the economic basis of the closely knit and intensely martial Highland clans. There was a long tradition of paternalistic care, but it was a feudal society for the simple harsh reason that a hundred strong men in times of crisis were of much greater use than a money rent.

The changing tide After the battle of Culloden the victorious Hanoverian government, frightened by the partial success of the Highland army that rallied to Bonnie Prince Charlie, determined to control this militant society. They proscribed firearms, the martial kilt and the strong legal powers of the clan chiefs – and they were undeniably thorough. Within a few years the Highlands were at peace and money rents began to replace feudal tenures. For a few glorious decades everything seemed rosy – the potato provided a new cheap staple crop for the poor, corn prices stayed down and livestock prices soared. Capitalists built iron foundries, fishing harbours, piers, linen and woollen mills, partly financed by enormous profits made by gathering kelp. The population quickly doubled but the plots of farming land became ever smaller.

The Clearances The end of the Napoleonic wars brought a violent depression with the total collapse of fish, cattle and kelp prices and the near extinction of rural industries. Only sheep brought in a handsome profit. Sheep farming, however, was incompatible with thousands of tenants packed into the glens and coastal strips. And so began the infamous eviction of crofters from their land to make way for sheep. They were moved south to the slums of the industrial cities or packed off to Canada, Australia, New Zealand and the US. Gladstone's Crofting Act of 1886 gave the surviving tenants a guaranteed tenure and allowed strong communities to survive in the Hebrides, but many big estates turned over to deer hunting and grouse shooting. With forestry, fish farming and tourism, this still plays a major part in the Highlands' economy.

TRAVEL FACTS

Arriving

By air London has four airports. The largest is **Heathrow** (one of the largest in the world). Airbuses and underground trains connect to central London; the underground is cheaper and generally quicker, but neither runs all night. Allow 45–60 minutes for the underground ride to central London. The next largest airport, **Gatwick**, is generally more manageable than Heathrow; access to London is much better too, with a direct rail link to Victoria Station. **Luton** (north of London) has a bus link to the railway station, and **Stansted** has trains to London Liverpool Street. **Birmingham**, **Edinburgh**, **Glasgow**, **Leeds/Bradford** and **Manchester** also serve international flights.

By boat Numerous ports have cross-Channel services to the rest of Europe. Dover in east Kent (114km/71 miles from London) is the main cross-Channel port connecting with Belgium and France; if you get stuck here for the night, there are plenty of bed and breakfast establishments along the main roads.

By rail Trains via the Eurotunnel run from the European mainland. Services from Brussels and Paris to London Waterloo take about 3 hours.

Camping

Campsites are abundant in Britain, ranging from small fields with just a single cold tap by way of facilities to large-scale sites with shower blocks and shops. Useful sources of information include the *Freedom* brochures published by the English Tourist Board (for a free copy tel: 01452 413041) and the list published by the Camping and Caravanning Club (Greenfields House, Westwood Way, Coventry CV4 8JH, tel: 01203 694995). Tourist information centres can help with lists of local sites.

If you have escapist whims and are thinking of camping in the wilds, be aware of all that the British climate can throw at you, and remember that even open moorland is owned by someone – try to ask permission first if possible.

Children

Many **hotels**, particularly larger ones, provide babysitting services, and baby-listening devices are often available. Enquire when booking about child discounts, and if there are any special facilities; British hoteliers are generally not too good about providing entertainment for the youngest travellers – toy boxes, children's books, emergency medical supplies and interesting children's meals are in short supply. Some establishments operate a 'no children' rule.

Child **discounts** are offered for many admission fees. On the rail network, up to two children under five years of age may travel free with each fare-paying passenger, while children of five and over and under 16 travel at half the full price. Anyone travelling by train with children should invest in a Family Railcard: up to four under-16-year-olds travel anywhere in the country for £1 and up to four accompanying adults have a

FOR TRAVEL DETAILS

London Heathrow, tel: 0181-759 4321
London Gatwick, tel: 01293 535353
European Rail Travel Centre,
Victoria Station, tel: 0171-834 2345
Eurostar, tel: 0345 881881

discount of either a third or a quarter.

Currently the law in **pubs** is that children under 14 are not allowed in the bar area. Some pubs allow accompanied children on to the premises (in the restaurant, for instance) and in the garden, but practice varies enormously and the licensing laws are likely to be reformed. You have to be 18 or over to buy or consume alcohol in a pub.

Theme parks and safari parks include Alton Towers (Staffordshire), Camelot Theme Park (Preston, Lancashire), Chessington's World of Adventures (Surrey), Knowsley Safari Park (Prescot, Merseyside), Legoland (Berkshire), Lightwater Valley (Ripon, North Yorkshire), Lions of Longleat Safari Park (Warminster, Wiltshire), Thorpe Park (Chertsey, Surrey), West Midland Safari and Leisure Park (Bewdley, Herefordshire)

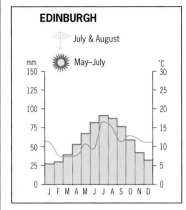

EDINBURGH

July & August

May–July

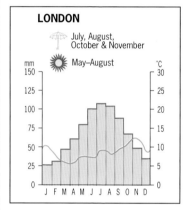

LONDON

July, August, October & November

May–August

November since records began'). In short, the British climate is a fascinatingly fickle beast: the seasons are distinctive but fuse into each other; brilliant mornings often cloud over as they proceed. No wonder the umbrella is such a national institution. Be prepared for sudden changes in temperature: chill winds as well as heatwaves, and bring rainproof footwear and clothing.

The prevailing wind comes from the west, bringing most rain to western Britain; a rain-shadow effect causes eastern areas to have considerably lower rainfall. The south coast gets less rain than the far north, and the climate tends to get warmer the further south you go. In mid-June it stays light until 10pm (later in northern Scotland); conversely, in winter it gets dark early, and the very far north stays gloomy all day.

Travel in spring and you could

and Woburn Wild Animal Kingdom and Leisure Park (Woburn, Bedfordshire).

London, the South Coast (Devon, Dorset and Sussex in particular), the North Yorkshire coast and Cornwall are among the most appealing **areas** for families; older children may also enjoy the Lake District, Exmoor, Pembrokeshire, York, Edinburgh and the Scottish Highlands.

The Family Holiday Guide *Children Welcome* lists places to stay and visit for those travelling with children.

Climate and seasonal considerations

Britain is a temperate country – the weather is seldom extremely hot or extremely cold and there is no prolonged rainy or dry season – yet where every year seems to break some meteorological record ('the coldest May this century'; 'the driest

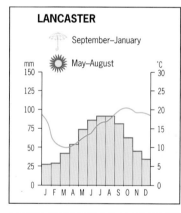

LANCASTER

September–January

May–August

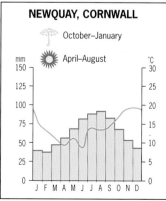

NEWQUAY, CORNWALL

October–January

April–August

encounter blustery squalls and sleet or fragrant whiffs of nature reawakening in benign sunshine; May and June can be excellent times for a holiday, with the long daylight hours and comparatively uncrowded roads and sights (except at Bank Holiday weekends). Oxford and Cambridge colleges are mostly closed in the weeks running up to examination time in late May and early June.

Summer school holidays make late July and all of August extremely busy in many areas, including national parks and coastal areas – Devon, Cornwall, the Lake District, the South Coast, the Scottish Highlands (also cursed by midges over this period) and Snowdonia are among the most crowded regions. Some historic cities fill almost to capacity, York, Chester and Canterbury among them. Other places are happily quite manageable, including the Welsh borderlands, Eastern England, East Anglia and the Scottish borders. September can have fine late summer weather; if you do not have school-age offspring often this can be a good time to travel.

Visitor numbers drop appreciably along with the temperature in October and November (the West Country stays reasonably mild), but Christmas is busier, with many hotels offering special Christmas break deals. Many attractions close between October or November and Easter (including most National Trust properties). Scottish winters usually have enough snow for skiing to be feasible in places, notably the Cairngorms.

During the grouse-shooting season (12 August to 10 December) and deer-stalking season (1 July to 15 February) access is barred to many tracts of open land in Scotland.

Crime

Violent crime is still rare in Britain and city centres are mostly quite safe, but minor offences against property have risen over recent years, particularly in some inner city areas. Even in remote countryside, it is wise to be on guard against car theft, and to ensure all valuables are locked out of sight. Be extra vigilant of your belongings at airports and major railway stations: do not let them out of your sight. Because of the spate of terrorist bombs, unattended parcels are likely to be removed.

Customs

Note the distinction between **duty-free** and **duty-paid** allowances; duty-free goods (bought at duty-free shops in airports, ferry terminals on ferries and on airplanes, even those in the EU) have had no duty paid on them and do not entitle you to the higher allowances now set for duty-paid goods bought in the EU. The countries of the EU are Belgium, Greece, the Netherlands, Denmark, Italy, Portugal, France, the Republic of Ireland, Spain (not the Canary Islands), Germany, Luxembourg and the United Kingdom (not the Channel Islands).

Visitors with Disabilities

The English Tourist Board grades hotel, farmhouse, inn and guesthouse accommodation according to suitability for visitors with disabilities from Category 3 (suitable for a wheelchair user who is also able to walk short distances and up at least three steps) to Category 1 (accessible for a wheelchair-user travelling alone). You can get help finding suitable accommodation from the Holiday Care Service, 2nd floor Imperial Buildings, Victoria Road,

A clock in Chester commemorates Queen Victoria's diamond jubilee

DUTY FREE ALLOWANCES

Duty-free allowances (for goods bought in or outside the EU) and duty-paid allowances for goods bought outside the EU.

Cigarettes	200
or cigarillos	100
or cigars	50
or tobacco	250g
Still table wine	2 litres
Spirits, strong liqueurs over 22% volume	1 litre
or fortified or sparkling wine	2 litres
Perfume	60cc/ml
Toilet water	250cc/ml
All other goods including gifts and souvenirs	£136 worth for travellers from outside the EU £71 for those coming from EU countries

Horley, Surrey RH6 7PZ, tel: 01293 774535, and from the Royal Association for Disability and Rehabilitation (RADAR), 12 City Forum, 250 City Road, London EC1V 8AF, tel: 0171-250 3222; RADAR publishes annually *Accessible Holidays in the British Isles – A Guide for Disabled People* as well as *Country Parks – A Guide for Disabled People.* The AA publishes *The Guide for the Disabled Traveller,* including restaurants and accommodation.

Some hotel chains (Crest, Holiday Inn, Novotel, Swallow and Forte) have bedrooms adapted for people with disabilities. Many museums and tourist sites have toilets for wheelchair-users; a booklet showing toilets for people with disabilities is available from RADAR.

Wheelchair-users planning train travel should first contact the rail network that they will be using – telephone numbers are in the *Yellow Pages* or through directory enquiries (192) – so that arrangements can be made for boarding and seating. RADAR has addresses of local disability associations.

Driving

Driving in Britain can be a delightful way to see the country, or a diabolically frustrating experience. In many remote country areas it is the only feasible way of getting around; for village-to-village pottering (such as the Cotswolds, the Weald and Constable Country), where the local public transport is limited, the car really comes into its own. The huge network of narrow, crooked lanes (many very ancient indeed) is a particular feature. Rural honeypots such as the Lake District and the Cornish coastal towns and villages can get so busy in summer that finding somewhere to park requires ingenuity; consider using local buses (if there are any) or finding a footpath (often possible by using coastal paths).

Breakdown Car rental companies normally provide cover with one or other of the major motoring organisations in Britain, the AA or the RAC. On motorways, there are emergency telephones at the side of the hard shoulder every 1.6km (1mile).

GUIDE LEVELS

Guide levels for duty-paid goods bought in the EU. These quantities include items bought duty free. You can bring in any amount of goods, but beyond these guide limits you have to be able to show the items are for your own personal use (this includes gifts); if you are receiving any payment in return for these goods (including payment of your travel expenses) you will be liable for duty.

Beer	110 litres
Cigarettes	800
Cigarillos	400
Cigars	200
Tobacco	1kg
Spirits	10 litres
Intermediate products (sherry, port etc)	20 litres
Wine (of which not more than 60 litres to be sparkling wine)	90 litres

Arrows on posts indicate the direction of the nearest one.

Car rental Large firms with numerous branches and desks at airports include Avis tel: 0181-848 8733, Europcar tel: 0181-568 5606 and Hertz tel: 0990 996699. These may not be the cheapest; telephone around for the best deal.

Licences (permits) Australian, Canadian, Irish, New Zealand and US driving licences or permits are acceptable. Holders of permits written in a foreign language are advised to obtain an official translation from an embassy or recognised automobile association, or an international driving licence before they leave their country. Car rental firms all require you to have held your licence or permit for at least a year.

Motorways These link most major cities; service areas are indicated well in advance. On some motorway stretches, however, there is a serious dearth of stopping places, e.g., the M25 (London's busy orbital route), the M11 and M20.

Parking restrictions Never park on a double yellow line; parking on single yellow lines is generally permitted on Sundays and at other times as displayed. Wheel clamps are increasingly used to combat illegal parking and beware, the fee/fine to release your car is hefty.

Ramblers dressed wisely for winter

Traffic regulations Traffic drives on the left (hence clockwise at roundabouts, which are common features at intersections). Speed-limit and destination signs use miles (one kilometre is roughly ⅝ of a mile). Speed limits for cars are 110kph (70mph) for motorways and dual carriageways, 95kph (60mph) for other roads, and 50kph (30mph) in built-up areas unless otherwise indicated. Front-seat passengers and drivers must wear seat-belts; rear-seat passengers must wear seat-belts if the vehicle has them. Drivers must be at least 17 years of age.

Electricity
The current in Britain is 240 volts, alternate current. Plugs have three square pins.

Embassies and consulates in London
Australia Australia House, Strand, WC2, tel: 0171-379 4334
Canada 1 Grosvenor Square W1, tel: 0171-258 6600
Republic of Ireland 17 Grosvenor Place, SW1, tel: 0171-235 2171
New Zealand New Zealand House, Haymarket, SW1, tel: 0171-930 8422
USA 24 Grosvenor Square, W1, tel: 0171-499 9000

Health
Most visitors receive free treatment under the National Health Service. However, visitors from countries which do not have a reciprocal agreement with Britain may find they are charged. Accident victims must be admitted via casualty departments in hospital. Local doctors (GPs) will see visitors; ask at your hotel or a chemist's for details. If you take medication, make a note of the medicines you use. A charge is made for dental treatment.

Hitch-hiking
Hitch-hiking is not illegal in Britain, although the occasional report of violent crime associated with hitching deters many people. It is illegal to stand on the hard shoulder of motorways; however, you may wait near roundabouts by motorway slip roads.

Holidays

Summer school holidays generally last from late July to early September; the country virtually closes down from Christmas Day to New Year.

Jan 1 New Year's Day
Jan 2 New Year's Day (Scotland only)
Late March to early April Good Friday, followed three days later by Easter Monday
First Monday in May May Day Bank Holiday
Last Monday in May Spring Bank Holiday (Whitsun)
First Monday in August Bank Holiday (Scotland only)
Last Monday in August Bank Holiday (England and Wales only)
December 25 Christmas Day
December 26 Boxing Day

Insurance

Travel insurance should cover accident or illness, loss of valuables, injury or death while driving, and holiday cancellation or curtailment. Travellers may be covered for personal items through their house contents insurance. Be sure to leave the original policy details at home and take only a photocopy on your travels. Shop around for the best buy: prices and what is covered vary enormously.

Language

Although there is nowhere in Britain where English is not understood, in certain parts it is very much the second language. Welsh is the main tongue in parts of Mid West and North Wales, but less so in South Wales and the Welsh borders. Throughout Wales signposts and so on are in both languages. Gaelic is spoken in a few parts of Scotland, notably the Hebrides. Britain's cultural diversity is often simplified into the notion of a land of two cultures, separated by a north/south divide. But to simplify accents this way would not be possible. In whatever area of the country you visit, you will come across marked regional accents; from 'Scouse' in Liverpool to 'Brummie' in Birmingham, from 'Geordie' in Newcastle to 'Cockney' in London.

Beach umbrellas and windshields may be handy for a day at the sea

Certain accents seem to be seen as common, harsh and ugly, while others are seen as educated, soft and beautiful. But which accents are ugly, and which are beautiful? The answer to this question seems to be simply who you are asking. A study in the 1970s showed that British English speakers placed 'the Queen's English' first out of ten, with Brummie ninth and Cockney tenth. However, North American English speakers placed Cockney second, and surely these 'onlookers' are far more objective. British people make their decision from cultural backgrounds, for example it cannot be coincidence that the accents perceived as common and ugly belong to the heavily industrialized cities.

Lost property

Items are often handed into police stations; they pass on information about lost items to other branches. To make life easier for you and the police, make sure your address in Britain is shown on all your valuables. For items lost while on public transport, contact the bus station, train station or airport involved.

The London Transport Lost Property Office is at 200 Baker Street, NW1, tel: 0171-486 2496 (recorded message).

Maps

The Automobile Association (AA) publishes a comprehensive road atlas of Great Britain and an atlas of town plans.

Britain has been mapped accurately by the Ordnance Survey (OS). If you intend to spend some time exploring a region, invest in the pink-covered OS Landranger maps, 1:50,000 scale (2cm to the km): contours show relief, and footpaths are mapped. For hiking, the green-covered OS Pathfinder maps, 1:25,000 scale (4cm to the km), showing field boundaries, are best; for some of the most popular walking areas (including many national parks) the yellow-covered OS Outdoor Leisure and orange-covered Explorer maps, both at 1:25,000 scale, are available instead. Most bookshops have local OS maps; the full range is sold at Stanfords Map and Travel Bookshop, 12–14 Long Acre, London WC2, tel: 0171-836 1321.

Media

Newspapers Britain is sometimes said to have the best and the worst newspapers in the world. The style contrasts between the 'quality' broadsheets (the *Independent*, *Guardian*, *Times*, *Financial Times* and *Daily Telegraph*) and the more widely selling 'popular' tabloids (the *Daily Mail*, *Daily Express*, *Sun*, *Mirror*, *Star* and *Sport*). For London, the weekly *Time Out* gives the low-down on eating places and entertainment. There are several regional dailies.

Television There are five channels: the government-funded BBC1 and BBC2, and the commercial channels ITV, Channel 4 and the more recent Channel 5. Many hotels now have cable and satellite TV, giving access to foreign stations.

Radio There are five BBC radio stations, Radio 1 (pop music), Radio 2 (light music), Radio 3 (classical music), Radio 4 (news, drama and general interest) and Radio 5 (sport and news). Classic FM, broadcasting lighter classical music, is the most popular independent radio station. There are also numerous local stations. Frequencies can be found in newspapers and the weekly *Radio Times* and *TV Times* magazines.

Money matters

Credit cards are widely accepted, at nearly all filling stations, most restaurants and many shops. Travellers' cheques (try to get £ sterling ones) and Eurocheques are a safe way of carrying money. The pound (£) is divided into 100 pence (p). Denominations are 1p, 2p, 5p, 10p, 20p, 50p and £1 coins, then £5, £10, £20 and £50 notes. Banks in Scotland issue their own banknotes; they are legal currency throughout the UK.

VAT refunds Nationals of countries outside the EU may claim refunds for Value Added Tax (VAT) on goods bought within the EU; ask for a form when you make your purchase.

Tipping Generally, tip 10–15 per cent in a restaurant if service has not already been added (if in doubt, ask whether service is included), or not at all if you think the meal and/or service was not up to scratch; total payment boxes on credit card slips are often left empty, leaving you to add a tip (whatever you decide, remember to fill it in!). Taxi-drivers expect 10 per cent; minicab drivers (whom you order by telephone and are told a price before you travel) generally do not expect anything. Porters in luxury hotels expect £1. Hairdressers and barbers can be tipped 10 per cent.

Opening hours

Standard office hours are Monday to Friday, 9am to 5pm; shops generally stay open until 5.30 or 6pm, and operate 9am to 5.30pm on Saturdays. Some are now opening on Sundays. In central London and certain other cities many stores are open until late in the evening on Wednesday or Thursday.

Banks are open Monday to Friday; most close at 4.30pm; a few stay open on Saturday mornings.

Pubs may stay open from 11am to 11pm seven days a week, but in England and Wales some close in the afternoons. Note, however, that on Sundays Scottish pubs open mostly from 12.30 to 2.30pm and 6.30 to 11pm.

Until recently Sundays in England and Wales were still regulated by the anachronistic Sunday trading laws, which had become absurdly complex – to the point that it was illegal to buy a Bible on a Sunday, but legal to buy pornography. Similarly, a fish and chip shop could not open on a Sunday, but a Chinese takeaway restaurant could sell fish and chips! In practice the laws were often flouted, and the big supermarkets and a few main stores gambled on Sunday opening. Despite the legal changes that have taken place, this 'day of rest' remains mainly quiet – regional town centres and even parts of London look pretty dead then; theatres generally make a habit of staying closed on Sundays too.

A 'bobby' on the beat

Organised tours

Tourist information centres stock information on privately run excursion buses. Day tours can be a good way of seeing the sights, particularly for those with a crowded itinerary. Tour buses frequently circuit the sights of Oxford, Stratford-upon-Avon, Windsor, Bath, Cambridge and certain other historic centres.

In London Special **sightseeing buses** tour the centre (with guided commentary); the Original London Sightseeing Tour makes a 1½-hour round trip (join it at Piccadilly Circus, Victoria or Baker Street), while the London Plus tour enables the user to get on and off at will over a two-day period. Tickets for both are available on the buses or at a discount rate from the Piccadilly Circus travel information centre. The **Riverbus** service makes a speedy trip along the Thames. **Canal trips** are offered from Camden Lock to Little Venice by Jenny Wren Cruises (tel: 0171-485 4433) and from Little Venice to Camden Lock by Jason's Trip (0171-286 3428). Special interest **walking tours** are given daily by Original London Walks (0171-624 3978). Themes among the 300–350 walks each week include pubs, ghosts, the Beatles and royalty, and there are trips to Salisbury and Stonehenge. Walks last about two hours, usually starting from an underground station; reservation is not necessary.

271

Pharmacies

Usually called chemists, these have a fair range of medicines you can buy without a doctor's prescription. Opening time rotas are often maintained; details of locations of the duty chemist are posted in the windows.

Places of worship

The established churches in Britain are Protestant but there are numerous Roman Catholic churches. In London, all major religions are represented. Denominational headquarters include **Westminster Abbey** (Church of England), Deans Yard, SW1, tel: 0171-222 5152, **Westminster Cathedral** (Roman Catholic), Victoria Street, SW1, tel: 0171-834 7452, **United Synagogue**, Upper Woburn Place, WC1, tel: 0171-387 4300, **Methodist Central Hall**, Storeys Gate, SW1, tel: 0171-222 8010, **London Central Mosque**, 146 Park Road, NW8, tel: 0171-724 3363.

Police

Telephone 999 for emergencies only; police stations are listed in the *Yellow Pages* under 'Police'.

Traffic wardens (black and yellow uniforms) deal with everyday parking matters and sometimes direct traffic.

Letterboxes vary in size and shape but are always red

Post offices

Main post offices open from 9am to 5.30pm, Monday to Friday and 9am to 12.30pm on Saturday. Many newsagents and corner shops sell stamps in booklets. Inland letters bearing first-class stamps generally take a day less than those with second-class ones. First-class letter rate is the same as the rate for EU countries. Postcards and letters are charged at the same rate.

Public transport

Air travel There are over 30 regional airports in England, Scotland and Wales. British Airways guarantee a place on the next available flight for Shuttle services between London Heathrow, Manchester, Edinburgh and Glasgow; a seat on a British Midland flight will normally be available on the same day that you buy your ticket. For reservations ring British Airways tel: 0345 222111, British Midland tel: 0345 554554. Off-peak, stand-by and advance ticket discounts are available.

Buses Generally speaking, services in rural areas are infrequent. An exception is the Isle of Wight, where bus services are excellent.

Coach Long-distance buses and coaches serve the towns the railways cannot reach; fares are lower than rail, but the journey may not be as comfortable. The main London terminus is Victoria Coach Station, Buckingham Palace Road (near Victoria railway station), SW1, tel: 0171-730 3499 (reservations), 0990 808080 (for general information about National Express services); for some trips, tickets are purchased on board.

Rail The national network has recently been taken over by private operators. In theory this should not affect the quality of services, but it is not guaranteed. Information can be unreliable, and you may have to change operator during your journey. Grumbling about the railways, in the land where they were invented, is a favourite British pastime; in fact rail is a comfortable, though not particularly cheap, way of seeing the country, although delays and cancellations do occur. Beware of weekend engineering works: regional maps showing affected services for each weekend ahead may be posted at stations: special bus services fill in for the closed sections of line but they add significantly to the journey time.

Railway tickets are subject to numerous special deals; day return or saver tickets (return within a given period) are much cheaper than two single tickets for the same journey, but are subject to time restrictions (typically not to be used before 9am); Saver tickets are more expensive on Fridays and certain other days. Apex tickets give discounts for booking seven days or more in advance on InterCity (long distance) journeys. (BritRail passes are only available to non-UK residents but will save money for those intending to make more than one long train journey.) Young Persons' Railcards (for under-26s and students) and Senior Citizens' Railcards (for over-60s) give a one-third discount. Bicycles are carried free of charge on most services (check before travel).

Apart from the London–Scotland and London–Cornwall lines at peak periods, it is seldom necessary to reserve. First-class travel is available. Train information can be obtained by telephone: look in the *Yellow Pages* under 'Railways'.

Season tickets

Those intending to visit a number of stately homes and castles should consider taking out a season ticket for the **National Trust** (NT) and **National Trust for Scotland** (NTS) (see panel, page 102; note that membership of the NT entitles you to entry to NTS properties, and vice versa) and/or **English Heritage** (EH), **Cadw** (for Wales), **Historic Scotland** (HS) (see panel, page 124). Membership is available for all of these at any staffed property. Many other houses are under the umbrella of the Historic Houses Association, (2 Chester Street, London SW1X 7BB; tel: 0171-259 5688).

Senior citizens

Anyone aged 60 or over is entitled to a Senior Citizens Railcard and can get discounts for numerous admissions.

Student and youth travel

Youth hostels These offer bargain basement accommodation; Britain is the birthplace of the Youth Hostels Association (YHA) and has an excellent network of hostels ranging from primitive converted primary schools to manor houses and medieval castles. These can be better places for meeting people than guesthouses and hotels, especially the smaller and more personal youth hostels; some have stunning locations, such as in the Lake District, Snowdonia and the Scottish Highlands. There is no upward age restriction. Accommodation is simple, usually in dormitories, although some hostels have family rooms; food is served at most hostels, at set times, although it is always possible to cater for yourself. Few establishments allow hostellers to stay in during the day; at peak times and weekends it is advisable to reserve. You must join the YHA (unless you hold a youth hostel card from another country) in order to stay; membership can be taken out at any hostel.

The central London information outlet is the YHA shop and YHA travel, both at 14 Southampton Street, WC2, tel: 0171-836 1036. The Scottish YHA is based at 7 Glebe Crescent, Stirling FK8 2JA, tel: 01786 451181.

The familiar red British telephone box is almost a thing of the past. A few have been retained – some pre-war specimens were listed as architecturally important structures, and rather more were kept on in Conservation Areas; now the utilitarian British Telecom steel model (considerably more reliable than its predecessor) is here to stay.

International student cards These are useful to help gain reduced admission fees to tourist sights and places of entertainment. Young Persons' **Railcards** give under-26s and students a third off the price of rail tickets.

Telephones

In emergencies tel: **999** (police, fire and ambulance); calls are free. Operator tel: **100** (free). Directory inquiries tel: **192** (free from payphones only).

Calls on freephone numbers and numbers prefixed 0800 are free.

To make a call from a public telephone, put the money in before dialling (if you put in large denomination coins, beware: you will not get change), and collect any unspent coins when you hang up. Phone cards can be bought from newsagents and corner shops. Mercury phonecards enable calls to be made using the Mercury network to any British Telecom number.

The dial tone is a continuous purr, the ringing tone is a repeated brr-brr, and a repeated single tone indicates the line is engaged; a continuous tone means the number dialled is unobtainable.

To telephone abroad, dial 00 followed by the country's code, followed by the local number minus the initial 0.

Australia 61	New Zealand 64
Canada 1	US 1
Republic of Ireland 353	

Time

When it is 12 noon in Britain between the last Sunday in October and the last Saturday in March it is 8–10pm in Australia, 4–8.30am in Canada, 12 noon in the Republic of Ireland, midnight in New Zealand

273

CONVERSION CHARTS

FROM	TO	MULTIPLY BY
Inches	Centimetres	2.54
Centimetres	Inches	0.3937
Feet	Metres	0.3048
Metres	Feet	3.2810
Yards	Metres	0.9144
Metres	Yards	1.0940
Miles	Kilometres	1.6090
Kilometres	Miles	0.6214
Acres	Hectares	0.4047
Hectares	Acres	2.4710
Gallons	Litres	4.5460
Litres	Gallons	0.2200
Ounces	Grams	28.35
Grams	Ounces	0.0353
Pounds	Grams	453.6
Grams	Pounds	0.0022
Pounds	Kilograms	0.4536
Kilograms	Pounds	2.205
Tons	Tonnes	1.0160
Tonnes	Tons	0.9842

MEN'S SUITS

UK	36	38	40	42	44	46	48
Rest of Europe	46	48	50	52	54	56	58
US	36	38	40	42	44	46	48

DRESS SIZES

UK	8	10	12	14	16	18
France	36	38	40	42	44	46
Italy	38	40	42	44	46	48
Rest of Europe	34	36	38	40	42	44
US	6	8	10	12	14	16

MEN'S SHIRTS

UK	14	14.5	15	15.5	16	16.5	17
Rest of Europe	36	37	38	39/40	41	42	43
US	14	14.5	15	15.5	16	16.5	17

MEN'S SHOES

UK	7	7.5	8.5	9.5	10.5	11
Rest of Europe	41	42	43	44	45	46
US	8	8.5	9.5	10.5	11.5	12

WOMEN'S SHOES

UK	4.5	5	5.5	6	6.5	7
Rest of Europe	38	38	39	39	40	41
US	6	6.5	7	7.5	8	8.5

274

and 4–7am in the US. The rest of the year, clocks go forward one hour to British Summer Time.

Toilets

Normally marked 'WC' or 'Toilets', these are divided into 'Men' or 'Gents' and 'Women' or 'Ladies'. Paper should always be provided and with a few exceptions, such as main London railway stations, entry is free. Public lavatories, or 'loos', are usually in fair supply and it is not generally the done thing to march into a pub or restaurant as a non-customer and expect to use this facility.

Tourist offices

There are over 800 tourist information centres in Britain, run by tourist boards for England, Wales and Scotland: most are well-signposted (look for the *i* sign). Many offer accommodation booking services. Additionally, national parks have visitor centres with good local information.

Walking and hiking

Britain has a lifetime of opportunities for the walker, ranging from easily managed waymarked trails to challenging mountain terrain. England and Wales are served by a unique network of public rights of way, which criss-cross private land but are open to walkers; Scotland has an informal rule tolerating access to open land except in the shooting seasons (see page 266). Public footpaths (waymarked with yellow arrows) are for walkers only; public bridleways (waymarked in blue) are open to horseriders and cyclists too. National trails (official long distance paths) are indicated with acorn motifs. Some walks are suggested in this guide: further routes, with excellent OS maps, are described in detail in the AA/Ordnance Survey Leisure Guides. Guided walks are offered by numerous bodies, including national park authorities (contact information offices for details). If you prefer to branch out on your own and devise your own walks, you need a good map (see Maps), and proper equipment: do not underestimate the perils of the mountains (see page 168).

HOTELS AND RESTAURANTS

When writing to hotels listed, please include the postcode given *after* the name of the county. Hotels are grouped according to the gazetteer arrangement in the A to Z section of this guide. Some of the areas, such as the Lake District and the Cotswolds, are our own groupings and should appear in the address: such areas are marked with an asterisk (*). As an example, Oxenham Arms on page 277 should be addressed South Zeal, nr Okehampton, Devon EX20 2JT. (Dartmoor, which is asterisked, is omitted from the address.)

ACCOMMODATION

Tourist information centres can help with local accommodation lists, and many provide a reservation service. Bed and breakfast ('B&B') establishments are ubiquitous and often excellent value: typically they consists of a room in a private house (some have separate bathrooms).

Regional tourist boards publish lists of farmhouses, inns and guesthouses offering B&B (including the English Tourist Board's book *Where to Stay*). Country house hotels give you the chance to stay in period country homes; many are privately run by families. Many pubs have a few rooms for overnight visitors (some are included under Restaurants, pages 281–4). Generally, supply outstrips demand: provided you are prepared to drive to the next town, you will always find a bed, although be warned that the most popular resort towns and the Scottish Highlands can get very busy in season.

The following recommended hotels and inns are divided into three price categories, based on bed and breakfast for one person sharing a double- or twin-bedded room:
budget (£): generally under £35
moderate (££): generally £35–£60
expensive (£££): generally over £60

The **AA Hotel Booking Service** is a new service exclusively for AA personal members. It is a free, fast and easy way to find a place for a short break, holiday or business trip; tel: **0990 050505**. Full listings of British and Irish hotels and B&Bs available through the service can be booked at the AA's Internet Site http://www.theaa.co.uk/hotels

LONDON
Chelsea, Knightsbridge and Victoria
Basil Street (£££) 8 Basil Street, SW3 1AH (tel: 0171-581 3311). Formal, old-fashioned yet stylish.
Quality Eccleston (£££) 80–3 Eccleston Square, SW1V 1PS (tel: 0171-834 8042). You have a choice of 3 bedroom categories.
The Rubens at the Palace (£££) Buckingham Palace Road, SW1W 0PS (tel: 0171-834 6600). Overlooks the Royal Mews; comfortable, well-equipped rooms.

Bayswater, Kensington and Hyde Park
Barkston Gardens(£££) 34–44 Barkston Gardens, SW5 0EW (tel: 0171-373 7851). Conveniently close to Earl's Court Exhibition Centre and the Underground.
Delmere (£££) 130 Sussex Gardens, Hyde Park W2 1UB (tel: 0171-706 3344). Friendly staff, well-equipped bedrooms and a particularly comfortable lounge are all pluses.
Forte Posthouse Kensington(££) Wright's Lane, Kensington, W8 5SP (tel: 0171-937 8170). Offers comfortable bedrooms, a leisure club and several eating choices.
Gloucester (£££) 4–18 Harrington Gardens, SW7 4LH (tel: 0171-373 6030). The style is contemporary and chic, the amenities are good and the eating is cosmopolitan.
Parkwood (££) 4 Stanhope Place, W2 2HB (tel: 0171-262 9484). Pretty hotel in quiet street fronting on to Hyde Park; very popular with families.
Whites (£££) 90–92 Lancaster Gate, W2 3NR (tel: 0171- 262 2711). Elegant 'town house' style hotel with good-sized bedrooms.

Regents Park
Ibis Euston (££) 3 Cardington Street, NW1 2LW (0171-388 7777). Convenient for Euston Station, this good-value hotel also has a secure covered car park.
Kennedy (£££) Cardington Street, NW1 2LP (tel: 0171-387 5122). Modern hotel, close to Euston Station; 2 categories of bedroom.

Bloomsbury and West End
Bloomsbury Park (£) 126 Southampton Row, WC1B 5AD (tel: 0171-430 0434). Cosy hotel catering to all markets. Small dining area and two bars.
Royal Trafalgar Thistle (£££) Whitcomb Street, WC2H 7HG (tel: 0171-930 4477). Good, popular hotel by the National Gallery and handy for West End theatres.

Beyond the centre
The Barbican (££) Central Street EC1V 8DS (tel: 0171-251 1565). Large, modern, near Barbican arts complex and the City.
Sandringham (££–£££) 3 Holford Road NW3 1AD (tel: 0171-435 1569). Small, friendly with garden, on edge of Hampstead Heath.
Tower Thistle (£££) St Katharine's Way E1 9LD (tel: 0171-481 2575). Modern, very convenient for City; fine views of Tower Bridge.

THE WEST COUNTRY
Bath, Somerset
Paradise House (£) 86–8 Holloway, BA2 4PX (tel: 01225 317723). Quietly located in an elevated position, near the centre.
Royal Crescent (£££) 16 Royal Crescent, BA1 2LS (tel: 01225 9823333). In Bath's most famous street; the interior matches the splendour of the setting.
Somerset House (£) 35 Bathwick Hill, BA2 6LD (tel: 01225 466451). Homely and friendly Regency house.

Bradford-on-Avon, Wiltshire
Bradford Old Windmill (£) 4 Masons Lane, BA15 1QN (tel: 01225 866842). Converted windmill with amusing décor.

Bristol, Bristol
Berkeley Square (£££), 15 Berkeley Square, Clifton, BS8 1HB (tel: 0117 9254000). Smart Georgian hotel, peacefully situated near the university and art gallery.
Rodney (££), 4 Rodney Place, Clifton, BS8 4HY (tel: 0117 9735422). In a listed building, convenient for the city centre and M5.

Cornwall
Carbis Bay (£££) Carbis Bay, St Ives, TR26 2NP (tel: 01736 795311). Long-established, family-run hotel with fine seaside location.
Hotel Rotorua (££) Trencrom Lane, Carbis Bay, TR26 2TD (tel: 01736 795419). Modern hotel in well-tended gardens; heated pool.
Pedn-Olva (££) The Warren, St Ives, TR26 2EA (tel: 01736 796222). Right at the water's edge – glorious views from most rooms.
Port Gaverne (££) Port Gaverne, nr Port Isaac, PL29 3SQ (tel: 01208 880244; free-phone 0500 657867). Pleasant inn by a cove on an unspoilt coast.
Skidden House (£££) Skidden Hill, St Ives, TR26 2DU (tel: 01736 796899). Said to be St Ives's oldest hotel. Cosy and friendly.

Dartmoor*, Devon
Holne Chase (£££) nr Ashburton, TQ13 7NS (tel: 01364 631471). Peacefully located by the River Dart; well-appointed rooms.
Oxenham Arms (££) South Zeal, nr Okehampton, EX20 2JT (tel: 01837 840244). Pleasant 15th-century inn in village street.

Dartmouth, Devon
Royal Castle (£££) 11 The Quay, TQ6 9PS (tel: 01803 833033). 17th-century coaching inn on quayside.

Dorset
Crown (£££) West Street, Blandford Forum DT11 7AJ (tel: 01258 456626). Attractive former coaching house in the centre of this Georgian town.
Plumber Manor (£££) Hazelbury Bryan Road, Sturminster Newton, DT10 2AF (tel: 01258 472507). Jacobean manor with 16 rooms. Restaurant.
Priory (£££) Church Green, Wareham, BH20 4ND (tel: 01929 551666). 800-year-old priory, now a comfortable hotel; river gardens.

Exeter, Devon
St Olaves Court (£££) Mary Arches Street EX4 3AZ (tel: 01392 217736). 19th-century Georgian-style house near cathedral.

Exmoor*, Somerset and Devon
Ashwick House (£££) Dulverton, Somerset TA22 9QD (tel: 01398 323868). Turn-of-the-century country house in large grounds. Log fires, spacious bedrooms, good food.

Halmpstone Manor (££) Bishop's Tawton, Devon EX32 0EA (tel: 01271 830321). You get sherry on arrival at this lovely manor house offering informal, friendly comfort.
The Oaks (£££) Porlock, Somerset , TA24 8ES (tel: 01643 862265). Elegant Edwardian country house overlooking Porlock Bay. Relaxed atmosphere and thoughtful extras.

Salisbury, Wiltshire
Stratford Lodge (££) 4 Park Lane, SP1 3NP (tel: 01722 325177). Small, quiet Victorian house with period furnishings, near city.

Scilly, Isles of, Cornwall
Island Hotel (£££) Tresco, TR24 0PU (tel: 01720 422883). Modern hotel; island a tonic for escapists.

SOUTHERN ENGLAND
Brighton, East Sussex
Adelaide (£££) 51 Regency Square, BN1 2FF (tel: 01273 205286). Small hotel in elegant square facing on to the seafront.
Courtlands (££) 23 The Drive, BN3 3JE (tel: 01273 731055). Near town and seafront; swimming pool.
Grand Hotel (£££) Kings Road, BN1 2FW (tel: 01273 321188). The grandest of the grand seafront hotels.

Canterbury, Kent
Falstaff (£££) 8–12 St Dunstan's Street, CT2 8AF (tel: 01227 462138). Old coaching inn near Westgate Tower.
Thruxted Oast (££) Mystole, Chartham, nr Canterbury CT4 7BX (tel: 01227 730080). Five converted oast houses; rustic furnishings, open fire; country setting.

Dover, Kent
Wallett's Court (£££) West Cliffe, St Margaret's at Cliffe, nr Dover, CT15 6EW (tel: 01304 852424). Old-fashioned rooms in manor house, newer ones in barn annexe.

Isle of Wight
Albion (££) Freshwater Bay, PO40 9RA (tel: 01983 753631). Large hotel in prominent position on seashore; sunny balconies.
Seaview Hotel: (££) High Street, Seaview, PO34 5EX (tel: 01983 612711). First-class, ideal for families; nautical trappings.

Rye, East Sussex
Jeake's House (££) Mermaid Street, TN31 7ET (tel: 01797 222828). Part tile-hung 17th-century house in a pretty cobbled street.

The Weald*, Kent
Kennel Holt (£££) Goudhurst Road, Cranbrook TN17 2PT (tel: 01580 712032) There are 10 individually styled bedrooms in this engaging country house hotel.
Tanyard (££) Wierton Hill, Boughton Monchelsea, nr Maidstone, Kent, ME17 4JT (tel: 01622 744705). Fine 14th-century, half-timbered house in charming grounds.

HOTELS AND RESTAURANTS

Windsor, Berkshire
Oakley Court (£££) Windsor Road, Water Oakley, Windsor SL4 5UR (tel: 01628 74141). Neo-gothic country house; grounds extend to the Thames.

HEART OF ENGLAND
Chiltern Hills*, Oxfordshire
Beetle and Wedge (£££) Moulsford-on-Thames, Oxfordshire OX10 9JF (tel: 01753 609988). Ideally placed for exploring the Thames Valley; by the river.
Stonor Arms (££–£££) Stonor, Henley-on-Thames, Oxfordshire RG9 6HE (tel: 01491 638866). 18th-century inn in peaceful village beside deer park and good walking country. Two restaurants.

Cotswolds*
Bibury Court (££) Bibury, nr Cirencester, Gloucestershire GL7 5NT (tel: 01285 740337). Old-world Jacobean mansion by River Coln, offering a relaxed and not over-manicured retreat.
Buckland Manor (£££) Buckland, nr Broadway, Hereford & Worcester WR12 7LY (tel: 01386 852626). In a quiet backwater village beneath the escarpment: a medieval manor adjoining the church; supreme class, priced accordingly.
Collin House (££) Collin Lane, Broadway, Hereford & Worcester WR12 7PB (tel: 01386 858354). Exemplary country house hotel, quietly set behind main street.
Cotswold House (£££) The Square, Chipping Campden, Gloucestershire GL55 6AN (tel: 01386 840330). Formal elegance; murals and antiques.
Painswick (££) Kemps Lane, Painswick, Gloucestershire GL6 6YB (tel: 01452 812160). Stylish former rectory in handsome small town.
White Hart (£££) High Street, Dorchester, Oxfordshire OX10 7HN (tel: 01865 340074). Relaxed Thames-side inn with rooms; noteworthy modern cooking in the restaurant.

Ludlow, Shropshire
Cliffe Hotel (££) Dinham, Ludlow, SY8 2JE (tel: 01584 872063). Friendly small hotel with home-cooked food. Jazz at weekends.
Feathers (£££) Bull Ring, SY8 1AA (tel: 01584 875261). Famous half-timbered building which has functioned as a hotel since 1600s.

Malvern Hills* Herefordshire
Hope End (£££) nr Ledbury HR8 1JQ (tel: 01531 633613). A country house amid green, rolling hills; stylish décor; home-grown produce and accomplished cooking.

Oxford, Oxfordshire
Cotswold House (££) 363 Banbury Road, OX2 7PL (tel: 01865 310558). Well-run B&B 3km (2miles) from city centre; frequent buses; eating places near by.

Linton Lodge (££) 13 Linton Road, OX2 6UJ (tel: 01865 553461). Large hotel comprising several houses in a quiet residential area close to colleges and River Isis.
Randolph (£££) Beaumont Street, OX1 2LN (tel: 01865 247481). Large, comfortable and long-established hotel in city centre.

Stratford-upon-Avon, Warwickshire
Falcon (£££) Chapel Street, CV37 6HA (tel: 01789 279953). Traditional inn with nice bedrooms and atmospheric public rooms.
Stratford House (£££) 18 Sheep Street CV37 6EF (tel: 01789 268288). Friendly Georgian hotel ideally located for theatre-goers.
Stratford Manor (£££) Warwick Road, CV37 0PY (tel: 01789 731173). Purpose-built hotel catering largely to a business clientele.
White Swan (£££) Rother Street, CV37 6NH (tel: 01789 297022). Half-timbered building with modern facilities close to town centre and the Bard's birthplace.

EASTERN ENGLAND
Cambridge, Cambridgeshire
Arundel House (£–££) 53 Chesterton Road, CB4 3AN (tel: 01223 367701). Victorian terrace by Jesus Green; near centre.
Garden House (£££) Granta Place, Mill Lane, CB2 1RT (tel: 01223 259988). Modern hotel, nicely sited by river and within a short walk of the city centre and colleges.
Gonville (£££) Gonville Place, CB1 1LY (tel: 01223 366611). Traditional hotel in centre, by Parker's Piece park.

Constable Country*, Essex/Suffolk
Great House (££) Market Place, Lavenham, Suffolk CO10 9QZ (tel: 01787 247431). Georgian exterior belies an ancient timber-framed structure; just four bedrooms.
Maison Talbooth (£££) Stratford Road, Dedham, nr Colchester, Essex, CO7 6HN (tel: 01206 322367). Top-notch B&B.

Lincoln, Lincolnshire
D'Isney Place (££) Eastgate, LN2 4AA (tel: 01522 538881). Redbrick house begun 1735, near cathedral; B&B only.

North Norfolk coast*
Beaumaris (£££) South Street, Sheringham NR26 8LL (tel: 01263 822370). Established hotel 5 minutes from seafront and town.
Morston Hall (£££ inc. dinner) Morston, Holt, Norfolk NR25 7AA (tel: 01263 741041). By marshes, a 17th-century brick-and-flint house; four rooms; excellent restaurant.

Norwich, Norfolk
Maid's Head (££) Tombland, NR3 1LB (tel: 01603 209955). Dating from 1272, England's oldest hotel in continuous use; the best bet in the city.
Quality Friendly (£££) 2 Barnard Road, Bowthorpe, NR5 9JB (tel: 01603 741161). Modern hotel on outskirts of city; pool and gymnasium.

Southwold, Suffolk
Swan (£££) Market Place, IP18 6EG (tel: 01502 722186). Traditional hotel; considerable standards of comfort.

Stamford, Cambridgeshire
George (£££) 71 St Martins, PE9 2LB (tel: 01780 55171). Splendid coaching inn; elegant public rooms and restaurant.

WALES
Brecon Beacons*, Powys
Gliffaes (£££) nr Crickhowell, Powys NP8 1RH (tel: 01874 730371). Traditional family-run hotel, overlooking River Usk and set in parkland; good fishing near by.
Llangoed Hall (£££) Llyswen, Powys LD3 0YP (tel: 01874 754525). Stylishly Edwardian, rebuilt by Clough Williams Ellis (of Portmeirion fame); personal touches; classic cooking.

Gower Peninsula*, Swansea
Fairyhill (£££) Reynoldston, Swansea, SA3 1BS (tel: 01792 390139). Mansion in woodlands with own trout stream; restrained décor; local dishes feature on an ambitious menu.

Llangammarch Wells, Powys
Lake (£££) LD4 4BS (tel: 01591 620202). Established as a spa hotel in the 1890s; now a graceful rural retreat overlooking a small lake near Llandrindod Wells.

Snowdonia National Park*, Gwynedd
Maes-y-Neuadd (£££) Talsarnau, nr Harlech, LL47 6YA (tel: 01766 780200). Ancient granite and slate building with splendid vistas; open fire.
Old Rectory (£££) Llansanffraid Glan Conwy, nr Conwy, Conwy LL28 5LF (tel: 01492 580611). Fine views of mountains and Conwy Castle; gourmet dinners add to the enjoyment.
Portmeirion Hotel (£££) **and village** (££) Portmeirion, LL48 6ER (tel: 01766 770228). Extraordinary Italianate village (see page 169); the hotel fronts the estuary and has a lavish interior; also offers rooms in the 'village'.
St Tudno (£££) Promenade, Llandudno, Conwy, LL30 2LP (tel: 01492 874411). Bay-windowed hotel standing on a handsome Victorian seafront; outstanding hospitality.
Sygun Fawr (££) Beddgelert, LL55 4NE (tel: 01766 890258). Stone manor up steep lane from village; popular with climbers and walkers.

Tenby, Pembrokeshire
Penally Abbey (£££) Penally, nr Tenby, SA70 7PY (tel: 01834 843033). Georgian Gothic house, near coast, high-ceilinged rooms, four-poster beds, ruined chapel; modern annexe; French influence to cooking.

Wye Valley*, Monmouthshire
Crown at Whitebrook (££–£££) Whitebrook, Monmouthshire, NP5 4TX (tel: 01600 860254). Country hotel with pretty bedrooms and comfortable lounge, in a valley near the River Wye.
Kings (££) High Street, Newport, NP9 1QU (tel: 01633 842020). Privately owned, town centre hotel; some family bedrooms
Marriott St Pierre Hotel & Country Club (£££) St Pierre Park, Chepstow NP6 6YA (tel: 01291 625261). Modern comfort in elegant surroundings; championship golf course.
Parva Farmhouse (££) Tintern, nr Chepstow, Monmouthshire, NP6 6SQ (tel: 01291 689411). Cosy without being twee.

NORTHWEST ENGLAND
Chester, Cheshire
Green Bough (££) 60 Hoole Road, CH2 3NL (tel: 01244 326241). On tree-lined main road into centre; personal service; antique beds (with modern bases).
Grosvenor (£££) Eastgate Street, CH1 1LT (tel: 01244 324024). Four-star luxury hotel at the heart of this historic city.

The Lake District*, Cumbria
Mill (£££) Mungrisdale, nr Penrith, CA11 0XR (tel: 01768 779659). Cosy and informal, former mill cottage, in quiet rolling moors of northern fells (not the same establishment as the nearby Mill Inn).
Old Vicarage (£££) Church Road, Witherslack, nr Grange-over-Sands, LA11 6RS (tel: 015395 52381). High standards of cooking and comfort; beneath Whitbarrow Scar.
Patterdale Hotel (££) Patterdale, CA11 0NN (tel: 017684 82231). Roadside hotel at the southern end of Ullswater. Mainly caters for tours; functional, practical standards.
Rothay Manor (£££) Rothay Bridge, Ambleside, LA22 0EH (tel: 015394 33605). Elegant Regency house; charming veranda; renowned cuisine; secluded site.
Sharrow Bay (£££) Ullswater, nr Penrith, CA10 2LZ (tel: 017684 86301). One of Lakeland's most celebrated hotels, highly rated for comfort and its cuisine.
Skiddaw (££) Main Street, Keswick, CA12 5BN (tel: 017687 72071). Set in the heart of town with views of Skiddaw from upper rooms (binoculars provided).
The Trout (£££) Crown Street, Cockermouth, CA13 0EJ (tel: 01900 823591). Long-established hotel, right next to Wordsworth's birthplace, offering executive, standard or economy rooms.
Wasdale Head Inn (££) Wasdale Head, nr Gosforth, CA20 1EX (tel: 019467 26229). Long-established haunt of walkers and climbers; in a spectacular isolated position.
White Moss House (£££–inc. dinner) Rydal Water, Grasmere LA22 9SE (tel: 015394 35295). Small, elegant house (formerly belonged to Wordsworth family); English cuisine.

HOTELS AND RESTAURANTS

The Peak District National Park*, Derbyshire
Callow Hall (£££) Mappleton Road, nr Ashbourne, Derbyshire DE6 2AA (tel: 01335 343403). Grand country house outside Ashbourne.
Cavendish (£££) Baslow, Derbyshire DE45 1SP (tel: 01246 582311). High-class comfort and in the best taste; a civilised retreat in the Chatsworth estate.
Riber Hall (£££) nr Matlock, Derbyshire DE4 5JU (tel: 01629 582795). Elizabethan manor above Derwent Gorge; plenty of period character with modern facilities.

NORTHEAST ENGLAND
Co Durham and Northumberland
The Postchaise Hotel (££) 36 Market Place, Bishop Auckland, DL14 7NX (TEL: 01388 661296) Old town centre hostelry with a lively atmosphere.
White Swan (£££) Bondgate Within, Alnwick, NE66 1TD (tel: 01665 602109). Interesting 300-year-old town centre hotel.

Durham
Royal County (£££) Old Elvet, DH1 3JN (tel: 0191-386 6821). Ample, comfortable hotel, extending on to river bank.
Three Tuns (££–£££) New Elvet, DH1 3AQ (0191-386 4326). Old-established, comfortable city centre hotel.

North York Moors*, North Yorkshire
Lastingham Grange (£££) Lastingham, YO6 6TH (tel: 01751 417345). Old-fashioned and welcoming, in tranquil village.
Mallyan Spout (£££) Goathland, nr Whitby, YO22 5AN (tel: 01947 8960486). Located in a village in fine walking countryside. Cottagey rooms.

York, North Yorkshire
Abbots Mews (£) 6 Marygate Lane, YO3 7DE (tel: 01904 634866). Just outside city walls, converted coachman's cottage.
Cottage (££) 3 Clifton Green, YO3 6LH (tel: 01904 643711). View of Clifton Green, close to city centre; very friendly.
Mount Royale (£££) The Mount, YO2 2DA (tel: 01904 628856). Two early 19th-century houses with antiques, and a welcoming atmosphere. South of centre.

Yorkshire Dales National Park*, North Yorkshire
Amerdale House (£££) Arncliffe, nr Skipton, BD23 5QE (tel: 01756 770250). Beautifully set manor house in Littondale; friendly and run with flair.
Ashfield House (££) Grassington, nr Skipton, BD23 5AE (tel: 01756 752584). Small-scale hotel off the Square: rustic pine décor; country cooking.
Miller's House (£££) Middleham, Wensleydale, DL8 4NR (tel: 01969 622630). Off an enchanting village square; elegantly furnished rooms; accomplished cooking.

SOUTHERN SCOTLAND
(Scottish) Borders
Cringletie House (£££) Duncar Road, Peebles, Scottish Borders EH45 8PL (tel: 01721 730233). Romantic-looking country house, family-run.
Tweed Valley (£££) Galashiels Road, Walkerburn, Scottish Borders EH43 6AA (tel: 01896 870636). Traditional comfort; elevated site above the River Tweed.

Dumfries and Galloway
Balcary Bay (£££) Auchencairn, nr Kirkcudbright, DG7 1QZ (tel: 01556 640217). Small, lone hotel by shore, overlooking the Solway Firth and Lake District mountains.
Knockinaam Lodge (£££) Portpatrick, Rhinns of Galloway, DG9 9AD (tel: 01776 810471). On the west coast, looking towards the Mountains of Morne in Ireland; well-equipped and spacious bedrooms.

Edinburgh
Bruntsfield (£££) 69/74 Bruntsfield Place EH10 4HH (tel: 0131-229 1393). Hotel overlooking links; south of city centre.
Caledonian (£££) Princes Street, EH1 2AB (tel: 0131-459 9988). 90-year-old former railway hotel affectionately known as 'The Cally', grand foyer, attractive rooms, friendly service.
Howard (£££) 32–6 Great King Street, EH3 6QH (tel: 0131-557 3500). High-class comfort: a Georgian terrace in the New Town.
Rothesay (££) 8 Rothesay Place, EH3 7SL (tel: 0131-225 4125). Keenly priced, family-run terraced hotel.
Roxburghe (£££) 38 Charlotte Square, EH2 4HG (tel: 0131-225 3921). Fine example of Adam architecture minutes from Princes Street; range of bedrooms.

Firth of Forth*
Greywalls (£££) Duncar Road, Gullane, Muirfield, East Lothian, EH31 2EG (tel: 01620 842144). Splendid house designed by Lutyens, overlooking golf links east of Edinburgh.

Glasgow
Deauvilles (££) 62 St Andrew's Drive, Pollockshields, G41 5EX (tel: 0141-427 1106). Imposing house in a leafy suburb with well-equipped bedrooms and elegant restaurant.
Ewington (£££) 132 Queens Drive, Queens Park, G42 8QW (tel: 0141-423 1152). Well-equipped and friendly hotel in terrace overlooking Queens Park.
One Devonshire Gardens (£££) 1 Devonshire Gardens, G12 0UX (tel: 0141-339 2001). Supremely elegant hotel occupying a terrace of houses; mahogany, rich fabrics.

St Andrews, Fife
St Andrews Old Course (£££) Old Station Road, KY16 9SP (tel: 01334 474371). By the famous golf course and the sea; elegant, well equipped and comfortable.

Scores (£££) 76 The Scores, KY16 9BB (tel: 01334 472451). In two 1880s fashionable town houses, overlooks seafront and convenient for Old Course.

Trossachs*, Stirling
Roman Camp (£££) Main Street, Callander, Stirling FK17 8BG (tel: 01877 330003). Enlarged manor house on banks of River Teith.
Terraces (££) 4 Melville Terrace, Stirling, KK8 2ND (tel: 01786 472268). Convenient and welcoming hotel in a tree-lined terrace; popular with business people.

NORTHERN SCOTLAND
Deeside*
Banchory Lodge (£££) Banchory, Aberdeenshire, AB31 5HS (tel: 01330 822625). Refreshingly unpretentious Georgian house in secluded gardens; antiques; hearty Scottish fare.
Kildrummy Castle (£££) Kildrummy, Aberdeenshire, AB33 8RA (tel: 01975 571288). Victorian mansion by castle ruin; tapestries, oak panelling.

Inverness*, Highland
Dunain Park (£££) nr Inverness IV3 6JN (tel: 01463 230512). Friendly country house outside Inverness, good food.
Knockie Lodge (£££) Whitebridge, IV1 2UP (tel: 01456 486276). Restful, with sheep and cattle for company; 'lived in' rather than smart; unpretentious cooking.

Lochaber*, Highland
Ardsheal House (£££) Kentallan, Glencoe PA38 4BX (tel: 01631 740227). Well placed for exploring Loch Linnhe and Glen Coe; furnished with flair.
Arisaig House (£££) Arisaig PH39 4NR (tel: 01687 450622). West coast views from its terrace. Imaginative menu, and helpful staff.
Kilcamb Lodge (£££) Strontian, Acharacle PH36 4HY (tel: 01967 402257). Friendly, family-run hotel, with fine views of Loch Sunart; close to shore; log fires.

Oban and Argyll and Bute
Airds (£££ including dinner) Port Appin, Appin PA38 4DF (tel: 01631 730236). Small hotel north of Oban with stunning views of Loch Linnhe; unassuming from outside, but extremely welcoming and comfortable.
Isle of Eriska (£££) Eriska, Ledaig by Oban PA37 1SD (tel: 01631 720371). On an island connected by bridge to mainland; putting green, croquet lawn, plus books and games. Pretty rooms.

Perth and Kinross
Dalmunzie House (£££) Spittal of Glenshee, Blairgowrie, PH10 7QG (tel: 01250 885224). Turreted house in its own private glen; offers fishing and golf; a favourite with families.

Guinach House (££) By the Birks, Urlar Road, Aberfeldy, PH15 2ET (tel: 01887 820251). Edwardian house, off A826, inviting lounge with open fire and books; excellent cooking, home-grown produce.

Shetland
Busta House (£££) Brae ZE2 9QN (tel: 01806 522506). 16th-century former laird's house overlooking Busta Voe. Well designed bedrooms and relaxing public areas.

Skye, Highland
Kinloch Lodge (£££) Isle Ornsay, Sleat, IV43 8QY (tel: 01471 833214). Peace and tranquillity in a friendly Gaelic atmosphere; small, old hotel.
Royal (££) Portree, IV51 9BU (tel: 01478 612525). Long-established hotel, popular with families for its health and leisure facilities; live entertainment in high season.

Spey Valley and Cairngorms*, Highland
Columba House (£) Manse Road, Kingussie, PH21 1JF (tel: 01540 661402). Converted 19th-century manse in elevated grounds; comfortable and relaxed; home cooking.

Sutherland*, Highland
Ceilidh Place (££) 14 West Argyll Street, Ullapool, IV26 2TY (tel: 01854 612103). Several cottages made into a local meeting-place: bookshop, coffee and wine bar, gallery and hotel; outgoing and friendly owners; simple bedrooms.

RESTAURANTS

Roast beef and Yorkshire pudding, plus apple pie and custard as a dessert, is the quintessentially British dish; but the nation's gastronomic tastes are becoming increasingly cosmopolitan.

Many hotels and restaurants offer French cuisine, while Indian and Chinese restaurants are the leading ethnic eateries. Fish and chips (known as 'fish supper' in Scotland) is the traditional, sustaining takeaway and is still very inexpensive.

Pub meals are among the cheapest sit-down options (an elaborate bread, cheese, pickle and salad platter is known as a 'ploughman's lunch').

In Scotland, high tea is often served in late afternoon and early evening – a hot dish, bread and butter, cake and/or scones, and a pot of tea.

The following restaurants are divided into three price categories:
budget (£): under £15 per head
moderate (££): £15–£30 per head
expensive (£££): over £30 per head

The following guides will help: AA *Best Restaurants 1998* and AA *Best Pubs and Inns Guide 1998*.

HOTELS AND RESTAURANTS

LONDON

The range of restaurants in London is unlimited, both in type of cuisine and price category. The selection given below is restricted to those that count among London's most highly rated or memorable eating places and those that offer a typically British meal. For further suggestions on where to eat, see page 59.

Alastair Little (££–£££) 49 Frith Street, W1 (tel: 0171-734 5183). Unassuming-looking Soho restaurant, minimalist décor, not luxurious; but high-quality dishes with Oriental and Mediterranean flavours.

Alfred (£££) 245 Shaftesbury Avenue, WC2 (tel: 0171-240 2566). Imaginative British cooking using quality ingredients. Rich puddings; good array of beers.

Capital Hotel (£££) Basil Street, Knightsbridge, SW3 (tel: 0171-589 5171). Stylish cocktail bar and dining room; provides good value set lunches and dinners.

Coast Restaurant (£££) Albemarle Street, W1 (tel: 0171-734 8040). Brash and smoky with a startling sci-fi décor. Daring menu offers inventive combinations of cuisines and ingredients; trendy house wines.

Four Seasons, Inn on the Park (£££) Hamilton Place, Park Lane, W1 (tel: 0171-499 0888). Smoothly executed cooking.

Gladwins (£££) Minster Court, Mark Lane, EC3 (tel: 0171-444 0004). Weekday lunch only, popular with City gents. Modern, flavourful cooking; complimentary mineral water flows freely.

Le Gavroche (£££) 43 Upper Brook Street, W1 (tel: 0171 408 0881). Superlative restaurant with a friendly atmosphere; set-menu options available.

Terrace, Dorchester Hotel (£££) 53 Park Lane, W1 (tel: 0171-629 8888). Renowned French cuisine.

The Hothouse (£) 78–80 Wapping Lane, E1 (tel: 0171-488 4797). Converted warehouse setting for modern English cooking; both elaborate and informal food.

Veronica's (££) 3 Hereford Road, W2 (tel: 0171-229 5079). Historically researched English food; British wines and cheeses.

Wilson's (££) 236 Blythe Road, W14 (tel: 0171-603 7267). High quality food with a Scottish bias. Booking essential.

THE WEST COUNTRY
Bath, Somerset

No 5 Bistro (££) 5 Argyle Street (tel: 01225 444499). True bistro ambience and confident, eclectic cooking. You can bring your own wine Mon & Tue evenings.

Royal Crescent (£££); see Accommodation.

Cornwall

Old Custom House Inn (££) South Quay, Padstow (tel: 01841 532359). Harbourside restaurant offering imaginative fixed-price menu. Bar meals too.

Port Gaverne (£–££). Bar food, and excellent buffets; see Accommodation.

The Kitchen (££) The Coombes, Polperro (tel: 01503 272780). Cosy cottage setting for a dazzling array of dishes, many using locally caught seafood.

Dartmoor*, Devon

Bel Alp House (£££) Haytor (tel: 01364 661217). Hotel restaurant offering splendid 6-course set dinner.

Gidleigh Park (£££) Chagford (tel: 01647 432367). Idyllic mock-Tudor hotel on edge of moor; cooking of international repute.

Holne Chase Hotel (£££). Country house hotel offering impressive cooking in the dining room; see Accommmodation

Oxenham Arms (£). Good-value pub food; see Accommodation.

Dartmouth, Devon

Carved Angel (£££) 2 South Embankment (tel: 01803 832465). French regional and British cuisine, with personal touches. Something of a national institution.

Dorset

Hambro Arms (£) Milton Abbas (tel: 01258 880233). Pub with low-beamed front bar with bow window looking onto village street of thatched estate cottages. Bar food and daily specials, plus Sunday roasts.

Three Horseshoes (£–££) Powerstock, nr Beaminster (tel: 01308 485328). Pleasant inn in centre of thatched village in hilly countryside; good fish dishes.

Exmoor*, Devon

Chough's Nest (££) North Walk, Lynton (tel: 01598 753315). Interesting dinners served in a bright, airy dining room.

Old Rectory Hotel (£££) Martinhoe, Parracombe, Barnstaple (tel: 01598 763368). The simple menu descriptions belie the scrumptious dinners served here.

Rising Sun (£–££) Lynmouth (tel: 01598 53223). This old-world former smugglers' inn has an oak-panelled restaurant and bar.

Taunton, Somerset

Nightingales (££) Bath House Farm, Lower West Hatch (tel: 01823 480806). Attractive food in comforting domestic setting. Restricted opening times (dinner Fri & Sat, lunch Sun).

SOUTHERN ENGLAND
Brighton, East Sussex

Black Chapati (££) 12 Circus Parade, New England Road (tel: 01273 699011). Minimalist décor, but you get a highly adventurous version of Asian cooking.

Terre à Terre (££) 7 Pool Valley (tel: 01273 729051). Popular spot for some of the most original vegetarian dishes in town.

Canterbury, Kent

Ristorante Tuo e Mio (££) 16 The Borough (tel: 01227 761471). Family-run Italian offering standard trattoria dishes.

Eastbourne, East Sussex
Star (££) Alfriston, nr Eastbourne (tel: 01323 870495). Famous old-world inn/hotel in charming village. Soup and ploughman's lunch, hot dishes, Sunday buffet.

Hastings, Kent
Roser's (££) 64 Eversfield Place (tel: 01424 712218). Intimate restaurant; small French-inspired menu, excellent wines.

New Forest, Hampshire
Le Poussin (££) The Courtyard, Brookley Road, Brockenhurst (tel: 01590 623063). Delicious ingredients, offered simply and sympathetically.

The Weald*, Kent
Rankins (££) Sissinghurst (tel: 01580 713964). Popular village restaurant providing eclectic, inventive cooking.
Royal Oak Hotel (£££) Upper High Street, Sevenoaks (tel: 01732 451109). Wide range of food in formal restaurant and bistro.
Thackeray's House (££) 85 London Road, Tunbridge Wells (tel: 01892 511921). Historic house, connections with William Thackeray; good, uncomplicated cooking.

Winchester, Hampshire
Wykeham Arms (£–££) 75 Kingsgate Street (tel: 01962 853834). Pub between the cathedral and Winchester College; open fires and cosy corners; interesting menu.

Windsor, Berkshire
Waterside (£££) River Cottage, Ferry Road, Bray (tel: 01628 20691). Splendid restaurant with rooms. French and Mediterranean influences; internationally renowned.

HEART OF ENGLAND
Cotswolds
Cotswold House Hotel (£–££) The Square, Chipping Campden (tel: 01386 840330). Good-value lunches; dearer dinners.
Feathers (££) Market Street, Woodstock (tel: 01993 812291). Gracious old hotel with daily menu. Close to Blenheim Palace.
Inn For All Seasons (££) The Barringtons, Burford (tel: 01451 844324). Generous portions of good home-cooked food.
Lamb (££) Shipton-under-Wychwood (tel: 01993 830465). Inn offering a short-set-price menu; local produce used.
The Lygon Arms (£££) Broadway (tel: 01386 852255). The main restaurant, in the stunning Great Hall, serves skilfully prepared dishes. Goblets Restaurant is less formal.
Marsh Goose (££) HighStreet, Moreton-in-Marsh, GL56 0AX (tel: 01608 652111). Daring menus in a genteel Cotswold setting.

Herefordshire and Worcestershire
Olde Salutation (£–££) Weobley, nr Hereford (tel: 01544 318443). Medieval inn in picturebook half-timbered village; good-value Sunday lunch.

The Evesham Hotel (££) Coopers Lane off Waterside, Evesham, Worcestershire (tel: 01386 765566). Friendly hotel with a well-deserved reputation for food.

Oxford, Oxfordshire
Le Manoir aux Quat' Saisons (£££) Great Milton (tel: 01844 278881). Cotswold mansion southeast of Oxford offering some of the finest, most inspired cooking in the land. Splendid accommodation.
Liaisons (££) 29 Castle Street (tel: 01865 242944). Popular Chinese restaurant with an excellent range of dim sum.
Munchy Munchy (£) 6 Park End Street (tel: 01865 245710). Idiosyncratic Southeast Asian gem, with stripped-bare décor and unpredictable combinations of herbs, spices and other ingredients.

Stratford-upon-Avon, Warwickshire
The Boathouse (£) Swan's Nest Lane (tel: 01789 297733). Forthright, flavourful food on the first floor of a working boathouse near the Royal Shakespeare Theatre.

283

EASTERN ENGLAND
Cambridge, Cambridgeshire
Cambridge Lodge Hotel (££) 139 Huntingdon Road (tel: 01223 352833). On the outskirts of the town, this spacious hotel restaurant serves classical cooking.
Midsummer House (££–£££) Midsummer Common (tel: 01223 369299). Worth seeking out: a short walk from the city centre. Accomplished cooking; excellent wines and cheeses.
Old Fire Engine House 25 St Mary's Street (tel: 01353 662582). Dishes of pigeon pie can be taken in the quarry-tiled rear garden.

Constable Country*, Essex
Le Tolbooth (££) Dedham (tel: 01206 323150). Half-timbered, on banks of Stour; seasonal menu.
White Hart Hotel (££) Market Place, Coggeshall (tel: 01376 561654). Traditional Italian cooking in a historic inn.

Lincoln, Lincolnshire
Wig and Mitre (£–££) 29 Steep Hill (tel: 01522 535190). Brasserie-style 14th-century inn close to the cathedral; good for inexpensive lunches and festive dinners.

Norwich, Norfolk
Adlard's (£££) 79 Upper Giles Street (tel: 01603 633522). Friendly service; fixed-price French menus; good value lunches.
Mange Tout (£) 22–4 White Lion Street (tel: 01603 617879). Comfortable bistro/coffee shop.

Southwold, Suffolk
Crown (£–££) 90 High Street (tel: 01502 722275). Elegant inn serving excellent fish dishes; tends to get crowded; reserve at busy times.

HOTELS AND RESTAURANTS

WALES
Brecon Beacons, Powys
Bear (£–££) Crickhowell (tel: 01873 810408). Old coaching inn serving imaginative food.
Griffin Inn (£££) Llyswen, Brecon (tel: 01874 754241). Popular country inn with good food (using local produce) and atmosphere.

Snowdonia National Park, Gwynedd
Castle Cottage Hotel (£) Pen Llech, Harlech (tel: 01766 780479). Delightful small hotel with a first-rate restaurant.
Tu-Hwnt i'r Bont (£) Llanrwst (tel: 01492 640138). Old-world, low-ceilinged tearoom; Welsh bara brith, cakes, baps, salads.
Y Bistro (££) 43–5 Stryd Fawr, Llanberis (tel: 01286 871278). Candlelit romance; the dinner menu's in Welsh with English subtitles;

NORTHWEST ENGLAND
The Lake District, Cumbria
Appleby Manor (£££) Roman Road, Appleby-in-Westmorland (tel: 017683 51571). Imaginative dishes and generous portions in this hotel above the town.
Britannia (£–££) Elterwater, nr Skelwith Bridge (tel: 015394 37210). Snug old pub by village green; restaurant attached.
Overwater Hall Hotel (£££), Ireby, Bassenthwaite (tel: 017687 76566). 5-course dinner makes good use of local produce.
Queens Head (£) Troutbeck, nr Windermere (tel: 015394 32174). Enterprising pub fare; friendly old coaching inn.
Sharrow Bay (£££); see Accommodation.

Cheshire
Broxton Hall Country House Hotel (££) Whitchurch Road (tel: 01829 782321). Good dining overlooking lovely gardens.
Cottage Restaurant & Lodge (£) London Road, Allostock, Knutsford (tel: 01565 722470). The food at this smart modern hotel has a large local following.

The Peak District*, Derbyshire
Fischer's (££–£££) Baslow Hall, Carver Road, Baslow (tel: 01246 583259). Innovative cuisine with Japanese touches; cheaper high teas and bistro meals

NORTHEAST ENGLAND
Northumberland
Linden Hall Hotel (££) Longhorsley, Morpeth (01670 516611). Anglo-French dishes feature here, as do fish and seafood.
Olde Ship (£) Seahouses (tel: 01665 720200). Harbourside inn, popular with fishermen; simple fare includes fish dishes.

North York Moors
Appleton Hall Country House Hotel (££) Appleton Le Moors, York (tel: 01751 417227). Reliable English-inspired dishes.
Milburn Arms Hotel (£££) Rosedale Abbey, Pickering (tel: 01751 417312). Priory restaurant offers fresh, local ingredients used imaginatively; wide range of bar food too.

York, North Yorkshire
Kilima Hotel (££) 129 Holgate Road (tel: 01904 658844). Intimate restaurant serving well-produced food using local produce.
Olde Starre (£) Stonegate (tel: 01904 623063). Oldest pub in the city; characterful and popular. Good value.

Yorkshire Dales, North Yorkshire
Devonshire Arms Country House Hotel (£££) Bolton Abbey, Skipton (tel: 01756 710441). Fine hotel; good-quality food.
Kings Arms (£–££) Market Place, Askrigg (tel: 01969 650258). Welcoming village inn.

SOUTHERN SCOTLAND
(Scottish) Borders
Burt's Hotel: (£–££) The Square, Melrose (tel: 01896 822285). Fine 18th-century inn situated in town centre with fixed-price and *à la carte* menus.

Edinburgh
Iggs (££) 15 Jeffrey Street (tel: 0131-557 8184). Unusual combination of Spanish and Scottish dishes; lively service.
L'Auberge (££) 56 St Mary's Street (tel: 0131-556 5888). A bit of France off the Royal Mile. Several menus; high standard food .
Martin's (££) 70 Rose Street North Lane (tel: 0131-225 3106). Unpretentious but accomplished cooking; light and airy décor; a firmly established favourite.

Glasgow
Buttery Restaurant (££) 652 Argyle Street (tel: 0141-221 8188). Fantastic Victorian setting for a menu that fizzes with ideas.
Ubiquitous Chip (£–££) 12 Ashton Lane (tel: 0141-334 5007). Ex-warehouse off Byres Road; choice ingredients (no chips!), Scottish dishes and salads.
Yes (££) 22 West Nile Street (tel: 0141-221 8044). Fine cooking at affordable prices.

St Andrews, Fife
Peat Inn (£££) Peat Inn, by Cupar (tel: 01334 840206). One of the best-known restaurants in Scotland, in rural location.

NORTHERN SCOTLAND
Perth and Kinross
Killiecrankie (£–££) Pass of Killiecrankie, nr Pitlochry (tel: 01796 473220). Scottish game, meat and fish.

Skye
Hotel Eilean Iarmain (£–££) Isle Ornsay (tel: 01471 833332). Small inn by natural harbour looking over Sound of Sleat; home cooking; good wines.

Sutherland and Wester Ross
Altnaharrie Inn (£££) Ullapool (tel: 01854 633230). Former drovers' inn; simple charm; virtuoso dinners.
Ceilidh Place (£) Pub, hotel, art gallery and live music venue; see Accommodation.

Index

285

INDEX

INDEX

Picture credits

The Automobile Association would like to thank the following for their assistance in the preparation of this book.
BRIDGEMAN ART LIBRARY 38a *Fitting Out, Mousehole Harbour, 1919* by Stanhope Alexander Forbes (1857–1947) (Bradford Art Galleries and Museums/Bridgeman Art Library, London), 149a *Wood Scene 1810* by John Crome (1768–1821) (By courtesy of the Board of Trustees of the V & A/Bridgeman Art Library, London), 149b *Fishing Boats off Yarmouth* by John Sell Cotman (1782–1842) (Christie's London/Bridgeman Art Library, London). BRITISH WATER-WAYS BOARD 128a Buckby Locks. MARY EVANS PICTURE LIBRARY 32a Charles II, 32b Elizabeth I, 32c Henry VIII, 33 Charles I, 39a J M W Turner, 40a Manchester 1870, 94b bathing machine at Brighton, 94c Hastings. J MORGAN 160a Royal National Eisteddfod of Wales, 161 Rhymney Valley. RITZ HOTEL 59b tea at the Ritz. SPECTRUM COLOUR LIBRARY (Spine) Queen's Head pub sign, Rye. THE MANSELL COLLECTION 216a Robert Burns, 246b Charles Stuart. ANDY WILLIAMS PHOTO-LIBRARY (Cover) cottage, Polperro.

All remaining pictures are held in the Association's own picture library (AA PHOTO LIBRARY) with contributions from: M ADELMAN 36a, 41, 227a, 238, 261a, 262b. M ALLWOOD-COPPIN 26–7, 130a, 130b. P AITHIE 151b. A BAKER 4, 20b, 64b, 69b, 112, 123c, 179, 198a, 198b, 198c, 208a, 212a, 230a, 230b, 231, 232, 236, 252, 256. P BAKER 21b, 23b, 26b, 44, 60, 63, 68, 73, 75a, 75b, 77, 106b, 140, 173, 174, 186a, 187, 197a, 203a, 206a. J BEAZLEY 16a, 186c, 190, 194a, 194b, 196b, 199, 200, 214, 216b, 217, 221, 222b, 237, 249a, 259. A W BESLEY 5b, 70c, 71a. M BIRKITT 5c, 28b, 65a, 84, 95a, 111b, 114, 115, 131, 135b. E A BOWNESS 18a, 173b, 243. P & G BOWATER 229b. P BROWN 12b, 86, 88b, 90, 91, 97a, 99, 104a, 105. I BURGUM 110a, 123a, 123b, 124b, 150, 152a, 152b, 155a, 156a, 157a, 157b, 162, 164a, 165a, 165b, 167, 168, 169a, 169b, 171b, 269. J CARNIE 233a, 245a, 245b, 253c, 258. T COHEN 263b. D CORRANCE 225, 233b. D CROUCHER 159a, 163, 164b, 222a. P DAVIES 146, 147. S DAY 8a, 176. P EDEN 100b. R ELLIOTT 224, 226–7. P ENTICKNAP 108. R FLETCHER 34b. D FORSS 15a, 30b, 50, 81b, 89, 92, 95b, 98, 102b, 103, 109a, 109b, 128b, 142a. S GIBSON PHOTOGRAPHY 213, 220, 228, 229a. J GRAVELL 166. V GREAVES 132. S GREGORY 202a. A GRIERLY 154b. J HENDERSON 211b, 235. A J HOPKINS 25, 82–3, 171a, 193. R JOHNSON 250, 251. P KENWARD 275b. A LAWSON 23, 61b, 69a, 70a, 70b, 74a, 74b, 116, 126–7, 144b. C LEES Back cover b. S & O MATHEWS 191b. J McCRAE 125b. E MEACHER 5a, 65b. C MOLYNEUX 209a. R MORT 12a, 14a, 54b, 272. J MORRISON 192, 209b. R NEWTON 21a, 37, 80a, 85, 143a, 158, 160b, 189, 206b. D NOBLE 17, 93, 104b, 106. K PATERSON 215, 249b. A PERKINS 156. J PERRIN 153. N RAY 3, 19, 62, 67. P SHARPE 3, 175, 178, 219, 240, 248. M SHORT 110b, 118a, 119. B SMITH 11a, 45, 56a, 59a. A SOUTER 10a, 24a, 72, 81a, 118b, 120, 136. F STEPHENSON 18b. R STRANGE 11b, 13b, 14b, 43b, 46, 48, 51, 57a, 57b, 185. R SURMAN Back cover a, 28a, 113. D TARN 207. M TAYLOR 223. T TEEGAN 79. T D TIMMS 27. M TRELAWNY 7a, 47, 54a, 58b, 96, 241, 271. P TRENCHARD 35b. R VICTOR 13a. W VOYSEY 9b, 16b, 22b, 34a, 35a, 38–9, 49, 53b, 78, 82b, 87, 88a, 101a, 107b, 156b. R WEIR 6, 7b, 239, 244a, 254, 257, 260. L WHITWAM 10b, 30a, 40b, 129, 138a, 138b, 143, 177, 182, 183a, 183b, 184a, 184b, 185a, 186b, 188a, 188b, 188c, 195, 201, 204, 206c, 208b, 266, 268, 275. H WILLIAMS 24b, 29, 64a, 122a, 122. P WILSON 55, 56b, 58a. T WOODCOCK 9.

Contributors

Original copy editor: Sue Gordon **Revision copy editor:** Sarah Hudson
Revision verifier: Tim Locke